Communication and Discourse Theory

Communication and Discourse Theory
Collected Works of the Brussels Discourse Theory Group

Edited by
Leen Van Brussel, Nico Carpentier, and Benjamin De Cleen

intellect Bristol, UK / Chicago, USA

First published in the UK in 2019 by
Intellect, The Mill, Parnall Road, Fishponds, Bristol, BS16 3JG, UK

First published in the USA in 2019 by
Intellect, The University of Chicago Press, 1427 E. 60th Street,
Chicago, IL 60637, USA

A catalogue record for this book is available from the
British Library.

Copy-editor: MPS Technologies
Cover designer: Aleksandra Szumlas
Production manager: Faith Newcombe
Typesetting: Contentra Technologies

Print ISBN: 978-1-78938-054-5
ePDF ISBN: 978-1-78938-056-9
ePUB ISBN: 978-1-78938-055-2

Printed and bound by Hobbs, UK.

This is a peer-reviewed publication.

Contents

Introduction

Discourse Theory, Media and Communication, and the Work of the Brussels Discourse Theory Group[1]

Nico Carpentier, Benjamin De Cleen, and Leen Van Brussel

Introduction

This book brings together a selection of work by the members of the Brussels Discourse Theory Group. Even if the label appears to be highly localized, it is the best possible term to refer to an international group of media and communication studies scholars, who work on the deployment of discourse theory (DT) within their field, and who have been, or are, affiliated to the Vrije Universiteit Brussel (VUB—the Free University of Brussels) in a variety of ways. What creates the coherence in this group is not their nationality, their presence in a particular city, or their position in the academic hierarchy, but their commitment to using DT to support media and communication research while fully respecting the theoretical sophistication of discourse theory.

In the last fifteen years, the Brussels Discourse Theory Group has drawn on the poststructuralist and post-Marxist DT first formulated by Ernesto Laclau and Chantal Mouffe (1985), in order to analyze media and communication. The Group has, as two group members described it in a 2007 article (Carpentier and De Cleen 2007), attempted to bring discourse theory into the field of communication and media studies, where it had been largely absent until then—at least explicitly, for as Dahlberg and Phelan (2011: 8) rightly indicate, DT's poststructuralism and post-Marxism do resonate with tendencies and concepts (discourse, for example) that have been present in communication, media, and cultural studies since the 1970s. In doing so, the Group has also aimed to contribute to the advancement of DT, by increasing its sensitivity to the importance of media and communication, by showing discourse DT's empirical applicability beyond politics, by strengthening the discourse-theoretical methodology, and through theoretical contributions to DT cross-fertilized by theories on, and analyses of, media and communication. This collection showcases some of this work, illustrating the benefits of a discourse-theoretical approach for the analysis of communication and media, and highlighting some of the contributions that the Group's work has attempted to make to DT more broadly.

Our aim in this introduction is to briefly reflect on the interaction between DT and the study of media and communication, and the Group's contribution to it. This introductory chapter starts with a concise discussion of the main tenets of DT that inform research carried out at the intersection of DT and media and communication studies, including the Group's own work. Building on this first section, we ask ourselves what it implies analytically and methodologically to perform discourse-theoretical research. We point out the specificity of discourse-theoretically inspired analyses, by first situating them in the field of discourse studies, and then describing the basic principles of discourse-theoretical analysis (DTA). We then discuss how DT has been put to use in the analysis of communication and media. We distinguish four thematic areas: (1) communication, rhetoric, and media strategies, (2) discourses in media organizations, (3) media identities, practices, and institutions, and (4) media and agonistic democracy. In the next part, we single out two areas that are currently being developed in the Group, and have thus far remained under-developed, theoretically as well as empirically, from a DT perspective: the relation between the discursive and the material, and the relation between media, communication, and audiences. Finally, we provide a short overview of the chapters in this book.

The main tenets of Laclau and Mouffe's discourse theory

The chapters in this book deal with topics ranging from journalistic identities to resistance to the radical right, and from the reality-TV program *Temptation Island*, to euthanasia and palliative care. All of these chapters make use of poststructuralist and post-Marxist DT, in one way or another, and combine DT with other theories, including political theory, political philosophy, sociology, cultural studies, audience studies, and journalism studies. What these chapters exactly use from DT depends on the needs of the specific research projects, but all of them take from DT its discursive (and thus deeply political) perspective on the social, as well as some parts of the DT conceptual framework, in order to perform their theorizations and analyses.

The major reference for Laclau and Mouffe's DT is the seminal *Hegemony and Socialist Strategy: Towards a Radical Democratic Politics* (1985). This remains one of the key works in the field of DT, next to Foucault's theoretical elaborations on discourse, which we can find especially in the *Archaeology of Knowledge* (1972). Laclau and Mouffe have, mostly in individually authored works, further developed their theoretical reflections, which features most prominently in Laclau's (1990, 1996, 2000) continuous development of a DT of politics and identity, and in his conceptualization of populism (2005), and in Mouffe's reflections on the political and her proposal for an agonistic democracy (1993, 2000, 2005, 2013). Laclau and Mouffe's work has also generated a considerable amount of secondary theoretical literature, most notably by students of Laclau at Essex University (e.g., Critchley and Marchart 2004a; Glynos and Howarth 2007; Howarth 2000, 2013; Smith 1999; Stavrakakis 2007; Torfing 1999) as well as empirical work, mainly situated within political studies (e.g., Howarth et al. 2000; Howarth and Torfing 2005) but also in the study of work, organizations, and management (e.g., Glynos 2008; Jones 2009; Grant et al. 2009), public health (policy) (e.g., Durnova 2013; Glynos and Speed 2012; Glynos et al. 2015), education policy (Rear and Jones 2013), and, of course, in media and communication studies (for an overview of some of the most important works in the latter area, see below).

In order to grasp how the work of the Brussels Group, and others' work in the field of media and communication studies, draws on DT, it is helpful to briefly consider some of the main tenets of Laclau and Mouffe's contribution to the development of a poststructuralist and post-Marxist DT. Somewhat schematically speaking, *Hegemony and Socialist Strategy* can be read on three strongly interrelated levels (Smith 1999): their ontology, their political identity theory, and their democratic theory of radical pluralism. Laclau and Mouffe's later work also fits into this basic model, as many of their later publications contribute to further developing one or several of these levels.

On the first level, Laclau and Mouffe make an ontological contribution (Howarth 2000: 17), by theorizing the discursive (Howarth 2000: 8-10).[2] DT looks at the social as a non-exclusively discursive reality, focusing on how it is constructed through these structures of meaning. This does not imply, for Laclau and Mouffe, that the discursive is all there is. Even if Laclau and Mouffe strongly privilege the role of discursive structures in their analytical focus, they never deny the existence of the material (or of human agency, for that matter). Their careful positioning between materialism and idealism allows them to acknowledge the significance of the material, while emphasizing that the discursive is needed to generate meaning(s) to the material world.

Discourses are then seen as always incomplete attempts to fix meanings within a particular structure of relations. Or, to use Howarth and Stavrakakis' (2000: 3) definition, a discourse is a "social and political construction that establishes a system of [meaningful] relations between different objects and practices, while providing (subject) positions with which social agents can identify." These significatory relations are generated through the practice of articulation, which implies the interlinking of different signifiers in networks of meaning. But, as Laclau and Mouffe's (1985: 105) definition of articulation entails, the process of articulation has consequences for all the components that are articulated into a discourse, and for the discourse as a whole. They define articulation as "any practice establishing a relation among elements[3] such that their identity is modified as a result of the articulatory practice." The articulation of the signifier freedom in different discourses is one example of this mechanism. Freedom, as a signifier, features in many different discourses, including neo-liberal and communist discourses, where it obtains very different meanings (even if it is the same signifier), which makes this signifier float. But inversely, the presence of the signifier freedom, in both discourses, affects both of them as a whole, albeit in different ways.

Importantly, Laclau and Mouffe take a non-essentialist position, and emphasize the always-present possibility of change, or, in other words, the contingency of the discursive. At the same time—and this is one of the significant merits of their work—they have a strong interest in how social structure is generated through the fixation of meaning. Their work balances a context of instability with practices of stabilization. It is important to stress this crucial role of contingency—which is very much in line with their poststructuralist position—which results in discourses being seen as overdetermined, never having the capacity to reach "a final closure" (Howarth 1998: 273). This is (partially—see later) because a discourse is never safe from elements alien to that discourse[4]: There is always a surplus (or a residue) of elements—which Laclau and Mouffe call the field of discursivity[5]—that offer themselves to articulation, and that thus prevent the full saturation of meaning (Laclau and Mouffe 1985: 112), allowing discourses to change. But this does not mean that discourses are necessarily and continuously unstable: Their articulation gives them a certain rigidity and viscosity, without which no meaning would be possible in the first place.

Furthermore, discursive stability is enhanced by the role of privileged signifiers, which Laclau and Mouffe call nodal points. Returning to the earlier example of liberal discourse: It is hard to imagine liberalism without the signifier, freedom. Torfing (1999: 88–89) points out that these nodal points "sustain the identity of a certain discourse by constructing a knot of definite meanings." Simultaneously, the field of discursivity has an infinite number of elements, which are not connected to a specific discourse at a given moment in time. Instability enters the equation through the idea that these unconnected elements can always *become* articulated within a specific discourse, sometimes replacing (or disarticulating) other elements, which affects the discourse's entire signification. Due to the infinitude of the field of discursivity and the inability of a discourse to permanently fix its meaning and keep its elements stable, discourses are vulnerable to re-articulation and/or disintegration.

Equally important for Laclau and Mouffe is the relationship between the discursive and the subject, which is mediated through the concept of the subject position, drawing on Althusser and Foucault:

> Whenever we use the category of "subject" in this text, we will do so in the sense of "subject positions" within a discursive structure. Subjects cannot, therefore, be the origin of social relations—not even in the limited sense of being endowed with powers that render an experience possible—as all "experience" depends on precise discursive conditions of possibility.
>
> (Laclau and Mouffe 1985: 115)

Laclau and Mouffe's DT has been criticized as both voluntarist/subjectivist—as denying structural constraints on the human subject (e.g., Therborn 2008), and as denying the subject's political agency by reducing the subject to mere subject positions constituted within discourse (Žižek 1990: 150–51, see Howarth 2000: 121; 2004: 264). We would argue that DT takes a middle position between structure and agency. It rejects both approaches to humans as rational self-interest-maximizing subjects and to approaches that deny agency by subsuming it under the reproduction of structures (Howarth 2000: 121; 2004: 254; Torfing 1999: 137–54). Instead, the DT position—strongly influenced by, among others, Althusser's theory of interpellation (see Laclau 1977; Laclau and Mouffe 2001; Sawyer 2002: 443), Foucault's decentering of the subject, and Lacan's psychoanalytical theory of discourse (see Sawyer 2002: 444)—is one that sees human subjects as *constituted as* subjects within discourses (Howarth 2000: 108), but simultaneously sees these discourses (and therefore the subject's identity) as contingent, changeable, and moldable (Howarth 2000: 121), which generates human freedom. Because of the plurality of discourses, an actor can identify at the same time with more than one subject position (e.g., woman, working class, black, feminist).

It is here that the space for agency lies (Howarth 2000: 108–09, 121). It is precisely the discursive contingency that creates the space for subjectivity and the particularity of human identity and behavior. In this way, a structuralist position is avoided, and a poststructuralist stance is taken.

The second—and strongly related—level on which *Hegemony and Socialist Strategy* and much other DT work can be read is what Smith (1999: 87) calls Laclau and Mouffe's political identity theory, which is tributary to conflict theory. Here, the focus is on the political nature of construction processes. The political is defined in a very broad way here, as "the dimension of antagonism that is inherent in human relations" (Mouffe 2000: 101). This allows seeing the fixation, sedimentation, and contestation of particular discourses, as well as the discursive struggle for hegemony between different discourses, as political interventions.

As mentioned before, discourses have to be partially fixed, because the abundance of meaning would otherwise make any meaning impossible. Laclau argues that contingency requires decisions to constantly supersede the undecidability (1996: 92). In Laclau's vocabulary, the notion of the decision is used to refer to the moment of fixation, where discourses are articulated in particular ways and discursive struggles are waged, leading to particular outcomes. But these fixations (or decisions) are also political interventions that privilege specific meanings over others. Mouffe (2000: 130) stresses this in her call for a "proper reflection on the moment of 'decision' which characterizes the field of politics." She adds to this idea that the decision—as a moment of fixation—entails "an element of force and violence" (Mouffe 2000: 130). Even when fixations appear to be permanent, because discourses will eventually lose their contested political nature and become sedimented in social norms and values, later in time they might become contested again, which implies their re-politicization (Torfing 1999: 70; Glynos and Howarth 2007).

In DT, fixations are not only intra-discursive, but also generated through inter-discursive political struggles. Discourses are often engaged in struggles, in an attempt to attain hegemonic positions over other discourses and, thus, to have their meanings (and not others) dominate the particular realm of the social. Through these struggles, "in a field crisscrossed by antagonisms" (Laclau and Mouffe 1985: 135–36), and through attempts to create discursive alliances, or chains of equivalence (Howarth 1998: 279), discourses are altered, which also produces contingency. In contrast, when a discourse eventually saturates the social as a result of a victorious discursive struggle, stability emerges. Laclau and Mouffe use the concept of hegemony for this stability, a concept that they borrow from Gramsci. Originally, Gramsci (1999: 261) defined this notion as referring to the formation of consent rather than to the (exclusive) domination of the Other, without however excluding a certain form of pressure and repression: "The 'normal' exercise of hegemony […] is characterized by the combination of force and consent variously balancing one another, without force exceeding consent too much." Following Laclau and Mouffe's interpretation of the concept, Torfing (1999: 101) defined hegemony as the expansion of the discourse, or set of discourses, into a dominant horizon of social orientation and action. In this scenario, a dominant social order (Howarth 1998: 279), or a social imaginary, is created, which pushes other discourses beyond the horizon, threatening them with oblivion.

On a third level, Laclau and Mouffe's post-Marxist plea for a radical democratic politics—and later for a left-wing populist strategy and for an agonistic democracy—contributes to democratic theory as well as to left-wing political strategy formation. Laclau and Mouffe (1985: 190) still situate themselves within the "classic ideal of socialism," but they argue for a "polyphony of voice" in which the different (radical) democratic political struggles—such as antiracism, antisexism, and anticapitalism—are allotted an equally important role and are linked to each other (Mouffe 1997: 18). From traditional Marxist positions, serious objections were launched against this post-Marxist decentralizing of the class concept. For example, Gledhill (1994: 183) called Laclau "a disillusioned Althusserian Marxist of the 1968 new left vintage who now declares himself a post-Marxist." This critique actually touches upon the heart of the theoretical project of Laclau and Mouffe, which aims to de-essentialize Althusser's and Gramsci's work (and thus indirectly also the work of Marx and Engels). The decentralization of the class struggle allows incorporating other relevant societal struggles and identities (for instance those related to ethnicity and gender) and thus correcting the traditional Marxist negligence for these areas, and allowing the construction of a broad progressive alliance (Torfing 1999: 291). Moreover, this post-Marxist position links up with a broader ontological rejection of classical Marxism's economic determinism.

Moreover, Mouffe's (2005, 2013) agonistic democracy is aimed at democratically transforming antagonism and violence in order to limit their damaging impact. In 1993, Mouffe (1993: 153) captured this idea as follows: "Instead of shying away from the component of violence and hostility inherent in social relations, the task is to think how to create the conditions under which those aggressive forces can be defused and diverted and a pluralist democratic order made possible." For Mouffe, the aim of democratic politics is "[…] to transform an 'antagonism' into 'agonism'" (1999: 755), to "tame" or "sublimate" (Mouffe 2005: 20–21) antagonisms,[6] without eliminating passion from the political realm or relegating it to the outskirts of the private. In other words, this implies the transformation of the other-enemy, to be destroyed, into an other-adversary, who can still occupy the same (political) symbolic and material space.

All of the contributions in this book draw on the first two levels—DT's discursive theorization of the social and its contribution to understanding the political; some chapters also draw on Laclau and Mouffe's contributions to democratic theory and to the development of a progressive political strategy.

Mapping discourse-theoretical analysis

Before we turn to a discussion of how DT has been, and can be, used in communication and media studies, and what the specificity of such analyses are, this section reflects more generally on the methodological translation of discourse theory (DT) into discourse-theoretical analysis (DTA). Of course, when discussing methodology, the multitude of approaches is reminiscent of the equally immense variety of conceptualizations and theorizations of discourse. Discussing both—conceptualizations and methods—in a structured way is helpful to provide a first map on which to situate DTA.

Here, it is important to keep the specificity of DT's approach toward discourse in mind, as it has a significant impact on its analytical and methodological operationalization. DT sees discourses as structures of meaning and aims to understand how these structures of meaning—or frameworks of intelligibility—work in society. This broad (and abstract) approach toward discourse also produces a particular perspective on language, which is seen in DT as one of the many ways that these meanings can be condensed, materialized, and communicated. Or, in other words, DT's interest lies in what is *behind* language, without ignoring the complexities and contingencies of the relationship between discourse and language. This, in turn, renders DT different from the discourse analyses that have their origins in the field of linguistics—or that are more hybrid—as these approaches remain more concerned with the close empirical analysis of written, spoken, or audio-visual texts, which they call discourse. Of course, DTA also draws on such texts as empirical material, and some of the more linguistic types of discourse analysis are also concerned with ideology, but DTA remains mainly concerned with the discursive (or ideological) constructions behind linguistic (and other signifying) practices.

This diversity of meanings of the signifier discourse is something that the field of discourse studies has always had to come to terms with. These meanings range from spoken language (as opposed to written texts), spoken and written language, the language use of a particular actor, language use associated with a particular institutional context or genre, text in context, a particular view on a particular part of the world, a structure of meaning, a particular perspective on the social in its entirety...This significatory diversity is caused by (1) the term being used by different disciplines (linguistics, psychology, literary and cultural theory, critical theory, political theory, organization studies, etc.) with rather different traditions, purposes, and ontological and epistemological assumptions, as well as (2) it being used in several ways and on different levels of abstraction within the same discipline and by one and the same author (see among many, many others: Blommaert 2005; Fairclough 1992: 3; Howarth 2000; Philips and Jørgensen 2002; Mills 1997; Sawyer 2002; Titscher et al. 2000: 25–27; Wodak 2008: 1–6).

Using Van Dijk's (1997: 3) definition of discourse studies as the study of "talk and text in context" as a starting point, this diversity of meanings can be structured—and the specificity of DTA explained—by distinguishing between micro and macro-approaches toward both text and context.

In the micro-textual approaches of discourse, the concept's close affiliation with language is emphasized, an approach we can also label, following Philips and Jørgensen (2002: 62), discourse-as-language. Van Dijk's (1997: 3) definition of discourse provides us with a helpful illustration: "Although many discourse analysts specifically focus on spoken language or talk, it is [...] useful to include also written texts in the concept of discourse."

Macro-textual approaches use a broader definition of text, much in congruence with Barthes (1975), seeing texts as materializations of meaning and/or ideology. In this macro-textual approach, where discourse becomes discourse-as-representation, or discourse-as-ideology, the focus is placed on the meanings, representations, or ideologies embedded in the text, and not so much on the language used. One related (but not entirely overlapping) strategy to distinguish between more micro-textual and more macro-textual approaches is Gee's (1990) distinction between "big D" Discourse and "little d" discourse, where the latter refers to "connected stretches of language that make sense, like conversations, stories, reports, arguments, essays [...]" (Gee 1990: 142). Big D Discourse is "always more than just language," and refers to "saying (writing)-doing-being-valuing-believing combinations" (Gee 1990: 142—emphasis removed). One could argue that "thinking" and "knowing" should be added to Gee's list, to describe the approaches at the very end of the macro-textual part of the micro/macro-textual spectrum, but Gee's approach remains important in mapping the diversity in the field of discourse studies.

A second distinction that enables us to map the different meanings of the discourse concept is that between micro- and macro-contextual approaches. Micro-contextual approaches confine the context to specific social settings (such as a speech act or a conversation). We can take conversation analysis as example, where—according to Heritage's (1984: 242—our emphasis) interpretation—context is defined at a micro-level: "A speaker's action is context-shaped in that its contribution to an on-going sequence of actions cannot adequately be understood except by reference to the context—including, *especially, the immediately preceding configuration of actions*—in which it participates." Heritage (1984: 242) continued: "every 'current' action will itself form the immediate context for some 'next' action in a sequence [...]." Another example is sociolinguistics' emphasis on the linguistic rule system, the syntactic and lexical planning strategies, and speech codes to define discourse, as Dittmar (1976: 12) explained. But it would be unfair to claim that micro-contextual approaches remain exclusively focused on the micro-context, even if that is where they are rooted. Sociolinguistics, with its emphasis on social groupings, class positions, social relations, and sociocultural and situational rules (Dittmar 1976: 12) is a case in point. Nevertheless, the role of context in macro-contextual is structurally different, as these approaches look at how discourses circulate within the social, paying much less attention to more localized settings (or micro-contexts). This leads to much broader analyses, for instance, how democratic discourse (which brings us back to Laclau and Mouffe) or gender identity (Butler 1997) is articulated within the social. Again, the emphasis on the macro-context of the social does not imply a complete disregard of the micro-contexts of language, social settings, or social practices, although the starting point of these approaches remains embedded in the macro-level. A more streamlined version of this debate, and the many different positions, can be found in Figure 1.

DTA, based on Laclau and Mouffe's work, is macro-contextual and macro-textual. The interest of this approach lies primarily with the analysis of the circulation, reproduction, and contestation of discourses-as-structures-of-meaning, not with language-in-use per se.

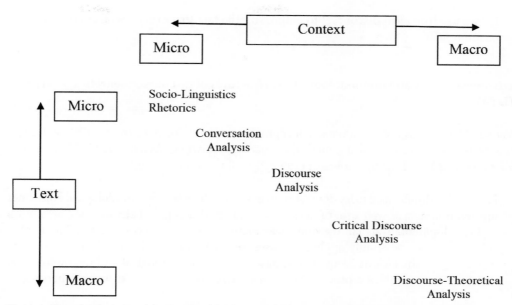

Figure 1: Textual and contextual dimensions of the discourse definition. Carpentier and De Cleen 2007: 277.

DTA uses a much broader definition of discourse than is common in linguistically inspired forms of discourse analysis. In contrast to, for example, CDA, that sees discourse as a dimension of the social that stands in a dialectical relationship to other dimensions that do not function discursively (Philips and Jørgensen 2002: 19, 61), DTA does not regard discourse "merely as a linguistic region within a wider social realm," but offers a more encompassing conceptualization of discourse that "insists on the interweaving of semantic aspects of language with the pragmatic aspects of actions, movements and objects" (Torfing 1999: 94). As Laclau and Mouffe (1990: 100) phrase it: "This totality which includes within itself the linguistic and the non-linguistic is what we call discourse."

In other words, DT "rejects the distinction between discursive and non-discursive practices" (Laclau and Mouffe 1985: 107). Although Laclau and Mouffe (1985: 107) (unrightfully, we would say) criticize Foucault for making such distinction, they are actually very much in line with Foucault and Hall by claiming that nothing meaningful exists outside discourse. Hall (1997: 44–45—emphasis in original) constructs his own language game in order to make this point, and to avoid the critique of idealism:

> Is Foucault saying [...] that "*nothing exists outside of discourse?*" In fact, Foucault does not deny that things can have a real, material existence in the world. What he does argue is that "*nothing has any meaning outside of discourse*". As Laclau and Mouffe put

it: "we use [the term discourse] to emphasize the fact that every social configuration is *meaningful.*"

Discourse theory and methodology: The procedures of discourse-theoretical analysis (DTA)

While DT provides a very valuable conceptual framework for poststructuralist analysis, it has been subjected to significant methodological critiques (e.g., Marttila 2015; Torfing 2005; Zienkowski 2012). In 1998, Howarth (1998: 291), for example, stated that:

> Laclau and Mouffe need to lay down, however minimally, a set of methodological guidelines for practitioners, as well a set of questions and hypotheses (à la Lakatos) for clarification and development. Thus far, the only clear methodological rule consists in a "non-rule": rules can never be simply applied to cases, but have to be articulated in the research process. [...] The lack of adequate responses to the epistemological and methodological questions pose significant problems for researchers working within discourse theory.

Since then, there have been considerable steps in the methodological development of DT. Glynos and Howarth's (2007) *Logics of Critical Explanation in Social and Political Theory* (see also Glynos 2008) proposes an analytical focus on the identification of social logics (that characterize practices in a particular field), political logics (that explain how practices emerge and normalized, and are politicized and contested), and phantasmatic logics (that explain how practices and ideologies "grip" subjects) as a way forward for discourse-theoretical research (for a critique of this logics approach, see Marttila 2015). Howarth and Glynos also reflect on what it means to analyze social reality from the perspective of DT, what kind of knowledge this might produce, and the kind of research strategies that are needed to make empirical analysis compatible with DT's ontological and epistemological principles. Such reflections can also be found in Philips and Jørgensen's (2002) work on social constructionist discourse analysis (which also discusses CDA and discursive psychology) and in Marttila's (2015) work on post-foundational discourse analysis. Some of the other notable advances in operationalizing DT-inspired discourse analysis include Glasze's (2007) proposal for combining qualitative and lexicometric methods in the identification of discourses, Nonhoff's (2007) hegemony analysis, which focuses on the detailed identification of hegemonic strategies, and Angermuller's poststructuralist discourse analysis (2014), which focuses on enunciative pragmatics.

In the work of the Brussels Group, a set of methodological procedures were developed to support what has been labeled DTA (Carpentier and De Cleen 2007; Carpentier 2010, 2017). Crucial in the development of DTA was (and is) the notion of the sensitizing concept, as it provided the methodological bridge between the DT framework on the one hand, and the empirical research data to be analyzed on the other hand. Sensitizing concepts help analysts, as Ritzer (1992: 365) explained, in "what to look for and where to look [...]." These concepts are not intended to dominate and foreclose the analysis, but are kept in the back of the mind of the analyst and provide support when interpreting particular social realities and applying the categorization logics of qualitative analysis (Maso 1989; Wester 1987, 1995). Within discourse studies, it is (not surprisingly) the notion of discourse that features as primary sensitizing concept, whether we are dealing with DTA, discursive-material analysis,[7] critical discourse analysis, or (linguistic) discourse analysis. DT itself then enables the production of a considerable list of secondary sensitizing concepts, which includes the concepts of articulation, nodal point, floating signifier, and subject position, but also contingency and overdetermination, chain of equivalence (and difference), antagonism, agonism, hegemony, and social imaginary.

Given the specificity of each research project, sensitizing concepts external to DT, but necessary for the theoretical grounding of the research project, remain also necessary. The latter set of theoretical notions form the third layer of sensitizing concepts, and these are indeed very much specific to each research project. To avoid an ontological and paradigmatic schism between the internal and external sensitizing concepts, there is a need to translate these external theoretical frameworks and bring them into the realm of DT. This re-reading of existing theories consists of a DTA of theory not dissimilar to Derrida's deconstruction, even though he takes aim at more philosophical texts. The outcome of these re-readings is discursive-theoretical versions of originally non-discursive-theoretical theories, which are made consistent, or calibrated with the ontological-paradigmatic assumptions of DT (see also Howarth 2005; Glynos and Howarth 2007 on the logic of articulation).

Discourse theory and the study of media and communication

In line with its history as a political-theoretical intervention in its own right, DT has mainly been used in the study of politics, focusing on political movements, parties, leaders, and ideologies. Discourse theorists have traditionally paid rather limited attention to media and their crucial role in contemporary politics and society more broadly (see Dahlberg and Phelan 2011; Dahlgren 2011: 224; but see Mouffe's (e.g., 2007) work on arts and politics). For example, the absence of much reflection on the role of media institutions and of mediated communication has been seen as a weakness of Laclau's theory of populism (Moffitt 2017; Simons 2011). DT can benefit from including communication and media in its analyses, and from engaging with literature on communication and media (and with some of the more linguistically and empirically inclined approaches to discourse studies that have focused more on media—especially critical discourse analysis—and that are more frequently drawn on in communication and media studies). Students of communication and media, for their part, have much to gain from engaging with DT. While DT still has a relatively modest place in communication and media studies, the last decade has seen the publication of a variety of work—some of which can be found in this book—that uses the DT framework to better understand aspects of communication or media.

While largely focused on political movements and ideologies, DT's conceptualization of discourse and its theory of hegemony are quite easily applicable beyond the field of politics proper. DT's stress on the so-called primacy of the political means that a particular social order, an identity or a practice that is sedimented, can always be questioned, and turned into an object of political struggle. In this respect, DT is rather more explicitly political than other forms of social constructivist thought (that are also used in communication and media studies) that stress how meaning is produced through social interaction. DT aims to make visible the political nature of the social, also exposing attempts to make that inherently political nature invisible.

This deeply political perspective on the social has great potential for the study of communication and media. For one, on an ontological level, the recognition of the contingent and profoundly political nature of the social urges communication and media scholars to turn their attention to how media representations and practices link up with hegemonic processes (e.g., in the representation of national groups or economic processes). But it also stimulates looking at what might seem like inevitable or evident communication and media *practices and institutions*, asking how these practices and institutions are underpinned by particular discourses (e.g., the public broadcaster as an institution rests on particular views on the role of the state in society, on the functions of media, etc., see Carpentier 2015). This ontological position also has an important critical potential, because it allows us to question the inevitability of particular representations of society, and the unchangeability of particular ways of doing and organizing communication and media. This, in turn, opens up spaces for envisaging alternatives (see Dahlgren 2011). The distinction between institutionalized politics and the political also makes clear that communication and media scholars can use DT not only for the study of the relation between communication, media, and the field of politics, but also for analyzing the ever-present political dimensions of media and communication in a broader sense.

Even if DT has not become a mainstream theoretical model in the field of media and communication studies, we can still identify four thematic domains in this field, where DT has effectively been deployed.

Communication, rhetoric, and media strategies

While often largely ignoring the role of mass media and the specificities of mediated and unmediated communication, the bulk of DT work analyzes political rhetoric or other forms of political communication in one way or another. As far as the study of political communication goes, DT has played a particularly prominent role in the analysis of populism. Drawing on DT in general and on Laclau's seminal discursive theory of populism (1977, 2005) in particular, a number of authors have further developed and empirically operationalized Laclau's work by putting it to use and confronting it with the empirical analysis of concrete populist political rhetoric and communication strategies. The work of Yannis Stavrakakis and the Populismus group in Thessaloniki is of particular importance here (e.g., Stavrakakis and Katsambekis 2014; Stavrakakis et al. 2017; also De Cleen and Stavrakakis 2017, but also Mouffe's (2018) latest book, *For a Left Populism*, has to be mentioned here). Some authors with a closer affiliation with communication and media studies have focused more specifically on the cultural and media dimensions of populism (see Moffitt 2016, 2017), asking for instance how social media relate to populist mobilization (Husted 2015) or how popular culture and high culture acquire political significance in the populist juxtaposition of the people and the elite and in attempts to reclaim "the people" and "the popular" from (radical-right) populists (De Cleen 2009, 2013, 2016; De Cleen and Carpentier Chapter).

The specificity of online communication and media strategies of political actors have been a topic of interest as well, also for some of the authors included in this collection (Akdoğan chapter; Filimonov and Svensson chapter). For example, the online strategies of the radical right have been scrutinized using the DT framework (Askanius and Mylonas 2015; Kompatsiaris and Mylonas 2015), as have progressive forms of activism, such as climate change activism (Askanius and Uldam 2011), the Occupy Movement (Husted 2015) and feminist activism (Filimonov and Svensson chapter).

Other areas of communication that take up a prominent place in media and communication studies have hardly been approached from a DT perspective. One example is medical communication, which has received more attention from within more linguistic approaches of discourse analysis (which have been far more concerned with interpersonal communication more generally than has DT) (e.g., Gotti and Salager-Meyer 2006; Roberts and Sarani 2005). Another area where a considerable potential for DT exist is advertising and marketing (see Stavrakakis 2007; Boje and Cai 2008; Carvalho 2008)—an area where good use could also be made of DT's connections with psychoanalytical theory.

Discourses in media organizations

Much of the DT work within the field of media and communication studies proper has been concerned with analyzing the presence of particular discourses in (mass) media organizations ("discourses in media"). A significant share of the work of the Brussels Discourse Theory Group can be situated in this realm. The DT framework has been applied in the analysis of the media representation of a wide range of topics—from the strictly political (political parties, economic policy, war, nationalism) to the political dimensions of the representation of life and death (Van Brussel 2012, 2014; Carpentier and Van Brussel 2012; Van Brussel and Carpentier 2012, 2017)—by and through a wide range of mass media related practices, from journalism to cinema. For example, in the wake of the 2008 financial crisis, a number of authors have used the DT framework in critical analyses of the role of mainstream journalism in reproducing neo-liberal capitalism by ignoring or undervaluing the systemic dimensions of the crisis, delegitimizing alternatives, and "culturalizing" the crisis. Especially the coverage of the crisis in Greece, by Greek as well as by international media, has received extensive attention, as in the work of Yiannis Mylonas, a text of whom is included in this collection (Mylonas 2012b, 2015, 2017, chapter; Mylonas and Kompatsiaris 2013; Doudaki 2015). The discursive construction of the self, the enemy, and the victim in the media representation of war has also been approached from a DT perspective, one of the areas of interest of one of the editors of this collection. These analyses have included mainstream journalism (Carpentier 2005; Cammaerts and Carpentier 2006, 2009; Carpentier and Trioen chapter; Bogaerts and Carpentier chapter), documentaries (Mylonas 2012a), film (Carpentier 2007), and alternative media, including also pro-war military blogs (Carpentier 2008). Nationalism and national identity has also been a topic of interest beyond the context of war, for example in studies of cinema (Martínez Martínez 2008), visual arts (Cuevas Valenzuela 2008), and of Chinese and Taiwanese journalism (Lams 2008), of the journalistic coverage of the 2015 "refugee crisis" (De Cleen et al. 2017; see also Phelan 2009).

Beyond these obviously political themes, DT has also been put to use in the study of the political dimensions of what could be called life-political domains, an expansion of the reach of DT to which the Brussels Discourse Theory Group has also contributed. Such analyses have included sexual fidelity, seduction, and hedonism (Carpentier 2009), the representation of death and dying (Van Brussel 2012, 2014; Carpentier and Van Brussel 2012; Van Brussel and Carpentier 2012, 2017), gender identity (e.g., Glynos 2000; Wang 2008), social care (West 2013), and ageing (West et al. 2017).

Media identities, practices, and institutions

DT has also been used to analyze discourses *about* media identities, practices, and institutions (that also partly circulate in media, of course). The Brussels Discourse Theory Group has been quite active in this domain. Our work has for example focused on discourses about public service broadcasting (Carpentier 2015) and about journalism (Carpentier 2005), on recording industry rhetoric about music piracy (De Cleen 2008), activists' discourse about the role of ICT in social change (Akdoğan 2012), and on the conceptualization of the audience in Chinese communication studies work on new media (Xu 2013). Other examples are the analyses of mainstream journalistic coverage of selfie photography (Tomanić Trivundža 2015), the discourse on the media-politics relation in Russia (Toepfl 2016), and the discursive construction of the "creative industries" (Mäe 2015).

These analyses of discourses about media have also been part of work that uses DT's conceptualization of the discursive construction of political identities to analyze media-related identities, not only through discourses about media, but also through media production practices and institutional arrangements. Here too, the Brussels Discourse

Theory Group has published a series of contributions. The Group has approached the identity of community media (e.g., Carpentier et al. 2003; Carpentier 2017a) in this manner, as well as journalistic identity and the identity of media professionals more generally (e.g., Bogaerts and Carpentier chapter; Carpentier 2005; Carpentier and Trioen chapter), the identity of media audiences (Carpentier 2004), the identity of "ordinary people" participating in media production (e.g., Carpentier 2011, 2014), and the identity of the visitor in museums (Lepik and Carpentier chapter in this book).

It is here that DT's conceptualization of discourse, as encompassing more than language, becomes most obvious. These analyses point to how media practices and institutions are strongly informed by, and contribute to, a variety of (also competing) discourses about the media. That is, discourses about what particular media are and should be (about what journalism is and should be: objective or explicitly critical, for example), about the role of different actors involved in media production (e.g., about the respective roles of media professionals and of ordinary people in talk shows), and about the audience (for example, do public broadcasters view the audience as consumers, as citizens, and/or as masses?).

Media and agonistic democracy

The discussion of the use of DT in the study of communication and media so far has pointed out the critical potentials of DT's ontological positions of contingency as well as of its conceptual framework for the study of hegemony and political identity construction. Beyond this, the radical democratic proposals formulated in *Hegemony and Socialist Strategy*, together with Mouffe's work on agonistic democracy have also inspired critical work in communication and media—some of which is less concerned with the DT framework itself. An early example is James Curran's (1997) attempt to articulate a radical democratic (normative) theory of the media, which he distinguishes from the more traditional liberal, Marxist, and communist theories. Although Curran does not explicitly refer to Laclau and Mouffe's work, a clear link with their radical democratic theory is present. Pieter Maeseele and his colleagues have drawn on Mouffe's work on agonism to analyze the degree of pluralism in mainstream and alternative media coverage of a range of topics, including economic policy and biotechnology (e.g., Maeseele 2011; Raeijmaeckers and Maeseele 2015). Schou (2016) explicitly reflects on the normative potential of Laclau's post-Marxism for the critical study of capitalist media—that is, its critical potential beyond the use of DT to deconstruct and reveal contingency. Phelan and Dahlberg (2014) also reflect explicitly on the relation between DT and critical political economy, considering the ontological differences between them. In the Brussels Group, the ideals of agonistic democracy have been put to use in the analysis of community media interventions in bridging antagonism in Cyprus (Carpentier 2015, 2017a) and the analysis of barter relations and the field of consumption (Airaghi 2013, 2014).

Some ways forward

As the discussion above indicates, DT has been used to analyze a range of communication and media phenomena. While the focus has mainly been on communication and media contents, there have also been considerable advances in the DT study of media professional identities and media production practices.

The Brussels Group is currently developing two areas that have remained under-analyzed as well as under-theorized in DT work on media and communication: the material and its relation to the discursive, and the ways in which audiences relate to media and communication. Both of these developments draw on media and communication theories and analyses, but both are relevant beyond the field of media and communication as well. The development of these two areas should be seen in the context of an (ongoing) process of a critical (self-)reflection on (lacks within) existing work within the field of DT research into media and communication—including the contributions gathered in this volume. There is a need to further develop both areas, and we will discuss them, focusing on how the theorization of these dimensions can be strengthened and how they can be analyzed empirically from a DT perspective.

The discursive and the material in media and communication

One area where progress can still be made is in further thinking through the entanglement of the discursive with the material. The strong emphasis on the discursive has provoked strong critiques, for instance, labeling Laclau and Mouffe's position as idealist. As Joseph (2003: 112) wrote: "the idea that an object only acquires an identity through discourse is a clear example of the epistemic fallacy or the reduction of intrinsic being to transformative knowledge." He continued that Laclau and Mouffe's idealism "reduce[s] material things to the conceptions, not of an individual or a *geist*, but of a community" (Joseph 2003: 112—emphasis in original). Others, in particular, Geras (1987: 65), were harsher in their language, accusing Laclau and Mouffe of a "shamefaced idealism." This critique in turn provoked responses of disagreement with Geras' rather extreme position, even if some maintained the idealism thesis. For instance, Edward (2008) argued that it was appropriate "to label Laclau and Mouffe as idealist because their discourse analysis concentrates on how interpretations and meanings are given to the world from humans. This is their 'constructivist idealism' [...]."

In Laclau and Mouffe's (1985, 1990) work, as mentioned before, we do find a rather clear acknowledgment of the materialist dimension of social reality, which is indeed combined with the position that discourses are necessary to generate meaning for the material. This—what Howarth (1998: 289) calls their—"radical materialism" opposes the "classical dichotomy between an objective field constituted outside of any discursive intervention, and a discourse consisting of the pure expression of thought" (Laclau and Mouffe 1985: 108).

Several other authors have defended Laclau and Mouffe's claim on a non-idealist position (e.g., Glynos and Howarth 2007: 109). Also Torfing (1999: 45–48) argues that Laclau and Mouffe's model is materialist because it questions the symmetry between the "realist object" and the "object of thought." This—what Torfing calls a—non-idealist constructivism presupposes "the incompleteness of both the given world and the subject that undertakes the construction of the object" (Torfing 1999: 48).

But there are also more specific traces of the material in Laclau and Mouffe's DT. A first trace can be found in Laclau's use of the notion of dislocation. Although this concept already featured in *Hegemony and Socialist Strategy*, it took a more prominent role in *New Reflections on the Revolution of Our Time*, where Laclau used it to further theorize the limits of discursive structures. In most cases, dislocation gains its meaning in relation to the discursive, for instance, when Laclau (1990: 39) claims that "every identity is dislocated insofar as it depends on an outside which denies that identity and provides its condition of possibility at the same time." At the same time, there is also a more material use of the dislocation, for instance, when Laclau (1990: 39) talks about the "dislocatory effects of emerging capitalism on the lives of workers": "They are well known: the destruction of traditional communities, the brutal and exhausting discipline of the factory, low wages and insecurity of work." This connection between the dislocation and material events becomes even clearer in Torfing's (1999: 148) description of the dislocation, which, according to him "refers to the emergence of an event, or a set of events, that cannot be represented, symbolized, or in other ways domesticated by the discursive structure—which is therefore disrupted." Despite the theoretical importance of the dislocation as a link to the material, its exclusive negative load necessitates an addition. One of us (Carpentier 2017a) has suggested using the concept of the invitation for this. The invitation captures processes where the material—through its materiality—calls upon the discursive to attribute particular meanings. Contingency remains present, as the invitation can always be declined, and other discourses can be used to provide meaning to the material.

There are other traces of the material in Laclau and Mouffe's work. As Biglieri and Perelló (2011) have argued, it is particularly in Laclau's *On Populist Reason* (2005) that the material[8] is introduced, through the concept of social heterogeneity. Laclau defines this concept as a particular exteriority: "the kind of exteriority we are referring to now presupposes not only an exteriority to something within a space of representation, but to the space of representation as such. I will call this type of exteriority social heterogeneity" (Laclau 2005: 140). Biglieri and Perelló (2011: 60) label it "a structure with a beyond." It is through the invocation of Lacan, for instance, when Laclau writes that "the field of representation is a broken and murky mirror, constantly interrupted by a heterogeneous 'Real' which it cannot symbolically master" (Laclau 2005: 140), that the material regains more prominence. Another trace of the material in Laclau and Mouffe's work occurs through the performative. For instance, in *Hegemony and Socialist Strategy*, they write "we will affirm the material character of every discursive structure" (Laclau and Mouffe 1985: 108—emphasis removed), a position they then illustrate by referring to Wittgenstein's famous language-game and the performative dimension of language.

Even if there are traces of the material, (mainly) in Laclau's work, and despite Laclau and Mouffe's plea for a position that Howarth (1998: 289) termed "radical materialism" as a "tertium quid," their strong orientation toward the analysis of the discursive components of reality, and more specifically toward the analysis of discourses such as democracy, socialism, and populism, remains. Practically speaking, this means that in their specific analyses they will pay considerably less attention to material components of reality (as for example bodies, objects, organizations, technologies, or human interactions). Here we would like to argue that there is a need for a non-hierarchical approach of the discursive and the material, which theorizes the entanglement of both, in what has been called the *discursive-material knot* (Carpentier 2017a).

Discourses, audiences, identifications

While discourse theorists have analyzed media representations, media politics, media organizations, and media professionals, the way audiences relate to media and communication has largely remained outside the scope of DT. One of us recently carried out a discourse-theoretical reception study of media coverage of the right to die (Van Brussel 2018) and found this approach to be particularly useful in enhancing the understanding of how discourses operate on the level of the subject. The case study focused on media coverage of euthanasia and the right-to-die ideology, but it goes without saying that the discourse-theoretical approach to reception studies can be adopted to investigate how subjects invest in a variety of discourses and (political) ideologies. Discourse-theoretical reception studies also create opportunities to gain insight not only in audiences' investments in discourses that circulate *in* media coverage, but also in discourses *about* media, shedding light on how audiences relate to discourses of—for instance—public service broadcasting, media professionalism, objective journalism, and so forth.

Studying practices of identification is relevant also beyond the domain of media and communication, of course. Outside the domain of media and communication exist a variety of possibilities to delve into how subjects relate to discourses. To study how subjects invest in the right-to-die discourse, one could, for instance, also look at medical practices and legal frameworks. On a broader level, the study of identification can contribute, theoretically as well as empirically, to the development of discourse-theoretical studies into different forms of non-mass-mediated communication, including political rhetoric, cultural communication, organizational communication, but also interpersonal communication in, for instance, the medical field that thus far largely remained outside the gaze of discourse theorists.

At the same time, audience reception is more than merely an entry point to the study of the way discourses operate on the level of the subject. Media texts of any kind— in traditional media, digital and social media, and all kinds of hybrid media texts—are omnipresent and play an important role in "mediating" between the discourse and the subject. Media are, and continue to be, important signifying machines. A key advantage of integrating reception studies and DT is that such an approach, by shedding light on how subjects relate to discourses, can answer to the need of DT to develop in a more *empirical way* the phantasmatic logics of discourse that, as Glynos and Howarth (2008: 165) argue, "furnish us with the means to explain the way subjects are gripped or held by a practice or regime of practices."

Through a better understanding of how media texts work, and are received, we can argue that media texts activate discourses; they operate as platforms for the struggle over meaning and the (attempted) construction of social imaginaries. As location of these struggles, which implies that they serve as catalysts of a multitude of discourses, they also offer audiences a multiplicity of identification points. The acts of identification, in which audiences engage when they encounter media texts, are to be seen as moments of human agency and individuality, where subjects invest in particular discourses (and not in others). It is precisely this notion of identification that theorizes the reception of media texts as phantasmatic sites where discourses work upon the subject, succeeding (or failing) in getting a hold on them.

But identification, in the context of audience reception, cannot be theorized in isolation from the process of *interpretation,* i.e. the process of allocating meaning to the text. From a DT perspective, two distinct logics affect the process of interpretation: the logic of *recognition* and the logic of *identification.* The logic of recognition is reminiscent of Hall's (1980) concept of preferred reading and refers to the way audiences tend to recognize the discourses that are put to work in media texts. The logic of recognition follows from the broader hegemonic discursive formation shared by media producers and media audiences, which indeed implies that the latter will often—without a high level of reflexivity— recognize the hegemonic meanings inscribed in the media text. The logic of recognition uses the framework of DT to rephrase the structured agency that Hall acknowledged, but which is also present in audience reception studies more in general. Along the lines of DT, Hall's decoding (1980) can indeed be seen as an active form of reception that "must be understood as a particular intervention, as minute as it may be, into the very meaning structures of a given hegemonic formation" (Marchart 2011: 75). At the same time, the logic of recognition draws attention to how textual openness and the possibility of polysemy ("many meanings") (Fiske 1998; Hall 1980) are not endless. While audiences may evaluate the media message in different ways, they often share a particular reading of its meaning. They produce what Hall (1980) called a preferred reading, which implies that they engage in the logic of recognition.

But recognition does not speak to how subjects *invest* in some of the identification points that are offered to them. The logic of identification, as mentioned earlier, refers to how discourses (that are activated in media coverage) get a hold on (a member of) the audience. When subjects identify with a subject position that interpellates them, through a media text, they invest in a discourse that they come to embody and enact. Still, contingency also lurks here. Identifications are always incomplete, and they never exactly coincide with

21

the subject position itself (Glynos 2012; Glynos and Howarth 2008). It is also through this process that human subjectivity and agency are achieved. As Marchart (2011: 75) argues, "no subject is fully 'subjected' to the force of interpellation." Identification is thus often partial, when audiences actively and creatively negotiate and combine discourses and subject positions in a way that caters to their sense of subjectivity. But human subjectivity can also manifest itself in the form of dis-identification, when audiences mobilize (and identify with) alternative discourses and subject positions. Identification, in this case, becomes a matter of de-subjection, subversion, disagreement, and dissent—thus allowing for "shifts within the hegemonic balance of forces" (Marchart 2011: 75). At the same time, subjectivity and agency are not completely disconnected from discourse; they "only proceed through the process of identification" (Laclau 1990: 44). Identification still creates connections between the subject and existing discursive structures and subject positions that are outside the subject (Carpentier 2011: 178). In identifying *and* in dis-identifying with discourses, activated in media texts, audiences remain reliant on the discourses that are "available" in media texts *and* in society—discourses that provide them with subject positions to identify with and which, in turn, allow them to "speak."

Outline of the book

The contributions to this volume are divided into five sections. The section concentrates on DT-inspired analyses of political ideologies, and their manifestation, reproduction, and contestation in media, communication, and culture. Yiannis Mylonas' article, "Crisis, Austerity and Opposition in Mainstream Media Discourses in Greece", deals with the ideological dimensions of how the Greek media have covered one of the defining moments in the recent history of the European Union: The financial crisis and its consequences for Greece. Kirill Filimonov and Jakob Svensson's chapter "(Re)Articulating Feminism: A Discourse Analysis of Sweden's Feminist Initiative Election Campaign" focuses on the hegemonic project of feminist politics in Sweden. Benjamin De Cleen's chapter, "The Stage as an Arena of Politics: The Struggle between the Vlaams Blok/Belang and the Flemish City Theaters," finally, analyzes how nationalism, conservatism, and populism are combined in the rhetoric of the radical-right-wing party Vlaams Blok/Belang, against the Flemish theaters.

The second section moves away from the strictly political to turn its attention to the political dimensions of life-political issues. Leen Van Brussel's chapter deploys DT to probe into the discursive struggles to define "The good death" in media representations of euthanasia. Nico Carpentier turns his attention toward the discourses on relationships and sexuality produced by reality television in "Putting Your Relationship to the Test: Constructions of Fidelity, Seduction, and Participation in *Temptation Island*."

The third section groups contributions that mobilize DT to perform critical-culturalist analyses of the role of discourse in media and communication production, the identities of media professionals, and media practices. In "The Postmodern Challenge to Journalism: Strategies for Constructing a Trustworthy Identity," Jo Bogaerts and Nico Carpentier analyze how the journalistic hegemonic discursive formations, build around a number of core journalist values, is being dislocated in the era of liquid modernity. The next chapter is Nico Carpentier and Marit Trioen's "The Particularity of Objectivity: A Poststructuralist and Psychoanalytical Reading of the Gap between Objectivity-as-Value and Objectivity-as-Practice in the 2003 Iraqi War Coverage." Carpentier and Trioen turn their attention to one of the central signifiers in mainstream journalistic discourse, objectivity, and analyze how war journalism creates tensions between rhetoric about objectivity and actual journalistic practices.

In the fourth section, the focus shifts toward audiences and how audiences are invited to participate in different media and communication contexts. In "The Articulation of 'Audience' in Chinese Communication Research," Guiquan Xu critically analyzes the construction of the identity of the audience in Chinese communication studies. Then, Krista Lepik and Nico Carpentier zoom in on the processes of "Articulating the Visitor in Public Knowledge Institutions." Nico Carpentier and Wim Hannot's "To be a Common Hero: The Uneasy Balance between the Ordinary and Ordinariness in the Subject Position of Mediated Ordinary People in the Talk Show *Jan Publiek*" focuses on the ambiguities of how media practices construct the identity of the participating audience.

A fifth and final section brings together analyses of the role of media and communication in activism, resistance, and empowerment. Giulia Airaghi's chapter on "Online Barter and Counter-Hegemonic Resistance" analyzes the practice of online barter as an emergent phenomenon of resistance and potential counter-hegemony. Itır Akdoğan concentrates on how Turkish activists perceive the role of ICT in social change, thereby mobilizing a number of "activist fantasies." In the last chapter of the book—"Contesting the Populist Claim on "The People" through Popular Culture: The 0110 Concerts versus the Vlaams Belang"—Benjamin De Cleen and Nico Carpentier turn their attention toward how popular culture acquires meaning in the discursive struggle against populist radical-right politics.

References

Airaghi, Giulia (2013), "The political practice of everyday life: The practice of barter," in I. Tomanić, N. Carpentier, H. Nieminen, P. Pruulmann-Vengerfeldt, R. Kilborn, E. Sundin, and T. Olsson (eds), *Past, Future and Change: Contemporary Analysis of Evolving Media Scapes: The Intellectual Work of ECREA's 2010 European Media and Communication Doctoral Summer School*, Ljubljana: University of Ljubljana Press, pp. 297–307.
—— (2014) "The political dimension of consumption: The case of online barter," Ph.D. thesis, Milan and Brussels: Catholic University of the Sacred Heart and Free University of Brussels (VUB).

Akdoğan, Itır (2012), "Digital-political fantasies in Istanbul: An analysis of the perceived role of ICT in changing institutional politics, activism, and identity," Ph.D. thesis, Helsinki: University of Helsinki.

Angermuller, Johannes (2014), *Poststructuralist Discourse Analysis: Subjectivity in Enunciative Pragmatics*, Houndmills: Palgrave Macmillan.

Askanius, Tina and Mylonas, Yiannis (2015), "Extreme-right responses to the European economic crisis in Denmark and Sweden: The discursive construction of scapegoats and lodestars," *Javnost—The Public*, 22:1, pp. 55–72.

Askanius, Tina and Uldam, Julie (2011), "Online social media for radical politics: Climate change activism on YouTube," *International Journal of Electronic Governance*, 4:1-2, pp. 69–84.

Bacchi, Carol and Goodwin, Susan (2016), *Poststructural Policy Analysis*, New York: Springer.

Barthes, Roland (1975), *The Pleasure of the Text*, New York: Farrar, Straus and Giroux.

Biglieri, Paula and Perelló, Gloria (2011), "The names of the Real in Laclau's theory: Antagonism, dislocation, and heterogeneity," *Filozofski Vestnik*, XXXII:2, pp. 47–64.

Blommaert, Jan (2005), "Critical discourse analysis," *Annual Review of Anthropology*, 29, pp. 447–66.

Boje, David M. and Cai, Yue (2008), "A discursive critique of 'McJob': Putting Laclau, Mouffe and Bakhtin to work," in N. Carpentier and E. Spinoy (eds), *Discourse Theory and Cultural Analysis: Media, Arts and Literature*, Cresskill: Hampton Press, pp. 169–78.

Butler, Judith (1997), "Contingent foundations," in S. E. Bronner (ed.), *Twentieth Century Political Theory*, New York: Routledge, pp. 248–58.

Cammaerts, Bart and Carpentier, Nico (2006), "The Internet and the Second Iraqi War: Extending participation and challenging mainstream journalism?," in N. Carpentier, P. Pruulmann-Vengerfeldt, K. Nordenstreng, M. Hartmann, P. Vihalemm, and B. Cammaerts (eds), *Researching Media, Democracy and Participation: The Intellectual Work of the 2006 European Media and Communication Doctoral Summer School*, Tartu: University of Tartu Press, pp. 157–71.

—— (2009), "Blogging the 2003 Iraq War: Challenging the ideological model of war and mainstream journalism?," *OBS**, 3:2, http://obs.obercom.pt/index.php/obs/article/view/276. Accessed 17 April 2008.

Carpentier, Nico (2004), "The identity of the television audience: Towards the articulation of the television audience as a discursive field," in N. Carpentier, C. Pauwels, and O. Van Oost (eds), *The Ungraspable Audience (Het On[be]grijpbare Publiek)*, Brussels: VUBPress, pp. 95–122.

—— (2005), "Identity, contingency and rigidity: The (counter-)hegemonic constructions of the identity of the media professional," *Journalism*, 6:2, pp. 199–219.

—— (2010), "Deploying discourse theory: An introduction to discourse theory and discourse theoretical analysis," in N. Carpentier, I. Tomanić Trivundza, P. Pruulmann-Vengerfeldt, E. Sundin, T. Olsson, R. Kilborn, H. Nieminen, and B. Cammaerts (eds), *Media and Communication Studies Interventions: The Intellectual Work of ECREA's 2010 European Media and Communication Doctoral Summer School*, Tartu: Tartu University Press, pp. 251–66.

—— (2011), *Media and Participation: A Site of Ideological-Democratic Struggle*, Bristol: Intellect.

—— (2015), "Who to serve and how? A discourse-theoretical analysis of public service broadcasting as a floating signifier," *Media and Communication (Mediji i Komunikacije)*, 2:4, pp. 7–23.

—— (2017a), *The Discursive-Material Knot: Cyprus in Conflict and Community Media Participation*, New York: Peter Lang.

—— (2017b), "Discourse-theoretical analysis," in J. Richardson and J. Flowerdew (eds), *The Routledge Handbook of Critical Discourse Studies*, London: Routledge, pp. 272–84.

Carpentier, Nico and De Cleen, Benjamin (2007), "Bringing discourse theory into media studies: The applicability of discourse theoretical analysis (DTA) for the study of media practices and discourses," *Journal of Language and Politics*, 6:2, pp. 265–93.

Carpentier, Nico, Lie, Rico, and Servaes, Jan (2003), "Community media—Muting the democratic media discourse?," *Continuum*, 17:1, pp. 51–68.

Carpentier, Nico and Spinoy, Erik (eds) (2008), *Discourse Theory and Cultural Analysis: Media, Arts and Literature*, Cresskill: Hampton Press.

Carpentier, Nico and Van Brussel, Leen (2012), "On the contingency of death: A discourse-theoretical perspective on the construction of death," *Critical Discourse Studies*, 9:2, pp. 99–115.

Carvalho, Anabela (2008), "Deconstructing a Portuguese city: Cement, advertising and the hegemony of 'green growth'," in N. Carpentier and E. Spinoy (eds), *Discourse Theory and Cultural Analysis: Media, Arts and Literature*, Cresskill: Hampton Press, pp. 179–206.

Critchley, Simon and Marchart, Oliver (eds) (2004a), *Laclau: A Critical Reader*, London and New York: Routledge.

—— (2004b), "Introduction," in S. Critchley and O. Marchart (eds), *Laclau: A Critical Reader*, London and New York: Routledge, pp. 1–13.

Cuevas Valenzuela, Hernán (2008), "Chilean traumatized identity: Discourse theory and the analysis of visual arts," in N. Carpentier and E. Spinoy (eds), *Discourse Theory and Cultural Analysis: Media, Arts and Literature*, Cresskill: Hampton Press, pp. 141–68.

Curran, James (1997), "Rethinking the media as public sphere," in P. Dahlgren and C. Sparks (eds), *Communication and Citizenship*, London and New York: Routledge, pp. 27–57.

Dahlberg, Lincoln and Phelan, Sean (eds) (2011), *Discourse Theory and Critical Media Politics*, Houndmills: Palgrave Macmillan.

Dahlgren, Peter (2011), "Mobilizing discourse theory for critical media politics: Obstacles and potentials," in L. Dahlberg and P. Sean (eds), *Discourse Theory and Critical Media Politics*, Houndmills: Palgrave Macmillan, pp. 222–49.

De Cleen, Benjamin (2008), "Downloading as piracy: Discourse and the political economy of the recording industry," in N. Carpentier and E. Spinoy (eds), *Discourse Theory and Cultural Analysis*, Creskill: Hampton Press, pp. 245–65.

—— (2009), "Popular music against extreme right populism," *International Journal of Cultural Studies*, 12:6, pp. 577–95.

—— (2015), "'Flemish friends, let us separate!': The discursive struggle for Flemish nationalist civil society in the media," *Javnost—The Public*, 22:1, pp. 37–54.

—— (2016), "The party of the people versus the cultural elite: Populism and nationalism in Flemish radical right rhetoric about artists," *JOMEC—Journal of Journalism, Media and Cultural Studies*, 9, pp. 69–91.

De Cleen, Benjamin and Stavrakakis, Yannis (2017), "Distinctions and articulations: A discourse-theoretical framework for the study of populism and nationalism," *Javnost—The Public*, 24:4, pp. 301–19.

De Cleen, Benjamin, Zienkowski, Jan, Smets, Kevin, Dekie, Afra, and Vandevoordt, Robin (2017), "Constructing the 'refugee crisis' in Flanders: Continuities and adaptations of discourses on asylum and migration," in M. Barlai, B. Fähnrich, C. Griessler, and M. Rhomberg (eds), *The Migration Crisis: European Perspectives and National Discourses*, Berlin: LIT-Verlag, pp. 59–78.

Dittmar, Norbert (1976), *Sociolinguistics: A Critical Survey of Theory and Application*, London: Edward Arnold.

Doudaki, Vaia (2015), "Legitimation mechanisms in the bailout discourse," *Javnost—The Public*, 22:1, pp. 1–17.

Durnova, Anna (2013), "Governing through intimacy: Explaining care policies through 'sharing a meaning'," *Critical Social Policy*, 33:3, pp. 494–513.

Edward, Mark (2008), "A (brief) critique of Laclau and Mouffe's discourse analysis," Struggleswithphilosophy.wordpress, 11 September, https://struggleswithphilosophy.wordpress.com/2008/09/11/a-brief-critique-of-laclau-and-mouffes-discourse-analysis/. Accessed 17 April 2008.

Fairclough, Norman (1992), *Discourse and Social Change*, Cambridge, MA: Polity Press.

Fiske, John (1998), *Understanding Popular Culture*, London: Routledge.

Foucault, Michel (1972), *L'Archéologie du savoir* (*The Archaeology of Knowledge*) (trans. Alan Sheridan), New York: Pantheon.

Gee, James (1990), *Social Linguistics and Literacies: Ideology in Discourse*, London: Falmer Press.

Geras, Norman (1987), "Post-Marxism?," *New Left Review*, I:163, pp. 40–82.

Glasze, Georg (2007), "Vorschläge zur Operationalisierung der Diskurstheorie von Laclau und Mouffe in einer Triangulation von lexikometrischen und interpretativen Methoden," *Forum Qualitative Sozialforschung* (*Forum: Qualitative Social Research*), 8:2, Art. 14, http://nbn-resolving.de/urn:nbn:de:0114-fqs0702143. Accessed 17 April 2008.

Gledhill, John (1994), *Power and Its Disguises: Anthropological Perspectives on Politics*, London and Boulder, CO: Pluto Press.

Glynos, Jason (2008), "Ideological fantasy at work," *Journal of Political Ideologies*, 13:3, pp. 275–96.

—— (2012), "Body, discourse and the turn to matter," in D. Radunovic and S. Bahun (eds), *Language, Ideology and the Human: New Interventions*, London: Ashgate, pp. 173–92.

Glynos, Jason and Howarth, David (2007), *Logics of Critical Explanation in Social and Political Theory*, London: Routledge.

—— (2008), "Structure, agency and power in political analysis: Beyond contextualised self-interpretations," *Political Studies Review*, 6:2, pp. 155–69.

Glynos, Jason and Speed, Ewen (2012), "Varieties of co-production in public services: Time banks in a UK health policy context," *Critical Policy Studies*, 6:4, pp. 4012–33.

Glynos, Jason, Speed, Ewen, and West, Karen (2015), "Logics of marginalisation in health and social care reform: Integration, choice and provider-blind provision," *Critical Social Policy*, 35:1, pp. 45–68.

Gotti, Maurizio and Salager-Meyer, Françoise (eds) (2006), *Advances in Medical Discourse Analysis: Oral & Written Contexts*, Bern: Peter Lang.

Gramsci, Antonio (1999), *The Antonio Gramsci Reader: Selected Writings 1916–1935*, London: Lawrence & Wishart.

Grant, David, Iedema, Rick, and Oswick, Cliff (2009), "Discourse and critical management studies," in M. Alvesson, T. Bridgeman, and H. Willmott (eds), *The Oxford Handbook of Critical Management Studies*, Oxford: Oxford University Press, pp. 213–31.

Hall, Stuart (1980), "Encoding/decoding," in S. Hall (ed.), *Culture, Media, Language: Working Papers in Cultural Studies, 1972–79*, London: Hutchinson, pp. 128–38.

—— (1997), "The work of representation," in S. Hall (ed.), *Representation: Cultural Representations and Signifying Practices*, London, Thousand Oaks, CA, and New Delhi: Sage, pp. 13–64.

Heritage, John (1984), *Garfinkel and Ethnomethodology*, Cambridge, MA: Polity Press.

Howarth, David (1998), "Discourse theory and political analysis," in E. Scarbrough and E. Tanenbaum (eds), *Research Strategies in the Social Sciences*, Oxford: Oxford University Press, pp. 268–93.

—— (2000), *Discourse*, Buckingham and Philadelphia: Open University Press.

—— (2004), "Hegemony, political subjectivity and radical democracy," in S. Critchley and O. Marchart (eds), *Laclau: A Critical Reader*, London and New York: Routledge, pp. 256–76.

—— (2013), *Poststructuralism and After: Structure, Subjectivity and Power*, Houndmills: Palgrave Macmillan.

Howarth, David, Norval, Aletta, and Stavrakakis, Yannis (eds) (2000), *Discourse Theory and Political Analysis: Identities, Hegemonies and Social Change*, Manchester: Manchester University Press.

Howarth, David and Stavrakakis, Yannis (2000), "Introducing discourse theory and political analysis," in D. Howarth, A. Norval, and Y. Stavrakakis (eds), *Discourse Theory and Political Analysis: Identities, Hegemonies and Social Change*, Manchester: Manchester University Press, pp. 1–23.

Howarth, David and Torfing, Jakob (eds) (2005), *Discourse Theory in European Politics*, Houndmills: Palgrave.

Husted, Emil (2015), "From creation to amplification: Occupy Wall Street's transition into an online populist movement," in J. Uldam and A. Vestergaard (eds), *Civic Engagement and Social Media: Political Participation Beyond Protest*, Houndmills: Palgrave Macmillan, pp. 153–73.

Jones, Campbell (2009), "Poststructuralism in critical management studies," in M. Alvesson, T. Bridgeman, and H. Willmott (eds), *The Oxford Handbook of Critical Management Studies*, Oxford: Oxford University Press, pp. 76–98.

Joseph, Jonathan (2003), *Hegemony: A Realist Analysis*, London and New York: Routledge.

Kompatsiaris, Panos and Mylonas, Yiannis (2015), "The rise of Nazism and the web: Social media as platforms of racist discourses in the context of the Greek Economic Crisis," in D. Trottier and C. Fuchs (eds), *Social Media, Politics and the State: Protests, Revolutions, Riots, Crime and Policing in the Age of Facebook, Twitter and YouTube*, London: Routledge, pp. 109–48.

Laclau, Ernesto (1977), *Politics and Ideology in Marxist Theory: Capitalism, Fascism, Populism*, London: New Left Books.

—— (1988), "Metaphor and social antagonisms," in C. Nelson and L. Grossberg (eds), *Marxism and the Interpretation of Culture*, Urbana: University of Illinois, pp. 249–57.

—— (1990), "New reflections on the revolution of our time," in E. Laclau (ed.), *New Reflections on the Revolution of Our Time*, London: Verso, pp. 3–85.

—— (1996), *Emancipations*, London: Verso.

—— (2000), "Identity and hegemony: The role of universality in the constitution of political logics," in J. Butler, E. Laclau, and S. Žižek (eds), *Contingency, Hegemony, Universality: Contemporary Dialogues on the Left*, London: Verso, pp. 44–89.

—— (2005), *On Populist Reason*, London: Verso.

Laclau, Ernesto and Mouffe, Chantal (1985), *Hegemony and Socialist Strategy: Towards a Radical Democratic Politics*, London: Verso.

—— (1990), "Post-Marxism without apologies," in E. Laclau (ed.), *New Reflections on the Revolution of Our Time*, London: Verso, pp. 97–132.

Laclau, Ernesto and Zac, Lilian (1994), "Minding the gap: The subject of politics," in E. Laclau (ed.), *The Making of Political Identities*, London: Verso, pp. 11–39.

Mäe, Rene (2015), "The creative industries: A discourse-theoretical approach," *International Review of Social Research*, 5:2, pp. 78–87.

Maeseele, Pieter (2011), "On news media and democratic debate," *International Communication Gazette*, 73:1-2, pp. 83–105.

Marchart, Oliver (2011), "From media to mediality: Mediatic (counter-)apparatuses and the concept of the political in communication studies," in L. Dahlberg and S. Phelan (eds), *Discourse Theory and Critical Media Politics*, Houndmills: Palgrave Macmillan, pp. 64–81.

Martínez Martínez, Germán (2008), "The changing national identity in contemporary Mexican cinema," in N. Carpentier and E. Spinoy (eds), *Discourse Theory and Cultural Analysis: Media, Arts and Literature*, Cresskill: Hampton Press, pp. 97–118.

Marttila, Tomas (2015), *Post-Foundational Discourse Analysis: From Political Difference to Empirical Research*, Houndmills: Palgrave Macmillan.

Maso, Ilja (1989), *Kwalitatief onderzoek*, Boom: Meppel.

Mills, Sara (1997), *Discourse*, London: Routledge.

Moffitt, Benjamin (2016), *The Global Rise of Populism: Performance, Political Style, and Representation*, Stanford, CA: Stanford University Press.

—— (2017), "Transnational populism? Representative claims, media and the difficulty of constructing a transnational 'people'," *Javnost—The Public*, 5 July, http://dx.doi.org/10.1080/13183222.2017.1330086. Accessed 17 April 2008.

Mouffe, Chantal (1993), *The Return of the Political*, London and New York: Verso.

—— (1999), "Deliberative democracy or agonistic pluralism?," *Social Research*, 66:3, pp. 754–58.

—— (2000), *The Democratic Paradox*, London and New York: Verso.

—— (2005), *On the Political*, London: Routledge.

—— (2007), "Artistic activism and agonistic spaces," *Art and Research*, 1:2, http://www.artandresearch.org.uk/v1n2/mouffe.html. Accessed 17 April 2008.

—— (2013), *Agonistics: Thinking the World Politically*, London and New York: Verso.

—— (2018), *For a Left Populism*, London and New York: Verso.

Mylonas, Yiannis (2012a), "Reinventing political subjectivities: Studying critical documentaries on the war on terror," *Social Semiotics*, 22:4, pp. 353–74.

—— (2012b), "Media and the economic crisis of the EU: The 'culturalization' of a systemic crisis and Bild-Zeitung's framing of Greece," *TripleC*, 10:2, pp. 646–71.

—— (2015), "Austerity discourses in *Der Spiegel* journal, 2009–2014," *TripleC*, 13:1, pp. 248–69.

—— (2017), "Liberal articulations of the 'Enlightenment' in the Greek public sphere," *Journal of Language and Politics*, 16:2, pp. 195–218.

Mylonas, Yiannis and Kompatsiaris, Panos (2013), "Culturalist explanations of the crisis in the Greek public sphere," in G. Pleios (ed.), *Crisis and Media*, Athens: Papazisis, pp. 387–419.

Nonhoff, Martin (2007), "Politische Diskursanalyse als Hegemonieanalyse," in N. K. Martin (ed.), *Diskurs, Radikale Demokratie, Hegemonie: Zum Politischen Denken von Ernesto Laclau und Chantal Mouffe*, Bielefeld: Transcript, pp. 173–93.

Peck, Janice (1995), "Talk shows as therapeutic discourse: The ideological labor of televised talking cure," *Communication Theory*, 5:1, pp. 58–81.

Phelan, Sean (2009), "The newspaper as political antagonist: Editorial discourse and the othering of Maori perspectives on the foreshore and seabed conflict," *Journalism*, 10:2, pp. 217–37.

Phelan, Sean and Dahlberg, Lincoln (2014), "Introduction: Post-Marxist discourse theory and critical political economy," *Critical Discourse Studies*, 11:3, pp. 255–56.

Philips, Louise and Jørgensen, Marianne W. (2002), *Discourse Analysis as Theory and Method*, London: Sage.

Raeijmaeckers, Danielle and Maeseele, Pieter (2015), "Media, pluralism, and democracy: What's in a name?," *Media, Culture & Society*, 37:7, pp. 1042–59.

Rear, David and Jones, Alan (2013), "Discursive struggle and contested signifiers in the arenas of education policy and work skills in Japan," *Critical Policy Studies*, 7:13, pp. 375–94.

Ritzer, George (1992), *Sociological Theory*, New York: McGraw-Hill.

Roberts, Celia and Sarani, Srikant (2005), "Theme-oriented discourse analysis of medical encounters," *Medical Education*, 39:6, pp. 632–40.

Sawyer, Keith R. (2002), "A discourse on discourse: An archeological history of an intellectual concept," *Cultural Studies*, 16:3, pp. 433–56.

Schou, Yannick (2016), "Ernesto Laclau and critical media studies: Marxism, capitalism, and critique," *TripleC*, 14:1, pp. 292–311.

Simons, Jon (2011), "Mediated constructions of the people: Laclau's political theory and media politics," in L. Dahlberg and S. Phelan (eds), *Discourse Theory and Critical Media Politics*, Houndmills: Palgrave Macmillan, pp. 201–21.

Smith, Anna Marie (1999), *Laclau and Mouffe: The Radical Democratic Imaginary*, London and New York: Routledge.

Stavrakakis, Yannis (2000), "On the critique of advertising discourse: A Lacanian view," *Third Text*, 14:51, pp. 85–90.

—— (2007), *The Lacanian Left: Essays on Psychoanalysis and Politics*, Edinburgh: Edinburgh University Press.

Stavrakakis, Yannis and Katsambekis, Giorgios (2014), "Left-wing populism in the European periphery: The case of SYRIZA," *Journal of Political Ideologies*, 19:2, pp. 119–42.

Stavrakakis, Yannis, Katsambekis, Giorgios, Nikisianis, Nikos, Kioupkiolis, Alexandros, and Siomos, Thomas (2017), "Extreme right-wing populism in Europe: Revisiting a reified association," *Critical Discourse Studies*, 14:4, pp. 420–39.

Therborn, Göran (2008), *From Marxism to Post-Marxism?*, London: Verso.

Titscher, Stefan, Meyer, Michael, Wodak, Ruth, and Vetter, Eva (2000), *Methods of Text and Discourse Analysis*, London, Thousand Oaks, CA, and New Delhi: Sage.

Toepfl, Florian (2016), "Beyond the four theories: Toward a discourse approach to the comparative study of media and politics," *International Journal of Communication*, 10, pp. 1530–47.

Tomanić Trivundža, Ilija (2015), "Are a thousand pictures worth a single word? The struggle between condemnatory and affirmative discourses on photographic change in Slovene and UK mainstream media news reports on selfies," *Javnost—The Public*, 22:1, pp. 93–109.

Torfing, Jacob (1999), *New Theories of Discourse: Laclau, Mouffe and Žižek*, Oxford: Blackwell.

—— (2005), "Discourse theory: Achievements, arguments and challenges," in D. Howarth and J. Torfing (eds), *Discourse Theory in European Politics: Identity, Policy and Governance*, Houndmills: Palgrave Macmillan, pp. 1–32.

Van Brussel, Leen (2012), "Autonomy and dignity: A discussion on contingency and dominance," *Health Care Analysis*, 22:2, pp. 171–91.

—— (2014), "A discourse-theoretical approach to death and dying," in L. Van Brussel and N. Carpentier (eds), *The Social Construction of Death*, Houndmills: Palgrave Macmillan, pp. 13–33.

—— (2018), "The right to die: A Belgian case study combining reception studies and discourse theory," *Media, Culture & Society*, 40:3, pp. 381–96.

Van Brussel, Leen and Carpentier, Nico (2012), "The discursive construction of the good death and the dying person," *Journal of Language and Politics*, 11:4, pp. 479–99.

—— (2017), "Closing the book of life: The hospice discourse and the construction of the dying role: A discourse-theoretical analysis," in V. Parvaresh and A. Capone (eds), *The Pragmeme of Accommodation: The Case of Interaction around the Event of Death*, Berlin: Springer, pp. 375–401.

Wang, Yow-Jiun (2008), "The 'outside' inside us: Antagonisms and identities in Taiwanese online gay forums," in N. Carpentier and E. Spinoy (eds), *Discourse Theory and Cultural Analysis: Media, Arts and Literature*, Cresskill: Hampton Press, pp. 169–78.

West, Karen (2013), "The grip of personalization in adult social care: Between managerial domination and fantasy," *Critical Social Policy*, 33:4, pp. 638–57.

West, Karen, Shaw, Rachel, Hagger, Barbara, and Holland, Carol (2017), "Enjoying the third age! Discourse, identity and liminality in extra-care communities," *Ageing and Society*, 37:9, pp. 1874–97.

Wester, Fred (1987), *Strategieën voor kwalitatief onderzoek*, Muiderberg: Coutinho.

—— (1995), "Inhoudsanalyse als kwalitatief-interpreterende werkwijze," in H. Hüttner, K. Renckstorf, and F. Wester (eds), *Onderzoekstypen in de communicatiewetenschap*, Houten and Diegem: Bohn Stafleu Van Loghum, pp. 624–49.

Wodak, Ruth (2008), "Introduction: Discourse studies: Important concepts and terms," in M. Krzyzanowski and R. Wodak (eds), *Qualitative Discourse Analysis in the Social Sciences*, Houndmills: Palgrave Macmillan, pp. 1–29.

Xu, Guiquan (2013), "The discourses of Chinese audience research: A discourse-theoretical analysis of the articulation of audience in Chinese academic texts," Ph.D. thesis, Brussels and Beijing: Free University of Brussels (VUB) and Communication University of China (CUC).

Zienkowski, Jan (2012), "Overcoming the post-structuralist methodological deficit: Metapragmatic markers and interpretative logics in a critique of the Bologna process," *Pragmatics*, 22:3, pp. 501–34.

Žižek, Slavoj (1990), "Beyond discourse analysis," in E. Laclau (ed.), *New Reflections on the Revolution of Our Time*, London: Verso, pp. 249–60.

Notes

1 Parts of this introduction have been published before (Carpentier and De Cleen 2007; Carpentier 2010; Carpentier 2017a, 2017b).

2 The term discourse then refers to more particular components, namely the many discourses that circulate in society, and that provide meaning to particular processes, phenomena, actors, objects, etc. It is here that the emergence, functioning, and changing of the multitude of analytically distinguishable discourses can be analyzed.

3 Laclau and Mouffe see elements as differential positions, which are not (yet) discursively articulated. Moments are differential positions that are articulated within a discourse.

4 Later on, (mainly) Laclau will refer to the Lacanian concept of lack to theorize this structural openness.

5 Differences in interpretation arise on the question whether the analyzed discourses are part of the field of discursivity or not. In this text the first interpretation is preferred (in contrast to Philips and Jørgensen 2002: 56), so the field of discursivity is defined here as the combination of actual and potential articulations.

6 In *Agonistics*, Mouffe (2013: 109) argues that "this antagonistic conflict can take different forms," in order to introduce the distinction between "antagonism proper" and "agonism," underneath the umbrella term of "antagonism."

7 See Carpentier (2017a, 2017b).

8 To do justice to Biglieri and Perelló's (2011) work, they refer to the Lacanian Real. Of course, with this argument we do not want to equate the Real with the material.

Section 1

Political Ideologies

Chapter 1

Crisis, Austerity, and Opposition in Mainstream Media Discourses in Greece

Yiannis Mylonas

Introduction: Crisis, discourse, and politics

This chapter presents a critical study of mainstream media representations of the EU's current economic crisis. The study focuses on hegemonic narratives of the crisis and the sociopolitical opposition to crisis-politics (such as austerity measures), as they appear in the Greek newspaper, *Kathimerini*. I characterize these media discourses as neoliberal, based on relevant literature analyzing the ideology of late capitalism (Brown 2003; Crouch 2011; Harvey 2005).

The study draws on both a critical political economic perspective on capitalism (De Angelis 2004; Harman 2009; Harvey 2010; Marx 1976) and a discourse-theoretical perspective on politics (Laclau 1996; Laclau and Mouffe 1985). I use discourse theory to analyze the hegemonic discourse of crisis capitalism in public articulations of mainstream visions and strategies to overcome the crisis. As discourse[1] has a material impact, discourse theory analyzes the myths of neoliberal capitalism in the crisis-context, while political economy addresses the materiality of the capitalist process itself. I understand the economy as political and understand politics as primarily discursive. The analysis departs from an understanding of political struggles and interventions as contingent. However, it also takes into account the politico-historical limits of social contingency that are due to sedimented (Laclau 1996: 88) power hierarchies, social relations, and social institutions, such as private property. In the course of time, hegemony produces forms of order, institutions, and social relations that become naturalized, established, and concrete grounds for human activity. Despite its essentialism, such naturalness and concreteness, however, is historically and socially constructed.

A capitalist crisis

The economy is always political, because it is organized by political interventions. Capitalism is a closed sociopolitical system that is established and naturalized by political interventions, norms, and narratives that organize social life according to capital's demands. The economic crisis (and its management) is thus deeply political, despite the reified character of a capitalist economy as a historical or natural entity. An apolitical understanding of the (capitalist) economy fails to acknowledge the political measures required for the establishment and maintenance of capitalist social relations. Simultaneously, it obfuscates the agency behind the massive destruction and inequalities capitalism produces worldwide. The crisis that Europe and the world are undergoing is a crisis of the late capitalist mode of production (that is neutrally described as "growth"). This is due to contradictions—both objective and subjective ones—that the capitalist process periodically reaches (Badiou 2012; Douzinas 2013; Hardt and Negri 2012; Harvey 2010).

Crises are inherent in the capitalist process[2] (Harman 2009; Harvey 2010). Crises are the limits that capital meets—the "challenges" that the managerial class refers to—that need to be overcome so that capitalist expansion and accumulation can continue. Such limits are met in the contradictions emerging during the strategic synthesis of the features putting capitalism into motion. Harvey (2010: 138) argues that these features include technology, organizational forms, social relations, institutional and administrative arrangements, production and labor processes, the uses of nature, mental concepts, and the reproduction of daily life. Capital is required to constantly revolutionize the ways in which the above features can be productively utilized, which requires a periodical destruction and re-invention of resources, institutions, or fixed, variable, and monetary capital (Harman 2009). Enclosures are capital's strategy of overcoming the limits it meets. Enclosures are organized by state policies. Marx used the term "primitive accumulation" to describe enclosures as an important step for the organization of capital. For De Angelis, enclosures concern the separation of humans from the means of production, and the construction of scarcities, which will tie societies to the sort of social relations favored by capital. De Angelis (2004: 68) recognizes two categories as limits to capital: (1) the frontier, which concerns areas of the social and natural world not colonized by capitalist social relations and rationales, and (2) the political limits placed by powers operating against capital. De Angelis argues that enclosures[3] have a disciplinary effect as they produce the social subjectivities necessary for the reproduction of the social relations and social myths characterizing the capitalist society. It is on this aspect of crisis-politics that this chapter focuses in particular.

The political crisis of contemporary Greece and Europe

To understand the politics of the crisis, one needs to address the advance of neoliberalism from the 1970s' "oil crisis" onwards (Harvey 2005). Neoliberalism is primarily a system of governance connected to the requirements of late capitalist growth. A neoliberal society is a market society run by economistic rationales, or, differently put, a biopolitical system of governance based on the primacy of the market mechanism (Foucault 2008: 30).

Žižek (2010) and Klein (2007) argue that the crisis provides a pretext for the development of a post-democratic form of governance, run by economistic principles. The advent of neoliberalism means the dismantling not only of the democratic pillars of liberal democracy (such as popular sovereignty in decision-making processes) but also of the liberal foundations of today's democracy (related to civil rights that are compromised or exempted in the emergency context of the crisis; Douzinas 2013). Rancière (2009), Lasch

(1996), and others (Agamben et al. 2009; Crouch 2004) argue that the economic elites are increasingly uncomfortable with democracy. The democratic horizon expresses the unlimited possibilities of politics to produce new forms of social constitution that could threaten established norms, institutions, and power relations. Democracy can challenge elite power and its aspirations for limitless profiteering and exploitation of labor or nature. Neoliberal interventions attempt to colonize democracy, demarcating its limits and neutralizing popular sovereignty. The neutralization of democracy requires the shrinking of the public spaces where politics are practiced. This occurs by the merging of state power and economic power under a scientific mode of governance that manages flows of finance and populations (Rancière 2009: 131). In this context, democracy is instrumentalized to legitimize the logics and decisions of society's most powerful.

From the beginning of Europe's economic crisis, neoliberal politicians and economists presented Greece as an exception within Europe, largely responsible for the Eurozone's crisis (Douzinas 2013). The pathologization of Greece provided the ground for exceptional policies to emerge. These surpassed constitutional rights and legitimized authoritarian and punitive policies for the country, whilst neutralizing and demonizing popular resistances (Mylonas 2012). Similar exceptional measures were to be adopted not much later in other countries quarantined according to the "crisis" political pretext, such as Ireland, Portugal, and Spain. Neoliberal discourses constructed Greece as a model of deviancy, where the rationales and sociopolitical constitutions for a post-crisis capitalism would be grounded and implemented. The economic crisis requires new political institutions, and Greece serves as an experimental laboratory (Badiou 2012), where the limits of crisis governance are tested and neoliberal reforms are implemented.

In this eschatological context, sociopolitical struggles are addressed as anomic, and dealt with through punitive measures, on the premise of an indefinite "national crisis-emergency." Sevastakis and Stavrakakis (2012) argue that "populism" is the umbrella term constructed by neoconservative and neoliberal elites in Europe to discredit leftist alternatives to neoliberalism. In this narrative, populism is discussed in moralistic terms, stressing personal responsibility, guilt, and obedience to expert systems. Citizens are configured as clients rather than as political subjects. Democracy itself thus becomes seen as populist as it is contingent to people's choices, aspirations, and struggles. The populist "evil" seems to block what is presented as essential and commonsense by politico-economic experts. However, as Laclau (2005) has argued, all politics bear a degree of populism, as they address—and also construct—the people. The elites' configuration of politics as populist, thus, masks the desire of a powerful oligarchy to rule without divisions of the people and without politics (Rancière 2009: 113).

The empirical field: (Neo)liberal constructions of the crisis in Greece

This chapter analyzes the articulations of the crisis by columnists of the Greek newspaper *Kathimerini* (Η Καθημερινή). The analysis will show how *Kathimerini* mediated the hegemonic meanings of the crisis and the prevailing modes of crisis-management to the Greek public sphere. It will also reflect on what the political implications of this are from a radical democratic perspective. Founded in 1919, *Kathimerini* is a mainstream daily newspaper of liberal and conservative political orientation. *Kathimerini* belongs to the Alafouzos group of companies, related to a major shipowner family of Greece. The Alafouzos group includes Skai group—one of Greece's largest media groups— and the Panathinaikos football club, and it is involved in other business activities. *Kathimerini* was one of the first Greek newspapers to host a public daily English edition at its website that is often cited by various newspapers outside Greece. According to available data,[4] *Kathimerini*'s average daily sales (including subscriptions) is 140,761, making it one of the most popular newspapers of the country.

Research (Pleios 2013) showed that *Kathimerini* and other mainstream Greek newspapers adopted the neoliberal explanation of the economic crisis as something that is due to pathologies of the Greek society. The articles analyzed here came from the newspaper's "permanent columns" section, featuring political analyses of contemporary events. The authors featured in *Kathimerini*'s permanent columns are public intellectuals enjoying the status of experts in the Greek public sphere with the authority to comment on the events and realities in Greece and abroad. Columnists include academics from Greece and abroad, politicians, journalists, writers, economic and political analysts, and academics and scholars related to research institutions and think tanks (such as the Constantine Karamanlis Democracy Institute related to the currently governing political party of Nea Dimokratia, ELIAMEP—The Hellenic Foundation for European and Foreign Policy, and the London School of Economics Hellenic Observatory). The ideas of these authors have a broad impact on the Greek public space and often become viral in a variety of online spaces such as blogs, news portals, and social media, triggering serious debate. The authors are often invited in mainstream television and radio programs to further explain their positions.

The research presented in this chapter focuses on relevant articles exemplary of the neoliberal crisis-discourse in Greece published during three important periods during the "Greek crisis." The first one is between 1 December 2009, when the "Greek debt crisis" appeared as an emergency problem in media and political discourse in Greece and abroad, and 31 May 2010, when the Papandreou government decided to subject the country to the EU's so-called "support mechanism," prescribed by the European Central Bank, the International Monetary Fund (IMF), and the European Commission (the notorious "Troika"). The second one concerns the period from 15 May 2011 until 30 October 2011, when a series of loan agreements, known as "Memorandums" (Μνημόνια), were made by the Troika and the Greek government. These agreements concerned aggressive austerity reforms and triggered massive protests. 15 May 2011 is the day when the Indignant citizens' movement that demanded "real democracy" erupted in Spain, which was followed by its Greek equivalent on 25 May 2011. The third period covers the time between 1 April 2012 and 30 November 2012. National elections took place on 6 May and on 17 June 2012, in which the conservative party New Democracy (ND) rose to power, with a very thin electoral victory against Syriza, by then the leading leftist opposition party. The criminal and Nazi organization Golden Dawn (GD) was also elected into parliament with almost 7 percent of the votes.

The keywords used to search on *Kathimerini*'s Greek-language web archive (http://search.kathimerini.gr/) were "δημοκρατία" (democracy), "δεξιά" (the Right), "ακροδεξιά" (the far right), "Ευρώπη" (Europe), "αριστερά" (the Left), "άκρα" (extremes), "κίνημα αγανακτισμένων" (indignant citizens' movement), and "λαϊκισμός" (populism). The search produced a very high number of results[5] that needed to be limited to a manageable corpus for a qualitative research. I therefore selected particular articles from all three periods, indicative of the newspaper's approach to the crisis.

Analytical method: Critical theory and discourse theory

Concepts from discourse theory are deployed to analyze the hegemonic constructions of the capitalist crisis by *Kathimerini*'s associates, as well as the ways in which sociopolitical opposition to austerity is addressed by neoliberal ideologues. A key concept of discourse theory is hegemony, which addresses the domination of particular political ideas, currents and interventions, norms and regimes of power in a given society. Hegemony conceals the power's interventions, thus reifying social relations, economic processes, and political regimes, and also the contingent character of social life more broadly. Furthermore, hegemony has material consequences regarding the organization of social relations, everyday life, and wealth distribution (Duménil and Lévy 2011: 9).

Simultaneously, the analysis is also informed by the Marxist critical tradition of social research as this offers indispensable concepts and ideas to criticize the deficiencies and power inequalities of contemporary societies. This may contradict discourse theory's ontology as Laclau and Mouffe were highly critical of Marxism (see below). Nevertheless, bridges between the two traditions (the critical and the poststructuralist) do exist, as both strive for social change and the deepening of democracy (Carpentier and De Cleen 2007: 275).

Critical political economy approaches understand discourse as one central moment of social constitution (Harvey 2010: 138), in a dialectic relation to the other processes that produce social reality. For political economy approaches, discourse is concerned with the legitimation of political decisions and with the social hegemony of specific interests and the ideological meanings naturalizing them. In contrast, discourse theory, developed initially by Laclau and Mouffe, presents the entire field of the social as discursively constructed. The discursive focus does not reject the materiality of social constructions and realities per se, but insists on the primacy of ideas and meaning in social life, "the materiality of discourse" (Laclau and Mouffe 1985: 108). We approach the material aspects of life through meaning making.[6] By studying the discourses that construct the social order, we can understand and critique the forces shaping our world in its historical, spatial, and political dimensions, insisting on the materiality of ideas and power relations.

Social contingency is the main theoretical concept I maintain from poststructuralism, while insisting on universal values of equality, fraternity, and freedom (as emancipation and not as free-trade), as central denominators of critique. The social is a contingent space, without any essentialist fundament in its organization. Historicity and power interventions organize different forms of social establishment. Moments of crisis and social turbulence produce ruptures in the discursive and institutional establishments of a given society, challenging their legitimacy and naturalness. Although capitalism is global, and resilient, the crisis reveals great contingency that cannot be fully contained by the discourses and structures of power. The current economic crisis, an occurrence that in Badiou's (2002) terms is a pseudo-event, provides the basis where true events—that are universal and based on people's political activity—can emerge.

Discourse analysis of *Kathimerini's* articles

The texts studied below are indicative of neoliberal articulations of the economic crisis, in the discursive struggle for hegemony over the public meaning of the "Greek crisis." The political and economic affiliations of mainstream media (like *Kathimerini*) make them effective distributors and amplifiers of neoliberal discourses in the public sphere (Couldry 2010: 73). The oppositional discourses I am interested in are those broadly related to democratic politics, challenging neoliberal configurations of the economic crisis, democracy, and economistic and technocratic rationales and "realisms." My main focus is to unfold the anti-political and anti-democratic culture and politics advanced by neoliberalism through mainstream media.

I use concepts drawn from discourse theory to analyze *Kathimerini's* selected texts. Social realities concern living agents, entail historical references, and include norms and beliefs. Discourses signify and systematize features of reality in particular ways preferable to the ideology of the social agents of articulation. In moments of crisis, concepts and meanings representing crucial social domains are under contestation by competing ideologies and agents (Laclau and Mouffe 1985: 131).

Ideology presupposes configurations of a problem: who produces it and who bears it, the problem's solution, the ideal and the worst scenario of a given social crisis/problem. Nodal points are key concepts of a discourse, whose signification relies on articulation. Discursive signs are vulnerable to discursive dislocations and re-articulations, despite their phenomenal stability or coherency. The categories of "chains of equivalence" and "chains of difference" (Laclau and Mouffe 1985: 127) demonstrate the identity constructions of political discourses, concerning us–them distinctions, denoting political enmity and alliances. Discourse analysis of the crisis' constructions is further elaborated with the use of critical theory.

Constructions of the "crisis"

The neoliberal understanding of the capitalist crisis is a moralist/culturalist one (Mylonas 2012) rather than a systemic one. The crisis is presented as a problem of specific countries and specific people that *lived beyond their abilities*, or are corrupted. Politicians, technocrats, the managerial and the business class (Duménil and Lévy 2011: 90), and mainstream media across the world presented Greece as a "sick body," a problematic infant or a deviant alien in the "Eurofamily." Such discursive constructions utilized many racial stereotypes, often related to the tourist industry, exoticizing the Mediterranean as a leisure zone where locals are supposedly living a permanent vacation. Stereotypes were taken as facts and were used analytically to prove a connection between (a fundamentally rotten) Greekness and the economic crisis.

The neoliberal construction of the crisis is eschatological: countries (or continents) are facing imminent destruction, unless harsh economic reforms are implemented. The Greek people are seen as fully responsible for the crisis because they cheated on their fellow citizens of the North. Austerity and media slandering took the form of moral punishments that would reform the corrupt Greek. The culturalist crisis rationales moralize austerity as a primarily educative or disciplinary program. Disregarding the fact that the average Greek worker worked many more hours than their colleague from the North, or that Greece was one of the countries with the lowest salaries in the EU before the crisis (OECD 2012), the elites blamed the Greek middle and lower classes for the whole Eurozone crisis. As Wacquant (2012: 73) argued, the neoliberal restructuring of state and society organizes punitive policies toward the poor in order to discipline the workforce for the new requirements of capital. The moral and material discrediting of Greeks thus has a rhetorical effect for the middle and lower classes of the North, preparing them for the indefinite regimes of austerity and exception due to a crisis that seems to become permanent. As Foucault (2008:147) argued, the free-market society is not a society based on the exchange of commodities, but one *based on the dynamics of competition*. Austerity is therefore imperative and is primarily a moral task; it concerns the reinvention of "our" identity, something central in the neoliberal restructuring of society, primarily grounded on *the withdrawal of the state from areas of provision* (Wacquant 2012: 69).

Kathimerini is positive toward neoliberal reforms (such as austerity, privatizations, and the reduction of social and political rights), seeing them as necessary evils for Greece to become "truly European" and "modern." Despite being moral, reforms are presented as a-political and rational. "Anomy," "delinquency," "irrationality," and synonymous terms are widely used by *Kathimerini*'s columnists, to ground the roots of the crisis in the (corrupt) essence of contemporary Greece. For example, on 25 December 2009, in an article entitled "the Greek case," Paschos Mandravelis argued:

state deficits and debts are just the tip of the iceberg [...] bigger than the financial, is the problem of delinquency [...] all these small irregularities accumulate as grains of sand in the gears of the economy paralyzing it [...] all these created a culture of anomy, accumulating an increasing anomy.

"Anomy" in this excerpt is a nodal signifier of a discursive construction of the crisis as the outcome of what is seen as an essentially lawless and irrational culture that dominates Greece. "State deficits" are not discussed; the article shifts the attention to "culture" as the deeper layer of the crisis' truth. Corruption appears as something cultural rather than structural, something that is not about the mingling of corporate with political power, but about the lifestyle and habits of laypeople. As Mandravelis further notes, big businesses "pay their taxes." Mandravelis does not consider debt or the crisis in relation to Greece's low taxation on big business, the off-shore "tax paradises" where many Greek business people deposit their money,[7] or to the global rise in wealth inequalities (Duménil and Lévy 2011: 74).

As a form of enclosure, austerity organizes the proletarianization and the dispropriation of the relatively independent Greek petty-bourgeoisie, and its disconnection from alternatives. Besides the privatization of anything public, austerity's main targets are the small and middle businesses that constitute the pillars of the Greek economy and the country's expanded middle class (Tsoukalas 2012). By attacking the lower and middle class through its effective indebtment by high taxation and market stagnation due to the mass loss of jobs and income reduction (the average Greek household lost 33 percent of its pre-2009 income in just 3 years[8]), austerity benefits core capitalist interests to further advance in the periphery, while local mainstream media rationalize the pretext for such economic restructuring in favor of multinational, oligopolistic capital.

Constructing "us" and "them" while addressing the crisis

Identity is connected to the symbolic dimension of political practices, which are usually based upon notions of commonality. Politics, in discourse-theoretical terms, is the strategy of systematizing and posing limits to difference, demarcating what one is not and thus (re)constructing one's identity and associated discourses. The crisis is a rupture that produces dislocations (Laclau 1996: 89) in the ideas and practices constituting contemporary Greekness. The rupture provides opportunities to both the Left and the Right for social change, through the reconstitution of identities and associated social relations. The analysis shows how the neoliberal Right attempts to achieve this, and how it positions itself in the struggle for hegemony.

Constructions of a positive Greek identity

The appeal to a common identity is central to all public discourses. *Kathimerini*'s texts speak about the common Greek identity of a people facing the same responsibilities and challenges.

Identity is anchored in signifiers of national homogeneity, such as "Greeks," "we," or "Greece." The national appeal provides a flattening version of identity that distributes responsibility equally. This way the elite's role and responsibility for the public indebtment of Greece (Douzinas 2013) is underplayed. Furthermore, the interests of the upper classes are presented as the interests of "the country." As Duménil and Lévy (2011: 28) argued, consensus on a commonness of interests between different economic classes was central to the establishment of neoliberal hegemony in the United States during the 1990s. The flattening of responsibility for the Greek public debt and important social problems of Greece follows the standard neoliberal crisis-narrative (Mylonas 2012): all Greeks were corrupted by consumerism and political clientelism, Greeks were not democratic enough, Greece had an abysmal, excessive, and dysfunctional public sector, and Greece deceived the EU. In a 5 June 2011, article entitled "Crisis' apocalypses," Angelos Stangou claims that:

> the reality was that before the crisis, Greece had a large state apparatus, which strangled society. Greece was essentially a lawless state, with limited social responsibility. Corruption and mediocrity determined everything […] Unfortunately, this is what Greece was and still is […] while populism is no longer simply a way of thinking and expressing, but a way of life.

Structure is blended with culture, with structure being culturalized. Such a narrative is fatalist, emphatic, and affirmative, and dismisses counter-explanations. "Corruption" is the nodal signifier denominating the Greek deficits that produced the crisis of Greece: corruption is denoted through generalizations that suggest (a) the oxymoron of a "lawless state" and (b) civil irresponsibility ("a way of life") and civil dependency on (excessive) state provisions. Identity emerges as the main reason of the crisis.

Crisis and austerity are presented as catalysts for a new Greek identity. Prolonged austerity appears as essential for a "new Greece" to emerge, that is (economically) dynamic, entrepreneurial, and more European. On 25 May 2010—two days after Greece's submission to Troika's so-called support mechanism—in an article entitled "The others want to help us, but do we?", Alexis Papachelas concludes that:

> I am optimistic because I believe that (a) the Greek has pride and an ego that can pull out of him incredible resources in a crisis, and (b) Greece's large middle class has a powerful instinct of self-preservation. But I'm also worried, because I know how inadequate a great part of our political staff is, and how low the level of the Greek public dialogue can be— with journalists also responsible for that—and, finally, how strong and parochial the post-dictatorship, populist monster is, that is now writhing because its end is approaching. I wish it won't manage to fatally injure Greece's remaining creative and positive entities.

In this excerpt, the Troika represents an opportunity for the "true Greek" to emerge, in *his* full creative and productive potential. Such a signification of "Greekness" is positively framed according to the individualist values and ethos of neoliberalism: "the Greek" has the entrepreneurial potential essential for the reproduction of late capitalism. Neoliberalism is a project concerning the production of specific social subjectivities to reproduce societies founded on economistic rationalities; "a fully realized neoliberal citizen is the opposite of the public minded citizen [...] a neoliberal citizenry is a group of individual entrepreneurs and consumers" (Brown 2003: 6).

Simultaneously, the missing fullness of "the Greek" to reach *his* full (entrepreneurial) potential is attributed to the impact of the Left in the country since the fall of the colonels' dictatorship. For neoliberals (as well as for the Greek fascists (Kompatsiaris and Mylonas 2014)), the Left is the big threatening Other prohibiting "us" from reaching our fullness. Drawing on Lacanian psychoanalysis, Stavrakakis (1999) argues that lack and fullness are caught in a circular relation. The imaginary of fullness is operationalized through its identified obstacle (e.g., the Left), which symbolizes what prohibits the materialization of fullness, the reaching of a nation's full capacities, etc.

The imaginary horizon orientating "our" missing fullness (Laclau 1996: 75) is anchored in the nodal signifier Europe. Europe, however, represents different legacies, totalitarian and democratic (Bauman 2004). A technocratic, market-orientated Europe relates to the totalitarian and undemocratic trajectories of Europe, due to the inequalities it produces.

The democratic social movements across Europe related to Occupy and Indignados, against the current technocratic and undemocratic turn of Europe (Hardt and Negri 2012; Harvey 2012), are discredited by *Kathimerini* as extremist and irrational. In an article dated 1 July 2011, entitled "The hour of truth", Angelos Terzis claims that:

> the same political system proclaiming change and the "end of Metapolitefsi"[9] seems essentially trapped in what it learned to do best during all these years. Although it tries to manage change, itself remains the same and unchanged. It does not listen to the voices— not even to the inarticulate cries of the "indignant" citizens—but also to the agony of the vast, silent majority. Whilst all of Europe was anxiously looking at the Greek Parliament, Syntagma Square was burning. Although the media was talking about the "most critical vote of all time", our politicians operated in terms of past decades, focusing on their own political survival and succession.

In this excerpt, Europe is reified into a panopticon, observing "us" from afar. Greece's symbolic relation to Europe has been tense and contradictory, both trying to fit western European norms and also negating them (Hamilakis 2007). *Kathimerini*'s discourse of Europe is deeply biopolitical, as "we" should internalize the norms that (neoliberal) Europe incarnates in order to reach our missing fullness. The form of Europeanness advanced by *Kathimerini* does not recognize difference and interprets the world according to neoliberal values of work, entrepreneurship, flexibility, consumerism, and private property (Harvey 2009: 72), aligning to the EU's technocratic diagnoses and remedies of the *Greek problem*.

The emphasis on expert-talk is connected to an objectivist understanding of social problems. Since the economy is neoliberalism's main denominator of the social, economists are the experts to solve social problems. In a 7 July 2011 article entitled "With trusted technocrats," Alexis Papachelas argues that:

Our politicians have finally realized that they cannot handle certain matters on their own, and that they urgently need help from technocrats to deal with privatization, the complex negotiations on debt, and many other important topics. Public Administration lacks the critical mass of people required [...] there are few who have the experience and expertise to handle critical cases with international dimensions. It is obvious that in order for them to leave their careers and to bear the risks of a political position, they should be compensated according to market standards, but also protected from possible court adventures, based on trade unionists or other "healthy forces'" complaints [...] Otherwise, the job will not be done and the same problems will confront any party asked to govern.

Constructions of the Other (within)

As discourse theory suggests, there is no essential foundation of identity (Laclau and Mouffe 1985: 111). Identity is always socially constructed. Simultaneously, identity is never full; its lack is inherent and the symbolic position of an Other is constitutive to the formation of any identity (including the identity of the Other).

The moralist/culturalist understanding of the Greek crisis perceives Left politics as the main reason for the moral/cultural deficits of the Greek people. The Left is the main obstacle to the implementation of austerity. If austerity is the main vehicle for the social and structural engineering required for the reinvention of Greekness, necessary for the post-crisis organization of capitalism, then the Left needs to be defeated ideologically and politically. In a 24 April 2010, article entitled "Excommunications and the IMF," Paschos Mandravelis argues:

If resorting to the support mechanism involving the IMF is bad, there is even worse: not to seek refuge there, as many irresponsibly argue for [...] The whole mythology of the Greek Left is based upon the diabolic capitalism, whose priests are international organizations such as the World Bank and the IMF [...] The IMF is neither destruction nor blessing. For some countries, it is necessary. For Greece, it is a supplement to the financial assistance of the EU, an assistance mechanism introduced so that the Germans would feel better [...] for 35 years we have moved forward tied to unreflected aphorisms. Now that these aphorisms brought us to the brink of bankruptcy, we need to change. Most of all, we need to start thinking.

The crisis, austerity, and Greece's subjection to the Troika are presented as opportunities to do away with the Left in Greece, which supposedly is the cause of Greece's problems. Critique of capitalism is discredited as a Greek particularity, based on leftist conspiracy theories. An ahistorical and uncritical position is assumed, discrediting the post-Junta period—the most stable liberal-democratic era of the Greek nation-state—as a trajectory that led Greece to (economic and moral) bankruptcy, due to a (supposed) hegemony of the Left. This way, contradictions are bypassed by an unreflective and monotonous, self-blaming narrative, bearing no interest in the historical complexity or the power relations shaping the Greek society.

Kathimerini presents the IMF as a neutral, technocratic, and credible institution, thus masking its deeply political role as a vehicle for the materialization of policies resulting in the plundering of countries' wealth by multinational corporations. In an article entitled "Austerity, debt and the IMF" (25 April 2010) written by Miranta Xafa—an investment consultant at Informed Judgement Partners—the IMF is presented as an opportunity for Greece to "buy time" in order to "return to the markets" with its "irrationalities" resolved, creating a more "extrovert," competitive economy. With an article from 22 April 2010, entitled "The demonization of the Fund," Athanasios Ellis discredits as prejudices public concerns against the IMF due to the catastrophes met by all countries submitted to its politics of social engineering. Such catastrophes include the augmentation of debt and dependency on foreign credit, the sellout of public infrastructures, the abolishing of social, labor, and political rights, or the massive pauperization, death, and immizeration (Harvey 2010; Kara 2009; Klein 2007).

Austerity's full failure in Greece—even by the IMF's standards—and the humanitarian crisis it caused, triggered massive social unrest. Sociopolitical struggles for justice were violently crushed by crude state (and para-state) violence, and slandered in Greece and abroad (Mylonas 2012: 662). In line with international mainstream media and tabloid press, a pathological, irrational, and cultural explanation of political struggles emerged as further proof of Greek irresponsibility.

Kathimerini addressed the social dichotomy that the crisis brought to the Greek society largely in apolitical terms: "reason," "reality," "populism," and "extremism" are nodal points signifying the crisis' social dichotomy. *Kathimerini*'s columnists organize a chain of equivalence of their preferable identity (the positive identity of "us") expressing the rational, realist, and (the supposedly) Europe-orientated social segments, understanding the crude reality of austerity as the only way for Greece. The oppositional chain of difference is signified by "populism" and "extremism," the nodal signifiers denoting those opposing austerity. This chain includes all those opposing austerity, identified as violent, lazy, well-off, anti-modern, or as serving anti-European and anti-Greek interests. In "The path towards ochlocracy" (2 June 2011), Stefanos Kassimatis perceived the then-emerging Indignant Citizens' Movement that transformed the Greek squares into spaces of public deliberation and direct democracy as a selfish, consumerist mob, manipulated by the Left and seeking scapegoats, while refusing to face its responsibilities and "reality." Kassimatis thus expresses the negation of the possibility of a different society and the memory of past struggles for emancipation (Marcuse [1956] 2005), in line to the regressive "no alternative" (to capitalism) narrative that epitomizes the political strategy of neoliberalism. In a similar fashion, Nikos Marantzidis in his 6 May 2012, article entitled "Tomorrow is another day" argued that:

it is very annoying and hypocritical that forces which [...] systematically cultivated violent rhetoric and insurrectionary anomic culture against constitutional legality, pretend to be surprised and angry about the rise of the GD [Golden Dawn]. All this time they contributed to the decay of democratic legitimacy. A datalytic role in these developments surely was played by the "Indignant citizens" [...] the osmosis of right-wing, populist and far left elements, forms a new political identity: the modern Greek indignant, a "black-red" amalgam of often contradictory values and attitudes that have one common feature: the contempt for representative democracy. The extremes are dangerous because they can be virtuous through tension and populism. As the tension (of the crisis) escalates, spiral polarization and anti- systemic behaviors, moderate ideologies and political behaviors find it increasingly difficult to stand up to the storm.

"Populist" is the nodal point of the discursive construction of the Left. Such discourse however is equally populist, in Laclau's terms (2005: 67). The aspiration of a society of individual entrepreneurs does not constitute a discourse as non-populist. The kind of populism detested by *Kathimerini*'s columnists is one that revolves around democratic demands. Although negated, *Kathimerini*'s "people" are constructed according to the political demands of the upper classes that benefit from the dismantling of labor, environmental or welfare laws.

Following the same line of argument, in a provocative article written on 16 September 2012, entitled "Golden Dawn's opportunity for democracy," Kassimatis claimed that:

Those believing in democracy owe a big "thanks" to the Golden Dawn - and I fully mean this. This derives from the opportunity it offered us ... to fix mistakes of decades and to make a fresh start in political life. It is the opportunity given to law and order to finally deal with the quasi-legitimate violence of the Left [...] which constitutes today the main obstacle of the country's transition from the era of "soviets with lobster-pasta" (the Greek model of socialism ...) to contemporary reality.

Nazi violence is here equated to Left politics. Everything outside the neoliberal framework is thus seen as unrealistic and extremist. Violence, though, is explained disproportionately. Rhetorical aggression against symbols—such as the Greek parliament—expressing a deep crisis of political representation, or calls for civil disobedience, are equated to the criminal acts of the Nazis. The Left appears as the true motivator of Nazi violence, which is presented as a reaction against leftist violence. Violence is thus relativized and violent acts trivialized, while the responsibilities of the Greek government and austerity for the growing popularity of the Nazis or the structural violence of austerity itself are silenced. In this way, the post-political horizon of what Balibar has framed as the "extreme center" emerges, that is indifferent to society's demise and hostile to calls for social justice and popular sovereignty.

Such discourses legitimize the presence of the extreme right in Greece's social and political life, while the "political center" is moving toward the far-right to implement austerity. The Greek government's exceptional prioritization of a law-and-order agenda, despite the growing desperation, pauperization and social cannibalism across Greece, is a clear indication of the reign of the post-democratic paradigm.

Conclusion

In this chapter, I used critical theory and poststructuralism reflexively in the empirical study of neoliberal discourse in the media. I focused on media because of their political and social importance in shaping our empirical reality, and their central role for the public legitimation and implementation of crisis-policies.

The neoliberal construction of the current economic crisis is eschatological: an imminent threat that is also an opportunity to resolve "our" problems and to reform our identity, our institutions. Capitalism has historically proven capable of overcoming the limits that put its process into a crisis (Harman 2009). The crisis is a crisis of accumulation and expansion of capital, so the way to resolve it is by creating new regimes of exploitation. "Greek identity" is both the key reason and solution of this crisis because the re-engineering of this identity is about the reform of the institutional context organizing work relations, property, and the collective-individual work and consumerist ethos.

Identity-based explanations of the economic crisis are central for the reproduction of capitalist imaginaries as common sense. This way, one will not seek to change the system but will only try to adjust oneself to systemic demands. Indeed, *Kathimerini*'s representations of the crisis contribute to the social engineering performed by crisis-politics in Greece. It normalizes the indefinite suspension of democracy by the emergency politics of austerity, and the unprecedented humanitarian, social, political, and environmental catastrophes the latter bring.

Neoliberal logics are based on reifications that reduce complex entities into calculable and controllable domains. Mainstream economics evaluates social reality according to its potential for capitalization. Decision-ability and determination count more than deliberation. Democracy is therefore a problem for neoliberal capitalism. Austerity is not compatible with democracy, as the expression of financial institutions openly suggests (Barr & Mackie 2013). The core EU leaders' dogmatic insistence on the Greek state to continue with what EU technocrats neutrally describe as "the program" (neoliberal reforms), for an indefinite period of time, makes the fearful Soviet five-year-plans appear as more democratic. Overall, technocracy and austerity mean the exclusion of citizens from participation in social and political life (Berardi 2009; Marcuse [1956] 2005), and the denial of the Right to even imagine an alternative future. *Kathimerini*'s columnists focus on the symptoms, refusing to address the systemic character of the crisis and the historical context of Greek specificities. For *Kathimerini*'s contributors, the problem is not capitalism, but political opposition to it. In this manner, they publicly reproduce neoliberal moralistic banalities that obscure the power structure of global capitalism and the corporate roots of contemporary misery. As Marx (1976: 756) argued, "to make the society happy and people easier under the meanest circumstances, it is requisite that great numbers of them should be ignorant as well as poor."

Emergency politics are connected to the disciplinary agendas of neoliberalism. Neoliberalism is a biopolitical project, reproduced through individuals' internalization and performance of its values and objectives, connected to strict atomization and antagonism, in a Hobbesian social realm.

Indeed, four years after the official beginning of Greece's crisis, Greek society finds itself in an extraordinary political, social, and humanitarian tragedy, with an impoverished middle class, a growing spiteful, excluded, and increasingly regressive population that supports racist, violent, and fascist ideas, a rich oligarchy, connected to global private monopolies profiteering from the crisis reforms while doing business-as-usual, an authoritative state ruling on the edges of constitutional legitimacy by a thin electoral majority—in full support of a conservative, German-led EU—succumbed to the Troika's "There-Is-No-Alternative" policies, and a public debt that continuous to grow despite draconian austerity.[10]

Kathimerini's discourses were largely challenged by the historical crisis-trajectory itself. The IMF recently admitted errors in its initial plans for Greece's restructuring, despite its religious dogmatism on austerity. The escalation of Nazi violence and the growing anti-Nazi indignation in Greece and abroad eventually forced Samaras' government to take moderate legal action against the GD leadership, after the murder of the artist Pavlos Fyssas, in September 2013. Until then, PM Samaras' party, ND, openly flirted with the idea of a future collaboration with the Nazis to curb the Left and continue with austerity. "GD is not a threat to Democracy, its supporters are not Nazis and should not be excluded," declared Viron Polydoras,[11] a former notable member of Samaras' party, on 1 July 2013. In the course of events, more members of ND were proven to have relations with GD, such as the government's former general secretary, Takis Mpaltakos, a self-declared "born anticommunist [*sic*]", who was forced to resign after records of secret discussions between him and GD members became public. The Greek government's instrumentalization of far-right extremists and neo-fascists, is openly supported by the EU's political elites as they openly support the same corrupt political establishment that has been ruling the country since 1974 (two previously rival parties that succeeded each other in power for 40 years, form today's [2014] government in Greece), and that is responsible for the country's political, economic, and moral bankruptcy. The authoritarian turn of Greek politics is best shown by the government's use of Makis Voridis—a former associate of Jean-Marie Le Pen and a leading member of a political party founded by Greece's former dictator Georgios Papadopoulos—and the TV persona named Adonis Georgiadis, known for advertising anti-Semitic and pseudo-scientific nationalistic books at marginal private TV channels. Both figures are former MPs of the far-right LAOS (Laikos Orthodoksos Synagermos—Orthodox People's Rally) who are currently in pivotal governmental positions. Consequently, *Kathimerini* and other neoliberal voices played their part in the rise of pauperization and fascism, and the degradation of democracy, in contemporary Europe.

References

Agamben, Giorgio, Badiou, Alain, Bensaid, Daniel, Brown, Wendy, Nancy, Jean-Luc, Rancière, Jacques, Ross, Kristin, and Žižek, Slavoj (2009), *Democracy in What State?*, New York: Columbia University Press.

Badiou, Alain (2002), *Ethics: An Essay in the Understanding of Evil*, London: Verso.

—— (2012), "Save the Greeks from their saviors!," The European Graduate School, http://www.egs.edu/faculty/alain-badiou/articles/save-the-greeks-from-their-saviors/. Accessed 3 July 2013.

Barr, Malcolm and Mackie, David (2013), "The Euro area adjustment: About halfway there," *Europe Economic Research*, 28 May, http://blogs.euobserver.com/phillips/2013/06/07/jp-morgan-to-eurozone-periphery-get-rid-of-your-pinko-anti-fascist-constitutions/. Accessed 3 July 2013.

Bauman, Zygmunt (2004), *Europe: An Unfinished Adventure*, London: Polity.

Berardi, Franco (Bifo) (2009), *The Soul at Work: From Alienation to Autonomy*, Los Angeles: Semiotext(e).

Brown, Wendy (2003), "Neo-liberalism and the end of liberal democracy," *Theory and Event*, 7:1, pp. 1–25.

Carpentier, Nico and De Cleen, Benjamin (2007), "Bringing discourse theory into media studies; the applicability of discourse theoretical analysis (DTA) for the study of media practices and discourses," *Journal of Language and Politics*, 6:2, pp. 265–93.

Couldry, Nick (2010), *Why Voice Matters: Culture and Politics After Neoliberalism*, London: Sage.

Crouch, Colin (2004), *Post-Democracy*, London: Polity.

—— (2011), *The Strange Non-Death of Neoliberalism*, London: Polity.

De Angelis, Massimo (2004), "Separating the doing and the deed: Capital and the continuous character of enclosures," *Historical Materialism*, 12:2, pp. 57–87.

Douzinas, Costas (2013), *Philosophy and Resistance in the Crisis: Greece and the Future of Europe*, Cambridge: Polity.

Duménil, Gérard and Lévy, Dominique (2011), *The Crisis of Neoliberalism*, Cambridge: Harvard University Press.

Foucault, Michel (2008), *The Birth of Biopolitics: Lectures at College de France, 1978–1979*, London: Palgrave McMillan.

Hamilakis, Yannis (2007), *The Nation and Its Ruins: Antiquity, Archaeology, and National Imagination in Greece*, Oxford: Oxford University Press.

Hardt, Michael and Negri, Antonio (2012), *Declaration*, New York: Argo-Navis.

Harman, Chris (2009), *Zombie Capitalism*, Chicago: Haymarket Books.

Harvey, David (2005), *A Brief History of Neoliberalism,* Oxford: Oxford University Press.

—— (2009), *Cosmopolitanism and the Geographies of Freedom*, New York: Columbia University Press.

—— (2010), *The Enigma of Capital and the Crises of Capitalism*, London: Profile Books.

—— (2012), *Rebel Cities*, London: Verso.

Kara, Siddharth (2009), *Sex Trafficking: Inside the Business of Modern Slavery*, New York: Columbia University Press.

Klein, Naomi (2007), *The Shock Doctrine: The Rise of Disaster Capitalism*, New York: Metropolitan Books.

Kompatsiaris, Panos and Mylonas, Yiannis (2014), "The rise of neo-Nazism and the web: Social media as platforms for racist discourses in the context of Greek economic crisis," in C. Fuchs and D. Trotier (eds), *Social Media, Politics and the State: Protest, Revolutions, Riots, Crime, and Policing in the Age of Facebook, Twitter and YouTube*, London: Routledge, pp. 109–30.

Laclau, Ernesto (1996), *Emancipations*, London: Verso.

—— (2005), *On Populist Reason*, London: Verso.

Laclau, Ernesto and Mouffe, Chantal (1985), *Hegemony and Socialist Strategy: Towards a Radical Democratic Politics*, London: Verso.

Lasch, Christopher (1996), *The Revolt of the Elites and the Betrayal of Democracy*, New York: Norton.

Marcuse, Herbert ([1956] 2005), *Eros and Civilization*, Abingdon: Routledge.

Marx, Karl (1976), *Capital: Critique of Political Economy Vol 1*, London: Penguin.

Mylonas, Yiannis (2012), "Media and the economic crisis of the EU: The 'culturalization' of a systemic crisis and Bild-Zeitung's framing of Greece," *TripleC—Cognition, Communication, Cooperation: Open Access Journal for a Global Sustainable Information Society*, 10:2, pp. 646–71.

OECD (2012), "Average annual hours actually worked per worker," http://stats.oecd.org/Index.aspx?DataSetCode=ANHRS. Accessed 10 March 2012.

Pleios, George (2013), "Τα ΜΜΕ απέναντι στην κρίση" ("The media against the crisis"), in G. Pleios (ed.), *Η κρίση και τα ΜΜΕ* (*The Crisis and the Media*), Athens: Παπαζήσης, pp. 87–134.

Rancière, Jacques (2009), *Hatred of Democracy*, London: Verso.

Sevastakis, Nicolas and Stavrakakis, Yannis (2012), *Λαϊκισμός, αντιλαϊκισμός και κρίση* (*Populism, Anti-Populism and Crisis*), Αθήνα: Νεφέλη.

Stavrakakis, Yannis (1999), *Lacan and the Political*, London: Routledge.

Tsoukalas, Constantine (2012), *Η Ελλάδα της λήθης και της α-λήθειας: από τη μακρά εφηβεία στη βίαιη ενηλικίωση* (*Greece of Oblivion and Truth: From a Prolonged Adolescence to a Violent Maturation*), Athens: Θεμέλιο.

Wacquant, Loïc (2012), "Three steps to a historical anthropology of actually existing neoliberalism," *Social Anthropology*, 20:1, pp. 66–79.

Žižek, Slavoj (2010), "A permanent economic emergency," *New Left Review*, 64, pp. 85–95.

Notes

1 Discourse is understood as central for the social construction of reality, as meaning is required to produce any kind of social form. Simultaneously, discourse materializes into processes, events, situations, and physical externalities of the world and develops in a dialectic relation to reality. Capitalism is therefore a social construction, a politico-economic project and historical condition that can nevertheless not be fully explained in discursive-theoretical

terms alone. Capitalism reaches crises due to "objective" conditions (which have a discursive foundation), relating to the fall of expected rates of profit, the changes in the composition of fixed and variable capital for the maximization of productivity, or to emerging contradictions related to catastrophes capitalism produces, and also due to subjective reasons, related to antagonism between rival capitalists and social classes. Discourse is central to all these features, objective and subjective ones, but a strictly discursive approach to the analysis of capitalist crises would be reductionist. A synthesis of critical and poststructuralist traditions of research can broaden the understanding of the crisis' complexity.

2 I maintain the term "crisis" other than the term "dislocation" to describe the event of the economic collapse that started in 2008 in the United States and later influenced the EU, because the concept of crisis is more engaging on a political and an analytical level. The idea of the crisis can maintain its discursive dimension (as explained by Kosseleck), and simultaneously allow one to endorse with Marx's understanding of capitalism, which challenges the naturalized and sedimented construction of capitalism, as a synonymous term to that of the "economy."

3 As a political strategy, enclosures are coined and decided through discourse, but then materialized through physical force. The material act of the enclosure has further discursive dimensions.

4 http://el.wikipedia.org/wiki/H_Καθημερινή. Accessed 5 December 2013.

5 A search from 1 December 2009, until 10 June 2013, using the keyword "αριστερά" (aristera—the Left) produced 1079 results (with several findings being irrelevant to the research); the keyword "άκρα" (akra—the extremes) gave 318 findings, "κίνημα αγανακτισμένων" (aganaktismenoi—indignant citizens) gave 629 hits, and "λαϊκισμός" (laikismos—populism) produced 278 hits (with a final search on the 15 June 2013). A search between 1 December 2009 and 31 May 2010, gave 106 results for the keyword "the Left," 33 for "populism," 70 hits for "the Right," 29 hits for "extremes," 203 hits for "democracy," and 329 hits for "Europe." A search during the second period, between 15 May 2011, and 30 October 2011, produced 83 hits for "extremes," 113 hits for "the Left," 50 hits for "the Right," 33 hits for "populism," 82 hits for "indignant citizens," 312 hits for "Europe," and 230 hits for "democracy." A search during the third period, between 1 April 2012 and 30 November 2012, produced 31 results for the term "indignant citizens," 586 for the term "Europe," 316 hits for the term "the Left," 147 hits for the term "the Right," 116 hits for the keyword "extremes," 430 hits for the term "democracy," and 62 hits for the keyword "populism." A different search, focusing on the weekends of the same third period studied, produced 141 relevant articles for all keywords.

6 And also through affects.

7 According to the research of International Consortium of Investigative Journalists—ICIJ, there are 107 Greek citizens that maintain accounts in offshore tax-free places. From those, only four are currently being taxed by the Greek state; http://left.gr/news/syzitisisti-voyli-zontani-metadosi-posoys-foroys-hanei-dimosio-apo-tis-ellinikes-offshore. Accessed 21 June 2013.

8 http://greece.greekreporter.com/2013/04/19/greeks-lose-33-of-disposable-income/. Accessed 21 June 2013.

9 "Metapolitefsi" is a term describing the era that succeeded the dictatorship of the colonels between 1967 and 1974, a period considered the most democratic in the history of the modern Greek state—which included many problems and excesses as well. The advent of the crisis allowed the proclamation of the "end of metapolitefsi" by conservative, neoliberal, and lately extreme right-wing agents.

10 Greece's public debt escalated from a 148% in 2009 to a 175% in 2013, after all the so-called "help packages" it received in exchange for austerity reforms: http://ec.europa.eu/eurostat/ tgm/refreshTableAction.do;jsessionid=9ea7d07d30db781d894ec7984dabb1e2e3429dc%20 e77f1.e34MbxeSaxaSc40LbNiMbxeNaNiRe0?tab=table&plugin=1&pcode=teina225&lang uage=en. Accessed 21 June 2013.

11 The statement can be heard here, in Greek: http://www.real.gr/audiofiles/244390.mp3. Accessed 3 July 2013.

Chapter 2

(Re)Articulating Feminism: A Discourse Analysis of Sweden's Feminist Initiative Election Campaign

Kirill Filimonov and Jakob Svensson

Introduction

Feminist politics have been a long-lasting source of inspiration in the field of gender research, yet questions regarding feminist politics do not often enter the public and political domains. This is, however, exactly what happened during the 2014 parliamentary election campaign in Sweden. The then-leader of the opposition (and the future prime minister) Stefan Löfven has repeatedly proclaimed himself to be a feminist (Holmqvist et al. 2013; Martikainen 2012). The Liberal Party selected "Feminism without socialism" as one of its campaign slogans, while the spokesperson for the Greens Gustav Fridolin called for a "feminist government" (Bie 2014). Furthermore, the foreign minister of the newly elected government Margot Wallström promised that under her leadership Sweden would be the only country in the world to conduct a "feminist foreign policy" (Rothschild 2014). On the forefront of this feminist discourse during the elections was the political party Feminist Initiative (Sw. *Feministiskt initiativ,* or FI), which in 2013–14 became Sweden's fastest-growing party (Orange 2014). In 2014, 20,740 new members were enrolled in FI, comprising half of the total number of new members enrolled in Swedish political parties that year (SvD 2015). FI won its first mandate in the European Parliament election in May 2014, becoming the second most active Swedish party online (Brandel 2014; on some platforms even the most active, see Filimonov et al. 2016) and was close to making it into the Swedish Parliament, but eventually failed. This chapter examines the FI phenomenon in Swedish politics, focusing on one specific aspect: the construction of the notion of *feminist politics* in their online campaign. By feminist politics we mean a hegemonic project (see theoretical framework) involving a variety of social movements, structured around the floating signifier feminism as articulated by FI. FI claimed to challenge the existing political order, positioning itself as an "ideologically independent feminist party" (Feministiskt initiativ 2014) that derives from intersectionality. FI focused on both feminism and antiracism, actively engaging the LGBTQ (lesbian, gay, bisexual, transgender, and queer) community and appealing to immigrants, racial minorities, and people with disabilities (Feministiskt initiativ 2014). This resulted in a broader definition of feminism compared to first and second feminist waves that focused almost exclusively on women (for an overview, see Bryson 2003). FI is thus an example of an intersectional, third-wave feminist organization.

For these reasons, we discuss the *re*-articulation of feminism in FI's online election materials during the 2014 election campaign. Our aim is to study how FI rearticulated feminism by including various social groups into the hegemonic project of feminist politics and who or what was asserted as its antagonist. The focus on articulation and the logics of contingency leads us to the theoretical and methodological framework of the chapter: the discourse-theoretical approach.

Theoretical framework

Laclau and Mouffe's (2014) discourse-theoretical approach (DTA), situated within poststructuralist and post-Marxist frameworks, has been used in this study. DTA offers a range of useful analytical tools—most notably hegemony and antagonism—that enable approaching the construction of an "us," a political identity, in this case the political identity of FI. Following Laclau and Mouffe, we define discourse as a "structured totality resulting from articulatory practice" (Laclau and Mouffe 2014: 91), in other words, an ensemble of articulated signifiers whose meaning is constantly (re)negotiated. Any social practice is articulatory, in the sense that it requires construction of meaning by fixing it relatively around particular signifiers called nodal points (Laclau and Mouffe 2014: 99). We refer to these articulatory practices as *hegemony*.

To articulate a signifier therefore implies ascribing it a certain meaning. Following the Gramscian tradition, in DTA hegemonic projects have the ultimate goal to "construct and stabilize systems of meaning" (Howarth 2000: 110). For Laclau and Mouffe (2014: 122), the two conditions for a hegemonic articulation are the presence of antagonistic forces and the instability of frontiers that separate them, i.e., a wide range of unarticulated elements floating within the discursive field. Laclau and Mouffe maintain that there are no necessary links between different signifiers of a discourse, as meanings always depends on a specific hegemonic articulation. This is an important analytical premise as it enables approaching feminism as a floating signifier, i.e., its various meanings being a result of various articulations rather than certain pre-given conceptions.

Hegemonic projects are articulated in a discursive field crisscrossed with antagonisms. No hegemony can ever be complete because there is always resistance to power emanating from an antagonistic force. At the same time, this force enables accentuating the difference of the project and in this way shapes it in a particular form (see Laclau and Mouffe 2014: ch. 3). The antagonist thus becomes a necessary prerequisite for the emergence of the subject, or, in the language of DTA, its *constitutive outside*. For Laclau and Mouffe (2014: 137), social antagonisms are part and parcel of the social, and, therefore, unavoidable and even desirable in a radical and plural democracy. The latter can therefore be described as "a form of politics that recognizes diversity and invites participation from a variety of social spaces" leading to "the continual proliferation of new voices, new communities, and new identities" (Sandilands 1993: 3).

We suggest that intersectionality is an example of this equivalent democratic logic encouraged by radical-democratic theory (see Mouffe 1993), i.e., collaboration of a variety of social struggles. The basic premise of intersectionality is that studying social stratification is reductionist and misleading if "structural axes of differentiation" (Peterson 1999: 53)—race, class, gender, sexuality, (dis)ability, age, and religion—are analyzed independently from each other. From the intersectional perspective, such an approach downplays specific problems of, for instance, women of color in western societies, who experience discrimination and abuse not only as women, but also as members of racial or religious minorities and, often, working-class individuals (e.g., Crenshaw 1991). The approach has, perhaps, been best summarized by Matsuda:

> When I see something that looks racist, I ask, "where is the patriarchy in this?" When I see something that looks sexist, I ask, "Where is the heterosexism in this?" When I see something that looks homophobic, I ask, "Where are the class interests in this?"
>
> (1990: 1189)

The critique of intersectionality has pointed at its potentially devastating effects for the unity of women and the idea of a common "sisterhood" (see Brah and Phoenix 2004). Indeed, intersectionality challenges the holistic approach to women, instead acknowledging differences existing within them as a sizeable social group. It reflects an understanding that people who belong to the same collective can be positioned differently in relation to a whole range of social positions. If the world is seen differently from each position, any knowledge based on just one position is incomplete (Yuval-Davis 1999), which intersectionality seeks to remedy.

The denouncement of essentialism and an amalgam of a variety of social struggles make it legitimate to bring together the theories of radical democracy and intersectionality under a common denominator. From a poststructuralist perspective, which informs radical-democratic theory, a stable notion of woman encouraged by first- and second-wave feminism is deeply problematic. We know from Derrida (1978) and Lacan (1994) that there is no "last word," but instead a constant play of signifiers, which makes the meaning slip out of reach. The word "woman," for instance, is simply unable to signify anything but "particular women in particular situations" (Soper 1990, cited in Mouffe 1995: 328). Soper rightly concluded (albeit in a critical manner) that the failure of signification of women results in the inability to construct a political community around women as such. For Mouffe, however, this opens up the opportunity to redefine feminist politics in accordance with her radical-democratic rationale:

> I argue that, for those feminists who are committed to a radical democratic politics, the deconstruction of essential identities should be seen as the necessary condition for an adequate understanding of the variety of social relations where the principles of liberty and equality should apply.
>
> (1995: 371)

In other words, rather than pursuing goals of women as women—a definable group with a shared identity—feminists should articulate their aims within a wider context of demands, struggling against various ways in which "the category of women is constructed in subordination" (Mouffe 1992: 382). Women should be understood as overdetermined social agents in contrast to the reductionist approach that ascribes women a single subject position based on their gender identity. As Emejulu (2011: 385) pointed out, this would lead to "building of solidarity between and amongst subjects who recognize themselves as radical democratic citizens."

From the radical-democratic and intersectional perspectives we suggest that FI's (re) articulation of feminism was based on the inclusion of several social groups into something that has traditionally been considered relating to (and produced by) women, understood as an essentialized biological (and social) category. We will study the discursive mechanisms behind the equivalent logic that expanded the hegemonic project of feminist politics. For that purpose, we have both singled out the nodal points that maintained the hegemonic project and analyzed the discursive construction of a constitutive outside. As Mouffe (2005: 15) reminds us, "in the field of collective identities, we are always dealing with the creation of a 'we' which can exist only by the demarcation of a 'they.'" It is thus indispensable to illuminate both the "we" and the "they" of a discourse under analysis.

The aim of this chapter is thus to study how FI articulated the hegemonic project of "feminist politics" in terms of intersectionality in their online election materials (website and Facebook page) during the 2014 election campaign. Two research questions were posed: (RQ1) How does FI try to include various social groups into the hegemonic project of feminist politics? (RQ2) What or who is constructed as an antagonist to feminist politics, and in what ways does it impede and make such politics possible?

Data and method

Because of a close intertwinement of theory and method in discourse analysis (Winther-Jørgensen and Phillips 2010), analytical categories attended to in the theoretical section, in a sense, define the methodological framework per se. Due to a lack of any common algorithm in DTA, it is always up to the researcher to define the structure of analysis using DTA's analytical concepts. Below we present our suggested analytical framework, preceded by the description of the empirical material and its selection.

Empirical material and data collection

Given FI's campaign strategy to use the internet and social media, as well as their relative success in doing so (compared to other parties, see introduction), we have focused on the online content. Online material is also easily accessible and often used by political parties (Svensson and Larsson 2016), which was also the case with FI who actively addressed voters with their campaign materials through social media channels. The empirical material of this study is a middle-sized, specialized corpus of texts (50,455 words), with compiled textual materials from:

- **FI's official website (www.feministisktinitiativ.se), making up about 90 percent of the data (44,150 words):** The website was chosen as the main source of data as it provided easy access to a wide range of campaign materials. Moreover, websites generally give an opportunity to express political stances and articulate identities more explicitly compared to traditional forms of campaigning such as leaflets. All of the texts related to FI's pre-election political program, available online as of April 2015, were selected and manually compiled into a single file. When quoting fragments from the website materials in the analysis, we shall refer to the document's full title in brackets.
- **Posts from the party's Facebook page (http://www.facebook.com/feministisktinitiativ) (6,305 words):** The collected Facebook posts comprise a one-month period prior to Election Day (14 August–14 September 2014). This is normally a period of intense campaigning when parties and candidates seek to communicate their election platform to voters; therefore, it was deemed the most appropriate period to study the discourse of the campaign. The same gathering procedure was carried out with the Facebook posts as with the website content: they were manually collected from FI's Facebook page in April 2015 and copied into a single file. When the posts contained a link to an article written by one of the party's top candidates for mass media, this article was also included in the corpus. Looking into the content of FI's official page on Facebook was particularly promising since, as we mentioned in the introduction, FI had outperformed most Swedish parties in the intensity of use of social networking sites in pre-election campaigning.

As the language of the empirical material was almost exclusively in Swedish (except for the text "Election platform", translated into English and other languages by FI), fragments quoted in this chapter were translated into English by the first author. The way the material was used and analyzed is explained in the section below.

Analytical procedure

As mentioned before, there is no single way of employing DTA. The analytical procedure is seldom a linear straightforward process often described in sections like this. Nonetheless, below we attempt to summarize our analytical procedure as transparently as possible. It can be described as an iterative in-depth text reading of the collected empirical material in order to identify central signifiers around which meanings were organized (RQ1) as well as what identities and groups are discursively constructed (RQ2) (see Winther-Jørgensen and Phillips 2010: 165–6). The analysis of the collected online material revolved around two DTA processes: institution of nodal points and construction of an antagonist.

The institution of nodal points

This part of the analysis corresponds to RQ1. We sought to identify central signifiers that FI had instituted in the discourse with an eye to fix the unstable meaning of feminism. We were interested in discursive mechanisms that enabled the expansion of meaning of feminism and construction of a political identity based on intersectionality. The discourse-theoretical perspective informed our assumption that the nodal points should sustain the expanded signifying chain of feminist politics, which now concerned numerous social movements as opposed to women as a definable and unproblematic entity. The intersectional/radical-democratic approach, in turn, made us take into account the differences within the elements of the signifying chain. Therefore, we were, on the one hand, searching for signifiers in the online material that could be considered central for structuring feminist politics as a single whole, while on the other hand looking for signifiers that enabled the expression of difference and particularity within the collective movement.

The construction of an antagonist

This step in the analysis helped answer RQ2. The aim here was to shed light on who or what was understood to be the constitutive outside that impeded full realization of the hegemonic project. Identifying the antagonist is crucial for understanding any hegemonic project, given DTA's point of departure that any identity comes into existence only when juxtaposed against an external force. A solid grasp of the constitutive outside, therefore, leads to a deeper understanding of the opportunities and limits of a hegemonic project. Two criteria were used to identify the antagonist (following Howarth 2000): (1) It should prevent the social agent (feminists) from attaining its identity, and (2) the social agent (feminists) constructs it as a foe deemed responsible for this failure.

Accordingly, the basic question posed to the collected material was: what is constructed as "us" and "them"? A concordance analysis, i.e., analysis of semantic context (see elaboration below) was conducted to see what function was ascribed to the antagonist in the texts (what it was said to *be* and to *do*) as well as how this function hindered FI's hegemonic project based on the nodal points elicited at the first stage of the analysis.

Previous studies (e.g., Baker and McEnery 2005; MacDonald et al. 2015) have shown evidence of how basic elements of quantitative analysis (namely, from corpus linguistics, see Baker, 2006) can support claims stemming from discourse analysis. This is particularly helpful in the analysis of larger corpora of texts, such as the one used in this study, albeit to be handled with care. In this study, two quantitative techniques—keyword analysis and concordance analysis—were used to navigate through the texts. Freeware AntConc, an analogue of Wordsmith (see http:// www.laurenceanthony.net/software/ antconc/), was used for quantitative operations with data. Below we attend to both analyses.

Keyword analysis

This analysis was used to make sense of the massive corpus rather than automatically generate ready answers to our questions. By keywords we mean the unusually frequent words in a given corpus compared to a reference corpus. To obtain a keyword list, AntConc conducts a log-likelihood test on each word from a given corpus and assigns it a keyness value; the higher the value, the stronger the keyness of that word (for the use of log-likelihood tests for corpus comparison, see Rayson and Garside 2000). As a reference corpus, to which the data were compared in order to identify unusually frequent words, two corpora of modern Swedish language, recommended by Gothenburg University (Språkbanken), were used: *August Strinbergs brev* (1,507,268 tokens) and *ASPAC svenska* (773,648 tokens). Thus, keyword analysis results present a list of unusually prominent words in FI's online election materials compared to their use in modern Swedish language (see Table 1).

Table 1: Keywords (most salient lexical words) in the corpus.

Rank	Word	Frequency	Keyness
1	Kvinnor [women]	164	1026.752
2	Initiativ	169	1016.704
3	Sverige [Sweden]	158	974.825
4	Våld [violence]	132	807.424
5	Människor [humans]	120	742.367
6	Rättigheter [rights]	88	548.767
7	Personer [people]	87	535.867
8	Diskriminering [discrimination]	66	431.181
9	Barn [children]	88	406.110
10	Resurser [resources]	61	380.935
11	Perspektiv	58	344.376
12	Män [men]	58	339.558
13	Hbtq [LGBTQ]	49	333.185
14	Samhället [the society]	55	330.376
15	Sexualitet [sexuality]	54	329.511

It should be noted that only lexical words, i.e., nouns, verbs, adjectives, and adverbs, were taken into account. Function words such as prepositions and pronouns were disregarded. The first column (Rank) numbers the keywords in the order they appear in the analysis results based on keyword strength. The second column (Word) presents each keyword. The third column (Frequency) indicates the number of times a certain word appeared in the corpus. The last column shows a keyness value.

Concordance analysis

This analysis was used to take a closer look at the context of broader discursive patterns that were identified by keyword analysis and during text reading. Concordance is "a list of all the occurrences of a particular search term within a corpus, presented within the context that they occur in" (Baker 2006: 71). It is arguably one of the handiest techniques of looking at the context of the use of words, which enables sorting a list of words with the same lemmas one by one. All in all, concordance analysis was deployed for an easier navigation through the texts and simpler access to a relatively large amount of data.

Findings

RQ1. Nodal points of feminist politics

In the case of FI, we deal with what Mouffe (1993: 13) labeled a "particularized universalism," meaning the importance of an open expression of differences in politics for the sake of expanding the application of the universalized notions of equality and liberty. Two nodal points in the discourse on feminist politics were extrapolated from the data: "human rights" and "experience of oppression."

The data revealed that FI emphasizes human rights as opposed to just women's rights. Concordance analysis revealed that in 47 percent of occurrences, the word *rättigheter* (rights) was linked to the word *mänskliga* (human), forming the collocation "human rights." This seems to confirm our hypothesis that, in spite of feminism's traditional preoccupation with women's issues, FI generally tends to go beyond the traditional articulation of feminist politics as a platform for the struggle for the rights of women *as* women. In order to test this hypothesis, a concordance analysis was conducted to identify the context in which the signifier "human rights" occurs. Out of 48 occurrences, only nine were directly associated with women, women's rights, and gender equality. By contrast, in 37 cases "human rights" was used in a broader, universalistic sense, embracing all people (see example below, emphases added):

Feminist Initiative works for *everyone's human rights*.

(Feministiskt initiativ n.d.a)

The European Convention on Human Rights, which has been Swedish law since 1995, states that *everyone has the right* to respect of their (private) correspondence.

(Feministiskt initiativ n.d.b)

As for the word *människor* (humans, people), it was used 185 times in comparison to 313 occurrences of the word *woman* in various lexical forms. Given that we are considering the discourse of a party with feminism in its name, we deem this quite a large ratio of the all-encompassing notion of *humans* compared to a more particular notion of *women*.

The second nodal point in FI's discourse on feminist politics is "experience of oppression." The signifier experience appears in various contexts, which, according to the concordance analysis, were predominantly negative. First and foremost, the experience concerns discrimination and oppression (emphases added):

> All of us have different *experiences* and body memories *of discrimination and oppression*.
> (Feministiskt initiativ n.d.c)

> Research shows that mental illness is higher among foreign-born individuals than among natives. It suggests that past traumas, but also racism, everyday discrimination, *experiences of injustice and degrading treatment* have effects on physical and mental health.
> (Feministiskt initiativ n.d.d)

Moreover, FI specifically touches upon the experience of exclusion from the mainstream public sphere (emphasis added):

> Many racialised women in Sweden and in other places, where whiteness gives power and privilege, have an experience of *being silenced, excluded* or told to "calm down" when they raise issues of racism.
> (Feministiskt initiativ n.d.e)

RQ2. The constitutive outside of feminist politics

An inevitable condition for a successful articulation of a political identity is an identification of the Other that constitutes and delimits identity (Mouffe 2005). Drawing on Howarth's (2000: 105) reading of *Hegemony and Socialist Strategy*, we use these two criteria to approach the articulation of a constitutive outside: (1) the social agent is unable to attain its identity due to the presence of an antagonist; (2) the social agent constructs an "enemy" deemed responsible for this inability.

Our findings demonstrated that the way in which FI was demarcating its constitutive outside was rather inexplicit. Formally, FI openly proclaimed its foe to be extreme-right-wing ideologies, particularly nationalist parties the Sweden Democrats (FI claimed to be "the most obvious opposition to the Sweden Democrats," see https://www.facebook.com/feministisktinitiativ/) and the Party of the Swedes. FI sees itself as a carrier of a new feminist ideology that "challenges the old ideologies in the Riksdag" with nationalists considered as the main threat to this ideology. FI constructs this opposition quite explicitly in most texts, from its slogan "Out with racists, in with feminists" to numerous statements:

Fascism and nationalism are always accompanied by limitations of the rights of women and LGBTQ persons.

(Feministiskt initiative 2015a)

Misogyny, homophobia, racism, fascism, and nationalism go hand in hand. FI challenges all of this.

(Feministiskt initiative 2015b)

Thus, on the one hand, Nazism, fascism, and nationalism (which in turn form a sort of chain of equivalence in FI's discourse) were explicitly proclaimed to be FI's ideological foes. It was paradoxical, on the other hand, that the respective signifiers were poorly presented in the corpus; each of them appeared only four times in various lexical forms (e.g., fascism, fascists, fascistic, etc.). If so little attention was paid to someone so important for self-identification, it is legitimate to question whether these ideologies are the actual Other. In fact, FI itself points at the blurred line between friends and foes with a somewhat unusual frankness for a political party:

Everyone is characterized by racism because we are part of racist society. The majority don't want to be labelled as racists, but one's actions and way of thinking can be racist, whether one wants it or not.

(Feministiskt initiativ n.d.e)

Judging from the above, everyone in society appears to a certain extent to be guilty for being racist without even noticing. This can be said to be in line with FI's general anti-essentialist approach to identities: racism is not ascribed to only one social group (which would make it, in discourse-analytical terms, a sutured and self-defined totality), but considered to be dispersed in society. Indeed, if society as a whole is "racist"—and racism threatens the project of feminist politics—then the constitutive outside cannot be represented simply by one social group.

After a closer reading of FI's campaign materials, we suggest that these are in fact *structures* and *norms* that are subjectified and constructed in antagonistic relation to FI's project of feminist politics. Both signifiers are quite salient in the texts: the corpus contains 54 occurrences of the words "structure"/"the structure/structures"/"structural" (*struktur/strukturen/ strukturer/strukturell/strukturella*) and 84 occurrences of various semantic forms of the word "norm" meaning social norms (*norm/normer/normal/normkritik/normkritisk/normkritiska/ normkritiskt*). A close look at collocations containing the root *struktur-* gives a clear idea of the context where it was predominantly used. FI uses, albeit never clearly defines, "structure(s)" as a set of complex relationships that organize and reproduce a social system. The intersections between different structures have often been underlined (our emphases):

We are going to show that feminism is not some special marginal interest, but a political force that is going to break down *patriarchal, sexist, and racist structures.*

FI is working to challenge the *established and discriminatory structures* that maintain ethnic privileges in society [...] and to make visible how *gender and racist structures* strengthen and maintain each other.

(Feministiskt initiativ n.d.f)

Concordance analysis of the word "strukturer" (structures) from the website revealed that it was predominantly used as a subject with agency. Abstract, depersonalized structures come to life and effectively become social agents per se. Namely, they are said to:

- *strengthen* other structures,
- *interact* with other structures,
- *create* conditions for discrimination in the workplace,
- *subordinate* certain groups systematically,
- *assign* men and women different positions,
- *maintain* ethnic privileges in society,
- *distribute* resources and influence inequitably,
- *create* power imbalance in society,
- *separate* individuals,
- *provide* men with benefits just because they are men, and
- be *manifest* in the concentration of power.

We see how structures are said to "maintain," "strengthen," and "interact with" each other, as well as to "subordinate" and "separate" individuals from one another. This means that, if feminist politics is based on the nodal point "human rights," the subjectified structures hinder it and prevent realization of the hegemonic project. In other words, FI's ultimate claim is that their antagonists are not nationalist or fascist political movements per se; the party sees structures behind them: "Perhaps the most important knowledge is that ... one can never stay outside social structures" (http://feministisktinitiativ.se/politik/sexualpolitik/).

By now, we have made clear what the structures are said to *do*; in Table 2 the adjectives used together with the word "structures" are presented in order to understand what they are said to *be*.

Judging from this data, "structures" are constructed in a way that is completely opposite to the feminist subject: in terms of gender (structures are "patriarchal" and "sexist"), race/ethnicity/nationality ("racist" and "colonial"), sexuality ("heteronormative"), and class ("socioeconomical"). Being what they are described to be, structures are a blocker of feminist politics situated at the intersection of the abovementioned categories. Structures are a serious enemy, described as "deep" and "comprehensive," and they function on a global scale. Most notably, structures directly relate to power and shape power relations, albeit "power" as such remains a vague and unattended signifier in FI's campaign materials. Yet, structures are not the only foe.

Table 2: Adjectives used with the word "structures" in the corpus.

Adjective	Occurrences (N)
Power	9
Racist	8
Sex (kön)	3
Patriarchal	3
Social	2
Discriminatory	2
Sexist	1
Heteronormative	1
Deep	1
Various	1
New	1
Global	1
Comprehensive	1
Socioeconomic	1
Colonial	1

A closely related concept to structures in FI's articulation is *norms*. Together with structures, they are constructed as the constitutive outside of feminist politics. Table 3 shows that the adjectives denoting *norms* are neutral or pejorative. Most of them, however, relate to feminism (as discussed above) in one way or another.

Norms are said to promote a white, western, gender-binary, and heterosexual standard, also stigmatizing disabilities; overall norms maintain an oppressive, patriarchal, and destructive order:

> Today oppressive gender norms are maintained at the state level and those who violate gender norms are often subjected to violence and stigma as well as suffer more from poverty.
>
> (Feministiskt initiativ n.d.g)

> If you, like us, wish [to live in] society where every person is free to live their life beyond the norms of masculinity and femininity, whiteness, abilities and sexual orientation, we have the policies to reach those goals.
>
> (Schyman 2014)

FI makes clear that all of the groups united in the project of feminist politics suffer from norms, which set exclusionary standards. They contradict feminist politics and, therefore,

Table 3: Adjectives used with the noun "norm(s)" *(norm/normer)* in the corpus.

Adjective	Occurrences (N)
Gender	5
Cultural	4
Social	3
Heterosexual	3
Sexual	2
Oppressive	2
Patriarchal	1
Destructive	1
Functional(funktionsnormer)	1
Gender-binary	1
White	1
Western	1
Stronger	1
New	1

are understood as its enemy. Norms can be social or cultural, but, importantly, they are *constructed*. This example illustrates FI's social-constructivist approach to the issue of masculinity and violence: "What we associate with masculinity is governed by cultural norms, not biological conditions" (Feministiskt initiativ n.d.a).

Considering how norms are constructed in the texts as a subject and object can help understand its discursively ascribed function. As with structures, FI subjectifies norms, which become a social agent per se. On the website, norms are said to (emphases added):

- "*underlie* abusive treatment,"
- "*contribute* to limiting women's and girls' space in public,"
- "*permeate* media, its content and appeal,"
- "*affect* young people's notion of their body and sexuality," and
- "*be able to be* significant for how violence is made possible, understood and addressed by society."

Interestingly, structures and norms are discursified differently, with the scope of the latter appearing much more modest than that of the former. Whereas structures are ascribed strategic functions such as creating a power imbalance in society and the very conditions for discrimination, norms are thought to function more tactically, with a supportive role in shaping power relations (e.g., *can* be significant, *contribute* to limiting rights).

Table 4 presents the list of verbs used in relation to "norms" and "structures" when they stand as object in texts. Once again, there is a certain similarity between "norms" and "structures" as objects in a sentence: both are conceptualized as social constructs that are created, can be made visible and altered. However, there is much more agency left to an individual in challenging norms rather than structures. Unlike structures, it is suggested that norms should be questioned, opposed, counteracted, criticized, violated—and are even possible to get free from.

Table 4: Verbs used with "norms" and "structures."

Norms		Structures	
Alter	Present	Break down	Stay outside (of)
Violate	Challenge	Alter	See
Make visible	Legitimate	Create	
Question	Entrench	Make visible	
Talk about	Oppose	Understand	
Fit (in)	Ponder	Illuminate	
Be freed (from)	Criticize	Challenge	
Counteract	Break	Become aware (of)	

FI actively involves itself in the hegemonic struggle and comes up with a remedy against the antagonist: a so-called norm-critical pedagogy (*normkritisk pedagogi*) in educational establishments. A closer look at this tool's expected results gives an understanding of FI's idea about the ultimate fixation of the discourse on feminist politics. Norm-critical pedagogy, inter alia, is supposed to do the following:

Make visible various norms and power structures that underlie abusive treatment.

Provide a tool to break down structures that shape power imbalance.

(Feministiskt initiativ n.d.h)

We may see that the FI's articulation of feminist politics is asserted in line with Foucault's (1978) *speaker's benefit*. By mere articulation (making structures and norms visible, deepening understanding of them, and "seeing" mechanisms behind discrimination), the antagonist is expected to be defeated, and those capable of articulating knowledge of the oppressive essence of norms appear to be liberated. However, the fact that both structures and norms remain purely imaginary constructs brings fundamental difficulties for FI's political identification. This is a point we turn to in the discussion.

Discussion

The analysis leads to two important conclusions. One concerns the radical expansion of meaning of feminism by FI. By articulating oppression as one of the nodal points that sustains the signifying chain of feminist politics, FI essentially leaves the door open for all discriminated groups in society: any of them could become a subject of feminist politics. Once again we are faced with the problem of shifting the focus away from women as a single group, as a "sisterhood"—although this time on a level of policies rather than theories. To be sure, there is nothing wrong about taking a complex approach to social inequalities. What seems problematic is the effect of FI's rearticulation of feminism as an analytical category. If feminism acquires the meaning that essentially makes it a synonym for anti-discrimination, we may well talk about emptying the concept. If gender is only one of the "axes of differentiation," does it mean policies for women's empowerment should be abandoned? Would it make the struggle for equal representation of women and men less significant because of its uncritical take on gender binary and negligence of, for instance, race as an equally substantial part of gender equality? It could, yet it does not. The reason is that FI, despite its proclaimed intersectional stance, often resorts to both liberal and radical feminist discourses that can mask possible contradictions between the deconstructive approach to womanhood and the struggle for women's rights. For instance, even though FI (in a poststructuralist fashion) acknowledges that "[not] all men have more power than women in all situations. Everyone can be inferior in once sense while being superior in the other," they go on to say:

> But it is important to see that there is a structure that provides benefits to men just because they are men, and that this structure cuts across all social classes.
>
> (Feministiskt initiativ 2014)

Notably, the latter statement represents an essentialist approach that is merely based on stable (and binary) gender definitions. FI's rhetoric, consciously or not, remains inconsistent, which brings us to the uneasy question of the possibility of concordance between an intersectional political agenda and election campaigning. Whether or not it is possible to match a political campaign context with intersectionality at all, it is apparent that FI failed to do so without falling into the trap of essentialism.

The second implication has to do with FI's construction of antagonism. That structures and norms are the constitutive outside of feminist politics brings us to Lacan's and Žižek's idea of a failed signification, with the signified slipping out of the signifier's reach (see overview in Stavrakakis 1999). We observe the same issue in FI's articulation of its antagonist, which is represented by a mere signifier: unable to fix the meaning around any particular "real" object, "structures" and "norms" do not transcend the symbolic register—the language— and remain essentially a void masked by a signifier. Following Lacan (1994), we may thus talk of *fantasy* guiding the articulation of feminist politics, which becomes dependent on purely imaginary concepts articulated as its antagonist. We argue that such articulation is highly problematic for the affirmation of FI's hegemonic project. From a radical-democratic perspective, a successful articulation of a political identity requires delineating the foe (the "big Other"); what FI does instead is blurring the line that separates "us" from "them," as we have seen in the example of racist structures that permeate society. However, with the signification of the foe failing, the identification process remains incomplete and the identity obscure. Operating in antagonistic terms of radical politics, FI nonetheless skips the crucial last step: defining its big "Other" in a way intelligible enough to gain support among voters and enter the Parliament.

Conclusion

In this study we asked two questions when examining FI's online campaign material: (1) how does FI try to include various social groups into the hegemonic project of feminist politics, and (2) what or who is constructed as an antagonist to feminist politics and how does it impede and make such politics possible? In regard to the first research question, we found that intersectionality essentially allowed FI to include every group/individual into the hegemonic project of feminist politics—as long as they had experienced oppression (it is up to each group/individual to define their experience as that of oppression). This also leads us to the second research question. Even though racists and nationalists in general, and the Sweden Democrats in particular, were singled out as the antagonist, it was mainly norms and structures that were addressed in the online material as standing in the way of FI affirming its hegemonic project of feminist politics.

The study of FI's articulatory practice goes to the core of the critique of intersectionality as potentially devastating for the unity of women (see Brah and Phoenix 2004). What happens to the idea of a common "sisterhood" when FI attempts to embrace everyone feeling oppressed by structures and norms? A hegemonic project challenging the holistic approach to womanhood—by revealing its contingency as opposed to the traditionally stable and unproblematic notion of women—proved difficult to communicate in a comprehensible manner during an election campaign. We do not aim to argue here against Mouffe's (1992) claim that feminism should be articulated within a wider context of demands, nor do we put forward the idea that women should be reduced to an essentialized (gender or sexual) category. Our point is that such a radical expansion of struggles constituting the project of feminist politics risks making it difficult to communicate, explain, and make the hegemonic project relevant, at least in the context of an election campaign. Hence, FI's initial appeal to a constituency looking for alternatives to grand narratives of "old ideologies" (to use FI's own expression) remained largely unnoticed as the election campaign proceeded to the traditional logic of the Left vs. the Right, with issues such as unemployment overshadowing matters of identity. FI managed to involve numerous social struggles into its hegemonic project, but did not succeed in structuring the discourse in a way that would cover the void behind its own political identity.

Acknowledgments

This chapter springs out of Kirill Filimonov's Master's thesis, written in 2015 under the supervision of Dr. Jakob Svensson at Uppsala University. Filimonov is the first and main contributor of this chapter. Kirill Filimonov's MA studies (and hence also this research) were possible thanks to a grant from the Swedish Institute.

References

Baker, Paul (2006), *Using Corpora in Discourse Analysis*, London: A&C Black.

Baker, Paul and McEnery, Tony (2005), "A corpus-based approach to discourses of refugees and asylum seekers in UN and newspaper texts," *Journal of Language and Politics*, 4:2, pp. 197–226.

Bie, Narok (2014), "Fridolin: 'Sverige ska få en feministisk regering," svt Nyheter, 31 May, http://www.svt.se/nyheter/inrikes/fridolin-hatarna-ar-politikens-huliganer. Accessed 21 November 2015.

Brah, Avtar and Phoenix, Ann (2004), "Ain't I a woman? Revisiting intersectionality," *Journal of International Women's Studies*, 5:3, pp. 75–86.

Brandel, Tobias (2014), "FI näst största på nätet," Svenska Dagbladet, http://www.svd.se/svd-lisslys-nya-valtjanst-visar-att-feministiskt-initiativ-ar-nast-storst-panatet. Accessed 21 November 2015.

Bryson, Valerie (2003), *Feminist Political Theory: An Introduction*, Gordonsville, VA: Palgrave Macmillan.

Crenshaw, Kimberlé (1991), "Mapping the margins: Intersectionality, identity politics and violence against women of color," *Stanford Law Review*, 43:6, pp. 1241–99.

Derrida, Jacques (1978), *Writing and Difference*, Chicago: University of Chicago Press.

Emejulu, Akwugo (2011), "Retheorizing feminist community development: Towards a radical democratic citizenship," *Community Development Journal*, 46:3, pp. 378–90.

Feministiskt initiativ (2014), "Election platform," http://feministisktinitiativ.se/sprak/english/election-platform. Accessed 21 November 2015.

—— (2015a), "Feministiskt initiative," Facebook, 23 May, https://www.facebook.com/feministisktinitiativ/. Accessed 21 November 2015.

—— (2015b), "Feministiskt initiative," Facebook, 14 July, https://www.facebook.com/feministisktinitiativ/. Accessed 21 November 2015.

—— (n.d.a), "Kvinnofrid, våld i nära relationer och våld i namn av heder," http://feministisktinitiativ.se/politik/vald-mot-kvinnor/. Accessed 21 November 2015.

—— (n.d.b), "Syn på brott och straff," http://feministisktinitiativ.se/politik/rattspolitik/. Accessed 21 November 2015.

—— (n.d.c), "Margaret om intersektionalitet," http://feministisktinitiativ.se/om/margaret-om intersektionalitet/. Accessed 21 November 2015.

—— (n.d.d), "Rätt omsorg oavsett kön," http://feministisktinitiativ.se/politik/halsa-och-sjukvard/. Accessed 21 November 2015.

—— (n.d.e), "Argumentationsguide för rasifierade feminister kombinerad med insiktsguide för andra!," http://feministisktinitiativ.se/om/argumentationsguide/. Accessed 21 November 2015.

—— (n.d.f), "Feministisk antirasism," http://feministisktinitiativ.se/politik/feministisk-antirasism/. Accessed 21 November 2015.

—— (n.d.g), "Sexualitet, sexuell och reproduktiv hälsa och rättigheter," https://feministisktinitiativ.se/politik/sexualpolitik/. Accessed 21 November 2015.

—— (n.d.h), "En jämlik skola," http://feministisktinitiativ.se/politik/utbildning/. Accessed 21 November 2015.

Filimonov, Kirill, Russmann, Uta, and Svensson, Jakob (2016), "Picturing the party—Instagram and party campaigning in the 2014 Swedish elections," *SM+S: Social Media + Society*, 2:3, http://sms. sagepub.com/content/2/3/2056305116662179. Accessed 21 November 2015.

Foucault, Michel (1978), *The History of Sexuality. Vol. 1: An Introduction,* New York: Vintage.

Holmqvist, Annette, Stenquist, Victor, and Karlsson, Pär (2013), "Fick största applåder—för feminismen," *Aftonbladet,* 1 May, http://www.alftonbladet.se/nyheter/artcile16702224.ab. Accessed 21 November 2015.

Howarth, David (2000), *Discourse,* Philadelphia: Open University Press.

Lacan, Jacques (1994), "The mirror-phase as formative of the function of the I," in S. Žižek (ed.), *Mapping Ideology,* London: Verso, pp. 93–99.

Laclau, Ernesto and Mouffe, Chantal (2014), *Hegemony and Socialist Strategy: Towards a Radical Democratic Politics,* 3rd ed, London: Verso.

MacDonald, Malcolm, Homolar, Alexandra, Rethel, Lena, Schnurr, Stephanie, and Vessey, Rachelle (2015), "Manufacturing dissent: The discursive formation of nuclear proliferation (2006–2012)," *Discourse and Communication,* 9:2, pp. 173–97.

Martikainen, Rebecka (2012), "Jag är en övertygad feminist, punkt slut," *Expressen*, 27 January, http://www. expressen.se/nyheter/jag-ar-en-overtygad-feminist-punkt-slut/. Accessed 21 November 2015.

Matsuda, Mari J. (1990), "Beside my sister, facing the enemy: Legal theory out of coalition," *Stanford Law Review*, 43, pp. 1183–92.

Mouffe, Chantal (1992), "Feminism, citizenship, and radical democratic politics," in J. Butler and J. W. Scott (eds), *Feminists Theorize the Political,* London: Routledge, pp. 369–84.

—— (1993), *The Return of the Political,* London: Verso.

—— (1995), "Feminism, citizenship, and radical democratic politics," in L. Nicholson, S. Seidman, and J. C. Alexander (eds), *Social Postmodernism: Beyond Identity Politics,* Cambridge: Cambridge University Press, pp. 315–32.

—— (2005), *On the Political,* London: Routledge.

Orange, Richard (2014), "Sweden's *Strictly* star adds charisma to feminist push for parliament," *The Guardian*, 23 August, http://www.theguardian.com/world/2014/aug/23/strictly-star-sweden-feminist- push-gudrun-schyman. Accessed 21 November 2015.

Peterson, V. Spike (1999), "Political identities/nationalism as heterosexism," *International Feminist Journal of Politics,* 1:1, pp. 34–65.

Rayson, Paul and Garside, Roger (2000), "Comparing corpora using frequency profiling," in *Proceedings of the Workshop on Comparing Corpora: The 38th Annual Meeting of the Association for Computational Linguistics (ACL 2000),* Hong Kong, 1–8 October, http://dl.acm. org/citation.cfm?doid=1117729.1117730. Accessed 21 November 2015.

Rothschild, Nathalie (2014), "Swedish women vs. Vladimir Putin," *Foreign Policy*, 5 December, http://foreignpolicy.com/2014/12/05/can-vladimir-putin-be-intimidated-by-feminism-sweden/. Accessed 21 November 2015.

Sandilands, Kate (1993), "Radical democracy: A contested/ing terrain," *Synthesis/Regeneration*, 5, pp. 5–13.

Schyman, Gudrun (2014), "Välj in Fi och skapa historia" ("Vote for Fi and make history"), *SVT*, 11 September, http://www.svt.se/opinion/article2308894.svt. Accessed 21 November 2015.

Stavrakakis, Yannis (1999), *Lacan and the Political*, London: Routledge.

SvD (2015), "Partierna växer—Fi allra mest" ("The Parties grows—Fi the most"), http://www.svd.se/nyheter/inrikes/partierna-vaxer-fi-allra-mest_4437927.svd. Accessed 21 November 2015.

Svensson, Jakob and Larsson, Anders O. (2016), "Interacting with whom? Swedish parliamentarians on Twitter during the 2014 elections," *International Journal of E-Politics*, 7:1, pp. 1–15.

Winther-Jørgensen, Marianne W. and Phillips, Louise J. (2010), *Discourse Analysis as Theory and Method*, 2nd ed., London: Sage.

Yuval-Davis, Nira (1999), "What is 'transversal politics'?," *Soundings*, 12, pp. 88–93.

Chapter 3

The Stage as an Arena of Politics: The Struggle between the Vlaams Blok/Belang and the Flemish City Theaters

Benjamin De Cleen

Introduction

Since the early 1990s, the Flemish populist radical-right party VB (Vlaams Blok; renamed Vlaams Belang after a legal conviction for racism in 2004) has been an important player in Belgian politics. Founded after the split of the more radical-nationalist and rightist wing delegates from the nationalist Volksunie (People's Union) party in the late 1970s, the VB became one of the most successful populist radical-right parties in Europe, although its heyday seems to have been from the early 1990s until the mid-2000s. This chapter discusses the VB by looking at the party's rhetoric about the Flemish city theaters in Antwerp, Ghent, and Brussels. These are the three largest Dutch-speaking theaters in Belgium, which are funded by the Flemish community and (to a lesser extent) by the respective cities. This choice is informed by the fact that these Flemish city theaters have been the cultural institutions most consistently criticized by the VB and have been among the most active opponents of the VB since the early 1990s. The VB's rhetoric about the theaters is characteristic of its views on the role of (subsidized) cultural institutions and of its ways of dealing with opposition from outside of political parties.

In order to lay bare the structure of the VB's rhetoric, a discourse-theoretical analysis (see Carpentier and De Cleen 2007) was carried out. Its main conceptual framework is drawn from the discourse theory of Ernesto Laclau and Chantal Mouffe (Laclau and Mouffe 2001; Laclau 2005; Glynos and Howarth 2007). Discourses are defined as systems of meaning that establish relations between identities, objects, and practices, and provide subject positions that people can identify with (Howarth 2000: 9; Howarth and Stavrakakis 2000: 3; Torfing 2005: 14). Every discursive practice builds on existing structures of meaning, for it would not make sense otherwise. In a concrete analysis, it is helpful to differentiate, analytically, the practice under study from the systems of meaning that existed before and that encompass much more than this practice under study (Jørgensen and Phillips 2002: 140–41). Therefore, a distinction is introduced in this chapter between rhetoric and discourse. *Rhetoric* refers to the structures of meaning produced through the discursive practices under study (the rhetoric of the VB, the rhetoric of the theaters). *Discourse* refers to the more encompassing and more stable structures of meaning on which rhetoric draws (and which are reproduced, contested, or altered by rhetoric). Rhetoric is the result of the articulation of (elements of) discourses. The notion of *articulation* refers to the combination of (elements of) different discourses within a particular rhetoric (see Howarth and Stavrakakis 2000: 3; Laclau and Mouffe 2001: 105). The central question of this chapter is: on which discourses (and which elements from which discourses) does the VB's rhetoric draw and how does the party articulate (elements of) those discourses?

In order to answer this question, the chapter analyzes texts using qualitative content analytical procedures of categorization, a process of sorting and organizing pieces of data and linking them together by grouping them into categories that are tied to the concepts used by the researcher (Coffey and Atkinson 1996; Titscher et al. 2000: 62). Three linguistic categories are of particular relevance to analyzing how discourses are articulated in texts: vocabulary, semantic relations between words and sentences, and assumptions and presuppositions (Fairclough 2003: 129–33). Empirical material consists of written texts produced in the period between 2005 and 2006, during which the struggle between the VB and the city theaters reached a peak. The corpus consists of external communication by the VB (28 texts)[1] and the theaters (97 texts),[2] VB interventions in the Flemish Parliament (20 texts), the Brussels Flemish Community Commission (10 texts), and the Antwerp City Council (2 texts), coverage in the Dutch-speaking Belgian press (241 texts), on Flemish television[3] (2 texts) and in theater magazines (34 texts).[4]

Each of the following sections discusses a discourse drawn on by the VB: nationalism, conservatism, populism, and authoritarianism. With each successive section the picture becomes more complete, as the way the VB articulates these different discourses becomes clearer. The focus is on the VB, but in order to get a good understanding of the party's objections to the theaters, the chapter touches upon the rhetoric of the theaters as well.

Flemish nationalism versus the theaters' rhetoric of cultural diversity

As is the case for other populist radical-right parties, an exclusive and radical nationalism lies at the heart of VB rhetoric (Eatwell 2000; Spruyt 2000; Swyngedouw and Ivaldi 2001; Mudde 2007). Nationalist discourse is built around the nodal point[5] nation, which is envisaged as a limited and sovereign community that exists through time and is tied to a certain space (e.g., Freeden 1998; Sutherland 2005; Anderson 2006). Because the nation has no positive identity—the members of a nation share no given essence that makes them a nation—it is constructed by opposing it to out-groups. These can be located outside the borders of the nation's territory (other nation states) and inside its borders but outside of the nation (foreigners) (Triandafyllidou 1998; Dyrberg 2003; Wodak et al. 2009: 27).

One of the main points of struggle between the VB and the Flemish city theaters is the theaters' Flemish character. The struggle revolves around the question of how strongly a Flemish city theater should occupy itself with the boundary around the nation, how the boundary is defined, and what this boundary implies for the relations between the nation and the outside. The struggle needs to be understood in light of the theaters' history. The establishment of the Flemish city theaters in the nineteenth century was rather closely tied to the history of the nationalist Flemish Movement—a label grouping the organizations and individuals striving for the emancipation and (later) autonomy of the Dutch-speaking population of the North of Belgium. In the first half of the twentieth century, the theaters were even more closely involved in Flemish nationalist politics, to the extent that they became involved in collaboration with the German occupier in two World Wars. After the Second World War, the city theaters were increasingly institutionalized within the developing autonomous political structures of the so-called Flemish community. At the same time, however, the theaters' history was never Flemish nationalist alone. Of particular interest here is that, after the Second World War, the theaters moved away from and became increasingly critical of Flemish nationalism as a political project (Geerts 2009; Vanhaesebrouck 2010).

It should come as no surprise then that the theaters reacted very negatively to the electoral breakthrough of the VB in 1991. In a first stage, this mainly gave rise to reactions *against* the VB structured around a rejection of the VB's racism and a defense of democracy. In a later stage, the theaters also started to focus on positive strategies to increase cultural diversity in their personnel, productions, and audience (Jans 2010). In the period under study, the theaters' position toward cultural diversity revolved around an opposition between their own openness and the closed character of the VB's nationalism. This openness has two aspects (that are often hard to disentangle): openness of the boundaries *around* the Flemish in-group and openness *of* the Flemish toward other groups. The VB's exclusive nationalism is contested by presenting immigrants and their descendants as part of Flanders, which is exemplified by plays that define minorities as part of Flanders and mix references to Flemish history with elements from minority cultures (see Vanhaesebrouck 2010). A vocabulary of dialogue, cross-fertilization, and contact is also used to signify the open position toward those who are non-Flemish. The theaters oppose what they consider the VB's treatment of Flanders as an "island" (Reyniers 2005). An open definition of Flanders is articulated with a city discourse. Particularly, the Brussels Koninklijke Vlaamse Schouwburg (Royal Flemish Theater, KVS) takes the cultural and linguistic diversity of Brussels—the officially bilingual French- and Dutch-speaking capital of Belgium and a city characterized by the strong presence of minorities—to mean that it should open its doors to French-speakers as well as to minorities.

The city theaters' position is not exactly applauded by the VB. To the city theaters' rhetoric of openness, contact, and dialogue, the VB opposes a radical nationalism. The party will not settle for anything less than an independent Flemish state, and demands strict protection of the boundaries around the nation. At the heart of the VB's criticism of the theaters' relation with Flanders lies an essentialist conception of Flemish identity. The task of the Flemish theaters, for the VB, is to protect that Flemish identity. This is particularly pertinent in Brussels, which the party considers a frontier zone in the defense of Flemish identity. From this perspective, the Brussels KVS is treated as a weapon in the "struggle for the preservation of the own identity" (Arckens 2004) in an environment that is defined by the "hostility" (Arckens 2004) of the Francophone majority and the purported threats of a large immigrant population. This reveals the view of a Flanders engaged in a constant struggle with other cultures/nations for the preservation of its own identity. Within the VB's nationalism, the theaters' attention for and openness toward "cultures" other than the

Flemish is profoundly problematic. The VB sees this as an unacceptable diversion from the role of the Flemish theater and a threat to the Flemish identity the theaters are supposed to defend. To the VB, the KVS should focus on producing Dutch-spoken theater for the Flemish population. Instead of being "ashamed" (Arckens 2006b) of their Flemish identity and Flemish nationalist history and embracing cultural diversity, the VB contends that the city theaters should be proud of and defend Flemish identity. As the VB's vocabulary of roots, history, threats, and preservation already indicates, its nationalism is profoundly conservative. But its conservatism goes beyond the defense of national identity. The next section looks at the VB's conservatism in more detail.

Conservatism versus cultural diversity and the avant-garde

A second discourse the VB draws upon is conservatism. This dimension of the struggle between the VB and the theaters revolves around the relation between past, present, and future. Unlike most definitions of conservatism, the definition of conservatism used here does not characterize conservatism as an attitude toward objectively identifiable change (e.g., Wilson 1973; Jost et al. 2003) or as a particular set of demands (e.g., Scruton 1980; Nisbet 1986; Eccleshall 1994, 2000), but as a particular structure of meaning that can be used to formulate and support very different demands (see Huntington 1958; Vincent 1994: 210). Conservative discourse is built around conservation, envisaged as a process of conserving into the future (part of) a present that has come to us from the past, and that is legitimated through reference to a desirable continuity between past, present, and future (see Narveson 2001: 10). It is the structure of the demand that counts, not its substance. Conservatism defines itself in opposition to what it presents as threats to the continuity between past, present, and future (Huntington 1958: 461).

The VB draws on conservative discourse to formulate its nationalist demands as well as its rejection of avant-garde theater. The party's nationalism is strongly articulated with conservatism, for its nationalism has at its core a Flemish identity rooted in the past. The division of the world into nations, each with their own state, is presented as natural. Flemish nationalism, to the VB, is about the defense and preservation of a pre-political identity, that is, an identity that has existed since long before any political party formulated nationalist demands. Against this, the theaters argue that their attention for cultural diversity is a matter of "tuning the artistic project to the culturally diverse and plurilingual reality" (Koninklijke Vlaamse Schouwburg 2005: 1). They oppose this to the VB that "turns its back on the challenges and continues to stare at an idealized Flemish past, as if it would be possible to turn back time" (Jans and Janssens 2005). Using a conservative discourse, the VB opposes the (currently existing) multicultural society, which it blames for uprooting the natural and preferable state of things, as well as the multicultural politics of the theater, which in the eyes of the VB is utopian. This strategy of delegitimizing opposition as utopian and of obfuscating its own profoundly political nature is characteristic of a conservatism that identifies itself as a "political position opposed to ideological politics" (O'Sullivan 1999: 52; Eccleshall 2000: 281–82).

Conservatism also plays a role in the VB's resistance to avant-garde theater. In Flemish theater, innovation has taken up a central position since the 1980s (De Pauw 2006). Although this focus on innovation is being criticized from within the theater by 2005, a taboo-breaking, innovation-centered tendency is still very prominent in the theater. The VB rejects what it considers as provocations to and insults of traditional values and long-standing identities (mocking Flanders, explicit sexuality, mocking religion). However, strongly voiced conservative arguments about the downfall of Western civilization and the crisis of society due to the morally, sexually, and otherwise deviant nature of culture and media, which in earlier times could be heard regularly from the VB, have become far less prominent by 2005. The party's rejection of experimental theater has become increasingly grounded in a populist discourse that criticizes avant-garde art because it is elitist.

Populism versus the artistic elite

The VB started out as an explicitly elitist party, but like other radical-right parties, it has become strongly populist (Rydgren 2005; Mudde 2007). Populism claims to speak for a powerless "down" (the people), whose identity is constructed by opposing it to a powerful "up" (the elite) (e.g., Mény and Surel 2000; Reinfeldt 2000: 51; Dyrberg 2003; Laclau 2005; Mudde 2007). The VB claims to be the party of the people, and seeks to delegitimize the so-called traditional parties (and especially the socialists) as an elite (Mudde 1995; Swyngedouw and Ivaldi 2001: 12–14; Jagers 2006: 219–52). The VB's populism also extends beyond its criticism of competing political parties.

The VB's nationalist and conservative objections to the city theaters' rhetoric of cultural diversity, as well as its conservative objection to their focus on experiment, are articulated with a populist criticism of the theaters as elitist. The city theaters, the VB argues, "must per definition aim at the entirety of the population—so also at the common man" (Pas 2005). The party argues that the program of city theaters is too experimental and too focused on a limited audience. The VB sometimes refers to the low attendance at the city theaters, but its objection against the élitism of the theater is mostly a qualitative one: the "[t]heatre is full, that's right, but it is always the same little group of people that returns" (Dewinter 2005a). This little group is presented as an elite and opposed to the people—"the ordinary man" (Dewinter 2005a) or "average Joe" (Dewinter 2005a).[6] The VB claims to defend the cultural needs of these ordinary people. Instead of focusing on "avant-garde" (Arckens 2004) and experiment, the theaters should give more space to "classic and popular repertoire theater" (Arckens 2006a) and "lower the bar" (Dewinter 2005a). Within this populist discourse, demands for more accessible theater are a matter of democracy. The VB's resistance to what it considered experimental theater is, by 2005, much more located in a populist rejection of high art as inaccessible to ordinary people than in a conservative protection of society against moral downfall. Still, populism and conservatism are articulated, for the definition of what is acceptable is situated in the taste and opinions of the majority of ordinary people, which the VB opposes to the progressive taste and ideas of a small artistic elite.

The VB also draws on populism to delegitimize the city theaters' pro-diversity stance, as well as their explicit opposition to the VB. To the VB, it is their elitist position that explains why theater-makers hold on to a positive view of cultural diversity and suffer from "identity shame." The Flemings that work for and are the audience of the theater in Brussels, for example, are argued to accept the dominance of French (and other languages) in Brussels and multiculturalism because of "a certain form of urban snobbism that has and creates an overly exaggerated idealistic image of city life" (Arckens 2006b). The party portrays them as "people who do not have problems in Brussels. They live in a protected cultural milieu" (Van den Eynde in Hillaert 2006). The VB opposes this elite's purported idealistic view on living in the city to the reality of living in a multicultural city for "the large majority" (Van den Eynde in Hillaert 2006). The theaters' explicit resistance to the VB is dismissed in even stronger populist terms. In reaction to a number of initiatives on the part of the theater and other artists in the run-up to the 2006 local elections, one of the party's leaders states:

> What more can I do than formulate the restrained complaint that the art world in Flanders one-sidedly and unanimously condemns the VB as heretic, with that in practice strengthening the cordon sanitaire[7] (that intellectual and democratic monstrosity) and de facto per definition and without nuance siding with the governing parties, so with the establishment. The Flemish art world is establishment. It marches out against the opposition and serves the powerful.
>
> (Annemans 2006)

Through a populist argument, artists and opposing political parties are presented as belonging to one and the same elite that is opposed to the party of the people and therefore also to the people. The VB also uses this populism to fend off the accusations of authoritarianism voiced against it. The final section looks at the VB's authoritarianism and its strategies to present itself as a democratic party in some more detail.

The VB, authoritarianism, and democracy

The opposition of the theaters to the VB has always drawn strongly on the accusation that the VB is undemocratic (as has the opposition to the VB in general). The theaters' reactions were no different in early 2005, when a Brussels VB representative ends his criticism of the KVS with the suggestion to "turn off the subsidy faucet for a certain period as ultimate instrument if need be?" (Arckens 2005). The theaters' argument goes as follows: the VB's criticisms of the theater (particularly when combined with demands to cut subsidies) are attacks on artistic freedom, and because artistic freedom is at the heart of democracy these impingements on artistic freedom prove the VB's authoritarian character. Authoritarianism can be defined as a discourse built around an authority, envisaged as an (individual or collective) actor who has the unquestionable right to take and enforce binding decisions. Authoritarianism is characterized by closedness, in that it constructs and maintains (a) a closed order governed by rules/norms that limit the liberty of the individual and in which the authority enforces the individual's compliance with the rules/norms if necessary, and (b) closes the space for politics by treating this order, its rules/norms, and the authority within that order as fixed and unquestionable (see Stenner 2005; Kitschelt 2007: 1179). From this perspective, the VB's rhetoric about the theater does indeed have authoritarian elements. The party's nationalism (the claim to speak for a pre-political nation), conservatism (the claim to defend unchangeable values, identities, and ways of life), and populism (the claim to speak for a homogeneous people against an illegitimate elite) serve to limit the freedom of theater-makers and to present their views as unacceptable and illegitimate. However, the VB refuses the accusation of authoritarianism and presents itself as a democratic party. The party rejects the parallels between the VB and the Nazis that are regularly drawn by the party's critics in the theater:[8]

Of course no one has to "shut up". We continue to defend freedom of speech. That freedom should apply to everyone. And that freedom should also include freedom of artistic expression. We do not want to prohibit books or theatre plays, we do not want to throw abstract artists in jail, we do not want to have "Entartete Kunst" burned, like the Nazis did.

(Vlaams Belang 2005a)

As this quote shows, the VB even presents itself as the defender of liberal democratic rights. At the same time, the party does argue for limitations to the freedom of the theaters to do as they wish. The VB deals with this tension mainly through a populist argument. The party presents its demands not as a matter of impinging on artistic freedom but as a matter of using subsidies in a way that reflects taxpayers' wishes. This argument supports not only the demand that the theaters play more popular theater but also (albeit more ambiguously) the demand that the theaters do not oppose the VB. Artists, according to the VB, have the right to speak out against the VB, but not when they are subsidized (Dewinter 2005b). Culture that is produced with the help of subsidies paid by taxpayers that include VB voters should not speak out "unanimously" (Annemans 2006) against the VB or should even *reflect* the political wishes of taxpayers. The first part of the following statement by Filip Dewinter, one of the electoral strongholds of the VB, exemplifies this:

Political engagement in the theatre, evidently, but then not one-sidedly against us, not one-sidedly pro the multicul [a wordplay on multiculture, "kul" means "bollocks" in Dutch], not one-sidedly pro a certain inclination and only against the other. Then *everything* should be possible [...] "where are the extreme right theatre makers?" I say:

luckily there are none. I am happy there are none. Because theatre does not have as a primary goal to serve a political purpose, but to be itself, and the purpose of the theatre must indeed be itself.

(Dewinter 2005a)

As the second part of this quote illustrates, the VB cannot accuse the leftist theaters of pushing out right-wing artists because of a lack of (radical-) right theater-makers who would *want* to speak out for the VB or its viewpoints. This might explain why Dewinter resorts to a *l'art pour l'art* discourse in arguing for a disconnection between theater and politics. In doing so, the VB uses the idea of the autonomy of art from politics in an attempt to limit precisely that autonomy. Even if the argument is based on the VB being a democratically elected party, this argument has an authoritarian character, for it gives the VB the right to determine what artists can and cannot say. The party's definition of democracy is limited to elections and does not accept the legitimacy of the non-electoral politics of artists. These are dismissed as the strategies of a leftist elite opposing a party it cannot beat democratically. The party even turns the criticism of authoritarianism around by arguing that the theaters' opposition to the VB "simply continue[s] a long tradition of abuse and manipulation of art for political goals and political indoctrination" (Vlaams Belang 2005b). This shows how populism does not merely serve to present the VB as the party of the people and to claim signifier democracy, but also to delegitimize political opponents as an elite that uses undemocratic tactics against the party of the people.

Conclusion

The aim of this chapter has been to shed light on the VB by analyzing its rhetoric about the Flemish city theaters. In VB rhetoric about the theater, nationalism, conservatism, and populism reinforce each other. This results in the construction of a strong antagonism. On one side there is the VB, the party of the (ordinary) people, who wish to protect their own identity from changes caused to their environment by increasing immigration, and who are not interested in and/or are offended by the experimental high art produced by the theaters. On the other side are the city theaters and their audiences, who form an artistic elite that lives a protected life, is ashamed of its Flemish identity and embraces immigration, produces difficult art for a small elitist audience, aims to offend the feelings of the majority of ordinary people, and supports the political establishment. In VB rhetoric, the two groups and what they stand for are almost completely opposed. This might explain the VB's strong criticism (and that of the theaters as well): there are many reasons to be displeased, and, in view of who the VB addresses as voters and how, the party has little to lose when it criticizes the theaters. While the VB presents itself as a democratic party, its attempts to enforce what it considers unquestionable nationalist, conservative, and populist demands, and the refusal to accept the legitimacy of opposing views and political opposition from outside of political parties, give VB rhetoric an authoritarian character.

References

Anderson, Benedict (2006), *Imagined Communities: Reflections on the Origin and Spread of Nationalism*, rev. ed., London: Verso.

Annemans, Gerolf (2006), "Over kunst en politiek…," *Vlaams Belang Magazine*, 3:12, p. 3.

Arckens, Erik (2004), "Interpellatie in Bespreking van de Beleidsnota Cultuur 2004–2009", Vlaams Parlement, stuk 15 (2004–5), nr. 7-D.

—— (2005), "Interpellatie van de Minister voor Cultuur, jeugd, sport en Brussel Bert Anciaux in de Commissie voor Cultuur, media en sport van het Vlaams Parlement over het beleid van de Koninklijke Vlaamse Schouwburg als Vlaamse culturele instelling in Brussel," *Handelingen van de Commissie voor cultuur, jeugd, sport en media*, 13 January.

—— (2006a), "Actuele vraag tot de heer Bert Anciaux, Vlaams Minister van Cultuur, Jeugd, Sport en Brussel, over de verklaringen van de minister aangaande een Cultureel Pact tussen werkveld, overheid en samenleving, wat het aspect diversiteit betreft," Vlaams Parlement, *Plenaire vergadering*, 24 January.

—— (2006b), "Interpellatie tot de heer Bert Anciaux, Vlaams Minister van Cultuur, Jeugd, Sport en Brussel, over het problematisch karakter van het gentrificatieproces in Brussel op sociaal-cultureel vlak," *Handelingen Commissie voor Brussel en de Vlaamse Rand*, 29 June.

Carpentier, Nico and De Cleen, Benjamin (2007), "Bringing discourse theory into media studies," *Journal of Language and Politics*, 6:2, pp. 267–95.

Coffey, Amanda and Atkinson, Paul (1996), *Making Sense of Qualitative Data*, London: Sage.

De Pauw, Wim (2006), "De Nieuwe Kleren van de Keizer?," Ph.D. thesis, Brussels: Vrije Universiteit Brussel.

Dewinter, Filip (2005a), interviewed on Ter Zake, VRT, Canvas, Brussels, 12 March.

—— (2005b), "Eigen stad eerst?" *De Standaard*, 26 February, p. 30.

Dyrberg, Torben Bech (2003), "Right/Left in a context of new political frontiers: What's radical politics today?," *Journal of Language and Politics*, 2:2, pp. 339–42.

Eatwell, Roger (2000), "The rebirth of the 'extreme right' in Western Europe," *Parliamentary Affairs*, 53, pp. 407–25.

Eccleshall, Robert (1994), "Conservatism," in R. Eccleshall, V. Geoghegan, R. Jay, M. Kenny, I. MacKenzie and R. Wilford (eds), *Political Ideologies: An Introduction*, London and New York: Routledge, pp. 60–90.

—— (2000), "The doing of conservatism," *Journal of Political Ideologies*, 5:3, pp. 275–87.

Fairclough, Norman (2003), *Analysing Discourse: Textual Analysis for Social Research*, London: Routledge.

Freeden, Michael (1998), "Is nationalism a distinct ideology?," *Political Studies*, 46:4, pp. 748–65.

Geerts, Ronald (2009), "De tachtigers schrijven," *Documenta*, 27:2/3, pp. 193–208.

Glynos, Jason and Howarth, David (2007), *Logics of Critical Explanation in Social and Political Theory*, London: Routledge.

Hillaert, Wouter (2006), "'Ik zou eens Shakespeare willen zien door Shakespeare': De theaterdrang van het Vlaams Belang," *Rekto:Verso*, 19, July-August.

Howarth, David (2000), *Discourse*, Buckingham and Philadelphia: Open University Press.

Howarth, David and Stavrakakis, Yannis (2000), "Introducing discourse theory and political analysis," in D. Howarth, A. Norval, and Y. Stavrakakis (eds), *Discourse Theory and Political Analysis: Identities, Hegemony and Social Change*, Manchester and New York: Manchester University Press, pp. 1–23.

Huntington, Samuel P. (1958), "Conservatism as an ideology," *American Political Science Review*, 51:2, pp. 454–73.

Jagers, Jan (2006), "De stem van het volk! Populisme als concept getest bij Vlaamse politieke partijen," Ph.D. thesis, Antwerp: Universiteit Antwerpen.

Jans, Erwin (2010), "Een regenboog boven het Vlaamse theater? Het multiculturele verhaal in de Vlaamse podiumkunsten," *Documenta*, 28:3/4, pp. 321–35.

Jans, Erwin and Janssens, Ivo (2005), "Een horizon van belangrijke vragen," *Etcetera*, 93, p. 16.

Jørgensen, Marianne and Phillips, Louise (2002), *Discourse Analysis as Theory and Method*, London: Sage.

Jost, John T., Glaser, Jack, Kruglanski Arie W., and Sulloway, Frank J. (2003), "Political conservatism as motivated social cognition," *Psychological Bulletin*, 129:3, pp. 339–75.

Kitschelt, Herbert (2007), "Growth and persistence of the radical right in postindustrial democracies: Advances and challenges in comparative research," *West European Politics*, 30:5, pp. 1176–1206.

Koninklijke Vlaamse Schouwburg (2005), *Terug van Weggeweest. KVS Seizoen 2005-6*, Brussels: Koninklijke Vlaamse Schouwburg.

Laclau, Ernesto (2005), *On Populist Reason*, London: Verso.

Laclau, Ernesto and Mouffe, Chantal (2001), *Hegemony and Socialist Strategy*, 2nd ed., London: Verso.

Mény, Yves and Surel, Yves (2000), *Par le Peuple, Pour le Peuple: le Populisme et les Démocraties*, Paris: Fayard.

Mudde, Cas (1995), "One against all, all against one! A portrait of the Vlaams Blok," *Patterns of Prejudice*, 29:1, pp. 5–28.

—— (2007), *Populist Radical Right Parties in Europe*, Cambridge: Cambridge University Press.

Narveson, Jan (2001), *The Libertarian Idea*, Peterborough, Ontario, Canada: Broadview Press.

Nisbet, Roger (1986), *Conservatism: Dream and Reality*, Milton Keynes: Open University Press.

O'Sullivan, Noel (1999), "Conservatism," in R. Eatwell and A. Wright (eds), *Contemporary Political Ideologies*, London and New York: Pinter.

Pas, Frederik (2005), "Het moest gezegd," *Vlaams Belang Magazine*, 2:4, p. 12.

Reinfeldt, Sebastian (2000), *Nicht-wir und Die-da: Studien zum Rechten Populismus*, Wien: Braumüller.

Reyniers, Johan (2005), "Brussel is de toekomst," *De Morgen*, 14 March.

Rydgren, Jens (2005), "Is extreme right-wing populism contagious? Explaining the emergence of a new party family," *European Journal of Political Research*, 44:3, pp. 413–37.

Scruton, Roger (1980), *The Meaning of Conservatism*, Harmondswood: Penguin.

Spruyt, M. (2000), *Wat het Vlaams Blok Verzwijgt*, Leuven: Van Halewijck.

Stenner, Karen (2005), *The Authoritarian Dynamic*, Cambridge: Cambridge University Press.

Sutherland, Claire (2005), "Nation-building through discourse theory," *Nations and Nationalism*, 11:2, pp. 185–202.

Swyngedouw, Mark and Ivaldi, Gilles (2001), "The extreme right utopia in Belgium and France: The ideology of the Flemish Vlaams Blok and the French Front National," *West European Politics*, 24:3, pp. 1–22.

Titscher, Stefan, Meyer, Michael, Wodak, Ruth, and Vetter, Eva (2000), *Methods of Text and Discourse Analysis*, London: Sage.

Torfing, Jakob (1999), *New Theories of Discourse: Laclau, Mouffe and Žižek*, Oxford: Blackwell.

—— (2005), "Discourse theory: Achievements, arguments, and challenges," in D. Howarth and J. Torfing (eds), *Discourse Theory in European Politics*, London: Palgrave, pp. 1–32.

Triandafyllidou, Anna (1998), "National identity and the 'Other'" *Ethnic and Racial Studies*, 21:4, pp. 593–612.

Vanhaesebrouck, Karel (2010), "The hybridization of Flemish Identity: The Flemish national heritage on the contemporary stage," *Contemporary Theater Review*, 20:4, pp. 465–74.

Vincent, Andrew (1994), "British conservatism and the problem of ideology," *Political Studies*, 42:2, pp. 204–27.

Vlaams Belang (2005a), "Geen censuur," 10 March, www.vlaamsbelang.org/0/381/. Accessed 14 April 2012.

—— (2005b), "Politieke Kunst," 24 February, www.vlaamsbelang.org/0/335/. Accessed 14 April 2012.

Wilson, Glenn D. (ed.) (1973), *The Psychology of Conservatism*, Oxford: Academic Press.

Wodak, Ruth, de Cillia, Rudolf, and Reisigl, Michael (2009), *The Discursive Construction of National Identity*, 2nd ed., Edinburgh: Edinburgh University Press.

Notes

1   Nine articles in the VB Magazine, three texts from the VB national website, three articles in the Antwerp VB magazine, seven articles in the Brussels VB magazine, three articles in the Ghent VB magazine, two articles in the electronic newsletter of the Antwerp VB; one election propaganda booklet for the 2006 elections in Antwerp.

2   Het Toneelhuis (Antwerp): three annual program booklets, eleven monthly magazines, seven promotional texts about plays; Koninklijke Vlaamse Schouwburg (Brussels): three annual program booklets, the bi-monthly magazine from January 2005 to December 2006 (twelve issues), seventeen printed press/promotional texts, three speeches at a presentation for the season 2005–06; ten KVS website blog posts; the KVS mission statement; a text about the history of the KVS; Publiekstheater/NTGent (Ghent): fourteen monthly brochures, three press/promotional texts for an installation.

3   The analysis is conducted on a literal transcript of the broadcast and does not take into account visual aspects.

4   Sixteen articles in *Rekto:Verso*, eighteen articles in *Etcetera*.

5   In Laclau and Mouffe's discourse theory, nodal points are "privileged discursive points that partially fix meaning within signifying chains" (Torfing 1999: 98). Other signifiers within a discourse acquire their meaning through their relation to that (those) nodal point(s) (Laclau and Mouffe 2001: 112).

6   "Jan met de pet," literally "Jan with the cap."

7   The cordon sanitaire (literally quarantine line) is an agreement between the other parties not to enter into coalition or make political deals with the VB on any level.

8   One example is the Antwerp city theater playing *Mefisto For Ever*—Tom Lanoye's play based on Klaus Mann's *Mephisto. Roman einer Karriere*, directed by Guy Cassiers—before the 2006 local elections in Antwerp.

Section 2

The Politics of Everyday Life

Chapter 4

A Discourse-Theoretical Approach to Death and Dying

Leen Van Brussel

Death, signs of: Relaxing of facial muscles, producing rather staring eyes and gaping mouth. Loss of curves of the back, which becomes flat against the bed or table. Slight discoloration of the skin, which becomes a waxy-yellow hue, and loses its pink transparency at the fingertips.

(cited in Ball 1976)

Introduction

Death is sometimes described as "the only certainty in life." It is often approached as the ultimate biological essentialism; the moment at which humanity's obsession with control finds an absolute limit (Giddens 1991). Such an essentialist view seems to result in a privileging of realist and materialist approaches over constructivist and idealist treatments. Obviously, death has a clear materialist dimension; it is an event/process that exists and occurs independently of human will, thought, and interpretation. We cannot reduce death to the way it is socially and culturally interpreted, but at the same death does remain loaded with meaning and we cannot detach it from the processes of social construction (Carpentier and Van Brussel 2012).

This chapter focuses on the social construction of the "medicalized death," referring to death as the result of a variety of medical decision made at the end-of-life. A high proportion of today's deaths are indeed directly linked to medical decision-making (see for instance Cohen et al. 2008; Slomka 1992). The permissibility of medical interventions in the dying process is subject to fierce political, medical, and ethical discussions. Central to contemporary discussions are signifiers such as "dying with dignity" and "the right to self-determination," which tend to entail quite polarized stances toward particular end-of-life interventions such as euthanasia and assisted suicide.

The chapter first sets forth a theoretical analysis, where discourse theory offers a lens through which the contemporary debates on end-of-life decision-making can be situated within specific dynamics of fixity and fluidity, emphasizing the contingent while allowing sufficient space for (temporary) fixation. Concretely, a twofold argument for the contingency of the discourse of (the medicalized) death is presented, which is based on two interlocking genealogies that illustrate the changing meanings of death over time. First, it is argued that a medical-rationalist discourse of death has (to a high degree) been replaced by a medical-revivalist discourse. Second, focus shifts to the historical changes in the articulation of a medicalized "good death," where the latter is defined in terms of the control, autonomy, dignity, awareness, and heroism.

The chapter then goes on to illustrate the empirical usability of discourse theory in the field of thanatology with an analysis of Belgian print media coverage of three euthanasia cases that gained considerable media attention in Belgium. Here, the chapter draws from the theoretical analysis of the articulation of death and the good death to support an empirical discourse-theoretical analysis (DTA) that follows the methodological principles of qualitative content analysis. The analysis shows how three main discourses—the discourse of autonomy, the discourse of hedonism, and the discourse of independence—are imported into news media texts and sheds light on the way these discourses privilege certain articulations of the good death over others.

Situating Laclau and Mouffe's discourse theory

Rather than regarding discourse "merely as a linguistic region within a wider social realm," Laclau and Mouffe offer a broader conceptualization of discourse that "insists on the interweaving of semantic aspects of language with the pragmatic aspects of actions, movements and objects" (Torfing 1999: 94). This broad definition of discourse can be described as discourse-as-representation or discourse-as-ideology, in contrast to approaches that use the discourse-as-language definition of discourse (Carpentier and De Cleen 2007: 277). An especially important concept for our analysis of the discourse of death is the concept of articulation, which also brings in the logics of contingency. Articulation is defined as "any practice establishing a relation among elements such that their identity is modified as a result of the articulatory practice" (Laclau and Mouffe 1985: 105). For discursive elements that relate to the subject, Laclau and Mouffe use a specific notion: the subject position, which refers to the way subjects are positioned within a discursive structure (Laclau and Mouffe 1985: 115). Crucial to Laclau and Mouffe's discourse theory is that discourses have to be partially fixed, since the abundance of meaning would otherwise make any meaning impossible: "a discourse incapable of generating any fixity of meaning is the discourse of the psychotic" (Laclau and Mouffe 1985: 112). The articulation of elements produces discourses that gain a certain, and very necessary, degree of stability, which is enhanced by the role of privileged signifiers or nodal points. Torfing (1999: 88–89) points out that these nodal points plan an important role in sustaining the identity of a discourse as they construct a "knot" of (temporary) fixed meanings. At the same time, the field of discursivity has an infinite number of elements that are not connected to a specific discourse. Due to the infinitude of the field of discursivity and the inability of a discourse to permanently fix its meaning, then, discourses are always liable to disintegration and rearticulation, which produces contingency.

Discourse theory and the contingency of death

On the following pages, Laclau and Mouffe's discourse theory is used to theorize the construction of death and the construction of the good death within a medical context. It will be argued that a medico-rational discourse, which was dominant until the mid-twentieth century, has become rearticulated in late-modernity, when a medico-revivalist discourse started to dislocate it. This impacted on the construction of the "good death."

Constructing death: The medico-rational and the medico-revivalist alternative

In the early middle ages and before, death was "tame": a familiar part of life not to be feared (Aries 1974, 1981). The modernization process, Aries (1981) argues in his well-known death-denial thesis, was accompanied by a shift from this tamed death toward an increasing denial of death. Aries asserts that from the beginning of the twelfth century, attitudes to death started to transform alongside the emergence of individualism. Tracing the history of death-related rituals, he noted another major transformation in attitudes toward death in the mid-nineteenth century, when the dying patient was, under the control of the doctor, moved to the hospital to die in an institutionalized setting rather than at home (see also Lupton 2010: 48). Drawing on Foucault's work on medicine and the body, Aries (1981: 562) states that death became hidden, mystified, and "driven into secrecy." He goes on to argue that the modern forbidden death reflects a "brutal revolution" in our attitudes toward death and dying (Aries 1974: 86). The tamed death was supplanted in modernity by a death that was consigned to medical care, as Illich (1975: 180) similarly asserts. Elias (1985: 85) remarks that "Never before, have people died so noiselessly and hygienically as today […]." According to supporters of the death-denial thesis, a new discourse of death thus emerged in modernity, and death began to be articulated as indecent, wild, dangerous, dirty, and polluting (Bauman 1992: 136) and needing to be sanitized.

Armstrong (1987) adopts a more discursive reading to challenge argumentations of the death-denial thesis, asserting that since the mid-nineteenth century, there has been a discursive explosion around death and dying, with the removal of death from the private to the public sphere of which the death certificate can be regarded as a key discursive symbol. The removal of the dying to hospitals, Armstrong (1987: 652) argues, rendered death into a publicly controlled event: "In the old regime knowledge of death was restricted to within earshot of the church bell: beyond there was silence, in the new regime no death was to be unknown." Arguably, it was not the simple replacement of speech by silence; rather, a new discourse of death emerged, which Walter et al. (1995: 581) summarize as "Death is publicly present, but privately absent." Unlike the death-denial thesis, counter-arguments assert that in the new epoch, a multitude of voices, including those of clinicians and pathologists, subjected the corpse to in-depth scrutiny to detect the "true" cause of death (Armstrong

1987: 652). Hence, instead of characterizing the modern period as an epoch of death denial, it should be described as an epoch when death was constructed in a medical-rationalist way.

In the modernist logic of medical-rationalism, dying was articulated as instrumentalist and impersonal; the dying process became a technical matter, bereft of its existential and personal significance. Because of the strong belief in medical progress, death was often regarded as an extreme example of illness (Seale 1998: 77). Thus, the medical-rationalist discourse constructed the dying subject as no more than a carrier of disease.

This construction of death marked an important reconfiguration of what could and could not be said about death and dying. From the late eighteenth century, a tendency developed to withhold the prognosis of imminent death from patients. Physicians and nurses were not trained to care for the dying and were uncomfortable with the idea of their patients dying. This led to a situation where the medical staff and the patient's family knew the truth about the patient's condition, but withheld it from the patient (Connor 2009: 3). According to Aries, this was "the lie" that dominated doctor–patient relationships between the mid-nineteenth and mid-twentieth century. But lie exists only in relationship to a regime of truth (that is the "types of knowledge a society accepts and makes function as true"; Foucault 1980: 131). Arguably, what is a lie now, in our society, in another society, within another "regime of truth," is not necessarily identified as such. To keep death a secret, Armstrong (1987) argues, was legitimate because it was believed that patients relied on the hope that the secret allowed. The silence was desired by the doctors who did not want to speak of death because it was distressing to them, and by the patients who did not want to be confronted with their worst fears (Armstrong 1987: 653–54). As the regime of truth began to transform during the late 1950s, the "secret" was exposed as a "lie" (Armstrong 1987: 653).

This was a major shift; from believing that it is in the patient's best interest to be kept ignorant of his or her condition, to believing that if patients are to participate in the organization of their dying process, they must be told the truth about their condition (Walter 1994: 31). In many western countries today, people's rights are considered to be violated if they lack the knowledge to make decisions concerning the last phase of their lives (Kearl 1989: 438).

This new discourse, dominant in late-modernity, can be termed the "medical-revivalist discourse." Within this discourse, death (again) becomes something that should be talked about without "taboo." Gradually, the former "conspiracy of silence" regarding death has been condemned. This resulted in a shift from the "interrogation of the corpse" to the "interrogation of the dying patient" who openly talks about his dying process without fearing or denying death (Armstrong 1987). From this point, Williams (2003: 131) asserts, "the truth of death ceased to be located in dark recesses of the silent corpse, and instead became embodied in the words and deeds of the dying patient." Several practices and organizations emerged during the last decennia, which responded and contributed to the changed discourse of death. One of these is the provision of modern day hospices directed toward "managing the anguish of the dying patient" (Prior 1989: 12). Others include legal–political developments such as laws on euthanasia that stress the value of reflexive and conscious planning of one's dying process. This aspect of reflexive and conscious planning is central to the medical-revivalist discourse of death that emphasizes this planning as a project of self-identity for the dying person (Seale 2000).

It could be argued, then, that death in late-modernity is increasingly "public." But, at the same time, medical institutions have not disappeared, which—according to critics (Williams 2003: 131; Somerville 2001)—causes death to remain hidden behind the walls of the hospital, or, more recently, the hospice and the care home. Regardless of this visibility–invisibility debate, it seems to be clear that a number of revivalist trends that emerged in recent decades are challenging the "rationalized death" and are becoming dominant in shaping contemporary discourses on the good death (Walter 1994; Williams 2003: 134).

Constructing the good death

The shift from a medical-rationalist discourse to a medical-revivalist discourse has impacted on the evaluative-hierarchical components that distinguish between good and bad deaths. While some components of a good death can be considered hegemonic and universalized (such as a death following a long and fulfilled life, during which children have been raised and provided for; see Seale 2004), there have been some considerable changes in the meanings attributed to the good death. To demonstrate the contingency of the articulation of the good death, we can use again a genealogical strategy and look at the meaning of the good death from a historical perspective.

The ideal of a peaceful death in the company of family and friends and at peace with God corresponds to the premodern attitude to death, which Aries described as the tamed death (Walters 2004: 405). The process of modernization made death something to be medically prevented, and its occurrence came to be regarded as failure (Walters 2004: 405). As already discussed, there are opposing theories regarding modern attitudes toward death. Whereas Aries (and also Bauman 1992) describes a privatization, Armstrong argues that death became more and more public after the late eighteenth century. Among these opposing views, however, there is agreement on the idea that death became highly medicalized in the modern period. This medicalization was accompanied by a new discourse of (the good) death, characterized by the withholding of the prognosis of imminent death from the patient. Thus, a modern good death was foremost a death that happened without the patient noticing it, such as dying quietly in one's sleep.

From the second half of the twentieth century onwards, the discourses on the good death started to change. According to Walters (2004), death is no longer a taboo subject in late-modern societies. Several authors describe this assumed "de-tabooing" with reference to the death-awareness movement (see, for instance, Bryant 2003: 53–54). By the late 1990s, the death awareness movement had become increasingly institutionalized, not only through the influence of palliative care and discussions on the right to die, but also through the organization of large-scale events concerning death-related topics. Moreover, the new awareness—or the revival—of death is reflected in the mass media, where death features as a main theme in films, TV series, plays, and novels (Bryant 2003: 54; Walters 2004: 405).

Although its hegemony is not total, today's dominant discourse of the good death is constructed around two groups of nodal points: control and autonomy; and awareness and heroism.

Control and autonomy

Specific to the medical-revivalist discourse is the articulation of the subject position of the dying person as someone in control of her/his own death. Indeed, it is believed in late-modernity that if individuals "are to make their own decisions about what remains of their lives, they must be told the truth about their condition" (Walter 1994: 31). A lack of decision-making power in this regard is considered a violation of the dying person's basic human rights (Kearl 1989: 438). This does not mean that control over death is total and that all social anxieties disappear. Somerville (2001: 11–12, 37), for example, asserts that the need to control death—referring mainly to the practice of active euthanasia—rests on an attitude of deep fear and denial. The contemporary idea of a death that is autonomously controlled allows it to be combined with the concept of dignity. In most late-modern western societies, dignity is mainly defined in terms of independence, autonomy, and control, especially (but not exclusively) within the framework of the right-to-die movement. It is regarded as highly desirable for the dying person to be free of excessive pain and to be in a state of awareness in order to preserve independence. The late-modern emphasis on autonomy and control is closely connected to a "civilized body discourse" that values self-mastery and self-care. As Lupton (2003: 57) argues: an ideal (dying) body is a body which is "tightly contained, its boundaries stringently policed, its orifices shut, kept autonomous, private, and separate from other things and other bodies."

Despite the centrality of the signifiers of autonomy and control in contemporary articulations of the medicalized good death, these same nodal points are very much surrounded by discursive conflict and struggle; they hence act as floating signifiers (Laclau and Mouffe 1985: 117) that are "overflowed with meaning" (Torfing 1999: 301) and can have different meanings within different contexts and discourses. While in the project of the right-to-die movement emphasizes the right of the dying patient to control the exact timing of death, the palliative care or hospice movement focuses on control over the symptoms that accompany the dying process, stressing the importance of fulfilling patients' wishes about how and where, rather than when, they choose to die.

Awareness and heroism

In order to control one's own (good) death, it is deemed necessary to have knowledge about one's condition. This implies that the subject position of the dying person is articulated as being aware and avoiding a state of denial. In contemporary western societies, an open awareness is often regarded as highly desirable. This open awareness refers to open communication among patient, the family, the doctor(s), and the professional carers (Kearl

1989: 428). Open awareness is required, first, for the dying person to make their own end-of-life decisions (Walter 1994: 31). Second, being aware of imminent death, the dying person can conduct reconciliations with loved ones, make confessions, and (re)tell and sometimes reconstruct personal biographies. In this way, the revivalist dying process becomes "a case study in the reflexive formation of a profoundly individualistic form of self-identity, of the sort described evocatively by Giddens" (Seale 2004: 967). The ideal of an aware death is closely connected to Seale's (1995, 1998) notion of the heroic death. According to Seale, a heroic death is highly valued in most western societies. Today, heroism becomes articulated as the deployment of skillful efforts of emotional labor. The capacity to gather support from family and friends and to make emotional progress in the process of denying, fighting, and accepting death (Seale 2002: 185) is a crucial aspect of what Seale (1998: 92) describes as the "inner-directed heroics of the self."

This new sort of heroic drama defines the subject position of the dying person as somebody who faces the inner danger and engages in an arduous self-search (Seale 1998: 92), and, eventually, after initial reactions of fear, shock, anger, or unfairness, demonstrates great courage in the eventual facing up to the final threat: death (Seale 1995: 599). This "inner-directed heroics of the self" is especially present in the project of the hospice movement, where death is often seen and spoken of as a "journey" (Banjeree 2005: 8). The hospice movement focuses on the heroism of dying naturally and of coping with the dying process while stressing the right of every dying person to be surrounded by a caring community. It is argued that this delays social death for as long as possible until biological death occurs (Seale 1995). The right-to-die movement acknowledges the importance of care, but argues also that the care of other people may not be enough to overcome the suffering involved in some forms of death. As Seale (1995, 1998: 190) argues, the right-to-die movement uses a different articulation of some of the core values of revivalism; a request for euthanasia is a statement that the care offered by other people is not enough to overcome suffering or that a different form of care (in the form of medical assistance with dying) is needed.

Articulations of the good death in Belgian media coverage

The remainder of the chapter aims to analyze the articulation of the good death in the media coverage of three euthanasia cases, and simultaneously illustrate the usability of discourse theory in the analysis of empirical material. The case at hands looks at media texts about euthanasia as materializations of discourses on death and the good death, which have been identified above. While the choice to analyze media representations is not compulsory and other empirical entry points, for instance, the analysis of legal texts, medical practices etc., are equally legitimate, there is a reason why analyzing media contents is particularly relevant. Media texts draw from "existing ways of making sense of the world" (McKee 2003: 46), and hence are important cultural resources that tell us something about the broader discursive framework in which they operate. Rather than being the origin of discourses, which then become further distributed throughout the social, media are an inseparable part of the social. Hence, media bring into circulation a variety of already existing discourses, making them both visible and tangible.

By means of a DTA (Carpentier and De Cleen 2007; Carpentier 2010), this chapter aims to answer the research question that inquires which constructions of the good death and of the subject positions of the dying persons the Belgian newspaper coverage offers. A DTA (and especially its second [empirical] phase) combines the basic principles of qualitative analysis—as captured, for instance, by grounded theory (Charmaz 2003, 2006)—with the conceptual framework of discourse theory. As argued elsewhere (Carpentier 2010), the sensitizing concepts, referring to those concepts that guide researchers in "what to look for and where to look" (Ritzer 1992: 365), act as methodological bridges between grounded theory and discourse theory. More particularly, discourse itself becomes the primary sensitizing concept. The discourse-theoretical framework (including concepts such as articulation, nodal points, subject positions, and hegemony), strengthened by the case-specific theoretical framework (the modern medical rationalist discourse, the late and postmodern revivalist discourse, and their nodal points of control, autonomy and dignity, and awareness and heroism) become the secondary sensitizing concepts for a textual analysis based on the methodological-procedural principles of grounded theory (including openness of interpretation and the cyclical nature of the relation between theory and analysis).

The analyzed corpus consists of the coverage in three mainstream Belgian (Dutch-speaking) newspapers (the quality newspapers *De Morgen* [DM] and *De Standaard* [DS] and the more popular newspaper *Het Laatste Nieuws* [HLN]) about three prominent euthanasia cases that derived considerable media attention in Belgium. These cases can be regarded as moments of increased discursive struggles around the meaning of dying "well." In 2008, the euthanasia of the well-known Belgian writer, Hugo Claus—the first case analyzed here—resulted in fierce societal debates. Claus was not terminally ill, but chose death because he was suffering from an early form of Alzheimer's disease. The debate on euthanasia was further inflamed by a second case in the same year. This was the Belgian politician, Marcel Engelborghs, who had incurable and terminal cancer and chose euthanasia. In 2009, the 93-year-old, non-terminally ill Amelie Van Esbeen, who was suffering from a range of geriatric ailments, requested euthanasia. Her struggle for her right to die stirred up debate on end-of-life decision-making and the (limits to) patient autonomy. Her request for euthanasia was rejected on the grounds that she was neither incurably ill nor suffering unbearably; her response was to go on hunger strike to protest the decision.

The final corpus comprises 126 articles (84 articles on the cases of Claus and Engelborghs [articles often deal with both cases at the same time], and 42 articles on the case of Van Esbeen), and includes a number of "press genres" (Bell 1991: 13): regular news items, commentary, reportage, and letters to the editor. This allows us to include the newspaper's "official voices," which "express an opinion, sum up the issues and make a moral judgement or decision upon the issue" (Lupton 1994: 148), as well as a diverse—although edited—variety of opinions from the newspapers' audiences.

Constructing euthanasia as the good death and celebrating the "heroic death"

The analysis points in the direction of a specific articulation of the good death. Euthanasia as a specific end-of-life decision is constructed as a particular form of dying well; it is articulated as a "heroic" way of dying, where the hero is defined rationally—emphasizing his braveness in choosing to die before illness and deterioration take over. This type of heroic death is somewhat different from the heroic death as defined by Seale, as it is very much articulated in terms of rationality rather than in terms of an inner emotional journey. The discursive construct of the "dying hero" is linked to the dominance of right-to-die ideals and is achieved by importing a series of discourses into the media coverage. More specifically, three main discourses through which the good death (with their respective nodal points and subject positions) becomes constructed have been identified; the discourse of hedonism, the discourse of control and independence, and the discourse of autonomy.

The discourse of hedonism

A first discourse that is imported into the analyzed media coverage is that of hedonism. This discourse is particularly relevant in the coverage of Claus and Engelborghs, where the focus is on the period prior to the euthanasia of both men. In this coverage, notions of enjoyment and happiness as well as activities associated with "the hedonist" such as drinking and dinning become associated with the choice for euthanasia. It is indeed the choice for euthanasia that allows the "bon-vivant" (Reportage HLN, 8–9 March 2008) to have a good death. One article about the euthanasia of Claus and Engelborghs, entitled "Euthanasia should not be horrible," opens as follows:

> Dining extensively and laughing with friends to encounter death in full awareness. Hugo Claus did it on Wednesday, and the alderman Marcel Engelborghs earlier this month. They could have postponed their death, but they didn't want to. To not lose anything of awareness, life enjoyment and dignity.
>
> (Regular news item HLN, 21 March 2008)

This quote illustrates the centrality of the nodal points discussed earlier in this chapter. It is above all the nodal point of awareness that is at the core to the discourse of hedonism; despite the rare use of the actual word awareness (or its derivatives), the analysis shows several assumptions that construct awareness as a key ingredient of a good death. One way in which an aware death is constructed as a crucial aspect of a good death is through the assumption that a conscious planning of own death allows the dying person to say goodbye to his family and friends in a "proper" way. The aware and active planning of their own deaths allowed Marcel Engelborghs and Hugo Claus "to enjoy their lives until the very last day" (Regular news item HLN, 21 March 2008).

The subject position of the hedonic dying person is also constructed in a number of journalistic narratives, sometimes through the voice of the dying person themselves: "I lived hard and well. I was a party type, loved to go out to dinner and travelled a lot" […] "I've had many girlfriends, but never have I wanted to give a woman the impression that I wanted to stay with her" (Reportage DS, 3 May 2008). The dying patient is not only constructed as a hedonist, but also as highly rational—not giving in to emotions such as fear of death. Encouraged by the tendency of journalism to construct "heroes," the coverage of the euthanasia of Engelborghs emphasizes the heroic facing of death: "Am I relaxed or what?" He laughs rhetorically, "I am really not afraid of dying. I never feared it, and at this moment I still don't" (Reportage HLN, 3 June 2008).

The discourse of hedonism as present in the analyzed media texts is part of a broader social reality where death is "on its revival." Not only is the high visibility of personalized euthanasia cases in the media *as such* an illustration of this reality, also the way death is constructed as familiar, not to be feared, demonstrates the way the analyzed media texts function as materializations of a more encompassing death-revival discourse. In the analyzed coverage, more concretely, we see how the dying person is represented as someone who is central to his own dying process, not only because he is physically involved, but also because the dying process becomes an opportunity for self-identity, where the dying patient dies in accordance with the way he lived. Dying, arguably, should not be horrible, it can equally be a final expression of hedonism—occurring after a final "farewell dinner" and taking place "in friendship and laughing" (Reportage HLN, 3 July 2008). It is clear, at the same time, that the analyzed media coverage privileges right-to-die articulations of the good death over hospice or palliative care articulations, constructing euthanasia or the self-chosen death as the ultimate hedonic death.

The discourse of independence and control

A second discourse imported into the coverage of the euthanasia cases is that of independence and control. A key signifier here is that of dignity, which is associated with the ideals of the "civilized" stringently controlled mind and body, and the "authentic" body–mind relationship, where the body reflects the inner-self.

In the coverage of Engelborghs, the deterioration of the body is constructed as a threat to dignity. The articulation of physical deterioration as impeding a dignified death is often imported into the coverage by directly quoting the dying patient. For instance: "I will not deteriorate, will not suffer, will not become dependent, will be able to die with dignity." In another article, Engelborghs is again quoted: "Then I can go to palliative care and be dependent, continue to suffer and deteriorate and be a burden to the whole society" (Reportage HLN, 3 July 2008). In both quotes, a discursive logic of difference is created, opposing deterioration and dependence to "dying with dignity." Not only the deterioration of the body is discursively constructed as an undignified way of dying, also the decline of mental awareness is constructed as a threat to dignity. For instance: "The certainty that I will get euthanasia and that I will die with dignity, mentally healthy, has given me the peace of mind" (Reportage HLN, 3 August 2008). By labeling the choice for euthanasia as "brave" and "courageous," dying before losing control and independence is positively evaluated and even elevated as a form of "heroic death." In similar vein, the coverage of Hugo Claus constructs Alzheimer's disease as a threat to the patient's dignity. In one article, it is for instance assumed that euthanasia was the only end-of-life decision allowing Claus to die with dignity: "Because he left us as a shining star, just in time, before he collapsed into a clumsy black whole" (Opinion piece DM, 20 March 2008).

The coverage of Claus and Engelborghs illustrates how the identity construction of "extraordinary" men, people whose political or artistic merits endow them with "great dignity," comes with certain assumptions about the way "great men" die (with dignity): before being affected by illness and deterioration. Losing consciousness, physical abilities, and as a result independence become represented as aspects of a bad dying process. In the cases of Hugo Claus and Marcel Engelborghs, the voices of the readers explicitly express the construction of such an undignified and bad death:

> Demented people are very often a burden to others, also to their own family. If I ever get the chance to opt for euthanasia before I forget I exist, I would immediately do so. Very brave what Claus did.
>
> (Letter to the editor HLN, 22 March 2008)

In the coverage of Van Esbeen, finally, the declining and deteriorating body is constructed as a threat to a dignified death because it can no longer represent the "authentic self"—that of a proud and independent woman who "lived alone until the age of 88 and took care of herself" (Regular news item DM, 2 April 2009). Indeed, the increasing dependence of Van Esbeen on other people is constructed not only as incompatible with her former self, but also as deeply shameful: "[...] decreased vision, hearing disorders, incontinence, and a limited independence. And all of that for a woman who had been extremely independent and very well surrounded during her whole life" (Regular news item DS, 6 April 2009).

What is potentially problematic is that these representations go hand in hand with the construction of euthanasia as the only possibility to a dignified death, which makes a palliative care based-death into an undignified death. The dominant articulation of dignity is only minimally challenged by an alternative, palliative care variation, which mainly comes from the medical field where voices of representatives of the medical field resist the articulation of dementia as undignified: "Dementia should not only be misery. Our sector works very hard to offer everyone a dignified existence" (Letter to the editor DM, 25 March 2008).

The discourse of autonomy

A final discourse that is imported into the media coverage is that of autonomy. Whereas the above-discussed construction of control and independence as components of a good death relates to the autonomous functioning of the mind and the body, the discourse of autonomy discussed below mainly is about autonomy in terms of decision-making.

The discourse of autonomy is present in all three cases, where a positive evaluation of controlling own death and to make own end-of-life decisions shows the hegemony of the right-to-die variant of the revivalist discourse and its nodal point of autonomy. The ideal of autonomy is most explicitly present in the voice of the readers of the newspapers. For example: "Of course I respect his choice to die. I find that a very great deed" (Letter to the editor DS, 3 June 2008—Hugo Claus), and "The most important thing about euthanasia is not death itself, it is knowing that as a human being, you have the choice, the possibility, the freedom" (Letter to the editor HLN, 3 August 2008).

The ideal of dying autonomously is not only present in letters to the editor; similar, yet often more subtle constructions are present in other press genres. The frequent use of agency-indicating signifiers such as wanting, deciding, choosing, and determining emphasizes the autonomy of Claus, Engelborghs, and Van Esbeen (see for instance regular news item HLN, 5 March 2008—Engelborghs; Opinion piece HLN, 20 March 2008—Claus; Opinion piece DM, 20 March 2008—Claus; Reportage DS, 2 April 2009—Van Esbeen), and the ways in which such signifiers are used often result in a subtle celebration of autonomy, as heralding the possibility of a "good" and even "joyful" death. For instance: "He left us the way he wanted to. When he fixed the date of his death, he didn't say goodbye, he celebrated goodbye" (Regular News item DM, 31 March 2008).

Autonomously determining the moment of death is often constructed as a brave, courageous, and exceptional act. In the case of Claus, this exceptionality is created through the construction of an identity of the "rebel artist," which is present in a number of articles. For instance, by combining the statement "He has always made his own decisions, until the last goodbye" (Opinion piece HLN, 20 March 2008), with an appreciative, admiring description of Claus ("A universal artist, painter, sculptor, director, and cineaste"), autonomous end-of-life decision-making is constructed as desirable, but also as a "courageous" need. Because of Claus' celebrity, his choice for euthanasia is represented as unusual and extraordinary. Euthanasia requires "an autonomous mind," "an example," "a master," "a rebel" (HLN, 31 March 2008; DM, 20 March 2008). Also the coverage of Engelborghs is often surrounded by a sphere of admiration, suggesting the choice for euthanasia to be an extraordinary one. For instance:

> The terminally ill alderman Marcel Engelborghs (61) has never been more determined than on the moment he chose to die when he wanted to, how he wanted to. And he remained determined until the very last.
>
> (Regular news item HLN, 27 December 2008)

In the coverage of Van Esbeen, the "ordinary" person is discursively constructed as a "heroic victim." This twofold subject position is first created by covering Van Esbeen's struggle to die in a pity-inducing way: "'I want to die. And rather today than tomorrow,' Amelie entrusts us, hooked to the bed of her too small room" (Reportage DS, 23 March 2009). In so doing, Van

Esbeen is represented as a "determined" woman (Regular news item DM, 2 April 2009) whose only wish is "to die" (Reportage DS, 23 March 2009), while the medical system is represented as a threat to the patient's autonomy. Second, the heroism of Van Esbeen is emphasized, focusing on the patient's victory over the medical system: "Eventually, Amelie went on a hunger strike and threw the media into gear to point to the gap in the legal system. Successfully: on 1 April, this brave lady acquired the end that she deserved" (Regular news item HLN, 25 December 2009).

Conclusion

While discourse theory and discourse-theoretical analysis have above all been applied in the study of political-social realities, death plays an all-too significant role within the social to be excluded from the analytical gaze of discourse theory (Carpentier and Van Brussel 2012). However, the discourse-theoretical approach to death and the end-of-life adopted in this chapter by no means had the ambition to explain the entire complexity of the dying process. A discourse-theoretical approach does, for example, not offer a framework to study the psychological and sociological aspects of the—often-disruptive—human awareness of inevitable mortality (Bauman 1992). But a discourse-theoretical framework, with its focus on the construction of meaning within a sphere of a struggle for hegemony, embedded within the dynamics of fixity and fluidity, does seem to be well suited for analyzing the construction of the master-signifier of the good death and how the subject position of the dying person becomes articulated within this construction. This chapter has drawn from Laclau and Mouffe's discourse theory to show how the impact of and the changes within the medical field affect the articulation of the discourse of death, first through a medical-rationalist discourse of death and, later, shifting to a medical-revivalist discourse, which structurally alters the way we think about death, the good death, dying, and the dying person. Answering to the methodological deficit in discourse theory as identified by a number of scholars (Torfing 1999; Zienkowski 2012; Howarth 2005; Glynos and Howarth 2007), the chapter also attempted to illustrate the usability of discourse theory in the analysis of concrete empirical material. In this chapter, DTA has been adopted as a method for the analysis of media texts. Defining media texts as specific materializations of more encompassing systems of meaning, three key discourses have been identified that are imported into the coverage of three prominent euthanasia cases: a discourse of hedonism, a discourse of control and independence, and a discourse of autonomy. It has been argued that the coverage of these three cases articulates euthanasia as a good death in specific ways, privileging the right to die of the dying person over processes of end-of-life care, thereby celebrating the hedonic dying person who (fearlessly) chooses to die before becoming dependent on care of others and before losing awareness, while constructing "other" ways of dying as "bad" or "undignified." We need to end this chapter by making some crucial reflections on the specificity of the sample. First of all, it should not be forgotten that although euthanasia is under certain conditions legal in Belgium, it also remains contested and subject to ongoing struggles and debates. The newspaper coverage, and its almost univocal support for the right to euthanasia, can only be seen as a contribution to the attempted hegemonization of the right to die, within the already hegemonic medical-revivalist discourse. Moreover, media logics such as intimization and dramatization make the analyzed sample specific, in the sense that they tend to privilege the extraordinary over the ordinary, and the conflictual over the consensual. Conducting a DTA on other texts, for instance, medical texts or legal texts, may point in the direction of other articulations of the good death.

References

Ariès, Phillipe (1974), *Western Attitudes Towards Death: From Middle Ages to the Present*, Baltimore: The John Hopkins University Press.
—— (1981), *The Hour of Our Death*, New York, NY: Alfred A. Knopf.
Armstrong, David (1987), "Silence and truth in death and dying," *Social Science and Medicine*, 24:8, pp. 651–57.
Ball, Samuel (1976), "Methodological problems in assessing the impact of television programs," *Journal of Social Issues*, 32:4, pp. 8–17.
Banjeree, Albert (2005), "Speaking of death: Representations of death in hospice care," Academia. edu, https://www.academia.edu/25618588/Speaking_of_Death_Representations_of_Death_in_Hospice_Care. Accessed 1 October 2013.
Bell, Allan (1991), *The Language of News Media*, Oxford: Blackwell.
Bauman, Zygmunt (1992), *Mortality and Immortality*, Cambridge, MA: Polity Press.
Bryant, Clifton D. (2003), *Handbook of Death and Dying*, London: Sage.
Carpentier, Nico (2010), "Deploying discourse theory. An introduction to discourse theory and discourse theoretical analysis," in N. Carpentier, P. Pruulmann-Vengerfeldt, K. Nordenstreng, M. Hartmann, P. Vihalemm, and B. Cammaerts (eds), *Media and Communication Studies Intersections and Interventions: The Intellectual Work of ECREA's 2010 European Media and Communication Doctoral Summer School*, Tartu: Tartu University Press, pp. 251–56.
Carpentier, Nico and Van Brussel, Leen (2012), "On the contingency of death: A discourse-theoretical perspective on the construction of death," *Critical Discourse Studies*, 9:2, pp. 99–116.
Carpentier, Nico and De Cleen, Benjamin (2007), "Bringing discourse theory into media studies," *Journal of Language and Politics*, 6:2, pp. 267–95.
Charmaz, Kathy (2003), "Grounded theory," in J. A. Smith (ed.), *Qualitative Psychology: A Practical Guide to Research Methods*, London: Sage, pp. 81–110.
—— (2006), *Constructing Grounded Theory*, London: Sage.
Cohen, J., Bilsen, J., Addington-Hall, J., Löfmark, R., Miccinesi, G., Kaasa, S., Onwuteaka-Philipsen, B., and Deliens, L. (2008), "Population-based study of dying in hospital in six European countries," *Palliative Medicine*, 22:6, pp. 702–10.
Connor, Stephen R. (2009), *Hospice and Palliative Care*, New York, NY: Routledge.

Elias, Norbert (1985), *The Loneliness of the Dying*, Oxford: Blackwell.

Foucault, Michel (1980), *Power/Knowledge*, Brighton: Harvester.

Gee, James Paul (1999), *The Language of News Media*, Oxford: Blackwell.

Giddens, Anthony (1991), *Modernity and Self-Identity*, Stanford: Stanford University Press.

Glynos, Jason and Howarth, David (2007), *Logics of Critical Explanation in Social and Political Theory*, New York, NY: Routledge.

Howarth, David (2005), "Applying discourse theory: The method of articulation," in D. Howarth and J. Torfing (eds), *Discourse Theory in European Politics*, Hampshire: Palgrave, pp. 316–50.

—— (1998), "Discourse theory and political analysis," in E. Scarbrough and E. Tanenbaum (eds), *Research Strategies in the Social Sciences*, Oxford: Oxford University Press, pp. 268–93.

Howarth, David and Stavrakakis, Yannis (2000), "Introducing discourse theory and political analysis," in D. Howarth, A. J. Norval, and Y. Stavrakakis (eds), *Discourse Theory and Political Analysis*, Manchester: Manchester University Press, pp. 1–23.

Illich, Ivan (1975), *Medical Nemesis*, London: Calder & Boyars.

Kearl, Michael (1989), *Endings: A Sociology of Death and Dying*, Oxford: Oxford University Press.

Laclau, Ernesto and Mouffe, Chantal (1985), *Hegemony and Social Strategy: Towards a Radical Democratic Politics*, London: Verso.

Lupton, Deborah (1994), "Discourse analysis: A new methodology for understanding the ideologies of health and illness," *Australian Journal of Public Health*, 16:2, pp. 145–50.

—— (2003), "The social construction of medicine and the body," in G. Albrecht, R. Fitzpatrick, and S. C. Scrimshaw (eds), *Handbook of Social Studies in Health and Medicine*, London: Sage, pp. 50–63.

—— (2010), *Medicine as Culture: Illness, Disease and the Body in Western Societies*, London: Sage.

McKee, Allan (2003), *Textual Analysis: A Beginner's Guide*, London: Sage.

Prior, Lindsay (1989), *The Social Organization of Death*, London: Macmillan.

Ritzer, George (1992), *The Blackwell Companion to Major Classical Social Theory*, Oxford: Blackwell.

Seale, Clive (1995), "Heroic death," *Sociology*, 29:4, pp. 597–614.

—— (1998), *Constructing Death: The Sociology of Dying and Bereavement*, Cambridge: Cambridge University Press.

—— (2000), "Changing patterns of death and dying," *Social Science and Medicine*, 51:6, pp. 917–30.

—— (2002), *Media and Health*, London: Sage.

—— (2004), "Media constructions of dying alone: A form of bad death," *Social Science and Medicine*, 58:5, pp. 967–74.

Somerville, Margaret (2001), *Death Talk: The Case Against Euthanasia and Physician-Assisted Suicide*, Quebec: McGill-Queen's University Press.

Slomka, Jacquelyn (1992), "The negotiation of death: Clinical decision making at the end of life," *Social Science and Medicine*, 35:3, pp. 251–59.

Torfing, Jakob (1999), *New Theories of Discourse: Laclau, Mouffe and Žižek*, Oxford: Blackwell.

Van Brussel, Leen and Carpentier, Nico (2012), "The construction of the good death and the dying person: A discourse-theoretical analysis of Belgian newspaper articles on medical end-of-life decision making," *Journal of Language and Politics*, 11:4, pp. 479–99.

Walter, Tony (1994), *The Revival of Death*, London: Routledge.

——— (2003), "Historical and cultural variants on the good death," *British Medical Journal: International Edition*, 327:7408, pp. 218–19.

Walter, Tony, Littlewood, Jane, and Pickering, Michael (1995), "Death in the news: The public invigilation of private emotion," *Sociology*, 29:4, pp. 579–96.

Walters, Geoffrey (2004), "Is there such a thing as a good death," *Palliative Medicine*, 18:5, pp. 404–08.

Williams, Simon J. (2003), *Medicine and the Body*, London: Sage.

Zienkowski, Jan (2012), "Overcoming the post-structural methodological deficit—Metapragmatic markers and interpretative in a critique of the Bologna process," *Pragmatics*, 22:3, pp. 501–34.

Chapter 5

Putting Your Relationship to the Test: Constructions of Fidelity, Seduction, and Participation in *Temptation Island*

Nico Carpentier

Introduction

The reality show, *Temptation Island*, was televised for the first time in 2001 on the FOX network in the United States. Many television networks bought the rights to this format, resulting in local variations of the original in for instance the United Kingdom, France, Australia, Brazil, and Italy. In Belgium and the Netherlands the local version was produced by Kanakna Productions for two SBS Networks broadcasters, namely VT4 in North-Belgium and Veronica in the Netherlands. The first Dutch *Temptation Island* was televised in 2002, and since then a new series has been produced almost every year of the first decade of the twenty-first century. The fifth and, at the time of writing, last series was televised in April 2006, on VT4 and Veronica, with Hans Otten (VT4) and Tanja Jess (Veronica) as presenters.

The format of *Temptation Island* is relatively simple, based on a clear and quasi-impenetrable categorizing of the participants. Eight couples, four men and four women, are housed separately in "resorts" on two tropical islands,[1] where they meet a number of so-called "bachelors" (or "tempters" and "temptresses"). The program format revolves around a relationship test, where each partner receives the attention of the "tempters" and "temptresses" for two weeks. As the Veronica TI website says: "During their stay they are seduced by attractive men and women who give rise to their ultimate fantasies."[2]

The eight partners (and their "tempters/temptresses") spend most of their time having fun, in smaller or larger groups, while every action is filmed and recorded by (sometimes hidden) cameras and sound recording equipment of *Temptation Island*'s production team. The different episodes consist of a montage of these clips, with commentary, as well as interviews with the participants.

The (group)interactions are alternated with two subformats. On the so-called "dates," which culminate in the "dream date," the partners choose one of the tempters/temptresses for a private date during which they undertake a romantic activity or an adventure. The *Temptation Island* production team thus attempts to heighten the pressure on the partners (and their relationships). In the second scenario the participants are shown video clips of their partners' escapades at the so-called "bonfires," while at the same time being interviewed by one of the presenters. The final meeting between the couples also takes place during such a bonfire. Both the video clips and the interview questions are aimed at increasing the pressure on the partners. In the final episode the couples are visited some months after their *Temptation Island* stay, and an inventory is made of the damage caused to the relationship.

In some programs the basic format was changed. For example, in *Temptation Island 2005* the barman and barlady—who played an important role in the festivities—took on the status of "tempter" and "temptress." In *Temptation Island 2006*, an extra "temptress" was invited (Rebecca Loos), and a new group of "tempters/temptresses" was brought to the island, including some of the previous participants (Tim De Pril, Gaby Visser, and Rowena Guldenaar[3]), and the participants had to choose which of the "tempters/temptresses" could stay. In addition, the mother of one of the participants came to visit her, and the respective "dream dates" of that couple was replaced by a "reconciliation date," where the couple could spend time alone to try and mend their relationship and "to make something special of their second last day on Temptation Island" (Veronica TI website).

Popular banality?

At first glance a program such as *Temptation Island* appears to be feeding a banal voyeurism on the side of the viewers, and to afford participants an opportunity for entertainment (as far as relationships go, as well as from a tourist perspective), with possible stardom as an added bonus.

At the same time popular culture is a site where social meanings are constructed, where we are offered definitions of what our society would tolerate, would strive for, or would sanction. These constructional processes are not always homogenous. In fact, popular culture is characterized by a crisscross of the many contradictions inherent in our culture. It is a place where attempts are sometimes made to transcend or transform rigid and impenetrable discourses. As John Fiske (1989) argues, popular culture serves as oxygen for these transgressions. At the same time it is also the stage where hegemony operates and finds foot. Hegemonic discourses can be contested, but such challenges can be dangerous because of the risk of social sanctions.

Television programs such as *Temptation Island* are microcosms allowing us to examine our boundaries as well as elements in our culture that we take for granted. It is in particular the emphasis on human relationships, gender, and sexuality, core elements of society that makes *Temptation Island* so relevant as research material. In addition, this program generates viewing pleasures for large audiences, and draws many online discussions. In one of the many discussion forums[4] viewing pleasure is summarized as follows: "Of course, it supplies viewers with sufficient 'suspense and sensation'. That's why we watch. And don't forget the lovely bodies" (Bobette, 2 May 2006, femistyle.be).

However, not all viewers are entertained by the program. As often happens with popular television—which was also emphasized in Ien Ang's analysis in *Watching Dallas* (1995)—there are two different discourses underlying the evaluation of popular television programs. On the one hand there is the discourse (or the ideology, as Ang calls it) of mass culture, condemning popular television as boring and irrelevant. We find examples of this perspective on some of the forums, for example one posting that says: "Never watch this rubbish" (jootje02, 4 July 2005, sbs.nl), or another: "I don't need this on TV" (LastHorizon, 2 July 2005, sbs.nl). In some instances the condemnation is somewhat less subtle, as in the following description of Temptation Island as "a fuck-around-programme with machos and sluts!" (kattekop, 30 March 2006, femistyle.be). On the other hand there is the discourse on popular culture that views these cultural expressions as legitimate and (even as) of cultural importance. The following posting on the Veronica website illustrates this very well: "Every Monday and Wednesday my housemates and I again sit on the couch with the three of us. This programme is fantastic. What I find a pity is that they show previews of later shows, so that you already know that some things go very badly. (In any case you know that already, but this only confirms it ;-))" (Lady_Y, 5 April 2005, veronica.nl).

These two discourses cannot be totally separated; they are reconciled by the ironic perspective, as is demonstrated by the following posting: "Of course it is pulp TV, but one has to agree, that can also be fun at times. Life is serious enough" (Angel45, 2 July 2005, sbs.nl). This reconciliation of the two discourses becomes even more noticeable when one looks at the question on a poster (from the mass culture perspective): "Is there really no-one who recognizes the sadness of the programme?" (calimero, 13 April 2006, vt4.be) The answer came the following day, and is telling evidence of the ironic perspective: "Sad? Sure. Pathetic? Definitely. Entertaining? Enormously!" (sugababe, 14 April 2006, vt4.be).

Therefore, an analysis of popular cultural products such as Temptation Island can never be made outside of the specific social contexts. As was already said, popular television programs are founded on numerous discourses about human interaction as well as about television and popular culture. In the case of Temptation Island these discourses include discourses related to (hetero)sexuality, gender, fidelity, and monogamy. Secondly, Temptation Island is an integral part of the television and media system(s). This implies in the first place that Temptation Island is embedded in chains of intertextuality. The fifth Temptation Island series is internally intertextual, as it refers to the previous series, allowing for a learning process of audiences, participants, and media professionals. There are also many forms of external intertextuality (or combined versions). Not only "ordinary" viewers produce texts about Temptation Island (via forums and blogs), but other media do so as well. The magazine, Humo, has for instance run a comic strip about Temptation Island. Magazines and newspapers regularly publish interviews with participants, or discuss how the program will develop or what new relationships have been formed. Some participants—such as Andries de Jongh,[5] one of the partners of Temptation Island 5—produced texts on their own websites or in newspaper or magazine columns.

Many references between Temptation Island and other programs and cultural texts exist, for instance through the (media)pre-history of the participants. Both Andries de Jongh (a partner in the 5th TI series) and Dennis van Solkema (a partner in the 4th TI series) took part in the Dutch Big Brother, and the couple, Sven and Sally (partners in the 4th TI series), previously participated in the VT4 program, The Block. Sometimes they also transcend the Temptation Island sphere, as in the case of Goedele van Ruysevelt, one of the partners from the first Temptation Island, who became a presenter on VT4 when the island series ended, or the music group, *Seduced,* whose members were all participants in the second series of *Temptation Island.*

A second consequence of *Temptation Island*'s embeddedness in the television system is that the series cannot be regarded as separate from the media production context. The television system is a commodified system, aimed at the production of a television program of such popularity that it can compete strongly on the television market of North-Belgium and the Netherlands. This political-economic context strongly affects its nature. It is also a professional system, grounded in media-professional identities, structured inter alia by means of—interrelated—ethical discourses, discourses on the hierarchy between participants and media professionals, discourses on the format of reality TV, and discourses on the quality of television. Of importance for this text are the power relations generated by this context, on the one hand in the interaction between the participants, as well as between the participants and the media professionals, and on the other hand in the interactions between participants, media professionals, and the discursive context. It is precisely from this power-laden interaction that the television text, *Temptation Island,* originates, and in turn will feed (as a televised discourse) into culture and society.

Power and the production of a television text

According to Foucault—in his analytics of power, in the *History of Sexuality* (1978)—power does not belong to a specific actor (or class), but it cuts across human relationships. However, this mobile and multidirectional character of power does not mean that power relations are by definition equally balanced. Foucault expressly recognizes the existence of unequal power relations, focusing on disciplining (of the Other and the self) in *Discipline and Punish* (1977). He states at the same time that no actor will ever fully realize his strategies and intentions, because there is always the possibility of resistance and contra-strategies. It is precisely this dynamic combination of strategies and contra-strategies, of hegemony and resistance, of creation and restriction, that power becomes so productive. Through this power logic new discourses and identities are produced, and old discourses and identities are transformed or in fact consolidated.

Applying Foucault's analytics of power on the television system implies that both the production sphere (the interaction between ideologies, participants, and media professionals) and the reception sphere (the interaction between ideologies, television texts, and viewers) are characterized by power relations that are not entirely controlled by a specific actor, so that resistance against unequal power relations is still possible. In *Temptation Island*'s production sphere the different actors—presenters, cameramen, sound engineers, technicians, directors, producers, partners, bachelors—effectively find themselves in unequal power relations. On the one hand the media professionals largely control the island context: they developed (*in casu* adapted) the format, they made the rules that have to be followed on the island, they chose (*in casu* cast) the participants, they concluded their contracts, for 24 hours a day their cameras (partly visible and partly hidden) are focused on the participants, they ask the interview questions, and they select the footage and edit it into a cohesive narrative that is broadcast on their respective stations. On the other hand, the participants are not totally powerless. The entire format of *Temptation Island* depends on their willingness to commit themselves to the interaction with the other participants, to answer the interview questions, to live with microphones attached to their bodies, and to try and forget the ubiquitous cameras and cameramen, and behave as "normally" as possible.

In the reception sphere the viewers also have their interpretative freedoms. Changing the television text cannot (in principle) be accomplished, but audiences do interpret the televised events and the personalities of the participants. In other words, as Stuart Hall also argues on the basis of his encoding/decoding model (1980), meanings that are generated in the production sphere are not necessarily the same as that generated in the reception sphere. People watching *Temptation Island* will not necessarily interpret the text in the way the producers intended. Resistance against the dominant interpretation always remains a possibility.

The idea is that the different power processes in the production and the reception spheres work productively. In the production sphere it is precisely the unequal power relations between the actors—co-determined by the circulating discourses that transcend the individuality of the actors—that ensures that a television text is produced. In the reception sphere it is the interaction between the viewers and the television text, once again co-determined by circulating discourses at the level of the social and the cultural, which creates new interpretations and meanings among the viewers.

Key discourses in *Temptation Island*

The interaction between the participants, stimulated by the production team's management thereof, leads to the creation of the television text. In this respect television is a discursive machine that transforms human interaction into (television) texts. As all texts, the *Temptation Island* texts are also ideological in character, containing a series of discourses that transcend individual statements and interactions cast in pictures and sounds. As we have said, these discourses cannot be separated from the cultural context whence they originated, and in this way *Temptation Island* thus makes these discourses—and therefore our cultural configurations—visible and tangible.

One of the most important discourses activated in (and through) *Temptation Island* is the discourse about sexual fidelity. In principle, human relationships can be organized in many different ways, but in *Temptation Island*—through the emphasis on the basic dichotomy of the couple—the bachelor, a specific form of heterosexual relational organization, is privileged, thereby ruthlessly excluding many other societal forms. But at the same time the status of the bachelors is acknowledged, without stressing the gender differences between the "tempters" and "temptresses," although their identity (as a category) stands in an antagonistic relationship with the partners, because the bachelors represent hedonistic pleasure, which at the same time is articulated as threatening. It is the forbidden fruit, which is in itself also a specific and reduced presentation of this social category.

It is noticeable that there are limits to the relationships that are subjected to the *Temptation Island* test. The following sentence from Kanakna productions'[6] call for participants indicates that married couples would not be considered: "Participants must be older than 20, unmarried, and must be free for two weeks." A second limitation—not mentioned in the call—is children. The impact (and evidence) of this limitation became clear during *Temptation Island 2* in 2003, when one of the couples (Cindy Stoop and James Serbeniuk) had to leave the island because Cindy Stoop was pregnant. In the *Temptation Island* discourse, marriage and children are seen as too important to be drawn into the game or even considered.

Moreover, the idea of the relationship test is reduced to one of resisting (physical) seduction and of sexual fidelity. On the Veronica TI website the end result of the 5th series (broadcast in episode 15) was summarized as follows: "Bianca was not the only one to stray; Liesbeth and Cheyenne also could not resist temptation, even though they denied this in the strongest terms. The pictures tell a different story." A specific and homogenous representation is offered of what is regarded as primordial in a relationship, and which criteria should be used to test a relationship. The problematic character of (sexual) infidelity and the intrinsic link between love and sexuality are strengthened by the recurrent references in the broadcasts to earlier crises between the partners as a result of infidelity. It is precisely this testing of mutual trust that is seen in the *Temptation Island* text as an important motivating factor for participating. This element is also emphasized on the VT4 website, where the couple, Bianca and Björn, was introduced as follows: "Bianca and Björn are from Willebroek. She has previously been unfaithful, and he often confronts her with this. She now wants to prove to him that one mistake means nothing, and win back his total trust."

Once this trust is backed up by practical evidence during the *Temptation Island* encounter, and the partners have proven their fidelity to each other, the way to an everlasting and harmonic relationship lies open. Sexual fidelity becomes proof of love that—once the "right one" has been found—is forever. This is well illustrated by the following sentence from the description of the couple, Lisette van Veenendaal and Len Konings, on the VT4 website: "They take part in Temptation Island to prove that they were born for each other." In this sense *Temptation Island* is articulated as a rite of passage, allowing people to enter the world of "genuine" relationships. Thus the program forms part of the hegemonic discourse of heterosexual monogamy, where relationships are regarded as exclusive, and where participants are perceived as striving for a lifelong unity.

When the partners fail the relationship test, another element takes precedence: honesty. The entire configuration (and power dynamic) of *Temptation Island* is in any case based on truth speaking. Participants who are interviewed (alone or during the bonfires) are trusted to be revealing their innermost feelings to others (the presenters, their partners, the viewers). If they are not honest, they run the risk of having their actions interpreted negatively by the production team, or being pressurized to be "honest," with the constant threat of being "unmasked" by the video clips. However, it is in particular when it comes to sexual infidelity that the pressure to be "honest" becomes extreme. Of course this emphasis on honesty forms part of the production team's management strategies, because the "struggle" followed by the "confession" creates "good television," and it can also be used to further undermine the position of the other partner. But these management strategies only strengthen the emphasis on the cultural importance of honesty, presenting it in the television text as an important regulatory mechanism in human relationships.

Apart from the emphasis on honesty, other cultural demands are made on human actions. The strong emphasis on the narration of the self, within the basic framework of the relationship test, presupposes consistent and rational (or rationalizable) action. Emotional fluctuations and (seemingly) inconsequent behavior are frowned upon in the commentary and in the interactions with other participants. For example, when Bianca Mommen at first held herself very aloof from the single males, and even reacted very emotionally to clips of her partner, Björn, holding hands with a "temptress." A few episodes later she was seen to have sex a couple of times with one of the bachelors. After these events, the other partners and singles, as well as the voice of the commentator, expressed their total lack of understanding.

The immediacy of the television system also plays a role here, because there is a time limit for filming, and participants do not have the opportunity of withdrawing to re-assess their positions and/or to rationalize their actions. Withdrawing from the group is in any event regarded as a problem, as the sociability of the participants is taken for granted.

Participants sometimes do isolate themselves, but this is articulated as a problem in the broadcasts, for example by referring to the grief of that specific participant. These emotions are the only legitimate explanations for voluntary social isolation. At the same time the individual responsibility of the participants is strongly emphasized. They take all decisions as mature and independent individuals, so that the entire structurizing context (and in particular the production team's management) moves to the background.

A second key discourse in *Temptation Island* is based on the ideal of physical beauty as source of, and catalyst for, attraction and seduction. On the Kanakna website the invitation to participate is expressly directed at "good-looking people (singles/couples)." According to the Veronica TI website the partners are exposed to seduction by "handsome single men and women," and it is not by chance that a tropical island is chosen as set for the series, resulting in an endless parade of scanty swimsuits, bikinis, and shorts. Here, the production team does revert to gendered stereotypes (although also the male bachelors do not escape from these processes of objectivation). An illustration of this choice is the scene where the female singles are introduced to the male partners. In an unsubtle reference to Kubrick's *Eyes Wide Shut*, the masked singles parade in long hooded gowns, clearly wearing only lingerie underneath. These images are also used on the front page of the VT4 website and in an affichage campaign. After this "revelation" the singles wrap themselves around the partners. This elicited the following remark from one of the partners: "They were touching us all over, and I thought: I hope they stay away from my business."

A significant number of the *Temptation Island* scenes support the idea of physical seduction, including the apparently inevitable wet T-shirt competition, the slapping of (female) buttocks, the selection rituals for the "dates" (reminiscent of beauty contests), and short-skirted or bare-chested dancing. In particular, the relationship test comprises exposing the partners to the physical component of sexuality, and to female and male beauty. It is thus also no accident that magazines such as *Maxim* and *P-Magazine*, which rely very strongly on the "babe" concept, as well as nude publications such as *Playboy* and *Penthouse*, published photo reports on the female singles. Examples of these are the photographs of Liesbeth van Muylem in *P-Magazine* (April 2006) and of Mieke and Rowena Guldenaar in *Playboy* (July 2006). In this respect the male participants received little publicity. With this emphasis on physicality, *Temptation Island*'s discourse also reinforces the classic ideals of (female) beauty, with symmetry and slimness as key components.

This somewhat exclusive focus on physicality and beauty is toned down by the notion of the "connection." Already attracted by the bodies of the singles, the partners quickly develop a preference for one or two singles. These individual preferences are legitimized by the concept of the "connection," which suggests that there is compatibility between the relevant personalities. This "connection" refers more to an attraction based on character than one based on the physical, and partly softens the exclusive focus on participants' bodies. The repertoire of "connection," however, mostly comes to the fore later, and thus does not really diminish the emphasis on the physical.

A third and last key discourse involves the "holy" rules of the game. As the direct interventions of the production team are supposed to remain hidden, their control is translated into the system of rules. The power of the media professionals is never directly seen in operation in *Temptation Island*; we only see the results of this power imbalance. Despite a number of modest manifestations of resistance, the entire program radiates obedience. The participants are docile bodies, disciplined by the production team. One example of this is the escape scene, where some of the partners decided to swim to the "women's resort" when they found that their boat had been approached to within reach. They effectively jumped into the water to swim the 500 meters to the "resort," but were then persuaded to return to their ship, with the escape ending as a failure.

Here the concept of the relationship test also plays an important role, as departing from the rules is equated to undermining the test. Therefore disobedience (or a critical attitude) is rearticulated into cheating, thus creating a Catch 22 situation for the participants. In this respect *Temptation Island* is a metaphor for normalization of media power as an impassive mover, the "primum movens immobile" that manages to hegemonize its own basic assumptions, principles, and methodologies. At the same time *Temptation Island* uses an alarming discourse of obedience, with participants prepared to let their relationships deteriorate for the sake of the rules of the game, and for the entertainment of the many.

Power in *Temptation Island's* production sphere

When the power relations between the participants and the production team are examined more closely, it is rather difficult to ignore the inequality of these relations. The production team use a number of sophisticated management techniques to place the partners under pressure. The most important of these mechanisms is the unlimited trial.

By basing the entire program concept on a relationship test to which the participants voluntarily subject themselves, the extreme interventions by the production team is legitimized. On the *Temptation Island* websites of VT4 and Veronica, the concept of the relationship test is explicitly mentioned. The first sentence of the introductory text on the VT4 website[7] is: "Four couples travel to Thailand, where they are separated for sixteen days, during which their relationships are subjected to extreme tests." On the Veronica TI website the first sentence was: "*Temptation Island*: the ultimate fantasy is a reality programme where four unmarried couples travel to an exotic location to test their relationships."

Based on the concept of the relationship test, *Temptation Island* becomes an unlimited trial, where not only the "tempters"/"temptresses" "do everything in their power to place as much pressure as possible on the women [and men]" (VT4 website), but where the production team as well try to influence the context in such a way that the carefully selected couples' relationships are placed under pressure, often resulting in a break-up between the partners when the program ends. By taking part in a program of this format, the participants relinquish their power over the nature and intensity of the tests to which they are subjected. At the same time this willingness to relinquish power legitimizes the production team's interventions and the intensity thereof. During the program participants often say that they underestimated the pressure on their relationship, without referring to those persons who— under the pretext of the unlimited trial—knowingly place their relationship under duress. In their discussions the participants strongly emphasize the "seduction" to which they are subjected by the presence of the tempters/temptresses. As often happens in the television system, the interventions of media professionals are not mentioned, but remain concealed.

The basic mechanism of the unlimited trial as a management technique is strengthened by the artificial setting, which is strongly reminiscent of a panopticon. The participants are cleverly isolated by housing them on a distant tropical island, which offers a wide range of tourist (and sexual) attractions, but at the same time strongly resembles a prison (including the occasional "escape"). Within the imaginary walls of the so-called "resorts," the participants are subjected to numerous surveillance techniques by means of which (almost) all their activities are captured day and night. These images are then shown to the viewers and their partners. Finally *Temptation Island* is "safeguarded" by numerous rules, contractually enforced, which direct and discipline the participants' behavior.

A third management technique is based on what Foucault has termed confessional power. Inter alia through interviews the participants are continually urged to describe their activities and emotional state, and to confess even the slightest "infringement" to the presenters and thus also to the viewers. The interview questions are (partly) enabled by the production team's Olympian perspective (due to the ubiquitous cameras). This not only results in an endless series of (self-)revelations, which the presenters of course do not reciprocate, but it also makes the presenters the first witnesses (and judges) of the, often inevitable, "lapses" of the partners. The culmination of the confessional power is found in the subformat of the bonfire, where the partners are not only questioned on their reactions when seeing suggestive or explicit clips of their partners, but where they also confess their own "bad behavior." It is in particular at the last bonfire, where the partners are re-united and have to confess their "sins" to each other (and to the presenter and viewers), that the most intimate details are confessed, often leading to emotional outbursts. One example of this was at a bonfire during *Temptation Island 5*, where the couple, Björn[8] and Bianca Mommen, were re-united already in the middle of the program so that she could confess—after the clips had already been shown to the viewers and to Björn—that she effectively had sex with one of the bachelors, Stephen. Björn stormed away raging: "Ten days, even that you could not do for me," and ran weeping to the beach. There he started shouting "Why?" so loudly that the sound quality of the recording was affected.

Two remarks have to be made regarding this analysis of the production team's management techniques. First, the interaction between the participants is important, but not only because the program is based on seduction of the partners by "tempters/temptresses." Here the power dynamics are also more complex, because the partners try to support and protect each other, but they also discuss and judge each other's behavior during the interviews. An example here is Tim De Pril's brief description ("fingering") of what in his view happened at a swim-party between one of the partners, Liesbeth de Lange, and the bachelor, Edwin Rutgers. As can be expected, such a delectable snippet is eagerly broadcast. Second, and more important, is the fact that resistance against the management of the production team is evident among all participants. Despite having very little opportunity, participants sometimes do manage to escape the cameras and microphones, for example, by swimming far enough out to sea, thereby becoming invisible and also inaudible, or by simply removing the portable microphone. Also refusing to participate in the interaction by locking themselves in, or by "going to bed early," can in some instances be seen as resistance. This is also true of the roles of the tempters/temptresses that were sometimes not performed with as much enthusiasm as expected. For example, in episode 12 of *Temptation Island 5*, the temptress Mieke at first accepted partner Len Konings' invitation to go on the dream date with him, but later returned the chain—the symbol of the "chosen one"—to him, saying that he was too arrogant, and that she no longer wanted to go on the dream date with him.

The television text and the viewer

The *Temptation Island* production process is aimed at creating a television text, which in turn has the objective of reaching as many viewers as possible. As has been said, the viewers engage with the text in their own interpretative manner, and not necessarily follow the intentions of the producers. However, the audience is not necessarily hyperactive, and might often be satisfied to accept this dominant reading of the television text.

The popularity of the program is not only evidenced by the many hundreds of thousands of viewers, but also by the many responses and discussions on online discussion forums, blogs, and feedback forms. And these online responses make it possible to involve the voices of the viewers in this analysis. But this method has its drawbacks, as online forums also are specific communicative systems with their own specific characteristics.[9]

As could be expected, these online responses are extremely diverse. A large part of the postings is purely informative, asking for or offering information on how the program is developing, but also on the private lives of the participants. This category of postings also includes the so-called "caps" (or stills of the broadcasts), which appear quite often in the forums, as well as quotations from the broadcasts. For example, when two of the "tempters" sing a snippet from the Carnival Medley by Hans Teeuwen, with this eminent text: "A stiff prick is made to pump with, falderie, faldera," this is eagerly quoted. Also partner Bjorn's cries: ("TEN DAYS!!!" (SEMTEX, 24-04-2006, fok.nl)), was a popular quote, in addition to references to older quotes belonging to *Temptation Island*'s standard repertoire, such as "No kissing no fucking" and "Drink is the devil" made by partner James Serbeniuk from *Temptation Island 2*.

These more informative postings are supplemented by a limited number of predictions of future developments and analyses of cultural[10] and gender differences (or expressions of cultural and gendered [lack of] comprehension). However, the main attitude displayed by the postings on the forums that were analyzed was of a judgmental nature. In other words, the posters expressed themselves on many different levels about the participants, their behavior, their physical appearance, their personalities, and their moral fiber.

It is in particular the idea of the (unlimited) trial that emphasizes the indisputable element of play. In a number of instances the words "play" or "game" are expressly used. It is a game in which the stakes that the participants will fail are high, and some viewers watch with drooling eagerness for the participants to "transgress." Others again strongly support certain participants, so that the program is turned into a race into decline, rather than a series of smaller and larger human dramas.

"I find it an amazing program; just cannot understand that there are still couples who want to participate, because by now everyone knows the game so well!! I would never participate, but I like to watch it." (praia, 12 May 2006, verionica.nl)

"It is very clear that this year they are doing their best to brew mischief and to make the couples uneasy about their partners (but OK, that is part of the game)." (Megara, 13 April 2006, vt4.be)

"I am curious whether it will again be heavy, and now I hope the women will make the mistakes haha." (lichtspeed, 15 July 2006, sbs.nl)

To be able to define this program as play, it is imperative (at least in part) to place the players in a not too favorable position and to avoid identification, so that pleasure can be derived from seeing their problems displayed on the screen. It is for this reason that so much emphasis is placed on the fact that the participants themselves carried the responsibility to decide whether they wanted to participate, or that they are discredited by calling them "mad," "silly," or "stupid." Via this mechanism some of the partners are reduced to jokers, so that the broadcasts can have legitimate entertainment value, and the participants can be judged. In exceptional cases posters (such as Bobette) have a more self-reflexive attitude toward this, or participants are defended against this type of criticism (even though it is not always easy to distinguish between supporters and critics).

The evaluations are largely on par with the key discourses described above. It is not surprising that the debate about sexual fidelity plays an important role in the discussions of the program. One of the words that are used most frequently to describe (at least some of participants) is the word

"Carl and Kim must stay together; only Eva must pull herself together; get real, girl, you cannot let your whole life revolve around one man." (ilonatjuh18, 11 July 2005, sbs.nl—more about Temptation Island 4*)*

"OK, the participants ask for this, but surely as a human being this would destroy you?" (believer, 28-04-2006, femistyle.be)

"What fool goes to an island with her boyfriend where she leaves him alone with single girls?? You're begging for it! And the single girls? I would die of shame." (Maartjj*, 30 May 2006, sbs.nl)

"Haha, I did not expect that! Carl is a real jelly-fish! With his silly talk, as if he is something! Bah!" (Nicole87, 16 July 2006, sbs.nl—about Temptation Island 4*)*

"A more stupid person is difficult to imagine … if she were to stand amongst a flock of sheep, I wouldn't notice hahahaha what a stupid woman!!!" (ZuseJ, 8 May 2006, belg.be)

"Let's be honest: Temptation Island *is an immoral program. And that's why we watch it: to be able to say 'I'll never do that,' and meanwhile we enjoy being a voyeur, hoping that, for example Len, will try and make amends in a following program, understandable in front of the camera." (Bobette, 7 April 2006, femistyle.be)*

"Bianca, if you read this, you are a very tough cookie!" (Rob, 14 May 2006, goedZO?!.com)

"Ah, is that one of the ten girlies who are part of the Slut Camp? Is there not enough going on in your lives? Is it

"slut," mostly oriented toward the female participants. On the strength of this, one of the posters calls the entire program "Slut Camp." One section of the viewers sees the female singles as "sluts," as their assumed promiscuity is in conflict with the traditional monogamous moral values, in the good old tradition of the double standard. While the television text portrays the hedonism of the singles in a mostly positive manner, the attitude of (some of) the posters is more negative. And the partners who (presumably) succumb are not spared the censure. One of the most striking postings (by Jayatonism) identifies each partner with a specific characteristic. Two are described as "whores." The same day a reaction appeared defending (only) one of the women.

It comes as no surprise that the second woman, Bianca Mommen, was not defended. Very soon after the first broadcast, the news that Bianca Mommen (aka Alana) was an erotic masseuse and prostitute was circulated on some websites, and it also appeared in an article in a major North-Belgian popular newspaper, *Het Laatste Nieuws*. Bianca Mommen defended herself

so boring? I find it only a 6/10." (Zagato, 11 April 2006, zattevrienden.be)

"I ask myself every year why the participants take part; it is not a real vacation, because there are cameras around you all the time. In effect you are all alone, or in any case together with 3 losers and 8 sluts, with whom you will never go on holiday. And then all the pathetic little kindergarten games; dancing with bananaleaf skirts, a little slutty performance behind a white sheet ... Get them away from me... And why do they get caught in the trap? Yes: litres of alcohol and 8 sluts who follow you all day long only to lure you into whoring ..." (MrBean, 11 April 2006, fok.nl)

"Kevin is smart. Matthieu is gross. Len is smart. Lisette has a sweet smile. Bianca is a whore. So is Cheyenne. Björn is naive." (Jaytonism, 22 May 2006, fok.nl)

"Ok, Cheyenne had sex with the Smoothy...but come on, this does not suddenly make her a whore? Though it is sad that she was not honest about this ... Kevin is far too good, and perhaps he would even have forgiven her." (hardsilence, 22 May 2006, fok.nl)

"I have been a client of Alana's. You will have to take my word that she is not a masseuse. She does just what the other girls do, and even better. When you enter the club, you can sit down and take your time making a choice from amongst the ladies. I immediately chose Alana, who was sitting on the couch wearing a see-through bra. When we were walking to the bedroom, I was already excited by the nice bum. In the room we at first had a relaxed talk, and then the action started. After going down quietly she asked whether I wanted to do it without a condom. I wanted that, but that would cost 30 euro more. Nothing was said about a massage,

in this newspaper article with the Clintonesque statement: "I only give massages with my breasts. That is not sex. I have never been paid to have sex with a client." These first articles generated an avid online investigation into Bianca Mommen's private life, creating a whole series of texts parallel to *Temptation Island*'s text. In addition, photos and a masturbation video were posted, and there were a whole series of testimonies by clients, contradicting her statement. More important than this privacy-infringing variation of which is sometimes called citizen journalism was the abusive tirade that broke over Bianca Mommen's head. An almost endless row of posters insulted her, and her initial reticence and emotionality were held against her. Whenever she was filmed making out with one of the singles, it was seen as final confirmation of her promiscuity. For most of the posters it was unthinkable that her professional work and her relational sphere could be separated. The fact that she was seen as a prostitute brought all the traditional registers about prostitution to the fore in the discussions, resulting in her being dehumanized and objectified,

but in any case I did not want that. She asked me not to come in her mouth. After sucking me very nicely, she quickly put on a condom and asked whether I wanted to fuck her doggy-style. Unfortunately, I was so excited that I came quickly. Afterwards we drank and talked a bit. She told me that she did this work mainly to pay for her studies." (de gele leeuw, 3 April 2006, whitelinefi rm.nl)

"An ugly whore who gives a stupid and prudish performance on TV. One should throw such a person in the Willebroek channel." (danzig, 11 April 2006, zattevrienden.be)

"I don't understand this female. On TV she does not even want to talk to a guest, there she is such a prude … what is the world coming to." (nXr, 11 April 2006, zattevrienden.be)

"I fear that her market price will rise now that she has been on TV." (electricpunk, 11 April 2006, zattevrienden.be)

"So, at last Bianca had a good fuck; perhaps she will now keep her stupid wits together. What an impossibly irritating person. Those who talk the most first get the chop. But of course, an escort girl cannot do without. Sorry, Veronica, that the program is now totally without credibility. It has always been fun to watch." (Angeliekje, 25 April 2006, veronica.nl)

"I find the whole business rather crude and mean, with all the comments. Bianca's occupation is her business, and it does not mean that the child is a slut." (sugababe, 11 May 2006, vt4.be) "Yes? Then what is your definition of a slut?

defined as abnormal and deviant, and stigmatized. A small number of posters spoke out in defense of Bianca Mommen, for example by trying to make a distinction between a "slut" and a prostitute, but these postings were ignored or countered. Bianca's denials of both her professional activities and her sexual escapades with Stephen also elicited negative responses. However, it was not only this one participant who was subjected to such condemnatory responses. Other participants who were suspected of lying were also condemned, and their deceived partners then received messages of sympathy. These participants were expected to confess and apologize. If they did not do so, the postings got even more condemnatory. This again emphasizes the cultural importance—or even the hegemony—of the traditional monogamous relationship, of sexual fidelity, and of honesty. In addition to the debate on fidelity, the debate on physicality and beauty is paramount in the postings. In some instances the clips of specific body parts (especially female) were applauded, for example in the posting by eronmiller. Another example

If a prostitute is not slut, then I don't what is." (Kuifer, 16 May 2006, vt4.be)

"There are also porno actors who are married and see sex as business, but who only 'make love' with their wives." (executegirl, 28 April 2006, femistyle.be)

"People who lie so glibly do not deserve better." (Shirley, 2 May 2006, fok.nl)

"I ask myself … if Bianca sees the clips again… how does she feel? Not because of the sex scenes, you know, but because she lied so shamelessly." (Amourath, forum moderator, 28 April 2006, vt4.be)

"hihi, I'm also watching TV:D Really sad for Andries:(Stupid woman that she is! All this lying, I so hate that! Good luck, Andries!)" (Direct_gek, 24 May 2006, veronica.nl)

"Melon time again." (FreCas, 11 April 2006, zattevrienden.be)

"To quote HUMO: TITS, TITS and again TITS! Whether it is Rebecca or Bianca, they are wiggling there for our visual pleasure…" (eronmiller, 12 April 2006, vt4.be)

"She walked face first into a wall, fell down, and afterwards a bus rode slowly over her face …" (Kenneth89, 12 April 2006, zattevrienden.be)

"I would rather go to a toothless crack whore than to stick my prick into Bianca with the cow spots on her

is the posting of a still of one broadcast showing the buttocks of one of the single females, and asking whose buttocks they were.

Often certain participants were singled out, and the attractiveness (or lack thereof) of their bodies exhaustively discussed and evaluated. In some cases this resulted in renewed attacks on participants, with Bianca Mommen once again being the target. These discussions are supported by the classic ideals of beauty and slimness. An example here is the debate on whether the "super-temptress" (Rebecca Loos) was "fat" or "stout." Those singles (and sometimes also the partners) who fit the beauty ideal were judged in positive light, and called "pretty," "nice," or "sweet."

Finally, some posters did also mention the production team's management, but these postings were rare. A number of postings showed that the viewers were aware of the production team's interventions. Posters referred to the suggestive pictures during the bonfire evenings, the creation of a specific "sphere" by means of music, the importance of the montage, the "mean" interview questions trying to fathom these interventions afforded added

legs and her crooked eye!" (mark25utrg, 21 April 2006, whitelinefirm.nl)

"And I must admit that Rebecca Loos looks better on film than on her photos, even though I find her rather heavy." (Amourath, forum moderator, 12 April 2006, t4.be)

"Liesbeth tops the show; a real pretty woman … and not a whore!!" (Tijnus, 17 April 2006, whitelinefirm.nl)

"Mieke is the nicest." (Quinten, 19 April 2006, whitelinefirm.nl)

"There is one nice guy and that is Len; a sweet thing, not so macho, a bit young, but if all goes well he will grow up." (Hetechick, 3 April 2006, whiteline-firm.nl)

"Ne me quitte pas [Jacques Brel's Don't leave me]… that is too sad. The director is a genius." (Fendy, 24 May 2006, fok.nl)

"It was again set up in such a way that Björn looked especially pathetic. He was let down by two women, and stayed behind on his own, smoking a cigarette." (kaos, 26 May 2006, fok.nl)

"What I find strange: everything Bianca does is broadcast, but Cheyenne's infidelity we apparently missed? Were we asleep, or are the participants strongly type-cast?" (charmed_angel, 23 May 2006, fok.nl)

"The presenters' questions were much meaner this year, but they missed the opportunity to make good use of the

entertainment value. This was also a way of displaying their media literacy (or "savvyness"). However, as *Temptation Island* is defined as a game that participants voluntarily take part in, the (sometimes) problematic character of these techniques can take a back seat. This key discourse sometimes even results in some posters criticizing the imperfect character of these management techniques.

In rare instances the posters critique the (legitimacy of) *Temptation Island*'s management via the concept of the game and the trial. The program (or a facet thereof) is then defined as "ridiculous" or "miserable," or the posters give vent to their annoyance. Sometimes the irritation is limited to para-social interactions with the television screen (as in the case of Mikkel), with the poster entering into a dialogue with the "personages" (participants). In a small number of instances this annoyance leads to fundamental criticism against the production team's (and in particular the presenters') behavior. The posting by "believer" is one of the few where the deontology of the program makers is indeed questioned. The criterion that is applied is based on the seriousness of the emotional and relational impact on the participants, but

footage of the partners having sex, in order to position the partners against each other, as they did the year before. Of course, we do not get a Kenny and a Sven every year." (_Boo_, 24 May 2006, fok.nl)

"The bonfires give us a good laugh. It is surprising what one can suggest with a little cutting and pasting. But they surely are discomfited by the clips." (Temmer, 25 April 2006, veronica.nl)

"I cannot help it, but I found the fact that Eyes Wide Shut *was imitated ridiculous. Complete with soundtrack, et cetera. I think that I would have died laughing, but well, in any case, I am not a man." (Megara, 6 April 2006, vt4.be)*

"Pity that people are thrown off balance by pictures and suggestive texts." (EI-Grande, 4 July 2006, sbs.nl)

"I always get irritated when they manipulate the clips during the bonfires. Then I sit and shout at the TV: 'No, that's not at all true!!!'" (Mikkel, 16 March 2006, femistyle.be)

"Was anyone else also so irritated by the lady-presenter (at the female camp)? I don't know who she was, but the ones from the previous years were at least a little sympathetic, and if they did instigate a bit of a fight, they were at least subtle about it. But this one TOO evidently stirred up trouble, also about unimportant things, and in fact exaggerated her input to such an extent that it no longer was trouble-stirring." (calcietje, 15 April 2006, femistyle.be)

131

once again they are reminded of their individual responsibility, and relatively little is said about the structural limitations. Most of these "critical" readings of the television text (with some exceptions, such as Bobette's postings on femistyle.be) in fact refer to a specific aspect, and ignore the all-encompassing character of the production management, which in any case remains hidden from most of the posters.

Besides the criticism leveled against the way in which the program is managed, as discussed above, the television text is also critically evaluated on a second level. This criticism goes to the heart of the program concept, as the authenticity and the real-life quality of *Temptation Island* as reality show is questioned. The contradictions in Bianca Mommen's behavior, the sensational news that she is a prostitute, and also the presence of participants who have taken part in other television programs and therefore are no longer considered "ordinary people" was enough for one group of posters to call the entire program a "put-up job." Despite a number of reflexive postings as defense against this criticism, together with testimonies and behavioral analyses, this criticism is

"You know, in this series I am overconscious of the way in which everything is directed: Mieke's letter with the key would really not have come without a tip (+ key) from the producers; trying to make the partners jealous was staged. The whole program is only insinuation, and if everything goes too well, the producers will intervene." (Bobette, 24 April 2006, femistyle.be)

"And I actually find that the whole thing can no longer be justified by the producers. OK, the participants ask for this, but surely as a human being, this must kill you?" (believer, 28 April 2006, femistyle.be)

"I always watch Temptation Island, *but I now heard that Björn and Bianca only acted. That they did this to ensure a large audience. Is this true? Can someone mail me?" (Carlijn, 10 May 2006, belg.be)*

"The TV show is thus totally fake ... they are not at all so prudish as they seem to be." (blueprint1979, 12 April 2006, zattevrienden.be)

"Ugh, how bad, to see your fake relationship go down!" (TheVulture, 21 April 2006, fok.nl)

"O well, perhaps Veronica did pay her...clever marketing concept..." (Iola, 21 May 2006, goedZo?!.com)

*"Ridiculous that there is again an Ex-*BigBrother *in the show. And that Rebecca woman also has to go. I always liked the program very much, when everything was not yet so fake, but this time I'll pass. It is simply ridiculous. I don't watch it any more. Veronica: continue like this and*

echoed by many posters. In this roundabout way, the production management then comes under fire (and heavy, at that) because the credibility of the program is prejudiced through interventions from the production team—negating the idea of fair play, or the idea of "ordinary people." This type of resistance is not aimed against the productions team's deontological code, but against the fact that they transcended the program format, and it is sometimes extremely radical in form and content.

will chase all (loyal) viewers away ..." (kimmetje18d 4 April 2006, veronica.nl)

"A total put-up job, that Temptation. And an ex-participant of Big Brother is also there! They are all actors!" (Tim, 1 April 2006, whiteLineFirm.nl) "Not true ... a friend of mine, temptress Mavis, is NO actress! She works in an accounting office. So, keep your prejudices for yourself!!!" (Sinneke, 4 April 2006, whiteLine-Firm.nl)

"I don't know if everything always is prearranged, as hetchick [another poster] said. Björn was really very sad, and most actors in the Netherlands and Belgium on average cannot act so well. I may be wrong, but his grief looked very real to me." (Lucky Luke, 2 May 2006, whiteLine-Firm.nl)

Conclusion

Besides entertainment, *Temptation Island* offers many viewers an in-depth look at our culture. The conclusion that they draw from this viewing is often not very optimistic. Both the program and the viewers who responded online show a rigid moral perspective on sexual fidelity and monogamy. While the television text still offers scope for hedonism (through the central, and legitimately defined role of the singles), the online discussions are dominated by a conservative perspective that in some instances escalates to moralization, intolerance, sexism, and stigmatization, mostly aimed at the female participants.

Through the logic of photo-negativism, where visions of order are photo-negativized into stories of disorder (see Hartley 1992), *Temptation Island* confirms the hegemonic interpretation of the ideal relationship. The partners, who one after the other succumb to the pressure, present negative points of identification against which the viewers can measure themselves, enabling them to confirm their own moral value system as presented on the (television) plate. That is the source of the malicious satisfaction as well as the pleasure that the viewers experience when they see how people whom they consider (with all their faults) as inferior fail. When the partners do succumb, the viewers in addition await the catharsis of the final confession that has to restore social order.

In order to legitimize the pleasure, the viewers enter into a social contract with the program, allowing them to ogle the (female) bodies, and in particular to tolerate emotional abuse in the name of the game. The program cleverly creates a distance between the viewers and the participants, discouraging identification through the participants' articulation as "stupid" (for entering into a situation that will unavoidably lead to their downfall), and through their articulation as being individually responsible. This is further strengthened by conferring an element of play on the happiness (or unhappiness) generated by human relationships. In this respect *Temptation Island* is truly an anti-empathetic program.

Temptation Island also (once again) illustrates how the television system manages to hide its power very effectively, and how it makes the production team's management role largely invisible. The discussion about the authenticity of *Temptation Island* is an important exception in this regard, as it shows that too much intervention from the production team can have a boomerang effect.

All this raises the deontological question of how the members of the production team can justify treating other people in such a destructive manner. The question is not whether the participants should be protected "against themselves," which would place us in a paternalistic position. The question is how media professionals can justify—both for themselves and toward the entire media sector—spending two weeks (and more) trying to destroy people's relationships. The argument that it is "only a game" and that participants voluntarily take part is in my opinion not a satisfying answer to this ethical question. In this respect, *Temptation Island* shows the need for human-interest journalism, or entertainment-oriented journalism (see Meijer 2001; Campbell 2004), so that reality TV and human-interest programming can be firmly embedded in journalistic ethical systems. In other words, it requires the inclusion of these journalistic ethics in the world of media professionals, beyond the strict definition of journalist identities.

References

Ang, Ien (1985), *Watching* Dallas: *Soap Opera and the Melodramatic Imagination*, London: Methuen.

Campbell, Vincent (2004), *Information Age Journalism: Journalism in an International Context*, London: Arnold.

Fiske, John (1989), *Understanding Popular Culture*, London: Routledge.

Foucault, Michel (1977), *Discipline and Punish: The Birth of the Prison*, New York: Pantheon.

——— (1978), *The History of Sexuality. Vol I: An Introduction*, New York: Pantheon.

Hall, Stuart (1980), "Encoding/decoding," in S. Hall, D. Hobson, A. Lowe, and P. Willis (eds), *Culture, Media, Language: Working Papers in Cultural Studies, 1972-1979*, London: Hutchinson, pp. 128–38.

Hartley, John (1992), *The Politics of Pictures: The Creation of the Public in the Age of Popular Media*, Routledge, London.

Meijer, Irene C. (2001), "The public quality of popular journalism: Developing a normative framework," *Journalism Studies*, 2:2, pp. 189–205.

Appendix: forums, blogs, and feedback pages analyzed

belg.be:
http://www.belg.be/leesmeer.php?x=3457 (no longer accessible)

femistyle.be:
http://www.femistyle.be/ubbthreads/showflat.php?Cat=0&Number=311289 &page=0&fpart=
1&vc=1

fok.nl:
http://forum.fok.nl/topic/840554, 844298, 848519, 849903, 851659, 852485, 854457, 854746,
856631, 858232, 860619 and 863794

goedZO.com:
http://www.goedzo.com/index.php/2006/04/26/filmpje_temptation_island_deelneemster_b

sbs.nl:
http://www.sbs.nl/modules.php?name=special&site=televisienieuws&sid=13 26

veronica.nl:
http://veronica.sbs.nl/modules.php?name=special&site=televisienieuws&sid
=4835&rubrieknaam

vt4.be:
http://www.forum.vt4.be/display_topic_threads.asp?ForumID=11&TopicID= 17887&Retu
rnPage=&PagePosition=1&ThreadPage=1

whitelinefirm.nl:
http://www.whitelinefirm.nl/node/202

zattevrienden.be: http://www.zattevrienden.be/Alana_aka_Bianca_uit_Temptation_Island_
de_verboden_fotos

Notes

1 The television text hardly makes any reference to the locality of these resorts, disconnecting
   them from their (post)colonial realities.
2 http://www.temptation-island.nl/. Accessed 28 December 2018.
3 Tim De Pril was a partner in *Temptation Island* 2. Gaby Visser and Rowena Guldenaar were
   "temptresses" in, respectively, *Temptation Island* 3 and 4.
4 This text is based on an analysis of the broadcasts combined with an analysis of the postings
   on *Temptation Island* on the following forums, blogs, and feedback pages: fok.nl, sbs.nl, belg.
   be, zattevrienden.be, whitelinefirm.nl, veronica.nl, goedZO?!.com, femistyle.be en vt4.be.
   The online postings are quoted verbatim. The author does not necessarily agree with them

as to form and content. Please note that the postings from the forums are all translated from the original Dutch.

5   http://www.big-andries.nl/ (currently offline).

6   This text can still be read on the following website: http://www.rotationz.be/new/news. php?newsid=1949. Accessed 28 December 2018.

7   At the time of writing, this website was no longer online.

8   It was not possible to discover all the participants' surnames, and where this was the case, only first names are used.

9   For example, a number of these forums were moderated, so some postings were removed or only partially shown. Sometimes the moderation policy was explained, such as that of the vt4 forum on *Temptation Island*: "Our aim is to talk about the programme, not let participants hang their dirty washing on the line! We will be very strict in this regard [...] such postings are removed because of their aggressive and offensive nature" (Amourath, forum moderator, 1 April 2006, vt4.be).

10   The focus of this text is not on cultural differences. Differences between the North-Belgian and the Dutch broadcasts are not considered, as are the differences in online culture between Northern Belgium and the Netherlands, and the difference in status between the posters ("ordinary viewers" and participants).

Section 3

Production

Chapter 6

The Postmodern Challenge to Journalism: Strategies for Constructing a Trustworthy Identity

Jo Bogaerts and Nico Carpentier

Introduction

The first decades of the twentieth century led to a period of high modernism[1] in (American) journalism because of the increasing professionalization of journalists and the consolidation of a shared occupational ideology, as authors such as Hallin (1992, 2006) and Zelizer (2004) have argued. Hallin shows that both political and economic factors contributed to the virtually uncontested status of journalism in providing what was accepted as truthful and direct access to reality. Even though journalism remained "caught between the competing imperatives of freedom of the press" and the "laws of the market" (Champagne 2009: 48), these tensions did not seem to affect the truth claims of high-modernist journalism. Indeed, characteristics of journalists' attitudes toward their work during the era of high modernism were an apparent self-confidence and an "absence of a sense of doubt or contradiction" (Hallin 1992: 14).

However, in subsequent decades this "sense of wholeness and seamlessness" (Hallin 1992: 14) in journalists' self-image has been thoroughly shaken. By taking a cue from the field of tension between its modernist legacy and contemporary developments in journalism, this chapter wishes to address journalistic identity politics in the face of threat. Departing from the challenges that journalism has been confronted with in the past few decades and the dwindling trust of audiences, we will first discuss the building blocks of the mainstream professional journalistic identity. We then discuss a number of strategies that journalists deploy in order to protect their professional identity to maintain trust in the profession and to reaffirm themselves as "society's truth-teller[s]" (McNair 1998: 65). This focus on journalistic identity is aligned with a still underdeveloped "cultural turn" within journalism studies, showing how collective identities (and their rigidities and fluidities) structure the journalistic field.

The theoretical backbone of our analysis is provided by a discourse-theoretical perspective. This allows us to focus on the discursive building blocks (or nodal points) of the modernist journalistic identity, and to analyze how these elements have become threatened in the contemporary era of liquid modernism. This will allow us to foreground a series of discursive coping strategies, which show how journalism attempts to protect its position as a vital societal field.

Given the broadness of the journalistic field, we will focus on one specific location, namely online journalism. This is one of the sites where these truth claims are both maintained and contested, which renders professional identities and the coping mechanisms to protect them visible. Without aiming to create a clear-cut dichotomy between online and traditional journalism, we would nevertheless argue that online journalism is a useful object of investigation because "professional consciousness emerges at least in part around ruptures where the borders of appropriate practice need renegotiation" (Zelizer 1993b: 223; cf. Matheson 2004: 446).

The passing of the "high modernism" of journalism

Since the late 1960s journalism has met the same fate as science, as the era of high modernism of journalism gradually shifted to what Deuze (2006a, 2006b)—following Bauman (2000)—has called "liquid journalism."[2] A diversity of processes lies at the root of this shift. This includes broader contextual changes such as detraditionalization, individualization, and globalization (Krotz 2007). Others point to the end of a consensus-based politics and an increasing economic insecurity that severely undermined the public's trust in institutions and authorities. Such distrust in the core values, norms, rhetoric, and practices of journalism (Deuze 2006a; Jones 2009) has challenged the monopoly on truth held by news institutions. Moreover, changes within the journalistic institution—such as a tendency toward commercialization, cross-media mergers and concentration, and the changes triggered by the rise of new media technologies—have contributed to the breakdown of journalism's monopoly status as a news institution. Such developments might have led journalism to doubt its own rationality, but instead it has remained mostly faithful to its high-modernist convictions and beliefs.

Journalism, as Zelizer (2004: 112) puts it, is still indebted to the "modernist bias of its official self-presentation" and has not adapted itself to changed circumstances. Despite the "passing of the era of high modernism" (Hallin 1992), journalism tends to hold on to its self-proclaimed authority. In order to face such severe challenges and to maintain trust in itself and generate trust in its audiences, journalism has developed a series of coping strategies that reaffirm its professional authority. Indeed, "abandoning the objectivity norm and confessing that journalism is unable to accurately represent reality, would undermine its authority" (Broersma 2010: 30).

The ways in which journalism maintains this position have been a widely researched topic in journalism studies. By claiming professionalism (Tuchman 1971; Soloski 1990), orienting their actions toward a certain habitus (Matheson 2003; Benson and Neveu 2005) and sharing interpretations of the profession (Zelizer 1993b), journalists maintain an image of competence and authority in spite of their apparent lack of self-criticism (Lule 1992: 92; Zelizer 1993a: 81, 1993b: 222). Strategies of self-confirmation in the face of threat and challenge have also been researched since Tuchman's introduction of the concept of "news repair" in her 1978 book *Making News* (e.g., Bennett et al. 1985; Reese 1990). In this chapter, we want to complement the focus on institutional reactions with a theoretical reflection on identity work and politics (Hall 1989; Reger et al. 2008) that modernist journalism and the threats to its position produce. To support this reflection, we will turn to discourse theory, which will allow us to develop a discourse-theoretical perspective on journalism.

A discourse-theoretical perspective on journalism

Discourse theory, most prominently formulated by Foucault, Žižek, Butler, and Laclau and Mouffe, regards the social space as discursively constructed. This means that its meaning is the temporary and contingent result of a *process of signification* (see Carpentier and Spinoy 2008: 5). As Ernesto Laclau (1988: 254) explains, a discourse is "a structure in which meaning is constantly negotiated and constructed." Any discourse consists of a number of discursive elements that are taken from a reservoir that Laclau and Mouffe call the field of discursivity. These elements are related to each other through articulation. This process of *articulation* involves linking up discursive elements around (a number of) privileged signifiers that temporarily stabilize discourses. Such privileged signifiers act as *nodal points*, i.e., they arrest the unceasing deferral of meaning and structure the dominant discourse in a rigid, even if structurally contingent, way. Even though nodal points "sustain the identity of a certain discourse by constructing a knot of definite meanings" (Torfing 1999: 88–89) that does not mean they are in some way more fully saturated with meaning than any other signifier. On the contrary, nodal points are characterized by a certain emptying out of meaning, which is exactly what accounts for their structural role in the unification of discourse.

From this perspective, journalism, like any social field, is seen to acquire its meanings through discursive processes. A discourse-theoretical perspective stresses that there is no inherent meaning to the concepts and practices of journalism, but that journalism acquires these in the process of articulation, i.e., the relations established among signifiers. Of course, in spite of this contingency, discourses aim to become hegemonic by concealing their particularity and claiming universality. The more natural and self-evident a discourse appears, the stronger its claim on universality and the better it is in maintaining its hegemonic status.

Such a claim to universality is based on the articulation of a range of signifiers that together construct "good journalism" through an "equivalential chain of particularities" (Laclau 2000: 304). In keeping with the literature (in particular Carpentier's [2005] and Deuze's [2005] work on journalistic identity), we regard the following values as the core nodal points of the journalistic ideology: public service, ethics, management, autonomy, membership of a professional elite, immediacy and objectivity. At the same time, "good" (mainstream) journalism needs a constitutive outside; it can only be established in opposition to other possible forms of journalism whose values are systematically excluded as "bad," "undesirable," or "unwanted." This does not only (evidently) mean that hegemony always involves the rejection of alternatives, but—more importantly—that this rejection is a constitutive moment in the production of identity. These other models of journalism, as well as the particular values that constitute them, are not necessarily "bad," but are rather considered as unacceptable in a given ideological, temporal, and spatial context. Obviously, different journalistic traditions, communities, and cultures will contain different articulations of these discursive elements, but it is contended here that the elements that are discussed below remain crucial building blocks for the professional identity.

The public service ideal (not to be restricted to public service broadcasting) points to journalism's (self-)perceived role as a cornerstone in democratic society at large. Journalists regard themselves as bringing a service to the public that mainly consists in "working as some kind of representative watchdog of the status quo in the name of people" (Deuze 2005: 447). Especially in the discourse of the liberal and social responsibility models of the media, journalists have been attributed such a key role in offering citizens the means to participate in democratic regimes (see Hutchins 1947; Siebert et al. 1956; Merrill 1974; McQuail 1994).

In order to justify this public service role, journalism points to the existence of a sense of ethics that guarantee the integrity, reliability, and status of journalists. Most often this ethical consciousness is identified with a commitment to objectivity and truth (see below), but the ethical framework is broader. Belsey and Chadwick (1992: 1), for example, call journalism an "honourable profession," while Frost (2007: 11) emphasizes the need to gather information in a "morally justifiable way." Because of journalism's emphasis on the nodal point of autonomy, it has often privileged the principle of self-regulation as a guarantee for ethical behavior. Such professional-ethical principles "replace censorship and other barriers to communication […] with compelling reasons for journalists regarding self-limitation in democratic societies" (Pöttker 2004: 84).

Another nodal point that is closely linked to the public service ideal is the journalist's role perception as gatekeepers who manage the flow of information. This is inextricably linked to journalists' main source of professional distinction: their ability to decide what news is and what is not (see Zelizer 1993b: 220). But journalists do more than managing the news; they also manage and control a wide series of resources. In order to achieve their objectives—which originate from their "responsibilities for the professional production of specific media products" (Carpentier 2005: 204)—journalists can make use of the production facilities that are owned (in the strictly legal sense of the word) by the media organization.

Autonomy is another nodal point that structures mainstream journalistic identity. Journalists emphasize that in order to carry out their work in a professional manner and to be journalistically creative they must be independent, have editorial autonomy, and enjoy freedom both from internal and external pressures (see McQuail 1994). However, in this insistence on autonomy and freedom, editorial independence has been elevated to "the status of an ideological value in that it functions to legitimize resistance to […] change" (Deuze 2005: 449). In avoiding interference from marketing, corporate ownership, and even public criticism, journalists claim that only journalism itself can judge its news products (Singer 2003: 145). As a result, the insistence on autonomy points to the autopoietic nature of journalism and has played an important role in its attempts to maintain hegemonic status and to legitimate increasingly aggressive styles of newsgathering (see Clayman 2002).

This sense of autonomy, however, does not mean that the links between media professional and news institutions are irrelevant. On the contrary, what constitutes a journalist as a professional is exactly his position within a hierarchically structured organization. Indeed, as Singer (2003: 153) illustrates, "organizational affiliation has largely defined the professional journalist in the past: one qualifies as a professional precisely because of a loss of individual control over the publication or broadcast of one's work." However, even within the constraints of this institutional organization, journalists imagine themselves to be independent truth-seekers. Such an image of "professionalism," as Soloski (1990) has convincingly shown, has been an efficient means to discipline journalists' behavior while at the same time conveying the idea of autonomy within the organizational structure. Within this structure, journalists are acquainted with the media organization through socialization and with peers through informal networks ("a private world," as Burns [1969] labeled it in his article about the BBC, entitled "Public service and private world"). Moreover, journalistic identity is also constructed through a broader sense of belonging, which relates to the existence of a professional group and professional bodies (Zelizer 1993b: 223; Naït-Bouda 2008).

Linking up with journalists' self-perceptions as elite professionals that are responsible for the means of the production of news is the nodal point of immediacy. Though the main professional trait of journalists is deciding on newsworthiness (see above), part of that ideal is also to get that news across as quickly as possible (Weaver and Wilhoit 1996: 263), albeit within segmented time zones. Dealing with time is indeed embedded in what Schlesinger (1987: 83–105) calls a "stop watch culture" that is organized around an efficient organization of labor according to "beats," deadlines, and cycles. Important in this regard is the value attributed to the "scoop" and other ways of gaining prestige by covering a news item first.

However, the key element that defines the self-perception of journalists (especially, but not exclusively, those working in a more Anglo-American(ized) context, see Carpentier and Trioen, (Chapter 7 in this book) is the notion of objectivity (see Schudson 1978, 2001; Reese 1990; Ognianova and Endersby 1996; Mindich 1998; Broersma 2010). By insisting on the value of objectivity in their work, to varying degrees, journalists claim to have unmediated access to reality and the ability to represent it in a factual and truthful manner. Of course, objectivity is not all-encompassing, as the distinction between "facts" and "opinion," and the explicit toleration toward specific ideological positions, shows. Moreover, "the concept of objectivity has been so mangled it now is usually used to describe the very problem it was conceived to correct" (Kovach and Rosenstiel 2001: 12). This does not resolve the fact that "the embrace, rejection as well as critical reappraisal of objectivity all help to keep it alive as an ideological cornerstone of journalism" (Deuze 2005: 448). Related notions such as fairness, professional distance, detachment, or impartiality (see among others Westerståhl 1983) can be considered supportive elements of this nodal point, crucial for establishing the hegemonic discourse of "good" journalism.

Objectivity and its related notions presuppose that a news event is intrinsically newsworthy rather than the result of a process of news-selection and writing procedures.

"While most news texts are the result of the processing and editing of other texts […], they are constructed within a set of conventions that aim for 'a unified text which conceals the editor's intervention'" (Bell 1991 cited in Matheson 2004: 455). As a result, the notion of objectivity has often become so pervasive and self-evident that it appears as if there is no other way of practicing "good" journalism.

However, in recent decades this discourse has become increasingly incapable of symbolizing journalism work. Such a failure to accommodate to a changed reality is apparent in the problems posed to journalism in the era of liquid modernity where its modernist discourse, centered on the representation of reality, is under constant threat. One site where such a change becomes most conspicuous is the online environment that has had an impact on journalism in a number of ways. First of all, the internet has become used as a resource for traditional journalistic practices such as source-gathering. Second, and more important here, the internet offered non-professional journalists the opportunity to distribute their material. Third, it spawned a distinct possibility for providing news, for professionals and non-professionals alike. Such characteristics may confront mainstream journalism with non-professional online news projects that destabilize traditional journalism: "[a] s newsgathering expert systems become available to the general public the gate-keeping function of news people will diminish and as a group, they will probably experience deprofessionalization" (Broddason 1994: 241 cited in Singer 2003: 147).[3] Even though the era of liquid modernity should not be equated with the breakthrough of the internet, it is clear that the technological realm, and more specifically the features of the online environment such as accessibility, hypertextuality, multimediality, and interactivity (see Deuze 2003: 205), pose a challenge to traditional and mainstream news work.

From the wider perspective of discourse theory, we regard online journalism as provoking a break in the discursive framework of mainstream journalism, bringing the particularity of its universalist claims to light.[4] In order to theorize such a break, discourse theory uses the concept of dislocation, which points toward the failure of a discursive structure to fully symbolize reality. Even though dislocation is seen by Laclau as an inherent aspect of any discourse, he also uses it in a more specific way to theorize a changed reality or a particular crisis event with which a discourse cannot cope. Confronted with such dislocatory events, a new "plane of inscription" or *myth* is required, which "involves forming a new objectivity by means of the rearticulation of the dislocated elements" (Laclau 1990: 61). In the context of this chapter, the end of high modernism in journalism is a prime example of such a dislocation.

Contested journalism in the era of liquid modernity

The self-evident function of journalism in democratic society is still paramount to journalism's self-understanding. However, journalism's truth claims are strongly contested, partially because increasingly cynical audience members no longer take it for granted and do not want to be told what to think (see, among others, Cappella and Jamieson 1997; Kovach and Rosenstiel 2001; Singer 2003, 2007). Since neither formal training, affiliation to an association, or licensing and agreed-upon ethics are mandatory in the exercise of journalism, it derives its authority mainly from the aforementioned modernist discourse, i.e., its self-justifying logic of public service and ethics, its self-proclaimed autonomy, a monopoly on the management of information and resources, and the ideology of objectivity. However, this is exactly what is being challenged in the era of liquid modernity. The seven nodal points that make up the discourse of mainstream journalism (namely public service, ethics, management, autonomy, membership of a professional elite, immediacy, and objectivity) all share this dislocation, triggered by the end of high modernism in journalism.

The challenge to the notion of public service, and the related gatekeeper role and elitist position in journalism, may be related to the emergence of a "redactional society" (Hartley 2000). In such a society, citizens are expected to possess "journalistic" qualities that help them find their way in an increasingly complex information society rather than depend on expert systems such as journalism. Indicative of this shift in the balance between the elite professional and the passive consumer are practices of *disintermediation* or the bypassing of cultural intermediaries like advertisers and journalists, exemplified by the practices of citizen journalism. Although some prudence is warranted, the possibilities for responsiveness that are a result of the internet's interactive features have also increased, shifting away the emphasis that solidly resided with the medium and the content. Both processes increase audience members' agency (in different degrees), and undermine journalists' privileged position to exclusively provide a public service.

The notion of objectivity, too, becomes subject to dislocation as its indisputability is affected and the way in which it conceals its own genesis is brought to light. News articles can no longer be regarded as self-enclosed narratives that reflect reality. Internal and external contradictions become more apparent, sometimes supported by the activism of news fact-checking organizations and media-watch organizations (e.g., FAIR) and by journalist weblogs that deconstruct the narrations of mainstream media, and in some cases question journalists' autonomy and their ability to resist external and internal pressures. Moreover, j-blogs offer news with different formal characteristics: news is ordered chronologically rather than formally (in descending order of importance); written in a more informal style; and can be reworked according to user's comments (Matheson 2004: 455). Even within traditional news articles, the use of hyperlinks may break open the rigid claims on "truth" and move toward a conception of the audience that is more in line with a "redactional society." Indeed, in offering a range of sources to draw from, "the weblog moderates the traditional claim of news journalism to know, on behalf of readers, what is happening in the world" (Matheson 2004: 455).

In this piecemeal construction of a news event, online mainstream journalism radically breaks with the traditional notion of immediacy in journalism. Whereas traditional journalism has always been deadline-oriented and attached much prestige to covering an event as quickly as possible within the news cycles, in the online environment (and in the

24-hour news television stations) the traditional approach to immediacy has transgressed into an ever-ongoing flux. As a result, the "scoop" logic seems less urgent online. Indeed, some critics have argued that the absence of technical production deadlines for online news means "the story's 'firstness' is of minimal market value in this new media landscape" (Hume 1999, as cited in Matheson 2004: 458). But more importantly, the increased speed puts pressure on the verification procedures to ensure information reliability and source credibility. "[T]he speed with which information is rushed onto the Web, a medium in which deadlines are perpetual and competition is intense, has been cited repeatedly as a problem" (Singer 2003: 152). This increases the likelihood of erroneous reporting, which (when discovered and discussed) further undermines the truth claims of traditional journalism.[5]

Coping strategies in mainstream journalism

Such dislocations that disrupt discursive unity may be regarded as traumatic events that threaten the stability of the identity of the mainstream media professional (Carpentier 2005). Laclau notes that "although the fullness and universality of society is unachievable, its need does not disappear [...]" (Glynos and Stavrakakis 2004: 207). As a result, we may assume that both journalists and the journalistic institution engage in coping strategies that attempt to protect and re-establish the claims of universality, and re-establish their authority as professionals. Of course, in suggesting this, we proceed from the premise that journalists mainly identify with a professional model of work that not only conveys prestige, but also causes trauma. However, one may equally regard journalism as a "mere" trade. From this perspective, journalists may not be confronted with a gap between values and practices. On the other hand, journalists may identify too strongly with the value system of journalism, causing the gap to appear unbridgeable. Such may be the case for the growing number of journalists who leave the job, either through dissatisfaction with the organizational structure or through serious mental issues such as burn-out and depression (Reinardy 2011). Still, in relation to the dislocation produced by online journalism, traditional journalism deploys at least three kinds of coping strategies: marginalization of rivaling media (through the logics of the constitutive outside); normalization of the mainstream online environment; and rearticulation of the nodal points embedded in the mainstream discourse.

A first set of coping strategies aims at marginalizing online media (professionals) with regard to professionalism, ethics, autonomy, and objectivity/accuracy. Testifying to this attitude is the acknowledgment that "scholars and professionals alike use the discourse of the internet's unique characteristics as a way in which to define online journalism as something different to other journalisms—as a fourth kind of journalism" and as "a breed apart" (Deuze 2003: 207). This stance is reminiscent of the logic of the constitutive outside: online journalism is regarded as a threat to the identity of mainstream journalism while at the same time it allows it to constitute this very identity. This is illustrated by the BBC's (initial) stance that "Blogging is not journalism. [...] Without editors to correct syntax, tidy up the story structure or check facts, it is generally impossible to rely on anything one finds in a blog without verifying it somewhere else—often the much-maligned mainstream media" (Thompson 2003 cited in Berry 2008: 15–16).

This strategy is also reminiscent of the critiques that have been launched by mainstream media against alternative media, calling them unprofessional and amateurish (Carpentier et al. 2003). And even as mainstream journalism itself engaged in practices of online journalism such as blogging, it still testified to a similar strategy of marginalization. Initially, it often regarded online journalism as an easy means to generate more profit since it has "consistently offered shoveled, repurposed and windowed content for free, cannibalizing on its core product while treating its Web presence as an advertisement for the offline product" (Deuze 2008: 856). But even as it gained more importance within mainstream journalism, it has remained a constitutive outside (see Jones and Himelboim 2010: 275).

As Singer—quoting Lasica (2001)—shows,

> Perhaps the most persistent criticism of online journalism, and the clearest line traditional journalists have sought to draw between themselves and those working online, has involved [the nodal point of] ethical behavior. There seems to be a generalized, unspoken notion in some newsrooms that online journalism is the gangly, misfit cousin of "real" journalism, that the Internet is a breeding ground for kooks and charlatans, and that perhaps Web journalism operates at a level below the standards of traditional news media.
>
> (Lasica in Singer 2003: 140)

In this manner online journalists are regarded as less professional than journalists working for print news, which disarticulates them from the professional elite (or makes them "lesser" members). Indeed, they are chided for not possessing the same cognitive (and thus professional) skills required to make news, such as deciding on newsworthiness, information gathering, and source checking.

Likewise, online mainstream journalism has been attacked for not being autonomous and for failing to assume a non-partisan attitude. In the j-blog, it is the lack of objective language and a distanced attitude toward the audience that has caused unease and actually led in some cases to journalists being fired (cf. Matheson 2004: 452; Singer 2005: 178). Such events also testify to the problem that "stepping outside that set of [linguistic] conventions risks stepping outside the claim to be able to 'get at the truth'" (Matheson 2004: 446). However, in online journalism it is also fed by critiques on too much immediacy and too strong commercial interests (Singer 2003: 155). Online journalism has similarly been criticized for the problems associated with the notion of immediacy. As noted above, online journalism's speed in getting information across challenged one of mainstream journalism's competencies to which social prestige is accorded. Rushing news on the internet (even more than before) constitutes a process of communal truth-seeking practices that dislocated traditional notions of objectivity, public service, and gatekeeping.

A second set of coping strategies has been to incorporate the online environment. That is, to provide only limited use of the internet's interactive possibilities and to domesticate alternative voices by bringing them into the logics of the mainstream media. Such coping strategies testify to efforts to maintain the ideal of the gatekeeper. As such, it has often been noted that major online news sites offer only limited hyperlinks, especially to other news websites (Hermida 2001: 13; Deuze 2003: 212; Matheson 2004: 454; Oblak 2005; Mitchelstein and Boczkowski 2009: 567). As such, there is an ongoing process of normalization at work in which traditional notions of good journalism are being recuperated in the online world (Singer 2005; Robinson 2006; Vobič 2007). The limited incorporation of online journalism also relates to non-professional online journalism, which in some cases, like for instance the 2003 war reports of the Iraqi blogger Salam Pax (Cammaerts and Carpentier 2009), makes it into the mainstream media. Here, a strategy of containment is used, where the Otherness of the contribution is emphasized by a symbolic detachment from the other (mainstream) material. Similarly, in their "informal" and "personal" aspects, blogs have continued an existing tradition of commentary (e.g., in editorials and opinionated journalism) rather than actually establishing a conversation with the public (Singer 2005: 192).

However, practices of disintermediation have made a more complete hegemonization of traditional journalistic notions impossible. As a result, we witness a third coping strategy in which journalism tries to hold on to its authoritative claims. As indicated above, whenever a discursive structure fails to accommodate the dislocations with which it is confronted, it will rearticulate its signifiers in a structure that offers a new plane of inscription or myth. In light of the present concerns surrounding liquid journalism, journalists protect their claim on the discourse of "good" journalism by partially shifting their competencies away from the dissemination of news. The journalist moves closer toward a new gatekeeper function that is to direct audiences toward "valuable" information and to offer them interpretation of these resources (Steiner 2009: 383). As a result, new mechanisms of distinction come to the fore. Not only has online journalism instituted its own mechanisms of critical acclaim, but increasing value is now attributed to other professional skills such as breadth of knowledge and the use of appropriate links (Matheson 2004: 456). Such a shift of attention testifies to efforts "in finding alternative modes of newswriting that do not unravel [journalism's] power to tell authoritative stories" (Matheson 2004: 456).

One of these alternative modes may be the increasingly subjective tone in news reporting that is evident in the wealth of blogs that are written by journalists who are affiliated to either traditional print news or mainstream online journalism. Indicative as well are the large number of autobiographical writings of journalists in recent decades (Good 1993; Matheson 2003). Such a tendency may be said to constitute a new truth claim in journalism, turning from claims based on objectivity to those based on authenticity. In this, journalism is in tandem with the broad evolution toward a confessional society (Foucault 1998) that is characterized by what Richard Sennett (1986) calls a "tyranny of intimacy." Especially in the weblog and autobiographical writings, journalists exemplify a tendency toward externalizing their innermost feelings. Linking up with the new gatekeeper role, "this more interpretive style serves the desire of journalists to create a public persona as much as anything else" (Kovach and Rosenstiel 2001: 55; cf. Mathiesen 1997: 226). This personal way of engaging with the audience recuperates the journalist as a legitimate truth-speaker in society, and may at the same time allow the journalistic community to re-appropriate an estranged public that they were no longer in touch with (see Capella and Jamieson 1997; Kovach and Rosenstiel 2001).

Dislocatory challenges to the high modernism of journalism

During the era of liquid modernity, the modernist belief in rationality and progress has been deprived of its self-evident character. Indicative of this development is, as Lyotard (1979) has famously put it, the loss of the "grand narratives" in which such belief was expressed. In the wake of such growing skepticism, a range of discourses, among them that of journalism, have seen their legitimacy threatened.

Our rereading of the existing literature on this "crisis" from a discourse-theoretical perspective regards journalism as a discursive-social construction, caught in the dynamics of stability and contingency. As is the case with any discourse, modernist journalistic identity discourses are in principle reasonably stable, but can become confronted with destabilizations that challenge its very nature. These dislocatory challenges are not exclusively situated at the individual or institutional level; they are cultural phenomena that affect these levels but also transcend them. Because of their pervasiveness, they force journalism (more than usual) into practices of identity work and politics, working through these challenges, in part accepting some rearticulations, whilst fiercely rejecting and fighting others. In the specific case of the challenges presented by online journalism, we can see coping strategies that denounce the validity of the rivaling system of online journalism, or that try to incorporate and domesticate it. On the other hand, we can also see coping strategies that shift the traditional journalistic identity more toward an interpretive and subjective position.

In conclusion, we would like to argue for the importance of culturalist perspectives on journalism to provide us with more tools to counter the tendencies of normalizing modernist journalistic identities, and for black-boxing the contingencies that have characterized these identities from their insipience. Many other approaches toward journalism are of course possible, but journalism also needs to be seen as a social-discursive struggle that reaches far beyond the material dimension of individual or institutional practices. These culturalist perspectives, for instance, allow different sets of questions, transforming more traditional—but virtually unanswerable—questions about the death of journalism into questions about the coping strategies of journalism in dealing with a changing context that dislocates its core identities.

References

Bauman, Zygmunt (2000), *Liquid Modernity*, Cambridge, MA: Polity Press.

Bell, Allan (1991), *The Language of News Media*, Oxford: Blackwell.

Belsey, Andrew and Chadwick, Ruth (1992), "Ethics and politics of the media: The quest for quality," in A. Belsey and R. Chadwick (eds), *Ethical Issues in Journalism and the Media*, London: Routledge, pp. 1–11.

Bennett, Lance W., Gressett, Lynne A., and Haltom, William (1985), "Repairing the news: A case study of the news paradigm," *Journal of Communication*, 35:2, pp. 50–68.

Benson, Rodney and Neveu, Erik (eds) (2005), *Bourdieu and the Journalistic Field*, Cambridge, MA: Polity.

Berry, David (2008), *Journalism, Ethics and Society*, Farnham: Ashgate Publishers.

Broddason, Thorbjörn (1994), "The sacred side of professional journalism," *European Journal of Communication*, 9:3, pp. 227–48.

Burns, Tom (1969), "Public service and private world," in P. Halmos (ed.), *The Sociology of Mass Communications*, Sociological Review Monograph, 13, pp. 53–73.

Broersma, Marcel (2010), "The unbearable limitations of journalism: On press critique and journalism's claim to truth," *International Communication Gazette*, 72:1, pp. 21–33.

Cammaerts, Bart and Carpentier, Nico (2009), "Blogging the 2003 Iraq war: Challenging the ideological model of war and mainstream journalism?," *OBS**, 3:2, pp. 1–23, http://obs.obercom.pt/index.php/obs/article/view/276. Accessed 8 November 2009.

Cappella, Joseph N. and Jamieson, Kathleen H. (1997), *Spiral of Cynicism: The Press and the Public Good*, Oxford: Oxford University Press.

Carpentier, Nico (2005), "Identity, contingency and rigidity: The (counter-)hegemonic constructions of the identity of the media professional," *Journalism*, 6:2, pp. 199–219.

Carpentier, Nico, Lie, Rico, and Servaes, Jan (2003), "Community media: Muting the democratic media discourse?," *Continuum*, 17:1, pp. 51–68.

Carpentier, Nico and Spinoy, Erik (eds) (2008), *Discourse Theory and Cultural Analysis: Media, Arts, and Literature*, Cresskill: Hampton Press.

Champagne, Patrick (2009), "The 'double dependency': The journalistic field between politics and markets," in R. Benson and E. Neveu (eds), *Bourdieu and the Journalistic Field*, Cambridge, MA: Polity, pp. 29–47.

Clayman, Steven E. (2002), "Tribune of the people: Maintaining the legitimacy of aggressive journalism," *Media, Culture and Society*, 24:2, pp. 197–216.

Deuze, Marc (2003), "The web and its journalisms: Considering the consequences of different types of news media online," *New Media & Society*, 5:2, pp. 203–30.

—— (2005), "What is journalism? Professional identity and ideology of journalists reconsidered," *Journalism*, 6:4, pp. 442–64.

—— (2006a), "Liquid and zombie journalism studies," Journalism Studies Interest Group, http://www.icahdq.org/divisions/JournalismStudies/jsigweb4/newsletterS06/debatedeuzefull.html. Accessed 8 November 2009.

—— (2006b), "Liquid journalism," *International Communication Association & American Political Science Association*, 16:1, http://frank.mtsu.edu/~pcr/1601_2005_winter/roundtable_Deuze.htm. Accessed 8 November 2009.

——— (2008), "The changing context of news work: Liquid journalism and monitorial citizenship," *International Journal of Communication*, 2, pp. 848–65.

Foucault, Michel (1998), *The History of Sexuality: The Will to Knowledge*, London, Penguin.

Frost, Chris (2007), *Journalism Ethics and Regulation*, Harlow: Pearson.

Glynos, Jason and Stavrakakis, Yannis (2004), "Encounters of the real kind: Sussing out the limits of Laclau's embrace of Lacan," in S. Critchley and O. Marchart (eds), *Laclau: A Critical Reader*, London: Routledge, pp. 201–16.

Good, Howard (1993), *The Journalist as Autobiographer*, Metuchen: Scarecrow Press.

Hall, Stuart (1989), "New ethnicities," in K. Mercer (ed.), *Black Film, British Cinema*, London: BFI, pp. 27–31.

Hallin, Daniel (1992), "The passing of the 'high modernism' of American journalism," *Journal of Communication*, 42:3, pp. 14–25.

——— (2006), "The passing of the 'high modernism' of American journalism revisited," *Political Communication Report, International Communication Association & American Political Science Association*, 16:1, http://frank.mtsu.edu/~pcr/1601_2005_winter/commentary_ hallin.htm. Accessed 21 August 2011.

——— (2009), "Not the end of journalism history," *Journalism*, 10:3, pp. 332–34.

Hartley, John (2000), "Communicational democracy in a redactional society: The future of journalism studies," *Journalism Theory Practice & Criticism*, 1:1, pp. 39–47.

Hermida, Alfred (2001), "The BBC goes blogging: Is 'auntie' finally listening?," *9th International Online Journalism Symposium*, http://online.journalism.utexas.edu/2008/papers/Hermida. pdf. Accessed 5 November 2009.

Hiler, John (2001), "Borg journalism: We are the blogs. Journalism will be assimilated," *Microcontentent News*, 1 April, http://www.microcontentnews.com/articles/borgjournalism. htm. Accessed 5 November 2009.

Hume, Ellen (1999), "Wired world, wired learning: The serf surfs," *Net-Media Conference*, London, 1 July, http://www.ellenhume.com/articles/serfsurfs_printable.html. Accessed 8 November 2009.

Hutchins, Robert M. (1947), *Commission on the Freedom of the Press: A Free and Responsible Press*, Chicago: University of Chicago Press.

Jones, Jeffrey P. (2009), "Believable fictions: Redactional culture and the will to truthiness," in B. Zelizer (ed.), *The Changing Faces of Journalism: Tabloidization, Technology and Truthiness*, New York: Routledge, pp. 127–43.

Jones, Julie and Himelboim, Itai (2010), "Just a guy in pajamas? Framing the blogs in mainstream US Newspaper coverage (1999–2005)," *New Media & Society*, 12:2, pp. 271–88.

Kovach, Bill and Rosenstiel, Tom (2001), *The Elements of Journalism: What Newspeople Should Know and the Public Should Expect*, New York: Crown Publishers.

Krotz, Friedrich (2007), "The meta-process of 'mediatization' as a conceptual frame," *Global Media and Communication*, 3:3, pp. 256–60.

Laclau, Ernesto (1988), "Metaphor and social antagonisms," in C. Nelson and L. Grossberg (eds), *Marxism and the Interpretation of Culture*, Urbana: University of Illinois Press, pp. 249–57.

——— (1990), *New Reflections on the Revolution of our Time*, London: Verso.

—— (2000), "Constructing universality," in J. Butler, E. Laclau, and S. Žižek (eds), *Contingency, Hegemony, Universality: Contemporary Dialogues on the Left*, London: Verso, pp. 281–307.

Laclau, Ernesto and Mouffe, Chantal (1985), *Hegemony and Socialist Strategy: Towards a Radical Democratic Politics*, London: Verso.

Lasica, Joseph D. (2001), "A scorecard for net news ethics," *Online Journalism Review*, 20 September, http://www.ojr.org/ojr/ethics/1017782140.php. Accessed 8 November 2009.

Lule, Jack (1992), "Journalism and criticism: *The Philadelphia Inquirer* Norplant editorial," *Critical Studies in Mass Communication*, 9, pp. 91–109.

Lyotard, Jacques (1979), *La Condition Postmoderne: Rapport sur le Savoir*, Paris: Minuit.

Matheson, Donald (2003), "Scowling at their notebooks: How journalists understand their writing," *Journalism*, 42:2, pp. 165–83.

—— (2004), "Weblogs and the epistemology of the news: Some trends in online journalism," *New Media and Society*, 6:4, pp. 443–68.

Mathiesen, Thomas (1997), "The viewer society: Michel Foucault's 'Panopticon' revisited," *Theoretical Criminology*, 1:2, pp. 215–34.

McNair, Brian (1998), *The Sociology of Journalism*, London, New York, Sydney, and Auckland: Arnold.

McQuail, Denis (1994), *Mass Communication Theory: An Introduction*, London: Sage.

Merrill, John C. (1974), *The Imperative of Freedom: A Philosophy of Journalistic Autonomy*, New York: Hastings House.

Mindich, David (1998), *Just the Facts: How "Objectivity" Came to Define American Journalism*, New York: New York University Press.

Mitchelstein, Eugenia and Boczkowski, Pablo J. (2009), "Between tradition and change: A review of recent research on online news production," *Journalism*, 10:5, pp. 562–68.

Naït-Bouda, Faïza (2008), "From identity to identity strategies: The French pigiste group identity as an exemplary case study," in N. Carpentier, P. Pruulmann-Vengerfeldt, K. Nordenstreng, M. Hartmann, P. Vihalemm, B. Cammaerts, H. Nieminen, and T. Olsson (eds), *Democracy, Journalism and Technology: New Developments in an Enlarged Europe,* Tartu: Tartu University Press, pp. 84–96, http://www.researchingcommunication.eu/reco_book4.pdf. Accessed 8 November 2009.

Oblak, Tanja (2005), "The lack of interactivity and hypertextuality in online media," *Gazette: The International Journal for Communication Studies*, 67:1, pp. 87–106.

Ognianova, Ekaterina and Endersby, James (1996), "Objectivity revisited: A spatial model of political ideology and mass communication," *Journalism and Mass Communication Monographs*, 159, pp. 1–36.

Pöttker, Horst (2004), "Objectivity as (self-)censorship: Against the dogmatization of professional ethics in journalism," *Javnost—The Public*, 11:2, pp. 83–94.

Reese, Stephen D. (1990), "The news paradigm and the ideology of objectivity: A socialist at the *Wall Street Journal*," *Critical Studies in Mass Communication*, 7:4, pp. 390–409.

Reger, Jo, Myers, Daniel J., and Einwohner, Rachel L. (eds) (2008), *Identity Work in Social Movements*, Minneapolis: University of Minnesota Press.

Reinardy, Scott (2007), "Newspaper journalism in crisis: Burnout on the rise, eroding young journalists' career commitment," *Journalism,* 12:1, pp. 33–50.

Robinson, Susan (2006), "The mission of the J-blog: Recapturing journalistic authority online," *Journalism*, 64:7, pp. 65–83.

Schlesinger, Philip (1987), *Putting "Reality" Together*, London and New York: Methuen.

Schudson, Michael (1978), *Discovering the News: A Social History of American Newspapers*, New York: Basic Books.

—— (2001), "The objectivity norm in American journalism," *Journalism*, 2:2, pp. 149–70.

Sennett, Richard (1986), *The Fall of Public Man*, London: Faber and Faber.

Siebert, Fred, Peterson, Theodore, and Schramm, Wilhelm (1956), *Four Theories of the Press*, Urbana: University of Illinois Press.

Singer, Jane B. (2003), "Who are these guys? The online challenge to the notion of journalistic professionalism," *Journalism*, 4:2, pp. 139–63.

—— (2005), "The political J-blogger 'normalizing' a new media form to fit old norms and practices," *Journalism*, 6:2, pp. 173–98.

—— (2007), "Contested autonomy: Professional and popular claims on journalistic norms," *Journalism Studies*, 8:1, pp. 79–95.

Soloski, John (1990), "News reporting and professionalism: Some constraints on the reporting of the news," *Media, Culture & Society*, 11:4, pp. 207–28.

Steiner, Linda (2009), "Disambiguating the 'media' and the 'media plot'," *Journalism*, 10:3, pp. 381–83.

Thompson, Bill (2003), "Is Google too powerful?," BBC News, 21 February, http://news.bbc.co.uk/1/hi/technology/2786761.stm. Accessed 8 November 2009.

Torfing, Jakob (1999), *New Theories of Discourse: Laclau, Mouffe and Žižek*, Oxford: Blackwell.

Tuchman, Gaye (1971), "Objectivity as strategic ritual: An examination of newsmen's notions of objectivity," *American Journal of Sociology*, 77:4, pp. 660–79.

—— (1978), *Making News*, New York: The Free Press.

Vobič, Igor (2007), "The normalization of the blog in journalism: Online newspapers of Slovene traditional media," *Medij.Istraž*, 13:2, pp. 59–83.

Walker, Rob (2001), "The news according to blogs," *Slate*, 7 March, http://www.slate.com/id/102057/. Accessed 8 November 2009.

Weaver, Donald H. and Wilhoit, Cleveland G. (1996), *The American Journalist in the 1990s: US News People at the End of an Era*, Mahwah: Erlbaum.

Westerståhl, Jörgen (1983), "Objective news reporting," *Communication Research*, 10, pp. 403–24.

Zelizer, Barbie (1993a), "Has communication explained journalism?," *Journal of Communication*, 43:4, pp. 80–88.

—— (1993b), "Journalists as interpretive communities," *Critical Studies in Mass Communication*, 3:10, pp. 219–37.

—— (2004), "When facts, truth and reality are God-terms: On journalism's uneasy place in cultural studies," *Communication and Critical/Cultural Studies*, 1:1, pp. 100–19.

Notes

1 The concept of "high modernism" generally subsumes the thought, practices, and cultural forms (thus also journalism) of modernity (the era encompassing the nineteenth and the

first half of the twentieth century) that are broadly characterized by a conviction in progress, an inclination toward rationality and bureaucratization and a lack of reflexive criticism. High modernism is not to be confused with high modernity, which is used to indicate the period that starts, broadly speaking, at the second half of the twentieth century, and which radically breaks with the assumptions of modernity.

2 "Liquid modernity" is one among a number of concepts such as "postmodernity" and "late modernity" that designate (despite conceptual and temporal differences) the turn to "reflexive modernization," i.e., a tendency in the process of modernity to become self-referring, testifying to a loss of the self-evident convictions of the preceding era and the growing doubts and critiques against the latter's assumptions. This goes hand in hand with a number of transformations in the economic, social, and political field and reflects the disintegration of modernist institutions (one of which is journalism).

3 Even though "technological change has long been identified as promoting professionalization in modern society" (Singer 2003: 143), in journalism the most recent changes in technology seem to have the opposite effect.

4 Arguably, there are other dislocations within journalism. One other example is the dislocation caused by the economic-financial pressure on journalists.

5 Even though online mainstream journalism may dislocate traditional notions of journalism because of its use of time, this may at the same time challenge the hegemony of print over online journalism. After all, it may severely undermine traditional media's ability to gain prestige from "scoop news" since online journalism may record events faster than traditional media such as news agencies and television networks (Walker 2001), and even do so in more depth than traditional media (Hiler 2001).

Chapter 7

The Particularity of Objectivity: A Poststructuralist and Psychoanalytical Reading of the Gap between Objectivity-as-a-Value and Objectivity-as-a-Practice in the 2003 Iraqi War Coverage

Nico Carpentier and Marit Trioen

Introduction

The coverage of the 2003 Iraq War has been problematized by both journalists and academics (e.g., Thussu and Freedman 2005), criticizing the (mainstream) media for having played "a different, much more ambiguous and ambivalent role than hitherto" (Webster [2003] 2005: 57). As the war coverage is intrinsically part of the conflict itself through its presumed impact on society (Tumber and Palmer [2004] 2006: 1), many of these critiques pay attention to the question of objectivity in wartime coverage. Despite the political and legal state of exception (see also Agamben 2005) that war sometimes generates—also for journalists—objectivity remained articulated as a value under threat. And again, as was the case during and after past conflicts, we could hear that the war coverage (the 2003 Iraq War in this case) signaled the loss of journalistic independence and objectivity (Lewis 2004: 302).

However characteristic this claim of "objectivity lost" may be, it does not reduce the problematic nature of the objectivity concept, since this claim overlooks two crucial theoretical and methodological considerations. First, the notion of "objectivity lost" implicitly assumes that an objective coverage is possible, which tends to reduce the highly complex nature of the concept of objectivity to a one-dimensional concept. Second, both war coverage and journalistic objectivity are approached from an exclusively external point of view, thus ignoring the journalists' perspective.

In highlighting the complex nature of media coverage in general and of wartime coverage in particular and in integrating the voices of war journalists themselves, this chapter explicitly aims to contribute to the academic debates on objectivity by using a somewhat innovative and unusual point of view. To do this, the objectivity norm within journalistic professionalism will be conceptualized by relating it to Ernesto Laclau's discussion on universalism and particularism, and by connecting it to the theoretical reflections on the concepts of desire and fantasy of the French psychoanalyst Jacques Lacan. Through these reflections, the irreducible gap between objectivity-as-a-value and objectivity-as-a-practice can be theorized, arguing that this gap between concept and practice is constitutive for the journalistic identity.

In the second part of this chapter, we bring the journalists' voices into our discussion on objectivity, by analyzing the ego-documents of one North Belgian and two Dutch Iraq War journalists. Writing for and broadcasting to a North Belgian and Dutch audience, these journalists found themselves in a specific (political) context, as a major part of both populations and the Belgian government strongly opposed the war.[1] But, as argued elsewhere, this specific context did not prevent these journalists from still having severe problems avoiding the ideological model of war (Carpentier 2005a), given the Belgian and Dutch cultural, political, and journalistic affinities with the Anglo-Saxon world. Neither did it prevent the debates about the loss of journalistic independence and objectivity from occurring in Belgium and the Netherlands.

The combination of both theoretical frameworks mentioned above is used to analyze how these three journalists deal with the gap between objectivity-as-a-value and objectivity-as-a-practice. Our analysis shows that these three (highly critical) journalists use a variety of strategies to deal with their gap, but never manage to completely escape either from their gap or from the hegemonic discourse of objectivity.

The discourse of rigidity: The traditional conceptualization of objectivity and its critics

Finding its origins in the aim of journalists to differentiate their "truth-seeking" practices from the "truth-distorting" practices of publicity agents, the very notion of objectivity can be considered as the "cornerstone" (Deuze 2005: 448; Lichtenberg 2005: 216) or even "emblem" (Hackett 1984: 229) of journalism in many western liberal democracies for most of the twentieth and twenty-first centuries. A commonly accepted definition of objectivity that approaches this particular norm as an organizing concept in the newsroom, in the management of media organizations, in media policies, and in media studies is to be found in Schudson (2001: 150):

> The objectivity norm guides journalists to separate facts from values and to report only the facts. Objective reporting is supposed to be cool, rather than emotional, in tone. Objective reporting takes pains to represent fairly each leading side in a political controversy. According to the objectivity norm, the journalist's job consists of reporting something called "news" without commenting on it, slanting it, or shaping its formulation in any way.

This traditional, essentialized, and universalized[2] conceptualization of objectivity positions journalists as "society's truthtellers" (McNair 1998: 71), supposing that their particular practices are "neutral, unbiased, and balanced, and void of personal ideology, and impressions" (Fox and Park 2006: 37). This traditional discourse on objectivity, however, has also been heavily criticized. As it is argued by many of its critics, the exact underlying premises of this conceptualization should be questioned, inevitably leading to a deconstruction of the taken-for-grantedness of the traditional discourse. According to this critical discourse, not only the self-proclaimed objective journalist but also the traditional bias critic accepts the premise that there is an objective reality out there and that a "zero-degree unbiased or objective account" of this reality is possible (Hackett 1984: 232).

In general, two arguments are used to problematize the articulation of the objectivity concept in the traditional discourse, as well as its premises. First, these objectivity critics have pointed to the problems related with realist and empiricist thought. Reality cannot be considered as "simply a given set of facts" (Hackett 1984: 236) that can be objectively represented. To use a Lacanian phrase: the Real is inaccessible. The second argument follows from the first one, as every single journalist, far from being a "detached chronicler" or a neutral "stenographer"(Ward 1999: 7), inevitably interprets the world by turning it into news. A logical conclusion that results from this critical perspective is that the traditional conceptualization of journalistic objectivity as the "impersonal gathering and reporting of information"(Fox and Park 2006: 38) can no longer be accepted. A less self-evident conclusion that is drawn remarkably frequently in this critical discourse on journalistic objectivity is that this (meta)theoretical deconstruction of the traditional approach is followed by "a call to scrap objectivity" per se, rather than by a motivation to "search for a better way of thinking about it" (Cunningham 2003: 26).

However fundamental and legitimate the critiques may be, both those who claim that "journalism *isn't* objective" or that journalism "*cannot* be objective" and those who argue that journalism "*shouldn't* be objective" (Lichtenberg 2005: 216, emphasis in original) generally underestimate a crucial part of the discussion. Their conceptualization of objectivity as an absolute standard (whether or not legitimate) intrinsically fails to make the distinction between the particularity and the conditions of possibility of the objectivity norm within journalistic ideology on the one hand, and a more concrete exploration of objectivity as embedded in journalistic practices on the other. Exactly this distinction deserves further consideration.

The dynamics of objectivity: A two-dimensional conceptualization

Rather than turning objectivity into an absolute and compelling norm concerning journalistic ideology and everyday practice, a conceptualization that distinguishes between "norms as prescriptive rules" on the one hand, and "norms as prevalent practices" on the other seems more appropriate (Schudson 2001: 151). Similarly, Tumber and Prentoulis ([2003] 2005: 216) argue for a conceptualization that treats objectivity in two different ways: "as a theoretical imperative underpinning reporting and as a strategic ritual enabling the defense of the practice as a profession" (Tuchman, 1972). In the first perspective, objectivity is conceptualized from a meta-theoretical point of view: it explores the meaning and the possibilities of the notion of objectivity within journalistic theory. The second perspective tries to grasp the meaning of objectivity when it is actually practiced in everyday journalistic life. One way to further theorize this distinction and the relationship between these two perspectives, and between objectivity-as-a-value and objectivity-as-a-practice, is to use Ernesto Laclau's (1996, 2000a, 2000b, 2005) discussion on universality and particularity. This allows us first to show the complex dialectics between the universal and the particular that is embedded within objectivity-as-a-value, deconstructing the universalization of objectivity without having to abandon the(se) notion(s). Second, this also allows us to add the unavoidable particularity of objectivity-as-a-practice to the equation.

Laclau's conceptualization of universality and particularity

By pointing to the need for a "redefinition of the existing relation between universality and particularity," Laclau (1996: vii–viii) reacts against the definition of universality and particularity as two "extreme positions." According to Laclau (2000b: 301–02) this polarization should be rejected, since universalism and particularism "are not two opposed notions, but have to be conceived [...] as the two different moves ('universalizing' and 'particularizing') which shape a hegemonic, articulating totality." According to Laclau (2000a: 56) his relationship is a dynamic process where "the universal and the particular reject each other but nevertheless require each other."

For Laclau, the universal is an empty signifier (2000b: 304), which does not imply that it does not exist. On the contrary, the very emptiness of the signifier of the universal always requires a particular, so that this particular can be universalized in order to (attempt to) saturate the universal. The universal thus cannot exist without the particular: "Now, this universality needs—for its expression—to be incarnated in something essentially incommensurable with it: a particularity" (Laclau 1996: 57). This relationship between the universal and the particular, however, is unstable and undecidable, since the way the universal and the particular relate to each other is "in the strict sense of the term, a hegemonic operation" and thus necessarily depends on a specific context (Laclau 1996: 14–15), which is susceptible to change.

But how is this hegemonic "passage [of the universal] through the particular" (Laclau 2000a: 55) to be realized? The answer lies in Laclau's argument that "the only possible universality is the one constructed through an equivalential chain of particularities" (2000b: 304). In such an equivalential chain different particular elements are articulated together, being positioned against a constitutive outside. The importance of this constitutive outside for the construction of (hegemonic) identities cannot be overestimated in Laclau's thinking, as the following argument shows: "But the whole model depends on the presence of the dichotomic frontier: without this, the equivalential relation would collapse and the identity of each demand would be exhausted in its differential particularity" (Laclau 2005: 131).

Hegemony at work: The particularity of objectivity as a universalized value

When we look at the discussion on journalistic objectivity through Laclau's conceptualization of universality and particularity, we can first focus on objectivity as an ideological construct and stress its particularity at the level of the ideological. The much-cherished value of objectivity can be considered as what Laclau (1996: 57) labels one of these "so-called 'universal' principles." Objectivity, as one of journalism's main values that structures the journalistic identity, often seems even "inevitable" within contemporary journalism (Lichtenberg 2005: 229). Together with other universalized journalistic values, for instance membership of a professional elite, entitlement to resource management, autonomy, public service, immediacy, and ethics (Carpentier 2005b; Deuze 2005: 447), objectivity can be said to belong to an equivalential chain, which constitutes the content of the signifier good journalism. As should be acknowledged, however, objectivity takes a special place within this chain, since it is exactly on the basis of its pervasive and self-evident character that "objective journalism" has often even been uplifted to a condition of possibility and a quasi-synonym for "good journalism." From this point of view, objectivity is to be considered as what Laclau and Mouffe (1985: 112) call a nodal point: a privileged signifier that stabilizes the meaning of an equivalential chain in a given time and context. However, journalism's intense "honeymoon with objectivity" (Cunningham 2003: 26), which hegemonizes and universalizes objectivity, often successfully hides that objectivity is, like *any* value, an essentially *particular* value that acquires its meaning in relation to other particular values. And although all components of the equivalential chain are universalized as the values that lie at the heart of what journalism is, can be, and should be, they too remain *particular* in nature.

Alternatively, "good journalism" can also be considered as an empty signifier.[3] One cannot define what "good" (mainstream) journalism is, without referring to other possible forms of journalism that promote oppositional values that are systematically excluded as "bad," "undesirable," or "unwanted." The presence of such rejected forms of journalism acts as a constitutive outside, which forms an absolute condition for the identity of "good" journalism (and journalists), since it is exactly what Laclau (1996: 41) calls the "opposition to a common enemy" that makes the equivalential relation and the construction of "good journalism" possible. Here, different mechanisms construct the otherness of these "rejected" journalisms as constitutive outsides. First, the alternative and counter-hegemonic ideologies that attempt to rearticulate the dominant journalistic models are sometimes harshly contested and become constitutive outsides, as has for instance been the case with the Marxist–Leninist model (Carpentier 2005b: 201). Second, spatial differences play a key role in constructing otherness, as the articulations of "good" (mainstream) journalism is structured through place-based imaginary journalistic communities.[4] Despite (the traces of) the existence of a dominant global journalistic ideology, national and local differences (Deuze 2005; Wasserman and Rao 2008) still not only affect the articulation of "good journalism," but also construct constitutive outsides for these localized versions. Similarly, time also constructs difference. Journalistic identities, and their nodal points like objectivity, cannot be seen as stable over time. This of course includes the Anglo-Saxon notion of objectivity, which can be contrasted to nineteenth-century notions of partisanship. These evolutions of the journalistic profession and its identities again allow the construction of a constitutive outside, this time in the past and often embedded in a discourse of progress.

These other models, as well as the particular values that constitute them, are not necessarily "bad," but rather are considered as unacceptable in a given ideological, temporal, and spatial context. In this process of dominance and exclusion we can see the hegemonic operation at work: one possible model of journalism, i.e., "good" journalism with objectivity as its cornerstone and nodal point, is universalized and essentialized as the only natural and acceptable form of journalism. This subjection to a hegemonic articulation thus fixes the meaning of contemporary journalism as "objective journalism," which presents itself as a self-evident social horizon or frame of reference and which consequently pushes alternative (or even counter-hegemonic) models with their particular values to the background.

The claim of objectivity: The particularity of objectivity as a practice

Although Laclau's thought tends to focus on ideological constructs, his approach to universalism and particularism nevertheless also proves to be helpful in looking at objectivity as a practice, and in focusing on the particularity that is generated through the practice of journalism. The signifier objectivity is not only particular (but hegemonized) at the ideological level, but also needs to be turned into practice, thus adding a second layer to its particularity. Despite its pervasiveness, the "objectivity norm" cannot be disconnected from the particular journalistic practices that together constitute its meaning within journalism. Thus, the meaning of objectivity within journalism is fixed in a given context through a specific hegemonic articulation, but simultaneously and continuously requires to be translated into everyday journalistic practices, which in turn co-determine its articulation.

Objectivity is an ideological construct that aims to structure and govern specific journalistic practices through a number of procedures that support the "claim of objectivity" (Tumber and Prentoulis [2003] 2005: 216) and assist in the classification of these practices into "good" and "bad" practices. But as representation is a necessary condition to capture reality, but never coincides with the Real, the ideological construct of objectivity can never be fully captured by these practices. These practices will always evade and escape the ideological lure of the concept of objectivity, as it is exactly "the act of reporting" itself that "places limitations […] on the ability to report the whole known truth" (Tumber and Prentoulis [2003] 2005: 216).

The tension between the objectivity concept and its concrete realization in journalistic practice thus generates another paradox, which is implicit in the nature of journalistic professionalism and gives evidence of both the necessity and the impossibility of this very concept. On the one hand, journalistic practice needs this very horizon of objectivity, for it provides the journalistic identity with coherence and meaning in offering it a frame of reference. On the other hand, the meaning of objectivity does not coincide with these very practices. As a consequence, every single journalistic practice is to be considered as an imperfect one, since it necessarily fails in its claim to reach objectivity.

Within its everyday practices, we see journalism thus confronted with an unfillable gap between what journalists *want* to do on the one side and what they actually *do* on the other.

Lacan's theoretical reflections on desire and fantasy: The *objet petit a* as the driving force of subjectivity

Despite the usefulness of Laclau's conceptualization of universality and particularity in order to further our understanding of the complex relationship between objectivity-as-a-value and objectivity-as-a-practice, it leaves one fundamental question open. As the journalistic profession can indeed be said to have developed specific procedures that unavoidably fail in their purpose, one might wonder how journalists actually deal with this tension between their much-cherished value system, its ideological particularity, and the always imperfect particular practices.

In the work of Jacques Lacan,[5] we can (despite the embedded essentialisms) find a ground for the reconceptualization of this journalistic gap as a positive rather than a negative notion. In Lacanian psychoanalytical theory, the concept of desire takes a central place since it is considered as the organizing principle of subjectivity ([1964] 1979: 107). What defines the Lacanian subject is exactly its relation to what it is missing, which Lacan denotes as the *objet petit a*. This *objet petit a* is seen as the solely possible object of desire, but it can never be concretized ([1972–73] 1999: 94).

Crucial to fully grasp Lacan's argument is that the *objet petit a* cannot be considered as the object of desire, but instead needs to be seen as the object that generates desire, which is the very cause of desire ([1960–61] 1991). This is evidenced by the fact that the *objet petit a* is at the same time denoted as the object-cause of desire in Lacanian psychoanalytic theory. Desire is in Lacanian thought consequently conceptualized not as a relation to an object, but as a relation to a lack. What causes the desire is exactly the lack that lies at the core of all subjectivity (Kirshner 2005: 83; Lacan [1960–61] 1991: 139). Since the *objet petit a* cannot be reached or grasped, the lack can never be filled and desire is consequentially unsatisfiable. Desire, as the "lack of being whereby the being exists" (Lacan [1954–55] 1988: 223), is thus not to be considered as an eternal experience of frustrating powerlessness, but as an endless unconscious driving force.

Objectivity as journalism's *objet petit a:* In search of the gap

It is exactly the reversal of the relation in Lacanian psychoanalysis between desire on the one side and the constitutive lack on the other that offers us a framework to theorize how journalists may come to terms with the unfillable gap resulting from the tensions between ideology and practice. As our discussion of universalism and particularism has shown that the value of objectivity cannot be realized outside everyday journalistic practice, and that objective reporting remains an unattainable horizon, objectivity can be conceptualized as the *objet petit a* of the journalistic identity.

This approach to everyday journalistic practice as a continuous striving process is not new (e.g., Deuze 2005). The added value of our conceptualization of objectivity from a Lacanian point of view lies in the recognition of the *objet petit a* (or the object-cause of desire) as the motor of the desire for objectivity. What is crucial with regard to our understanding of everyday journalistic practice is thus that the approximation of objectivity is not to be considered the ultimate endpoint of the journalistic striving process, but that the unattainability of objectivity is a point of departure, which is constitutive for the journalistic identity. As Stavrakakis (1999: 35) argues, it is exactly the "irreducible character of this lack which in turn reinforces our attempts to fill it." The gap remains, but what counts is that it is a crucial, positive, and constitutive one that generates meaning and identity. From this point of view, objectivity (and its failure) may be thought of as an ultimate mainspring for everyday journalistic practice and identity, rather than of an ultimate goal.

However, this is not to say that the existence of the gap is unambiguously accepted or recognized in journalistic culture. Although the Real (i.e., objectivity) in Lacanian theory can never be reached and the subject remains locked in the symbolic, it never stops searching for "what was lost for him, the subject, the moment he entered into this discourse" (Lacan [1958] 1977: 16), in order to cover the constitutive lack. And it is here that Lacan's concept of fantasy comes into play. In Lacanian psychoanalytic theory, fantasy is conceptualized as having (amongst others) a *protective* function ([1964] 1979: 41). In providing the subject with (imaginary) frames that attempt to conceal and finally to overcome the lack (Lacan [1956–57] 1994: 119–20), fantasy functions as "the support that gives consistency to what we call 'reality'" (Žižek [1989] 1995): 44). Translated into our conceptualization of journalistic objectivity, the positions of journalists toward the traditional model of objectivity can be seen as unconscious fantasmatic constructions, which also implies the negation of the gap. In attempting to provide journalistic objectivity with an (illusionary) anchor in the Real, these journalistic ideologies and practices cover their fantasmatic nature, for instance by fiercely defending the traditional model of objectivity.

Of course, the negation of the gap does not solve the problem. Since the fantasmatic repression of the gap sustained by the traditional model of objectivity simultaneously and necessarily collides with the particularity of journalistic practices—but also with the particularity of the hegemonized journalistic ideologies—the universalized model is permanently affected with fissures and ruptures. This "encounter with the real," as Lacan ([1964] 1979: 53) would call such a confrontation, in turn unavoidably generates problems for journalists that adhere to the universalized model of objectivity, leading to frustration and sometimes to an embracing of the critical (one-dimensional) discourse of bias, which articulates objectivity as a potentially still attainable goal to which access is blocked by a series of practical problems. Here the notion of castration anxiety becomes useful. Translated into our discussion on objectivity, this anxiety could be seen as a symbolic fear of losing the sense of wholeness and the semblance of harmony provided by the universalized model of objectivity, and the threat of becoming the "other" journalist outside the hegemonic model and the ideal-typical journalistic identity it produces.

Nevertheless, it is a mistake to make absolute the search for wholeness and harmony, as the possibility of recognizing the irreducibility of the gap, as well as its constitutive nature, is always present. Some journalists are indeed very conscious about the gap, and a number of them have attempted to bring the (existence of the) gap into the realm of the public (or on the plane of the conscious). This transgression leads in many cases to antagonistic reactions and social sanctions to protect the universalized model of objectivity, and to avoid the symbolic castration that abandoning it might generate. Furthermore, care should also be taken not to dichotomize the journalist profession into believers and non-believers in the attainability of objectivity. As our analysis also shows, the relationship of journalists with their *objet petit a* is highly complex and contains sometimes overlapping and contradictory positions.

The case of the 2003 Iraq War

Our particular choice for war journalists is motivated by the increase in visibility of the practices and ideologies that lie at the root of media coverage, as wartime "highlights and intensifies many of the things that happen in peacetime" (Williams 1992: 158). The extreme nature of wartime makes the tensions between ideology and practices all the more tangible, as it stretches the particular practices of journalists, and the representations they produce, to their limits (see also Cammaerts and Carpentier 2006: 159–61). War also affects the war journalists themselves who are confronted with the hegemonizing strategies of propaganda, military censorship, and commerce (Tumber and Prentoulis 2005: 221), together with the impact of the ideological model of war (Carpentier 2007) and the institution of war (Knightley 1982) on their work.

The qualitative analysis of the ego-documents of one North Belgian and two Dutch "unilateral" journalists and/or correspondents, published in the aftermath of the 2003 Iraq War, provides us also with the opportunity to combine the theoretical reflections about objectivity with the voices of the journalists themselves. All three journalists have over time worked for different types of media, and combined positions as field and home reporters (which often happens in small countries). Arnold Karskens is a Dutch journalist who worked for the Dutch magazine *Nieuwe Revu* (2005–08) and then moved to the free newspaper *De Pers*. He also works as a freelancer for various radio programs and talk shows on different Dutch channels. He published in 2003, in Dutch, the book *Our Man in Baghdad: Journal of a Wartime Correspondent* about his coverage of the Iraq War for the Dutch and Belgian radio and television news from within Baghdad. The second Dutch journalist is Joris Luyendijk. He worked between 1998 and 2003 as a foreign correspondent in the Middle East, first for the Dutch newspaper *De Volkskrant* and for the Dutch *Radio 1*; later also for the newspaper *NRC Handelsblad* and the public broadcaster *NOS*. In 2006, he published *They're Just like*

Human Beings: Images from the Middle East, narrating his work as a correspondent in several Arab countries, including the coverage of the 2003 Iraq War. Finally, the North Belgian public broadcasting journalist Rudi Vranckx published *No News from the Front: Memories of the Wars in the Middle East* in 2003, about his time as a correspondent in the Middle East between 1990 and 2003. Although some of their books cover other conflict arenas (such as the Israeli–Palestinian conflict), Karskens, Luyendijk, and Vranckx are the only three Dutch-speaking journalists (working in Belgium and in the Netherlands) who covered the 2003 Iraq War as "unilaterals" and published an ego-document about their time as a war journalist.

Manifestations of the gap: The mapping of the narrative strategies of war journalists in their ego-documents

The three books deal in various ways with the notion of the gap. Our qualitative content analysis of these books focuses not so much on the differences between the three publications (which definitely exist, especially concerning the degree of self-reflexivity and their acknowledgment of the gap). Instead, it uses these three different publications to map the ways the gap manifests itself. In our analysis, we have distinguished four manifestations of the gap, where the authors (1) narrate the gap; (2) explain it; (3) (implicitly) hope to bypass it; and (4) try to reduce it. Of course, these four manifestations can be complemented by a fifth coping strategy, which consists of ignoring the gap. This non-manifestation is mentioned briefly later, but remains crucial to our analysis.

Narrating the gap: The act of writing an ego-document on war coverage and the process of "othering"

The first strategy consists of writing an ego-document in which the journalistic profession is opened up toward their readers. Characteristic of this first (meta-) strategy is a rather unusual openness about the practices of the journalistic profession, combined with a (form of) reflexivity on the journalistic identity. The existence of the gap is implicitly (by Karskens especially) or explicitly (by Luyendijk especially) communicated to their audiences by publishing a document (i.e., a book). Moreover, all three journalists mention in their books feelings of doubt (Karskens 2003: 88), inconvenience (Luyendijk 2006: 36), frustration (Luyendijk 2006: 97), or powerlessness (Luyendijk, 2006: 183; Vranckx 2003: 133) that come into play as a result of self-confronting the existence of the gap. By making these anxieties public, these journalists attempt to counter them and to almost therapeutically overcome them (at least partially).

As this strategy conflicts with the general closedness exerted by the journalistic professional culture in relation to the existence of the gap (Deuze 2004: 100; see also McNair 1998: 62) and with their defense of the universalized model, this meta-strategy is clearly to be considered as a (conscious or unconscious) counter-hegemonic one. The overt articulation of these critical reflections on both the journalistic profession and their journalistic identities can be considered as counter-hegemonic constructions of the "other" journalist in order to (consciously or unconsciously) come to terms with the constant pressure generated by the presence of the gap. At the same time, the degree to which the authors explicitly acknowledge the existence of a gap varies. Some narrations still contain the hope that objectivity might be rescued, if the practical problems that block its achievement have been resolved. In other narrations, objectivity is explicitly articulated as an impossible object (*petit a*). But in all cases, objectivity is deconstructed and becomes particular.

Explaining the gap: The educational–pedagogic project of war journalists

The three books not only disclose the existence of a gap between objectivity-as-value and objectivity-as-practice. Luyendijk's book in particular, but also that by Vranckx, aims to explain a number of reasons that led to this gap, both within and external to the media. This focus on allowing readers to understand these problems, as exemplified by the citation below, situates this second strategy at the educational-pedagogic level.

> I hope that this book will contribute to this openness, from the classical journalistic idea that the more we understand the world, the better it becomes—even when this would imply a better understanding of all that we cannot understand.
>
> (Luyendijk 2006: 218)

In the ego-documents, a range of restrictions that problematize the universalized value of objectivity is laid bare and illustrated. Often these restrictions are analyzed and critiqued by the journalists as being a cause for biased media representations. In other words, they still remain within the framework of the one-dimensional perspective on objectivity. Within this framework, the fantasmatic option of closing the gap still persists, as these bias critiques tend to imply that the dysfunctions of the media system can be addressed (at least in theory), and that representations can still completely capture the realities they describe (namely by avoiding misrepresentations). A number of restrictions that are discussed in the three books nevertheless exceed the bias critique, by pointing to the epistemological problems that journalism has to face. Here, the analysis of the gap is at its richest, since the limits the gap poses to representation are "encircled" (Stavrakakis 1999: 83) and the irreducibility of the gap is overtly recognized and explained.

Explaining the restrictions that are related to the "world of media"
Joris Luyendijk explicitly points to a series of media-intrinsic features that strongly restrict the possibilities of objective media representations. This broad range of features is not

necessarily limited to war coverage, but is related to media coverage in general. But all three journalists show (in varying degrees) that they are aware of these features, however taken for granted they are in the professional culture. As these features are rarely articulated toward their audiences, some of the authors aim to meticulously unravel them. Five different types of media-intrinsic restrictions can be traced in the three publications: (1) restrictions related to media format, genre, and technology; (2) the practical restrictions of a (foreign) correspondent; (3) access restrictions; (4) restrictions caused by commercialization and commodification; and (5) epistemological restrictions.

The restrictions related to media format, genre, and technology focus on the definition of news as "the exception that proves the rule" (Luyendijk 2006: 44), the existence of news and production values like *"If it bleeds it leads"* (Luyendijk 2006: 91, emphasis in original), and the "power of the image" in television news, as well as the bias that these values are causing (Luyendijk 2006: 44). The second type of restrictions incorporates the many practical problems that correspondents specifically have to face, mainly because of their dependence on the news flow originating from the home base and the press agencies. Third, as access is considered to be crucial for (war) correspondents, the consequences of problems of access (e.g., poor access to water, visa problems, safety problems) are intensively scrutinized. Fourth, the restrictions resulting from the commercialization and commodification of the media are seen as causes for the journalistic gap. For example, the more or less "clean" and patriotic image of the 2003 Iraq War the US media are said to have generated is explained by the logics imposed by the use of ratings (Luyendijk 2006: 213).

Finally, and most importantly, the epistemological restrictions are discussed. Some of these restrictions focus more on procedural problems in relation to knowledge acquisition and distribution. It is, for instance, explained to the readers that the images and ideas provided by news coverage have (to have) their complexity reduced, and are made more comprehensible and straightforward than the "real" state of affairs (Luyendijk 2006: 14). Also, the check and double check procedure often fails, as alternative sources are more often than not difficult to check (Karskens 2003: 46, 76), leaving the journalist with many unanswered questions (Vranckx 2003: 79). But in a number of cases the gap becomes fully present, when the authors explain that journalists are frequently confronted with different truths (Karskens 2003: 77; Vranckx 2003: 67), that news media can only tell one story (Luyendijk 2006: 16) and that they, as a consequence, only can offer one part of the puzzle (Vranckx 2003: 11). Even more importantly, journalists, editors, and press agencies are denied their Olympic overview, stressing that they always have to use their—per definition imperfect—recourses to produce their media outputs.

Explaining the restrictions that are related to the particular political-military context

A second type of restrictions that are explained to the readers arise from the political-military context in which the journalists have to live and which they have to cover. Besides the permanent threat of being in a warzone, the omnipresent (attempts of) manipulation by governments is seen as a problem for journalistic objectivity. In this "media war" (Luyendijk 2006: 194; Vranckx 2003: 128), the journalist feels as if they are "being used" (Karskens 2003: 71) by the belligerent parties. Of course, manipulation by the dictatorial Iraqi authorities is not the only problem confronting the journalists. The propaganda of the (western) allies is also explained as a factor that makes the gap between objectivity-as-value and objectivity-as-practice more than ever tangible.

Since language is used as a key instrument in the propaganda struggle for "the" truth, language is considered another restriction arising from the specific context. Both the warring parties and the journalists perceive language as a "site of struggle." The problem is not only that both sides manipulate the media in order to get their words and their perspective included (Vranckx 2003: 92), but also that journalists still have to use these words, which forces them—through the unavoidable partiality of language—into a similarly particular perspective. Here we find another trace of the epistemological problem, where language cannot represent the complete reality (or cannot provide access to the Lacanian Real), as is exemplified by the following comment on the Israeli–Palestinian conflict:

> When you wanted to be impartial in the Holy Land—to use that term—the first problem was that there were no impartial words. Simply putting all the terms next to each other was naturally impossible: "Today, in Ramallah on the occupied or disputed or liberated West Bank or Samaria, two Palestinians or Muslims or Arabian newcomers or terrorists or freedom fighters were killed or slaughtered by Israeli soldiers or the Israeli defence force or Zionist occupation troops [...]."
>
> (Luyendijk 2006: 132–33)

Hoping to bypass the gap: The creation of utopian and fantasmatic locations of truthfulness

A third coping strategy consists of the creation of utopian locations that might still offer some access to truthfulness. This strategy can be considered as an attempt to bypass the problems generated by the existence of the gap between journalistic ideology and practice by privileging some societal sites where truthfulness might still be within reach. In constructing these utopian and fantasmatic spheres, however, the position of the journalist becomes paradoxical. On the one hand, the explicit articulation of the existence of the gap implies the recognition of the particularity of journalistic practices. The belief in the existence of privileged sites of truthfulness, on the other hand, implies a utopian belief in the possibility of a "truthful" coverage. Interestingly, both positions can be found in the books analyzed here. This paradox again illustrates the complex nature of the journalistic identities in their relation to the one- and two-dimensional approaches of objectivity, the difficulty of accepting the gap, and the always-present hope that the gap can be bypassed or avoided.

In the three books, four utopian sites are constructed. A first utopian site is based on the world of statistics. Positioned in an antagonistic relationship to the partial and potentially manipulative nature of language, the (more) impartial statistics are considered to provide a (more) privileged access to truthfulness. Defined as (more) neutral touchstones, these quantitative data are constructed as (more) reliable sources of knowledge (Luyendijk 2006: 58). A second privileged site of truthfulness is the ordinary citizen. Whereas statistics' access to truthfulness is based on their perceived impartiality, ordinary citizens are approached as the embodiment of authenticity, in an antagonistic relationship to the official sources that are seen as corrupt and manipulative. The third site of truthfulness is the empirical observation and experience generated through the physical presence of the journalist. The authors consider a direct, personal, and long-term confrontation with the harsh conditions of war as a requirement in order to provide their audiences with the insights of the "true" face of war. Finally, professional skills also provide privileged access to truthfulness. The knowledge, frames of reference, and skills that were gathered by the "good" journalist throughout his career enable him to see (better) through the "fog of war."

Reducing the gap: A plea for rethinking journalistic ethics

A fourth and final strategy to deal with the gap consists of transforming (or suggesting to transform) the journalistic profession, in order to make it more open to acknowledging the (existence of a) gap in general and the concrete problems that arise from its existence more specifically. The "other" journalist thus questions the hegemonized journalistic ethics. Three such transformational strategies can be found in the ego-documents.

First, Joris Luyendijk argues for a radical openness of the journalistic profession. From his point of view, the educational–pedagogic strategy needs to be expanded. He pleads not only for "journalism about journalism" (Luyendijk 2006: 217), but also for a "radical other journalism" (2006: 175) that incorporates into the news coverage itself the reflections about the deficiencies, problems, uncertainties, or considerations that relate to objectivity. A second transformational strategy lies in exploring the possibilities and advantages of a form of journalism that does not consequently and necessarily exclude moral judgment and detachment. But unlike the overt plea for a radical openness, the possibility and the desirability of an engaged journalism is characterized by a rather ambivalent position combining personal acceptance and professional rejection. A final transformational strategy concerns the integration of the everyday into the media coverage. Media representations about the Middle East should focus not only on Arab politics and its (perceived) threats, so it is argued, but should also include the everyday, as this might reduce the one-sided representations and structurally enrich the representations of the Arab world that are currently produced.

Conclusion

In explaining the origin of the objectivity norm in western (Anglo-Saxon) journalism, Schudson (1978: 159) argues that "[j]ournalists came to believe in objectivity, to the extent that they did, because they wanted to, needed to, were forced by ordinary human aspiration to seek escape from their own deep convictions of doubt and drift." Despite the many changes journalism has undergone since the establishment of the profession, there is still a need for objectivity in contemporary journalism. Objectivity is hegemonically fixed as the nodal point of the (almost) only form of "good" journalism accepted as natural within contemporary society. Nevertheless, objectivity remains a value that is particular in nature, only receiving its meaning in relation to other particular values, and always depending on its concrete translation into everyday journalistic practices without ever coinciding with these practices. As a consequence, the gap between journalistic ideology on the one hand and journalistic practices on the other is unfillable.

Despite the continuous, latent pressure that this unavoidable gap generates, it should not necessarily be seen as a source of negativity or permanent frustration for each single journalist. In conceptualizing objectivity as the *objet petit a* of journalism, the objectivity norm—as the object-cause of desire—is transformed from an unattainable horizon into the ultimate starting point for journalism. Since it is exactly the gap itself that creates the need for its filling (Stavrakakis 1999: 68), the journalistic gap is to be seen as a generative driving force and an absolute requirement for the production of mediated meaning.

At the same time, this requirement leaves several options to deal with this gap, which may vary from cherishing the fantasy of the Real (which keeps the gap suppressed and unconscious) to making the existence of the gap conscious and public. As our analysis of the ego-documents shows, the three journalists have developed different strategies that allow them to deal with (the existence of) this gap: narrating it, explaining it, hoping to bypass it, and trying to reduce it by suggesting a number of transformations of the hegemonized journalistic ethics. As the publications of the war journalists provide the readers with a rather unusual openness about journalism in general, ranging from offering a clear insight into everyday journalistic practices, through overtly articulating feelings of doubt and frustration, to even stronger forms of self-reflexivity, self-criticism, and transgression, these four manifestations of the gap are to be considered as counter-hegemonic. These manifestations stand in an antagonistic relationship with the fifth coping device that consists of *ignoring* the existence of the gap, which implies the fantasmatic belief that objectivity is within reach. The hegemonized nature of this non-manifestation is evidenced by, for instance, the antagonistic reactions of several (other) Dutch journalists to the publication of Luyendijk's ego-document, as his book brings the gap very explicitly into the realm of the public.

Nevertheless, *all* manifestations, including the four "alternative" ones, give evidence of the inevitable dominance of the universalized model of objectivity. In explaining a range of restrictions that lead to the gap, the recognition of the inevitability of the gap is evidenced.

By contrast, the fantasmatic possibility of closing the gap is only seldom totally excluded. Very often, there is still some fantasmatic hope left that the gap might eventually be closed, as found in the attempts to bypass the gap by creating a number of utopian and fantasmatic locations of truthfulness, something which all three authors do. And even in arguing for a transformation of hegemonized journalistic ethics, where the problems that result from the existence of the gap are to be partially overcome, the "other" journalist finds it difficult to escape the hegemony of the universalized and one-dimensional model of objectivity. Here we can actually see the centripetal power of hegemony at work: both the hegemonic, universalized model of "good" journalism and the counter-hegemonic attempts to transform this model are sutured around the rigid nodal point of objectivity, structurally hindering the centrifugal attempts to radically transform (at least part of) this model and to allow for more (conscious) self-reflexivity about objectivity as journalism's *objet petit a*.

Of course, this is not to say that the attempts of the "other" journalist to break through the centripetal logics are irrelevant. What distinguishes these "other" journalists is exactly both their desire for and their articulation of the constructive need for journalistic openness. These processes are a requirement to allow for (and to increase the presence of) self-reflexive and self-critical dialogues in journalistic culture, where different and constructive forms of journalisms and meta-journalisms (both in plural) can meet and can cross-fertilize each other, in finding ways to deal with the unavoidable gap that will remain to define, enable, and haunt journalism.

References

Agamben, Giorgio (2005), *State of Exception* (trans. K. Attell), Chicago: University of Chicago Press.

Anderson, Benedict (1983), *Imagined Communities: Reflections on the Origin and Spread of Nationalism*, London: Verso.

Cammaerts, Bart and Carpentier, Nico (2006), "Blogging and the Second Iraqi War: Extending participation and challenging mainstream journalism?," in N. Carpentier, P. Pruulmann-Vengerfeldt, K. Nordenstreng, M. Hartmann, P. Vihalemm, and B. Cammaerts (eds), *Researching Media, Democracy and Participation: The Intellectual Work of the 2006 European Media and Communication Doctoral Summer School*, Tartu: University of Tartu Press, pp. 157–71.

Carpentier, Nico (2005a), "De vijand in de berichtgeving: Constructies van het zelf en de vijand tijdens de Irakese oorlog in maart-april 2003" ("The enemy in the news coverage: Constructions of the self and the enemy during the Iraqi war in March-April 2003"), in M. Hooghe, K. De Swert, and S. Walgrave (eds), *Nieuws op Televisie: Televisiejournaals als Venster op de Wereld*, Leuven and Voorburg: Acco, pp. 195–213.

—— (2005b), "Identity, contingency and rigidity: The (counter-)hegemonic constructions of the identity of the media professional," *Journalism*, 6:2, pp. 199–219.

—— (2007), "Fighting discourses: Discourse theory, war and representations of the 2003 Iraqi War," in S. Maltby and R. Keeble (eds), *Communicating War: Memory, Media and Military*, Bury St Edmunds: Abramis, pp. 103–16.

Cunningham, Brent (2003), "Toward a new ideal: Rethinking objectivity in a world of spin," *Columbia Journalism Review*, 42:2, pp. 24–33.

Deuze, Mark (2004), *Wat is Journalistiek?*, Amsterdam: Het Spinhuis.

—— (2005), "What is journalism? Professional identity and ideology of journalists reconsidered," *Journalism*, 6:4, pp. 442–64.

Fox, Julia R. and Park, Byungho (2006), "The 'I' of embedded reporting: An analysis of CNN coverage of the 'Shock and Awe' campaign," *Journal of Broadcasting & Electronic Media*, 50:1, pp. 36–51.

Hackett, Robert (1984), "Decline of a paradigm? Bias and objectivity in news media studies," *Critical Studies in Mass Communication*, 1:3, pp. 229–59.

Karskens, Arnold (2003), *Onze Man in Bagdad: Dagboek van een Oorlogsverslaggever (Our Man in Baghdad: The Journal of a Wartime Correspondent)*, Amsterdam: Meulenhoff.

Kirshner, Lewis (2005), "Rethinking desire: The *objet petit a* in Lacanian theory," *Journal of the American Psychoanalytic Association*, 53:1, pp. 83–102.

Knightley, Philip (1982), *The First Casualty of War*, London: Quartet.

Lacan, Jacques ([1958] 1977), "Desire and the interpretation of desire in *Hamlet*," *Yale French Studies*, 55&56, pp. 11–52.

—— ([1964] 1979), *The Four Fundamental Concepts of Psycho-Analysis* (ed. J.-A. Miller, trans. A. Sheridan), London: Penguin.

—— ([1954–55] 1988), *The Seminar – Book II: The Ego in Freud's Theory and in the Technique of Psychoanalysis* (trans. S. Tomaselli), Cambridge: Cambridge University Press.

—— ([1960–61] 1991), *Le Séminaire – Livre VIII: Le Transfert* (ed. J.-A. Miller), Paris: Seuil.

—— ([1956–57] 1994), *Le Séminaire – Livre IV: La Relation d'Objet* (ed. J.-A. Miller), Paris: Seuil.

—— ([1972–73] 1999), *The Seminar – Book XX: Encore, on Feminine Sexuality, the Limits of Love and Knowledge* (ed. and trans. J.-A. Miller), New York: Norton.

Laclau, Ernesto (1996), *Emancipation(s)*, London: Verso.

—— (2000a), "Identity and hegemony: The role of universality in the constitution of political logics," in J. Butler, E. Laclau, and S. Žižek (eds), *Contingency, Hegemony, Universality: Contemporary Dialogues on the Left*, London: Verso, pp. 44–89.

—— (2000b), "Constructing universality," in J. Butler, E. Laclau, and S. Žižek (eds), *Contingency, Hegemony, Universality: Contemporary Dialogues on the Left*, London: Verso, pp. 281–307.

—— (2005), *On Populist Reason*, London: Verso.

Laclau, Ernesto and Mouffe, Chantal (1985), *Hegemony and Socialist Strategy: Towards a Radical Democratic Politics*, London: Verso.

Lewis, Justin (2004), "Television, public opinion and the War in Iraq: The case of Britain," *International Journal of Public Opinion Research*, 16:3, pp. 295–310.

Lichtenberg, Judith (2005), "In defense of objectivity revisited," in J. Curran and M. Gurevitch (eds), *Mass Media and Society*, London: Arnold, pp. 216–31.

Luyendijk, Joris (2006), *Het zijn Net Mensen: Beelden uit het Midden-Oosten (They're Just Like Human Beings: Images from the Middle East)*, Amsterdam: Podium.

McNair, Brian (1998), *The Sociology of Journalism*, London: Arnold.

Schudson, Michael (1978), *Discovering the News: A Social History of American Newspapers*, New York: Basic Books.

—— (2001), "The objectivity norm in American Journalism," *journalism*, 2:2, pp. 149–70.

Stavrakakis, Yannis (1999), *Lacan and the Political*, London: Routledge.

Thussu, Daya and Freedman, Des ([2003] 2005), *War and the Media: Reporting Conflict 24/7*, London: Sage.

Tuchman, Gaye (1972), "Objectivity as a strategic ritual: An examination of newsmen's notions of objectivity," *American Journal of Sociology*, 77, pp. 660–79.

Tumber, Howarth and Palmer, Jerry ([2004] 2006), *Media at War: The Iraq Crisis*, London: Sage.

Tumber, Howarth and Prentoulis, Marina ([2003] 2005), "Journalists under fire: Subcultures, objectivity and emotional literacy," in D. K. Thussu and D. Freedman (eds), *War and the Media: Reporting Conflict 24/7*, London: Sage, pp. 215–30.

Vranckx, Rudi (2003), *Van het Front Geen Nieuws: Herinneringen aan de Oorlogen in het Midden-Oosten* (*No News from the Front: Memories of the Wars in the Middle East*), Antwerpen: Meulenhoff.

Ward, Stephen (1999), "Pragmatic news objectivity: Objectivity with a human face," Discussion Paper D-37, Harvard University, http://www.ksg.harvard.edu/presspol/research_publications/papers/discussion_papers/D37.pdf. Accessed 25 November 2018.

Wasserman, Herman and Rao, Shakuntala (2008), "The glocalization of journalism ethics," *Journalism*, 9:2, pp. 163–83.

Webster, Frank ([2003] 2005), "Information warfare in an age of globalization," in D. K. Thussu and D. Freedman (eds), *War and the Media: Reporting Conflict 24/7*, London: Sage, pp. 57–69.

Williams, Kevi (1992), "Something more important than truth: Ethical issues in war reporting," in A. Belsey and R. Chadwick (eds), *Ethical Issues in Journalism and the Media*, London: Routledge, pp. 154–70.

Žižek, Slavoj ([1989] 1995), *The Sublime Object of Ideology*, London: Verso.

Notes

1   The Dutch government expressed its support for the Iraq War, but did not provide military assistance, although the latter was contested by the Dutch (public) broadcasting program Argos in its 17 March 2007 broadcast (http://www.ochtenden.nl/afleveringen/32554009/. Accessed 28 December 2018).

2   These concepts are, of course, grounded in Laclau's discussion of the universal and the particular, which is discussed later in this chapter. To emphasize the process behind the construction of the universal, the concept "universalized" is preferred here.

3   A similar argument can be made to articulate objectivity as an empty signifier.

4   "Imagined journalistic communities" re-uses Anderson's (1983) concept in the more specific context of journalism.

5   The use of Lacan's concepts will not necessarily comply with the Lacanian orthodoxy.

Section 4

Audiences and Participation

Chapter 8

The Articulation of "Audience" in Chinese Communication Research

Guiquan Xu

Introduction

Three decades ago, when communication science was introduced to Mainland China,[1] Chinese scholars invented a new word: *shouzhong* (受众), which literally means "receiving masses."[2] This is used as the translation of the concept of audience(s) because in Chinese, although there are vocabularies referring to the specific terms "reader," "listener," "viewer," etc., no word exists equivalent to the collective term "audience" as the "receiver" in the communication process. This translation was not perfect, because it did not fully represent the meanings of "active user" in user studies and "meaning-maker" in cultural studies. Nevertheless, this notion inspired scholars and practitioners in the pursuit of media reform: the media should not only function as an ideological propagator, but also serve information to the "audiences" by all means. Audience awareness greatly stimulated China's journalistic reform since the end of the 1970s, and legitimized the status of Chinese communication research.

Nowadays, Chinese communication research faces new challenges, which are also represented by the concept of audience. One challenge is that it is difficult to cover with the term *shouzhong* the characteristics of active audience participation in the new technological environment, such as "user-generated content." Also, the meaning of "audience-consumer" has been emphasized during the media marketization reform in the past three decades, but the audience's identities as "citizen" and "public" have not been fully articulated in the academy. As Zhongdang Pan (2008) argued, a well-understood "publicness" of the media must be the basis for setting new goals for the media reforms, and Chinese communication studies must offer theoretical resources for the rejuvenation of the reforms. However, what does "public" mean for China and which road should reforms take? There is no explicit confirmation from researchers and policymakers. For both reasons, a comprehensive understanding of "audience" remains crucial to China's media reform and communication research.

Moreover, China's media reform and communication research was embedded in the broader societal context. As an oriental country with 3,000 years of history, ancient China was a super-stable system of civilization with its own knowledge about "people." After the mid-nineteenth century, China was pushed into the modern, colonial, capitalist world system, and began to seek its own way of modernization. The recent wave of modernization was launched in 1978, when the People's Republic of China (PRC) abandoned communism—the dominant ideology from the 1950s to the 1970s—and adopted economic reforms and opening-up policies. Since then, great changes have taken place in various aspects of Chinese society, including the media and communication. In politics, China was changing from a "totalist" state to a resilient authoritarian state, marking a new sense of the identity of "people." In its economy, it changed from a closed, planned economy to a globalized market economy, ushering in the notions of "market" and "consumer." In the social domain, it changed from the "total social system" under strict control of the state to a relatively open and diverse social-cultural space with an emerging civil society, which laid the foundations for the growth of "the public" and "citizens." Since mass media are an organic part of modern society, these distinctive changes altered the audience's experiences and identities, and simultaneously shaped the ideas of audience research.

As the recent reflections on de-westernizing communication research indicate (e.g., Wang 2011), all the "western" theories, when applied to other contexts, need careful consideration based on local knowledge. This also holds true for conceptualizations of the audience. Indeed, when Chinese media scholars published the results of the first large-scale audience survey conducted in 1982, Rogers et al. (1985: 190–91) noticed its distinction:

> The Beijing Audience Survey was planned within the philosophy and normative-theoretical framework of Marxism. But it followed the communication research methods and empirical-theoretical approaches of Western and Third World scholars. Special attention was paid to the adaption of these foreign methods and theories to Chinese conditions and to Marxist ideology.

After thirty years of development, Chinese audience research can no longer be considered a simple combination of foreign methods and local conditions. In order to unravel the inner complexity of the field, this chapter attempts to explore how the conception of "audience" has been articulated in Chinese communication research within the changing societal contexts in the past three decades. It does so based on a discourse analysis of major Chinese academic journals in the field of communication research.

Methodology

Five top scholarly journals were selected as data sources: (1) *Journal of International Communication* (1979–), published by the School of Journalism, Renmin University of China; (2) *Journalism Quarterly* (1981–), published by the School of Journalism, Fudan University; (3) *Modern Communication* (1980–), the former *Journal of Beijing Broadcasting Institution*, published by the Communication University of China; (4) *Journalism & Communication* (1989–), published by the Institution of Journalism and Communication, Chinese Academy of Social Science[3]; and (5) *Chinese Journal of Communication and Society* (2006–), published by the School of Journalism and Communication, Chinese University of Hong Kong and the School of Communication, Hong Kong Baptist University.[4] In this corpus, only the articles that focused on the notion of "audience" were selected, including both theoretical and empirical articles.

The chapter adopts a theoretical-discourse-inspired approach to discourse analysis to explore the meanings of audience in Chinese communication research. In discourse theory, "discourse" is defined as a structure of meaning that is constantly under negotiation and construction (Laclau 1988: 254). The structure of a discourse consists of a number of relative fixed central signifiers (which can be named nodal points), and the components of meaning surrounding these nodal points (Carpentier 2010).

In the analysis, I follow the principle of constructivist grounded theory methodology (Charmaz 2006), in that I aim to generate the concepts and discourses of Chinese audience research from an abundant data of academic texts, rather than starting from any theoretical hypothesis. The coding of texts focused on the construction of "sensitizing concepts" (Blumer 1954). In the stage of "initial coding," a variety of signifiers of audience in the texts were detected and listed, including Chinese terms that may be understood approximately in English as "reader," "listener," "viewer," "user," "people," "mass," "consumer," "class," "citizen," "public," and "crowd." It also contained the local concepts that may not be mentioned in western audience theories but indeed refer to a form of audience, such as *qunzhong* (群众, approximately translated as "masses" in English). In the advanced stage of "focused coding," I used these significant initial codes to sort and integrate the discursive data within the specific academic contexts and societal contexts. As such, the discursive structures were reorganized, including a variety of core signifiers of "audience" and groups of specific significance.

As for the narrative of the results, after a short prelude before 1978, I divided the timeline onward into three periods according to significant changes in the societal contexts. In each period, I interpreted the articulation of "audience" in different analytical discourses within the specific contexts. In this way, I have attempted to balance the diachronic and synchronic aspects of the discourses.

Prelude to the reform era: The heritage of "people" and "mass-line"

For Chinese traditional political culture, the ideal situation of politics was a *minben* (民本, monarchy). The term *minben* (people-base) originated in a chapter of a classic *Shangshu* about 2,000 years ago: "the people are the base of a country; when the base is firm, the country is tranquil" (*The Song of Five Sons*, 尚书·五子之歌). All the long-lasting regimes in Chinese history implemented this instruction, taking people's opinion seriously, although they also followed a principle, "Confucian in appearance but Legalist in substance," which meant that a regime could not be sustained permanently unless it kept the balance between benevolent governance and coercion by law.

Meanwhile, there is also a long history of the idea of *gong* (公, public and common) in Chinese political culture. Taken from "The conveyance of rites" in *the Book of Rites*

(礼记·礼运): "When the Great Moral was pursued, the spirit of gong [public and common] ruled all under the heaven; they [the kings] chose men of talents, virtue, and ability; their words were sincere, and what they cultivated was harmony." It meant that not only should the king rule a benevolent kingdom, but also talented men, who should always take common interests into consideration. This is also the requirement of the "people-based monarchy."

Since the mid-nineteenth century, along with the import of western civilization, the worldview of Chinese people has experienced great changes. This has included the conceptual contradiction between "people-base" and "democracy" (people's rule). When the term "democracy" was translated into Chinese, the translator coined the word *minzhu* (民主), which looked rather like the term *minben* (民本). This translation might have been intended to narrow the gap between "democracy" and "people-base," and implied that it was possible for China to be a democratic country. From a western modernization perspective, "democracy" is more advanced than "people-based" government because the former let the people become the real rulers and the government be their servant. But in modern China, there was no simple substitution relationship between these two conceptions; rather, it was a sophisticated mixing process. For instance, Sun Yat-sen, the founding father of the Republic of China (1912–49), liked quoting the old saying, "a public and common spirit ruled all under the heaven," but as a modern politician, his understanding of "public" had mixed with the western meanings of "democratic citizens." This hybrid status also appeared in the view of "Confucian-liberal" journalists, who considered the mission of the press as educating ignorant people to save the country, rather than empowering them as free citizens to participate in public discussions (Lee 2005: 108).

In the spectrum between "people-base" and "democracy," the "mass-line" of the Communist Party of China (CPC) was especially influential through its propaganda practice in the war and revolution era (from the 1920s to the 1940s). *Qunzhong* (群众), as a compound word in Chinese, appeared in the twentieth century; it literally refers to "crowd" and "multitudes," but is more frequently translated as "masses" in English. However, its political implication is more important than its literal meaning. As the CPC's leader, Zedong Mao ([1943] 1965: 119), explained:

In all the practical work of our Party, all correct leadership is necessarily "from the masses, to the masses." This means: take the ideas of the masses (scattered and unsystematic ideas) and concentrate them (through study turn them into concentrated and systematic ideas), then go to the masses and propagate and explain these ideas until the masses embrace them as their own, hold fast to them and translate them into action, and test the correctness of these ideas in such action. Then once again concentrate ideas from the masses and once again go to the masses so that the ideas are persevered in and carried through. And so on, over and over again in an endless spiral, with the ideas becoming more correct, more vital and richer each time. Such is the Marxist theory of knowledge.

In brief, mass-line is a political and organizational method of the CPC, claiming to be on behalf of the masses, rather than the power elites. Although mass-line seemed to be democratic and respected people's opinion in appearance, in essence the people did not have the rights of decision-making in the form of representation or participation. Rather, "mass-line" was a way of persuading the masses to accept policy implementation (Lee 2005: 116). Following the mass-line, the Party-press played the prominent role of propagandist. In the "Note to its Reader" on 1 April 1942, *Liberation Daily*, the central press channel of CPC, claimed that the characters of Party-press contained four points: "Party principle," "mass principle," "fighting spirit," and "organization." The Party principle was the primary character, asking the press to propagandize the Party's directives and policies without reserve. Second, this editorial asked for the *mass principle*, claiming that "the task of the press is not only to increase the knowledge of masses, raise their consciousness, educate them, organize them, but also to represent them, become their mouthpiece and friends." This mass propaganda strategy gained success in the revolutionary era, as many people in the lower classes were inspired by the CPC's revolutionary ideal and ideological mobilization.

The CPC seized political power and founded the PRC in 1949. In the view of political sociology, this regime was a "total social system" in which the "totalist" state monopolized all the economic and social resources (Sun et al. 2004; Tsou 1994). In the early years of the regime, the model of the Party-press was promoted to the media throughout the country. In such a system, the media were completely under the control of the state and functioned as the tool of policy and ideological propaganda. Especially during the Cultural Revolution (1966–76), many newspapers ceased publishing, as did the Party organs, and the rest became instruments of political struggle, resulting in the most severe disaster. By the end of the 1970s, the people suspected both the regime and its propaganda.

Political transition, economic reform, and the emergence of "audience" (1978–89)

In December 1978, the Third Plenary Session of the 11th CPC Central Committee was held in Beijing. This meeting decided to turn the focus of the CPC's work from class struggle to socialist modernization, marking the beginning of a new era of "reform and opening-up." This decision was widely supported by the people, and thence "socialist modernization" became the dominant societal discourse, instead of the revolutionary communist ideology.

In official statements, "socialist modernization" included "material civilization" and "spiritual civilization." For material civilization, the aim of "modernization" included four areas: agriculture, industry, national defense, science, and technology. Meanwhile, ideology and spiritual civilization remained crucial. In 1979, Xiaoping Deng delivered a speech titled "Upholding four cardinal principles." He claimed that to achieve "four modernizations" required upholding the socialist path, the dictatorship of the proletariat, the leadership of the CPC, and Marx–Lenin–Mao thought. Generally, the political climate in the 1980s was tolerant, and social thoughts were active, but these four cardinal principles were the unchallenged boundary. In this sense, China's regime was changing from a "totalist" to an authoritarian state, characterized by a guiding ideology but diverse discourses (Zhao 2001: 46). Moreover, the economic reform from planned economy to "planned commercial economy" and the opening-up policies stimulated the differentiation of the economic sphere and the social sphere, which also encouraged the diversification of social thoughts.

In such a political and economic environment, the news media propagandized the official ideology on the one hand, and within their own organizations carried out commercial reform on the other. At the end of 1978, the *People's Daily*, together with seven other presses in Beijing, tried out a new orientation of "state-owned enterprise, business management." This orientation was soon approved by the treasury department of the central government and gradually adopted by all the press, radio, and television. Economic reform and modernization building urged the media to satisfy the increasing information demand of readers, listeners, and viewers. Audience surveys and studies became necessary.

Encouraged by the open atmosphere, Chinese humanities and social sciences revived in the 1980s. The intellectuals were keen to learn new knowledge and to promote the country's progress. The media researchers, who witnessed the disaster of propaganda in the Cultural Revolution, were especially devoted to rectifying the propaganda mistake and to reform the media system. They found that audience research could be an effective approach. Based on the collected texts, the discourses about audience in media and communication research in this era can be divided into four clusters.

First, the Party-press discourse remained dominant, but adapted the articulation of "people" and "mass-line" to the changing social environment. In the National Forum for the Press in 1979, Jiwei Hu, editor-in-chief of the *People's Daily*, claimed that after the Cultural Revolution, the *People's Daily* became the people's press again, representing both the people principle and the Party principle. In another forum that year, he asked: "When the Party makes a mistake, as in the Cultural Revolution, could the press, which is controlled by the Party and serves as the Party's mouthpiece, be able to make no mistake, or even help and supervise the Party to rectify and minimize the mistake?" (Zhang 2000: 624). His implicit answer was that the press must follow people's will in order to avoid mistakes, and the people principle was even higher than the Party principle. The notion "people principle" aroused sensitive discussions, but was soon forbidden by the conservative forces since it threatened the Party's prior legitimacy.

Nevertheless, modest discussions were allowed in the academy. For instance, in Ruimiao Chen's article entitled "People's trust is the condition of survival for newspapers," he quoted Marx's words: "The trust of the people is the condition for a newspaper to live. Without this condition, the newspapers will shrivel." He further explained:

The newspaper, as the mouthpiece of the Party and the people, must be faithful to propagandize our lines and policies. However, the effect of communication depends on whether we follow the law of journalism, gain the trust of the people and achieve the unification between the communicators and the receivers. In order to gain the trust of people, we need to respect the democratic rights of the people, let the people know what they need to know and ought to know, let the people participate in and discuss the politics through the channel of opinion expression, let the people sense that the newspaper is trustable and worthy of trust.

(Chen 1988: 5)

This paragraph not only used the traditional words of "mouthpiece of the Party and the People," but also mixed in the emerging vocabularies of communication science such as "communication," "effect," and "receiver" (which were equivalentially translated from English to Chinese), as well as the popular media discourse such as "following the law of journalism" and "let the people participate in and discuss politics," thereby inputting the traditional concept of people with a fresh interpretation as "information receiver" and "political participants."

The second discourse—the democratic discourse—had partly appeared in the preceding paragraph. In the Chinese context, "democracy" is a discussable topic, because the CPC always claims that it aims to build a democratic country. However, the CPC rejected "capitalist democracy," since it "only represented the interests of capitalist classes." In contrast, "socialist democracy" was assumed to represent the interests of working classes and allowed the "people" to be the masters of the country. In the report of the 13th CPC's National Congress in 1987, the Chinese leaders stressed that "high democracy" was part of the aims of socialist modernization, claiming "let the people know the significant issues, let the people discuss the significant problems." They also declared that the news media should "serve a role of public opinion supervision, supporting the criticisms of the public and targeting errors and shortcomings [in government work], opposing bureaucratism, and struggling against various unhealthy tendencies." This positive attitude further encouraged scholars to study public opinion. In early 1988, the Public Opinion Research Institute of Renmin University of China launched a survey of 200 celebrities in Beijing. The findings displayed that 62 percent of the respondents warmly supported democratic reform and the media's role of "public opinion supervision" (Chen 1989). When the scholars interpreted the survey results, they generally quoted the official statement of "socialist democracy" as their justification in order to avoid political risks. However, the notion of "public opinion supervision" had expressed the preliminary significance of democratic participation.

The third discourse can be termed "media professionalist discourse." "Media professionalism" was also a term imported from the West. In the 1980s, this notion had not yet been clearly articulated in China, but the journalists had begun to reflect on their professional identity. At the beginning of journalistic reform, the media scholars urged the press to return to the tradition of "mass-line," getting rid of "falsity, exaggeration, emptiness" and seeking the truth and "liveness" of news. However, sticking to these principles was not sufficient—the media had to investigate the needs of audiences. In 1982, the first large-scale audience survey was conducted in Beijing. Its results revealed the rapid development of media use and the audience's dissatisfaction with media contents as well as their expectation for changes. This pioneering study resonated in both the press and the academy. More and more audience surveys were conducted from the middle to the end of the 1980s, ranging from national to local levels. When the researchers discussed the results, they adopted the concrete concepts of reader, listener, and viewer. It meant that the focus of inquiry had moved from the collective "masses" to the segmented "audiences," examining the users' characteristics of each medium type, thereby providing pertinent suggestions. For instance, Tianquan Shi (1986) suggested that television should make full use of the viewers' participation that included three levels: feelings of sympathy, sense of involvement, and real participation in television programs. This kind of discussion indicated that improving the service for the audience had been conceived as the duty of media professionals.

The fourth discourse was the scientific discourse, which mainly borrowed from the positivist discourse of media use and effect studies in the West. In the 1980s, both "administrative" and "critical" communication research were introduced into Chinese academia, but the former was more welcomed by media scholars and practitioners. The reason might be twofold. First, many researchers and practitioners had been bored with ideological indoctrination—even the critical theories seemed merely another version of "Marxist doctrine." By contrast, the fresh notions of "communication," "receiver," "feedback," "selective attention," and "comprehension" just met their interests in new knowledge. Second, these new concepts and the method of survey, with the focus on audience's structure and behaviors, were more convincing and inspiring for journalistic reform. Some articles interpreted the psychology of selective perception of the audience, and thereby instructed ways of improving newspaper layout and news broadcasting (e.g., Song 1988). The primary intention of these articles was not to explore pure knowledge, but to apply scientific knowledge to promote media reform.

In brief, this period was an era of change, from closed to open knowledge. The relatively tolerant social environments inspired scholars to explore ways to democratic and scientific decision-making and economic efficiency, which were also represented in audience research. Nevertheless, as Lidan Chen (2008) reflected, academia in this period was too close to the political trends, and lacked academic autonomy. Consequently, at the end of the 1980s, when a few liberal intellectuals broke the boundary of dominant ideology, the political climate was tightened up and communication science was criticized as a "bourgeoisie science" that ignored the Party principle and identity of social classes. Chinese communication research experienced unprecedented frustration, leading researchers to reconsider its orientations.

"Socialist market economy" and the expansion of "audience consumer" (1990–2000)

After the political disturbances in 1989 and a two-year economic adjustment, the CPC reactivated economic reform with the aim of "building a socialist market economy" in 1992. "Socialist" meant the dominant political framework would not be changed but consolidated, while an affirmative formulation of "market economy" reignited the flame of economic liberalization in the 1990s. As Xiaoping Deng ([1992] 1993: 373) said, "a planned economy is not equivalent to socialism, because there is also planning under capitalism. A market economy is not equivalent to capitalism, because there are markets under socialism. Planning and marketing are both economic means of controlling economic activity." This market pragmatist stance penetrated all aspects of the socio-economic spheres, framing an "interest-based social order" (Zheng 2004: 61).

The media and audiences were inevitably influenced by such a social order. Zhou He (2000) argued that China's Party-press was being transformed from a mouthpiece of the Party-state into "Party Publicity Inc.," which had to serve both the Party's propaganda and market interests. In this structure, the media practitioners and scholars became more concerned about audience ratings and market segmentation, adding the identity of "consumer" to the audience (Zhang 2000).

In this period, the discourses of communication research continued to parallel the changing contexts, highlighting the media industries and audience-consumers under the condition of a socialist market economy. This focus was not only the requirement of the broader environment, but also the scholars' conscious choice. Learning from the lessons of the 1980s, they paid more attention to the pragmatic issues of media operations than the grand design of media reform (Yu 1997). This characteristic was typically represented in audience research.

For the Party-press discourse, the "guidance of public opinion" became a prominent issue defined by the Party. As President Zemin Jiang ([1996] 2006: 563) said, "correct guidance of public opinion was good for both the Party and the people, and incorrect guidance potentially calamitous for both." It meant that the media must not print or broadcast content that in policy or spirit was at odds with the Party. Instead, they should actively promote the policies of the Party and facilitate public understanding of these policies. The scholars further interpreted these official statements. For instance, based on Xiaoping Deng's speeches, Lidan Chen (1994: 7) concluded the main points of "guidance of public opinion": "in the new situation of reform and opening-up, our propaganda must grasp the correct guidance of public opinion. Whatever our media report, social stability is the basic concern." Being aware of the essential stance of the Party, the academy had no intention to challenge the bottom line, but accepted these political requirements.

Contrasting with the emphasis of the "guidance of public opinion," the previous focus of "public opinion supervision" in the democratic discourse was much weakened. But a few researchers still expressed their concerns with public opinion as far as possible. For instance, Xun Ni (1993) claimed that public opinion could serve as a reference for economic policymaking; hence, the news media should make full use of the feedback from the audience.

Meanwhile, the market-driven discourse became another influential discourse, articulating the audience as "market" and "consumer." Guoming Yu (1994) compared the "administration" and "marketization" of the media system and obviously preferred the market system because the latter could better satisfy the audience's needs and include different opinions. Hongduo Zhou (1997: 37) also noted: "in the condition of socialist market economy, to satisfy the needs of consumers the media should not only be concerned with the quality of the products, but also be devoted to exploring the consumer market." As the research went further, the discussions became multifaceted, including media consumption behaviors, consumer culture, the impact of economic stratification on media consumption, and the protection of consumer rights, etc.

In this vein, the media professionalist discourse was located between the Party-press discourse and the market-driven discourse, but closer to the latter: serving the readers, listeners, and viewers was almost equal to serving the consumers. On the other hand, the norms of media professionals were further reflected. A few scholars began to caution against the negative impact of the media's profit-seeking activities, which was incompatible with the principles of media professionalism. For instance, Lidan Chen (1998) suggested that the media should play a role in encouraging public opinions toward healthy social lives, resisting the worship of money in the market economy.

Although media industries and audience markets became the emphasis of communication research, the autonomy of the academic field was also addressed. This was another lesson learned in the 1980s: scholars must stick to scholarship. In the scientific discourse of audience research, the focus of inquiry was moving from the description of the audience's structure and behaviors to the audience's deeper perception of information. For instance, from 1991 to 1993, the research group of "communication and people's modernization" in the Chinese Academy of Social Science conducted surveys on the relation between mass communication and the audience's conception of modernization. One of their findings was that the factor of education levels had a common effect on an individual's perception of modernity: the audience with higher education levels and more frequency of reading had a more significant conception of modernity, and vice versa; the audience who had a stronger conception of modernity were inclined to select the media forms and context that had stronger effects of modernity, and vice versa (Min and Chen 1991).

Other research on media and audiences' values proposed a hypothesis that was partly confirmed: as great changes took place in the social culture and media content during the process of China's rapid modernization, the audience's perception and cultural values were under significant transformation (Pan and Wei 1997). These studies implied that the audiences were not only information receivers and media users, but also the participants of China's modernization.

Academic autonomy was also represented in the discourse of cultural critique along with the rise of popular culture in the market economy. Some scholars adopted a critical attitude toward popular culture. By quoting the theories of the Frankfurt School, they argued that the media should resist the invading of consumerism in social lives. Tianquan Shi (1995: 36–37) wrote that

since our country entered into market economy, the contradiction between the economic criteria and the cultural criteria became obvious. On the one hand, to achieve the aim of modernization, we must emphasize the economic criteria and promote the market mechanism; on the other hand, we cannot live without the cultural criteria. Our socialist market economy must simultaneously embody the human dignity, feelings and morality.

Therefore, he argued that mass media should caution against the invasion of popular culture, thereby protecting the ordinary people. But still other scholars (e.g., Yang 1993) confirmed the social meanings of popular culture because it enriched the Chinese people's everyday lives; hence, they advocated an open but cautious position.

"Harmonious society," "civil society," and the construction of "audience-consumer-public" (2001–12)

For the third period, the year 2001 is a demarcation, not simply because it was the beginning of the twenty-first century, but due to changes in social context. First, China joined the World Trade Organization in 2001 and further merged into the global market economy, and its media industries became more marketized. Second, as sociological research indicates (e.g., Sun et al. 2004), social stratification, which was triggered by market economic reform, tended to be solidified by the end of the 1990s. Yet the new stage of social transformation was characterized by increasing social problems (e.g., corruption), conflicts, and civic protests due to the unequal distribution of socio-economic interests and rights. These social problems not only promoted the government's social policy adjustments, but also shaped the agendas of media and academic research.

In this period, the dominant societal discourse insisted on the "socialist market economy," but paid more attention to social inclusion and integration. In 2002 General Secretary Zemin Jiang ([2001] 2006: 272) redefined the guiding ideology of the CPC: "the Party must always represent the advanced productive forces, the advanced culture, and the fundamental interests of the overwhelming majority of the people in China." It implied that "the leadership sought to expand the social base of the CPC and to establish or at least accommodate an interest-based political order" (Zheng 2004: 81). His successor, Jintao Hu (2007: III), declared the aim of "building a socialist harmonious society" since 2004, which required "democracy and the rule of law, equity and justice, honesty and fraternity, vigor and vitality, stability and order, and harmony between man and nature." The rearticulation of ideology not only represented the leaders' flexible discursive strategy, but also reflected the urgency of social contradictions.

This dominant ideology set the tone of media coverage, but in public opinion there were other voices regarding the solution of social problems, one of which can be named "civil society discourse." It claimed that citizens had the right to political participation and that social organizations should be free from the state and the market's interventions and serve the public interest. The emergence of civil society discourse expressed the appeals of the new social classes and the bottom classes (Gao and Yuan 2008). They asked to rebuild state–society relations based on civil society, rather than state dominance.

Although communication research has addressed both the themes of "harmonious society" and "civil society," compared with scholars in mainstream social sciences, communication researchers have participated less in public debates, such as debates about the road to China's reform, instead focusing only on their professional studies. However, since the media have been embedded in the political economic system, communication research has inevitably related to broader themes. When the media scholars witnessed the over-commercialization of media industries and rampant media corruption, they advocated that the duty of media was not in making a profit for themselves, but serving the audience and public. This was exactly the starting point of media reform in the 1980s, but nowadays has tended to be overlooked in the wave of media marketization. Hence reflection on media reform has become urgent (Pan 2008).

In these social and academic contexts, some new characteristics have appeared in the discourses of "audience." For the Party-press discourse, the notions of "people" and "mass-line" have been rearticulated, mixing with the vocabularies of the official ideology and the meaning of "citizens." In 2007, President Jintao Hu claimed that the government should guarantee "people's rights to know, to participate, to express, and to supervise." This statement was soon quoted by scholars to discuss the communication rights of citizens, but more interpretations were added, such as "guarding against the criminalization of free speech should be the requirement of building democracy and rule of law in our country" (Chen and Wu 2009: 32). Similarly, Qinghe Zhu (2011) traced the history of "mass-line press," and argued that ensuring citizens' rights and promoting social justice should be the destination of the mass-line. This kind of mixed rhetoric strategy reflected the scholars' cautious attitude toward the conceptual heritages of Party-press discourse and their intention to maximize its inspiration for media reform toward publicness. Moreover, some articles discussed the way to improve the "art of guiding public opinion" and communication between the government and the people through the media, especially concerning issues of social conflict.

For the market-driven discourse, the audience market and media consumption continued to be the focus of study, while media economics gained legitimacy as a subdiscipline in the journalism education system. Guoming Yu (2003) claimed that the nature of media industries was the economy of influence, stressing the importance of attracting and sustaining the attention of audiences. Along with the development of new media, market analysis of the digital audience also became popular. Nevertheless, the scholars also realized that the media could not simply follow the market logic of profit maximization. The overemphasis on audience ratings was fiercely criticized in the mid-2000s (e.g., Shi and Lv 2006). After intensive discussions, more and more scholars and practitioners agreed that audience ratings were merely one indicator for media program evaluation, besides which the media needed to consider the audience's feelings and its social influence.

As the publicness of media became a critical concern of communication research, "the public" and "the citizens" were articulated in democratic discourse. The justification of democratic discourse had two aspects. First, it could adopt the "open-minded" notions of official statements, such as "public opinion supervision" and "people's rights" (e.g., Chen and Wu 2009), which were specifically applied to encouraging public discussion in the new media environment. Second, it could borrow the western concepts such as public sphere and citizen's rights. Some scholars agreed that the media should function as a "public sphere" between the state sphere and the market sphere, through which the public could express their diverse voices (e.g., Pan 2008). However, radical critiques on a Habermasian "public sphere" emerged in the late-2000s. Yuezhi Zhao (2007) argued that the "public sphere" in Chinese academia was usually understood as a liberalist stance, which indeed excluded the voices of the lower social classes. Therefore, she and other critics called for a more inclusive understanding of "public sphere," with more concerns of social equality. It is worth noting that in the democratic discourse, the notion of social classes embodied the reflection on social stratification and social justice, while in the market-driven discourse, economic stratification was taken for granted.

Meanwhile, as the notion of "media professionalism" was gradually accepted by Chinese media professionals and scholars (Pan and Lu 2003), the media professionalist discourse increasingly highlighted the media's duty of serving the public. When some scholars conducted large-scale surveys on the credibility of the media (Liao et al. 2005; Yu and Zhang 2007), they translated the term "credibility" as "the degree of public trust" in Chinese, which implied their expectation of the media's role as a "public service" and identified the audience as "public." Moreover, along with the rise of new media, "user-generated content" changed the relation between producers and audiences, hence stimulating media professionals to adopt the new concept of user. Because of the strengthening of the audience's activity, it was suggested that the media should pay more attention to the users' experiences and satisfy their diverse needs, thereby raising the media's competitiveness (e.g., Tian 2008).

These discourses had partly overlapped with the scientific discourse, namely with the use of scientific methods to investigate public opinion, the market, media credibility, etc. This implied that media use and effect studies remained practical. Nevertheless, some scholars of reflexive awareness began to explore theory building based on China's local situations. For instance, the project "Shanghai Audience in the New Media Technological Environment" by the Research Center for Information and Communication Research at Fudan University (2010) examined the relation between media use and the audience's perception of social stratification and integration. They formulated the theoretical arguments as follows:

1) the media resources or "capitals" were embedded in the constitution of media adoption and use behavior; 2) in this structural situation, the media become the resources for audience's perception of their belongings of social strata and classes, their identity of citizens and nationality; 3) both new media and old media by means of "mediation" had penetrated into the audience's everyday lives in terms of psychological and social needs. In sum, all of these embodied a norm proposition, namely the publicness of the media.

It means that the principle of social justice, open and integration must eventually be reflected in the constitution of media resources and audience's uses.

In these statements, we can see that the "audience" is represented in its complicated social relations: audiences are not only media users, but also citizens, social classes, and nationalities; the media's publicness is not merely a normative concept, but also represented in the audience's use of media recourses.

Concerning the culturalist discourse, the researchers adopted a more tolerant attitude to popular culture, such as the audience's reception of advertisements. The reasons for this change might be twofold. First, as popular culture had penetrated into everyday lives, including the rise of an online popular culture, the researchers observed that popular culture was not as bad as they had previously imagined, and the audience was able to actively decode meanings. Second, the theoretical knowledge of popular culture was growing; the knowledge of cultural studies in particular provided insight into the audience's capability of resistance and active meaning-making. Nevertheless, some critics warned that the overemphasis on audience rating would lower the quality of television programs, whose essence was the colonization of commercial logic in the culture field (Shi and Lv 2006).

Moreover, some articles discussed the necessity of promoting the media literacy movement in China as constructing "cultural citizenship" in civil society. Wei Pu et al. (2009: 5–6) argued that

the real concern of media literacy education is promoting the citizens to participate in society through media channels. In this sense, media literacy education is a social movement, namely advocating all the citizens to actively use media for social progress. During this process, it is necessary to pay particular attention to the rights of the children, the youth, the female and the NGOs [non-governmental organizations], ensuring they get equal opportunities to use media resources.

As such, this approach of media literacy study identifies the audience as "cultural citizens" in civil society, connecting the democratic discourse with the aim of enhancing civic pacifications.

Conclusion

The Chinese discourses of audience research of the three periods since 1978 are summarized in Table 1.

What can we learn, then, from China's experience? After over 30 years of exploration, the Chinese discourses of audience research were rather diverse. They were not a simple combination of scientific methods and "Marxist ideology" (Rogers et al. 1985), but deeply grounded in complicated societal contexts, including the interrelations between politics,

Table 1: The discourses of Chinese audience research.

Discourses		Main articulations		
		1978–1989	**1990–2000**	**2001–2012**
Societal discourse	Dominant discourse	Socialist modernization discourse	Socialist market economy discourse	Socialist market economy and harmonious society discourse
	Alternative discourse	n/a	n/a	Civil society discourse
Academic discourse in audience research	Party-press discourse	People's trust is crucial; following the mass-line	Ensuring the "guidance of public opinion"	Guaranteeing people's rights; improving the art of guiding public opinion
	Market-driven discourse	n/a	Investigating the market and serving the consumers	Investigating the market and serving the consumers
	Democratic discourse	Media's role of public opinion supervision (strong)	Media's role of public opinion supervision (weak)	Media's role of public opinion supervision; media as public sphere; the rights of citizens and social classes
	Media professionalist discourse	Serving the readers, listeners, viewers	Serving the readers, listeners, viewers	Serving the readers, listeners viewers, users, and the public
	Scientific discourse	Studying media use and effect for media reform	Studying media use and effect for science and practice	Studying media use and effect for science and practice
	Culturalist discourse	n/a	Critiquing or confirming the popular culture	Interpreting active popular culture; culturing media literacy

economy, civil society, and media. The sophisticated reality has resulted in multiple discourses about the audience, which were even contradictory in some situations, such as the coexistence of Party-press discourse and democratic discourse.

Although these discourses illustrated the changing reality about the Chinese media, audience, and society, their theoretical contribution seems limited. One of the reasons might be that social science is not in the intellectual tradition of Chinese culture. The traditional wisdom of Chinese culture is more concerned with moral principles, just like the saying: "when the Great Moral was pursued, a spirit of gong (public and common) ruled all under the heaven." It is difficult to explain what "Great Moral" and "public and common spirit" means, because they are more like "tacit knowledge" than theorized knowledge. It might be the case that although the media scholars emphasized the professional norm of media, they have not yet developed a theoretical model of their own.

Nevertheless, western social science has been imported into China for more than a century, and its academic norm has been accepted by the Chinese academy, especially in the past three decades. Indeed, Chinese communication research began to show an increasing convergence with internal communication studies in terms of the use of concepts and methodologies. But even nowadays, the autonomy of the academic field is not entirely guaranteed. In communication research in particular, there are still interventions by the political and the economic field. Related to this, we can see that the articulation of audience was mixed with "administrative" discourses with certain ideological or pragmatic orientations, which would be obstacles for building theory.

To be sure, theoretical innovation about Chinese society and communication is under exploration. Communication researchers have been talking about theoretical indigenization since the 1980s. One of the aims is to generate the logic of media and communication from the trajectory of Chinese social transformation—a progressive development started from the emancipation of economic productivity, followed by the differentiation of the pattern of social interest, and later by the claim of democratic citizenship (Chen 2006). The representation of audience, from the singular identity of "people" or "masses" to the multiple identities encompassing the "receiving audience," "consumer," "citizen," and "the public," was also the outcome of the process of social differentiations. Due to the distinctiveness of China's cultural tradition and transforming society, this kind of academic endeavor is worth observing, for both Chinese and other international scholars.

References

Blumer, Herbert (1954), "What is wrong with social theory?," *American Sociological Review*, 19:1, pp. 3–10.

Carpentier, Nico (2010), "Deploying discourse theory: An introduction to discourse theory and discourse theoretical analysis," in N. Carpentier, I. Tomanić Trivundža, P. Pruulmann-Vengerfeldt, E. Sundin, T. Olsson, R. Kilborn, H. Nieminen, and B. Cammaerts (eds), *Media and Communication Studies: Interventions and Intersections*, Tartu: Tartu University Press, pp. 251–65.

Charmaz, Kathy (2006), *Constructing Grounded Theory: A Practical Guide Through Qualitative Analysis*, London: Sage Publications.

Chen, Chongshan (1989), "Public opinion surveys in China," *Materials of Journalism Research*, 2, pp. 1–18.

Chen, Lidan (1994), "The guidance of public opinion under the condition of socialist market economy: Learning *Deng Xiaoping's Selected Works*," *Journalism & Communication*, 2, pp. 2–7.

—— (1998), "On the media's guidance of public opinion in contemporary China," *Journalism Quarterly*, 1, pp. 10–3.

—— (2008), "The rectification in journalism research," in L. Tang (ed.), *Thirty Persons' Views in the Thirty Years*, Beijing: Zhongxin Press.

Chen, Lidan and Wu, Lin (2009), "On the legal guarantee of people's right of expression," *Journalism Quarterly*, 2, pp. 26–32.

Chen, Ruimiao (1988), "People's trust is the condition of survival for newspapers," *Journalism Quarterly*, 1:5.

Chen, Wenhong (2006), "Communication, civil society and social transformation of China," *Global Framing of Democracy Conference*, Philadelphia: Annenberg School for Communication, University of Pennsylvania.

Deng, Xiaoping ([1992] 1993), "The speech during the Southern Tour," in X. Deng, *Deng Xiaoping's Selected Works, vol. III,* Beijing: People's Press, pp. 370–83.

Gao, Bingzhong and Yuan, Ruijun (eds) (2008), *A Blue Book of the Civil Society in China*, Beijing: Peking University Press.

He, Zhou (2000), "Chinese Communist Party press in a tug of war," in C.-C. Lee (ed.), *Power, Money, and Media: Communication Patterns and Bureaucratic Control in Cultural China*, Evanston, IL: Northwestern University Press, pp. 112–51.

Hu, Jintao (2007), "Hu Jintao's report at 17th Party Congress," Xinhua News Agency, http://www.china.org.cn/english/congress/229611.htm. Accessed 9 March 2013.

Jiang, Zemin ([1996] 2006), "Correct guidance of public opinion is good for the Party and the people," in *Selected Works of Jiang Zemin*, vol. 1, Beijing: People's Press, pp. 563–68.

—— ([2001] 2006), "Jiang Zemin's report at the 80th Anniversary of the CPC," *Selected Works of Jiang Zemin*, vol. 3, Beijing: People's Press, pp. 264–99.

Laclau, Ernesto (1988), "Metaphor and social antagonisms," in C. Nelson and L. Grossberg (eds), *Marxism and the Interpretation of Culture*, Urbana: University of Illinois, pp. 249–57.

Lee, Chin-Chuan (2005), "The conception of Chinese journalists: Ideological convergence and contestation," in H. de Burgh (ed.), *Making Journalists: Diverse Model, Global Issues*, London: Routledge, pp. 107–26.

Liao, Shengqin, Li, Xiaojing, and Zhang, Guoliang (2005), "A study of the media's credibility in China," *Journalism Quarterly*, 1, pp. 19–27.

Mao, Zedong ([1943] 1965), "Some questions concerning methods of leadership," in *Selected Works of Mao Zedong*, vol. 3, Peking: Foreign Languages Press, pp. 117–22.

Min, Dahong and Chen, Chongshan (1991), "The relation between audiences' media contact and the conception of modernity in Zhejiang Province," *Journalism Research Materials*, 3, pp. 14–46.

Ni, Xun (1993), "The influence of public opinion on economic decision-making," *Journalism Research Materials*, 1, pp. 1–11.

Pan, Zhongdang (2008), "The publicness of the media and rejuvenation of China's media reforms," *Chinese Journal of Communication and Society*, 6, pp. 1–16.

Pan, Zhongdang and Lu, Ye (2003), "Localizing professionalism: Discursive practices in China's media reforms," in C.-C. Lee (ed.), *Chinese Media, Global Context*, London: Routledge, pp. 215–36.

Pan, Zhongdang and Wei, Ran (1997), "After enriched media content: A tentative study of the relationship between mass media and values," *Journalism & Communication*, 4, pp. 38–50.

Pu, Wei, Pan, Zhongdang, and Lu, Ye (2009), "Media literacy: The international development and local experiment," *Chinese Journal of Communication and Society*, 7, pp. 1–24.

Research Center for Information and Communication Research (2010), "Introduction to the project 'Shanghai Audience in the New Media Technological Environment'," *Journalism Quarterly*, 2, pp. 1–3.

Rogers, Everett M., Zhao, Xyaoyan, Pan, Zhangdong, and Chen, Milton (1985), "The Beijing audience study," *Communication Research*, 12, pp. 179–208.

Shi, Tianquan (1986), "On the participation of television viewers," *Journalism Quarterly*, 13, pp. 82–86.

—— (1995), "Popular culture and mass communication," *Modern Communication*, 4, pp. 35–37.

Shi, Tongyu and Lv, Qiang (2006), "Critique on audience-rating orientation: Questioning its nature," *Modern Communication*, 2, pp. 1–5.

Song, Xiaowei (1988), "On the audience's sensitive mentality," *Journal of Beijing Broadcasting Institute*, 1, pp. 1–5.

Sun, Liping, Li, Qiang, and Shen, Yuan (2004), "The short-term and long-term of China's social structural transformation and latent crisis," in L. Peilin, L. Qiang, and S. Liping (eds), *China's Social Stratification*, Beijing: Chinese Social Science Publishing House, pp. 42–48.

Tian, Zhihui (2008), "On the impact of user-created-content to news communication," *Modern Communication*, 2, pp. 49–52.

Tsou, Tang (1994), *Chinese Politics in the 20th Century*, Hong Kong: Oxford University Press.

Wang, Georgette (2011), *De-Westernizing Communication Research: Altering Questions and Changing Frameworks*, London and New York: Routledge.

Yang, Ruiming (1993), "On the mass media in the wave of popular culture," *Journalism Quarterly*, 4, pp. 21–24.

Yu, Guoming (1994), "Administration and marketizaton: On the distribution of communication resources," *Journalism & Communication*, 3, pp. 16–20.

—— (1997), "The development and characteristics of journalism research on the Mainland of China since the 1990s," *Mass Communication Quarterly*, 55, pp. 272–90.

—— (2003), "Economy of influence: On the nature of media industries," *Modern Communication*, 1: 1–3, n.pag.

Yu, Guoming and Zhang, Hongzhong (2007), "Assessing the credibility of mass media channel," *Journal of International Communication*, 5, pp. 29–34.

Zhang, Yong (2000), "From masses to audience: Changing media ideologies and practices in reform China," *Journalism Studies*, 1, pp. 617–35.

Zhao, Dingxin (2001), *The Power of Tiananmen: State-Society Relations and the 1989 Beijing Student Movement*, Chicago: University of Chicago Press.

Zhao, Yuezhi (2007), "State, market, and society: Examining communication and power in China from a critical perspective," *Chinese Journal of Communication and Society*, 2, pp. 23–50.

Zheng, Yongnian (2004), *Globalization and State Transformation in China*, Cambridge and New York: Cambridge University Press.

Zhou, Hongduo (1997), "On the consumption of mass communication," *Modern Communication*, 6, pp. 35–39.

Zhu, Qinghe (2011), "The logical beginning and future destination of masses-run newspapers," *Journalism & Communication*, 3, pp. 21–27.

Notes

1   Unless otherwise indicated, contemporary "China" in this chapter refers to Mainland China.

2   To be precise, in Chinese 受 means "receiving," while 众 means "masses." Sometimes scholars also use the term 受传者 to describe an individual receiver, compared with 受众 as a plural noun. In Hong Kong and Taiwan, where communication research developed earlier than Mainland China, "audience" was translated as 阅听人, which means "readers and listeners," but this term is rarely used by scholars in Mainland China.

3   Journals 1–4 are included in Chinese Social Science Citation (CSSCI). *Journalism & Communication* can be traced back to the former *Materials of Journalism Research* (1979–93), which mainly focused on the history of journalism; the data of this journal on audience studies was not valid until 1989.

4   The *Chinese Journal of Communication and Society* is a new journal, but is well-known because of its high quality. The authors come from Mainland China, Hong Kong, Macao, Taiwan, and elsewhere. Since my research objects were the discourses in Mainland China, only the audience research papers about Mainland China were selected.

Chapter 9

Articulating the Visitor in Public Knowledge Institutions

Krista Lepik and Nico Carpentier

Introduction

For centuries, public knowledge institutions have been engaged in "collecting, organizing, retrieving and disseminating of documents" (Hjørland 2000). These institutions, including museums and libraries, are seen as places "accessible to the community" serving "as repositories for and disseminators of knowledge" (Dalsgaard et al. 2008: 93). Today, they still perform these roles, but also act as melting pots of various discourses and practices: educating (Hooper-Greenhill 1994; UNESCO 1997), marketing customer services (Corrall 2003; Hooper-Greenhill 1994), preserving cultural heritage (Commission of the European Communities 2005; ICOM 2006), and constructing identity clues for their users (Hooper-Greenhill 2000: 101). Eventually, as Hooper-Greenhill (1994: 1) has stated in relation to museums, "[they] are changing from being static storehouses for artifacts into active learning environments for people."

This broadening of the scope also strongly affects the relationship between public knowledge institutions and their visitors, and the respective discursive practices that will be analyzed in this chapter. In particular, we want to see how visitors are both articulated and governed through these articulations. Borrowing the concept of articulation from Laclau and Mouffe (1985: 105), who define it as the practice of combining discursive elements "such that their identity is modified as a result of the articulatory practice," we want to show how this discursive-articulatory dimension functions to constitute the visitor, but also how it becomes part of the logics of governmentality. Although governmentality studies strongly focus on discursive practices, analyzing "institutions, procedures, analyses and reflections, calculations and tactics" (Foucault 1991c: 102), with this chapter, we want to introduce elements of Laclau and Mouffe's discourse theory (1985) within the logics of governmentality (but without seeking a full integration of both approaches). This will allow us to emphasize the role of a specific signifier, in our case the visitor.

The empirical part of this chapter is based on analysis of manager interviews, management documents (statutes and strategic plans), and regulations of three prominent Estonian public knowledge institutions: the Estonian National Museum, the Estonian Literary Museum, and the University of Tartu Library. As Marstine (2005: 8) has also argued (for the case of museums): within contemporary culture, these public knowledge institutions take on "diverse and contradictory meanings." With our analysis, we want to show how this diversity is played out in relation to the concept of the visitor,[1] whose structurally different— sometimes overlapping, sometimes contradictory—meanings contribute to the positions that these public knowledge institutions (can) take toward the Estonian society in which they are embedded. Using the notion of visitor articulation as the main sensitizing concept, we have identified three specific and co-occurring visitor articulations in the analyzed material, which are each supported by theoretical discussions from the relevant academic fields: visitors as people, as target groups, and as stakeholders. These articulations activate different paradigms, and show how Estonian museum and library culture has sought to balance the more traditional educational paradigm with marketing-driven and democratic paradigms. At the same time, we will also argue that in all three articulations (including the participatory-democratic articulation of the visitor as stakeholder) the governing logics of the public knowledge institutions remain present. By analyzing how these articulations contribute to the discursive governing of visitors in and by the three public knowledge institutions, we will highlight the continued capabilities of public knowledge institutions to develop and deploy power strategies to govern their visitors and to maintain their societal position, even within the context of changing museum and library cultures.

Articulating the visitor: People, target group, and stakeholder

The earliest articulation of visitors in public knowledge institutions is the "(common) people." Both public museums and libraries have historically been seen as educators of "common people" in order to cure society of the social illnesses (Bennett 1995; Black 2005)—either of moral or politico-economic nature—"that threatened social order and *the* social order" (Black 2005: 423, emphasis in original). This notion has a longer history however, dating back to long before the foundation of public knowledge institutions, so a brief discussion of its discursive roots is helpful here.

In western culture, the concept of the people has often had a positive connotation, referring to "the whole political community" (Canovan 2005: 12) or the sovereignty of the common people and its ability to be involved in societal decision-making. In contrast, and with an exception in the socialist tradition (McQuail 1994), the "mass" has been generally considered the negative counterpart to the people, stressing the "uneducated, ignorant and potentially irrational, unruly and even violent" (Bramson 1961 cited in McQuail 1994: 36) nature of the "common people" to whom the education policies of early public knowledge institutions attempted to speak. Considering the "people-mass" dichotomy (Williams 1963), we can use the signifier of the people as a starting point for our analysis, keeping in mind possible negative connotations that may be activated when the people are articulated as a mass.

Today, the notion of (educating) the people continues to play a significant role in public knowledge institutions, even though the educational purposes and modes of learning in museums (and libraries) have changed (Hooper-Greenhill 2007) due to the long-term success of the civilizing process. Thinking of visitors as an "undifferentiated mass public" (Hooper-Greenhill 2011: 362) has evolved into conceiving visitors as "active interpreters and performers of meaning-making practices" (Hooper-Greenhill 2011: 362). However, the people are still being served, as museums are "shaping knowledge" and producing "views of the past and thus of the present" (Hooper-Greenhill 2007: 2). This also applies to libraries that provide their users with information skills so they would be more able to evaluate and manage information, solve problems, and "empower [themselves] and the community" (Lupton and Bruce 2010: 15). There is still a perceived need to guide people, but instead of distinguishing right answers from wrong, people are encouraged to find relevant information depending on their context or practices (Lupton and Bruce 2010: 12). These developments have been supported by visitor studies that have evolved correspondingly, signifying the changed attitudes toward visitors. While earlier studies (since the 1920s) aimed at detecting patterns of visitor behavior in exhibitions, in order to improve the effectiveness of exhibitions (Screven 2004), later research has focused more on visitors' interests, motivations, roles taken during the visit (Falk 2009), or their earlier experiences, preferences, and knowledge, with the objective of specifying visitor clusters, and the desire to "create more assured and memorable experiences [...] with longer-lasting impact" (Pitman and Hirzy 2010: 25).

This already brings us to the second notion that is (discursively) structuring the relationship between knowledge institutions and their visitors: the target group. This concept originates in marketing (but was also quickly introduced in education and communication studies), where it was developed to better understand customers and to maximize efficiency by serving them better. To do that, in the market segmentation logic, customers (or visitors in our case) are divided into target groups according to particular characteristics or behaviors, and provided "separate products or marketing mixes" (Armstrong et al. 2009: 221).

The attempts to import a marketing approach to public knowledge institutions were initially particularly successful in libraries. Here, Kotler's (1975) *Marketing for Nonprofit Organizations* can be considered a turning point[2]; after 1977, the number of articles published on the marketing of library (and information) services started to increase, and reflections on library marketing were introduced in marketing or library journals (Oldman 1977; Wilson 1977). However, marketing and particularly management techniques have had "no place in [the] museum world," as promoting public museum services could generate an excessive demand that might not be met by existing resources (Yorke and Jones 1984: 94). Only since the 1990s have marketing concepts gained more popularity in museums, often hand in hand with the education politics, keeping in mind the "educational and entertainment value" (Hooper-Greenhill 1992: 214) of the museum. This way, museums have responded to the "paradoxical situation" (DiMaggio 1985 cited in Rentschler and Hede 2007: XIX), adopting a nonprofit framework and yet coping with their existence in a free market economy (Rentschler and Hede 2007).

Today, the target audience is one of the areas that the exhibition policy has to address, as, besides allowing to deal with practical questions about "resources, types of provision, roles and functions of temporary exhibitions and permanent displays, etc." (Hooper-Greenhill 1994: 177), it is also seen to pose challenges related to the museum's identity. In this logic, studying target groups helps public knowledge institutions to understand their visitors better by, for example, enabling them to predict the effects of entrance fees on target groups (Lampi and Orth 2009) or by considering hard-to-reach target groups (Toner 2008), etc.

The third concept articulated by public knowledge institutions is the stakeholder. Recently, with the need to "reconnect with the public and demonstrate their value and relevance in contemporary life" (Simon 2010: I), the idea of museums and libraries as places for public engagement or participation (Dalsgaard et al. 2008; Simon 2010) has been gaining popularity (at least to some degree). Explaining what participation means in practice, Dalsgaard et al. (2008) and Simon (2010) have referred to various forms of collaborative activities wherein the visitor has been allowed and even invited to contribute to the public knowledge institution. Such forms of participation are not entirely new—for example, Simon (2010) refers to cases of "citizen science" dating back to the 1880s (Simon 2010: 185), in which amateurs were "invited to participate in formal scientific research" (Simon 2010: 185) as volunteers—but these instances have been exceptional for a long time. And although these ideas contain an explicit validation of visitors, the reconfiguration of the internal power balance is not to be taken for granted, and frequently participation—defined as a decision-making process where the different parties can influence the outcome, or hold equal power relations (Pateman 1970: 70–71)—is still reduced to "mere" access or interaction (Carpentier 2007: 227).

One way to capture the more participatory articulation of the visitor is the concept of the stakeholder, which has its origins in economic and marketing theory. Within these fields, the concept of the stakeholder already emerged in the 1960s, although it gained wider popularity in 1984 with Freeman's work. He defined stakeholders as "any group or individual who can affect or is affected by the achievement of the organization's objective" (Freeman 1984: VI). In recent years, the focus has shifted from corporate-centric stakeholder management to managing the relationships with stakeholders in order to engage them for "long-term value creation" (Andriof et al. 2002: 9). Stakeholdership holds a participatory dimension, as these relations are "interactive, mutually engaged and responsive" (Andriof et al. 2002: 9), allowing the inclusion of notions like "participation, dialogue and involvement to the centre of stakeholder theory, with a clear inspiration (and aspiration) from democratic ideals" (Morsing and Schultz 2006: 325).

Freeman's definition of stakeholders is, however, all-inclusive. Although Freeman (1984) mapped stakeholders according to types of power positions, additional attempts to differentiate various types of stakeholders have been made, by their power, proximity, or urgency (Walker et al. 2008: 652), or by their relation to the institution. In case of nonprofit organizations (including public knowledge institutions), we can distinguish "organizational, economic, and societal stakeholders" (Werther and Chandler 2006: 4). Following this categorization, organizational stakeholders (internal to the organization) include employees, managers, stockholders, and unions (Werther and Chandler 2006: 4). Volunteers can also be included as they help to increase "employee productivity and retention, while decreasing costs" (Werther and Chandler 2006: 141). Among economic stakeholders are customers, creditors, distributors, and suppliers; societal stakeholders are communities, government actors and regulators, nonprofit organizations, and NGOs (Werther and Chandler 2006: 4).

In studies about visitors of public knowledge institutions, the concept of stakeholder remains less common and as ambivalent as in the theoretical literature. Quite often the authors have drawn upon Freeman's all-inclusive definition (e.g., Legget 2009). In some cases, visitors are explicitly and strategically distinguished from stakeholders, who are seen to have a legitimate interest in a public knowledge institution (Davies 1994 cited in McLean 2003: 11). Apart from these examples, other publications use the stakeholder concept more implicitly, for instance, when the public knowledge institution is considering visitor involvement in the service development processes (Scupola and Nicolajsen 2010), engaging the visitor in a co-creative new exhibition project, drawing on the interest of the community (Simon 2010), or enabling the visitor to co-contribute knowledge (Dalsgaard et al. 2008).

Visitor concepts, governmentality, and power

The concepts of people, target groups, and stakeholders have emerged in different environments, periods, and discourses. However, in the world of public knowledge institutions, they share an attempt to capture and understand visitors, while simultaneously being discursive tools to govern visitors. This brings us to the logics of governmentality, as captured in the work of Foucault (1983, 1991a, 1991b, 1991c) and the governmentality school (Dean 1999; Gordon 1991; Miller and Rose 2008).

In Foucault's work, power is "conceived not as a property, but as a strategy," and we can "decipher in it a network of relations, constantly in tension" (Foucault 1991a: 26). Although Foucault paid attention to the logics of governmentality "by focusing on carefully defined institutions" (Foucault 1983: 222), he still avoided isolating these institutions from the social, as "the fundamental point of anchorage of the relationships, even if they are embodied and crystallized in an institution, is to be found outside the institution [...] rooted deep in the social nexus" (Foucault 1983: 222), and not wanting to attribute total power to these institutions. After all, as Dean (1999: 28) formulated: "those who might be thought to exercise authority (over clients, investment decisions, workers, students) are subject to the exercise of other forms of authority." To protect the multidirectional character of his analytics of power, Foucault (1983: 221) also emphasized the importance of freedom as a key condition, whereas "power is exercised only over free subjects, and only insofar as they are free." This is aligned with Foucault's more general stance on power, emphasizing that power is both restrictive and generative (Tucker 1998: 114). In the constant "power game," individuals face multiple contingencies to anticipate and exploit (Pottage 1998: 22), which in turn allows them to be actively "at stake" (Pottage 1998: 23) in these ever-emerging power relations.

Foucault "understood the term 'government' in both a wide and a narrow sense" (Gordon 1991: 2), so in addition to referring to political structures or management of states, "government" "designated the way in which the conduct of individuals or of groups might be directed" (Foucault 1983: 221)—the "action upon actions" (Foucault 1983: 222). Dean (1999: 11) captures the expanded definition of government as follows:

> Government is any more or less calculated and rational activity, undertaken by a multiplicity of authorities and agencies, employing a variety of techniques and forms of knowledge, that seeks to shape conduct by working through our desires, aspirations, interests and beliefs, for definite but shifting ends and with a diverse set of relatively unpredictable consequences, effects and outcomes.

The "multiplicity of authorities and agencies" can apply various forms of governmentality, such as caring, administering, counseling, curing, punishing, and educating (Dean 1999: 21). Arguably, this variety of forms incorporates and is enabled by an evenly wide set of both material and discursive practices. In other words, government as a social phenomenon also has "a discursive character," and "to analyze the conceptualizations, explanations and calculations that inhibit the governmental field requires an attention to language" (Miller and Rose 2008: 29). While we prefer to define discourse in a broader-ideological and not exclusively linguistic way (following Laclau's [1988: 254] definition of discourse as "a structure in which meaning is constantly negotiated and constructed"), the emphasis on the discursive component of governmentality forms the basic theoretical assumption of this chapter.

The chapter's focus on the visitor articulations in public knowledge institutions is in alignment with this discursive component of governmentality. Articulating the subject is a strategy with a clear power dimension, aiming to allow and disallow the subject to engage in practices in, and in relation to, public knowledge institutions. This strategy of articulating, or naming as it is sometimes called in this context, also aims to have an impact on the subject's identity. Governmentality "makes individuals subjects [...] subject to someone else by control and dependence, and tied to his own identity by a conscience or self-knowledge" (Foucault 1983: 212). Discussing this strategy, Couldry (2003: 43) emphasizes the struggle over symbolic resources by quoting Melucci's hyperbole (1996: 182): "The real domination is today the exclusion from the power of naming." Naming, or as we prefer, articulating the visitor, produces particular power relations, with both generative and restrictive components, between the public knowledge institutions and their visitors. This discursive power play will be the object of our analysis, within the specific context of Estonia.

Context and methods

Although—at the time of writing—it has been more than twenty years after Estonia regained its independence, the country can be still considered a (post-)transitional society (Lauristin and Vihalemm 2009). This is visible within Estonia's political realm, where the long period of authoritarian (Soviet) rule has left its traces. For instance, during the Soviet regime, the signifiers democracy and participation obtained negative meanings among the population, and they paradoxically continued to disappoint people afterwards (Masso 2001). In line with "the separation of official and unofficial opinions" (Vihalemm et al. 1997: 199), the homogenizing notion of "people" in Soviet ideology (as in "Soviet people"), combined with the definition of Russians as the "'leading nation' of the Soviet multi-national state" (Kuzio 2002: 242) was met with negative responses. Estonian independence in 1991 allowed the notion of "Soviet people" to be quickly replaced with an ethnic positioning of the (Estonian) people, which is only now slowly evolving into a definition of the people on the basis of residency.[3]

In addition, older attitudes toward culture are only slowly changing. In Soviet society, culture was seen as hierarchical, distinguishing "good" taste (involving "classical" high culture) from "poor" taste (found in "western" popular culture) (Lõhmus et al. 2009). Similarly, the difference between cultural experts and consumers was significant, giving the former the legitimacy to define and produce "culture." Although "ordinary" people could participate in cultural production as amateurs, the emphasis remained on "high" culture to be accessed through the guidance of cultural experts. The regained Estonian independence did add a crucial dimension to the understanding of culture. In the Soviet Union, national culture was deemed to be "socialist in content and nationalist in form"; in the Estonian Republic both the content and form of culture became nationalist. Culture fed into the country's nationalist sentiments (Lõhmus et al. 2009: 84), distinguishing primary Estonian culture from ethnic minorities' cultures (including the substantial Russian-speaking minority in Estonia). Finally, the relative smallness of Estonia also impacted on its cultural activities, as limits in the state budget demanded the prioritization of some forms of culture over others. The two dichotomies mentioned above ("high" versus "low," "national" versus "minority" culture) were used to justify these prioritizations.

The political and cultural changes impacted upon Estonian public knowledge institutions in more specific ways. During Soviet rule "the narrative in the museum representation" (Kuutma 2011: 233) was written according to the dominant (Soviet) ideology, while libraries experienced strict censorship. After regaining independence, national culture was introduced again, but through an emphasis on the "timeless romantic peasant past" (Runnel et al. 2011: 325) of the Estonians, and only recently has the inclusion of non-Estonian groups in these representations become visible. Also, the dominance of the cultural expert and the negative meanings attributed to democracy and participation still resonate in contemporary Estonian public knowledge institutions, although Estonian museums and libraries are striving to become more participatory (Runnel et al. 2011).

Estonian national culture is embedded in a plurality of cultural institutions among which we can also find the institutions that this chapter focuses on: the Estonian National Museum, the Estonian Literary Museum, and the University of Tartu Library.[4] They can be seen as litmus papers of Estonian official cultural policy. Their roles as *the* museums dedicated to Estonian cultural heritage "confirming the self-confidence of a nation" (Õunapuu 2011: 32), or as *the* oldest and largest research library in Estonia are hard to underestimate. Our analysis will focus on these three Estonian public knowledge institutions and their visitor articulations. We use interviews with top and mid-level managers, combined with management documents and regulations generated by these institutions. The corpus of texts (Table 1), first of all, consists of nineteen interviews. Ten interviews were conducted in the Estonian National Museum and the Estonian Literary Museum in 2008, seven interviews at the University of Tartu Library in 2010, and two additional interviews at the Estonian National Museum in 2011. Moreover, five key management documents (statutes and strategic plans) and nine regulations documents (containing the rules of usage of the collections) have been analyzed. The different status (and codifying power) of the documents and interviews has been incorporated in the analysis, although both sets of documents were aligned when it came to the ways in which they articulated the visitor.

To find answers to our two main research questions: (1) how visitors are articulated by these three knowledge institutions, and (2) how these articulations are used to discipline and govern these visitors (or, in other words, what is allowed and disallowed through articulations), the methodological principles of grounded theory, in particular Charmaz'

Table 1: Corpus of texts.

Interviews	Estonian Literary Museum: 6 interviews	Estonian National Museum: 6 interviews	University of Tartu Library: 7 interviews
Management documents (statutes and strategic plans)	(1) Charter of the Estonian Literary Museum (Eesti Kirjandusmuuseumi Põhikiri)	(1) Statutes of the Estonian National Museum (Eesti Rahva Muuseumi põhimäärus); (2) Strategic development plan of the Estonian National Museum (ERM, strateegiline arengukava 2008– 2013)	(1) Statutes of the University of Tartu Library (Tartu *Ülikooli* Raamatukogu põhikiri); (2) Development plan of University of Tartu Library (TÜR arengukava 2011– 2015)
Regulations	Regulations for using the collections of: (1) The Archival Library; (2) The Estonian Folklore Archives; (3) The Estonian Cultural History Archives	Regulations for using: (1) Object collections; (2) Archive; (3) Photo collection; (4) Library; (5) Audio-visual collection	(1) University of Tartu Library regulations

constructivist variation, are used, combining phases of initial and focused textual coding (see Charmaz 2006). As is the case in all qualitative research, the iterative nature of research and the interaction between the theoretical framework on the possible articulations of the visitor and the empirical analysis is respected (Blaxter et al. 2010). As argued elsewhere (Carpentier 2010), the notion of the sensitizing concept, referring to those concepts that guide researchers in "what to look for and where to look" (Ritzer 1992: 365), acts as a crucial methodological bridge between what can be established theoretically, and what can be observed in practice. This implies that in this chapter no theoretical framework was imposed on the data (even when the theoretical framework is still discussed first in this chapter). On the contrary, the sensitizing concept of visitor articulation was used to trace specific visitor articulations in the data. The analysis of the key articulations that emerged out of the data (people, target group, and stakeholder) and their governing capacities was then further supported by theoretical reflections on these specific articulations. Here, we should add that although the explicit mention of visitor articulations was obviously acknowledged in the analysis, the implicit occurrence of these articulations was also incorporated in the analysis.

Articulations of the visitor in three public knowledge institutions

The visitor as the people

The three public knowledge institutions refer to the visitor using the three articulatory frameworks (people, target group, and stakeholder) discussed before, showing the complexity of the articulatory process: these articulations partially overlap, but also frequently contradict each other. The first visitor articulation identified in the data articulates the visitor as the people and is used to stress the institutions' all-inclusive nature. Apart from the interviews, it is especially prevalent and well-developed in the managerial documents. For example, the mission of the Estonian National Museum is to be "an institution that collects, preserves, studies and disseminates primary sources about Estonian and Finno-Ugric peoples' culture and its development" (Strategic development plan of the ENM[5] 2008–13). However, the Statutes of the ENM, revised in 2010, also add "ethnic groups living in Estonia, and neighbouring nations" to this definition of the "people," revealing, therefore, the shift in approach to the notion of "people" (from an exclusive ethnic basis to a combination with a more geographical basis). In this way, museums and libraries as public institutions are seen to be working for their society, which is translated as working for all, and educating all. Thus, the articulations of people include cases when visitors are mentioned explicitly as "everyone" or "all," as for example: "archival documents can be used by all who have expressed the wish to do so" (Regulations for using the ENM's collections).

This emphasis on "all" also defines the visitors as independent individuals, having their own sets of practices and opinions, made palpable by public knowledge institutions through visitor research. These practices vary at the level of acceptability or predictability—for less preferred yet predictable actions, rules have been developed by public knowledge institutions to define a problem, establish order, and sanction people. People are also allowed to present critique on public knowledge institutions. The critique is usually deemed acceptable for public knowledge institutions; the visitors are encouraged and enabled to present these critiques—even if the institution does nothing in response. An illustration is the following statement: "when it is a reasonable suggestion and it is feasible for us, then we have taken these wishes into consideration" (Interview 6, UTL). Only in a few extreme cases ("inept usage of old photos" (Interview 1, ENM), "spying on other laptops in public networks" (Interview 4, UTL), or "pieces of newspapers have been cut out using manicure scissors" (Interview 11, ELM)) are visitor practices perceived as a threat.

When visitors are articulated as people their interest is emphasized, as this is (seen as) the main reason why they visit a museum or a library. As the "people" is too broad to be fully embraced by public knowledge institutions, it is assumed that this interest is general. People attending public knowledge institutions are believed to visit various exhibitions, without having a particular topic of interest. People could visit another establishment—"a shopping centre" (Interview 17, ENM), for example—but their interest is seen as explaining their decision to visit the museum.

The third trait of the visitors as (part of the) people is based on their perceived need for guidance, which poses a positive challenge for the staff as the need for guidance can have faces varying in depth and form. It is tempting for staff members to relate the need for guidance to age. For instance, some respondents (Interview 1, ENM; Interview 5, UTL) suggested that especially after the "technical revolution," during the past decades, younger people are smarter, and can easily cope with developments in ICT, while elderly people need more guidance.

These characteristics (all-inclusiveness, a general interest, the need for guidance) also articulate the people as outsiders, opposite to the staff of the public knowledge institutions. Most visibly, this border between insiders and outsiders is physical: there are interior elements that create separate spaces (service counters, special repository rooms). There is also a temporal distinction, regulating when the people can visit knowledge institutions, manifested in opening hours present in regulations of public knowledge institutions. Moreover, the people are articulated as outsiders because of the lack of knowledge about (the performance of) public knowledge institutions. Despite the position as outsiders, there are still modest attempts to have people's voices heard, through visitor surveys, for instance. Obviously, the right to interpret these data is seen as the prerogative of the knowledge institution staff members (or their consultants).

The visitor as target group

Target groups constitute the second important visitor articulation in the analyzed material, standing for particular visitor groups that may be aggregated into the people. Of all articulations, this concept had explicit identifying moments[6] when interviewees were asked about "typical visitors." In some cases, the respondents listed an entire array of target groups, such as "students, faculty members, employees, [etc.]" (Interview 10, UTL). As this concept is framed by marketing discourse, it provides a relatively "safe haven" for the public knowledge institutions—at least to manage their visitors, and provide them with well-calculated products and services. This may happen even before they actually visit the public knowledge institution. As targets of a particular kind of product or service they are expected to receive customized information from and about public knowledge institutions.

Looking for the first clue to identify this articulation, we can distinguish a target group from an arbitrary group of people. It appears from the analyzed material that target groups can be formed on the basis of various "typical" features, some of which are predetermined, while others are generated through visitor research. In some cases it may be age (children), in other cases it is occupation (student or faculty member) or activity (tourism) that distinguishes one target group from another. The target group may also be formed geographically, by treating inhabitants of a particular town (e.g., Tartu) as a target group. Even if a particular group of people is heterogeneous, it is treated internally as homogeneous. Sometimes, merely one relevant feature can ground this homogeneity (for example, in case of a student target group, the focus is on the occupation of a person, not on her or his age nor town of residency; on this basis, students can be compared to "historians, […] journalists" (Interview 16, ENM) or "faculty members, scientists" (Interview 8, UTL).

Second, the members of target groups are seen to share a specific interest in a particular topic that distinguishes them from the "people," who are articulated as having a general interest in the information that a knowledge institution can provide. This is especially evident in the case of public knowledge institutions that have unique collections (rarities, manuscripts, original objects, etc.) and particular "regular customers" (Interview 8, UTL) interested in these collections.

Through the definition of the target group, its members are considered to be in need of specific knowledge, as defined beforehand by public knowledge institutions. The knowledge is thus "packaged" and served as a marketing or educational product or service. In some cases, this kind of product can be developed, considering various politics that concern knowledge institutions. In case of the Estonian public knowledge institutions, the education politics has the strongest impact on public knowledge institutions as they see themselves as trustworthy partners for schools in providing education, for example, when "teachers relate the introduction of permanent exhibition with the program of their own subject" (Interview 19, ENM).

The aggregation of all target groups still covers the variety of all people, who remain outsiders, interested in the specific products and services provided by public knowledge institutions, and they are still seen as in need. The rules meant for the people also apply to target groups. They, too, are defined through the physical and temporal constraints they are subjected to in public knowledge institutions. Moreover, their knowledge about the institutions is not deemed sufficient to become an insider, and through marketing discourse they are supposed to consume what public knowledge institutions offer them.

The visitor as stakeholder

The third visitor articulation identified in the data is the visitor as stakeholder. Following Werther and Chandler's (2006: 4) stakeholder categorization, we distinguish organizational, economic and societal stakeholders. However, not all of them concern visitors. Organizational stakeholdership often only refers to the staff (of institutions)—therefore, practically excluding visitors from this (sub)category. Nevertheless, there is one important exception, where the visitor (nearly) becomes an organizational stakeholder, and that is as volunteer, a position that combines visitorship with semi-membership of the institution's staff. Visitors can also be articulated as economic stakeholders, including correspondents, professional contributors, donors,[7] and (expert) customers, all involved in improving the quality of products and services of the public knowledge institution. Third, the material also contains references to societal stakeholders in two different ways. The first group of social stakeholders is administrations, other public knowledge institutions, or the media, although they rarely visit the public knowledge institutions,[8] an absence that complicates their position as visitors, although it does not nullify it. The second group of stakeholders is the representatives of communities (which are often defined in traditional ways, as geographical or ethnic-linguistic communities), nonprofit organizations, and NGOs; these actors are more clearly articulated as public knowledge institution visitor-stakeholders.

Despite the multifarious nature of the visitor-as-stakeholder articulation, this set of articulations still has a number of common characteristics. The first distinguishing trait is their position among all visitors: only a few specific visitors are defined as stakeholders and attributed representative power. Stakeholders (mainly economic and societal) are seen to represent the interests of other visitors, although the mechanisms of representation may vary. Because of their symbolic capital, consisting of their knowledge (about the other visitors they represent) and their ability to channel the multiplicity of visitor voices to public knowledge institutions, their opinions gain more weight. This is particularly notable at the university library that relies heavily on "specialists of particular fields: professors, associate professors and so on, who, with librarians, were checking in repositories for more up-to-date books" (Interview 10, UTL) or "have specific knowledge to buy books for research groups" (Interview 5, UTL). Economic stakeholders represent the interests of various types of professional groups, such as "faculty members demanding that all necessary materials would be near them, in their own faculty" (Interview 5, UTL). Societal stakeholders derive legitimacy from their representation of society (or parts of it), sometimes in a legal-political way, but, in other cases, in a more symbolical-political way, for instance, in relation to specific geographical or ethnic-linguistic communities.

The second characteristic of the visitors as stakeholders is related to their interest and involvement in public knowledge institutions (and not so much in their collections). One example, at the level of organizational stakeholders, is volunteering. Although public knowledge institutions are cautious to use the help of volunteers, they are accepted and acknowledged for tasks such as "inputting the data into information systems" (Interview

18, ENM) or "cutting, pasting, drawing, guarding, [...] so we let them do the work we do ourselves" (Interview 19, ENM). Apart from providing free labor, stakeholder contributions take on several other forms. Stakeholders are sometimes seen to function as information suppliers, capable of providing knowledge institutions with new information (see also the examples of collaboration between faculty members and university librarians presented in the previous paragraph). They may also be involved in the evaluation of (the quality) of products and services. A third role is the representational role mentioned before, in which stakeholders generate access to, for instance, specific societal groups and communities, providing information about them and promoting public knowledge institutions with these groups and communities. The interests of stakeholders and public knowledge institutions are seen to overlap largely, facilitating dialogue and symbolic transfers between these parties and enabling them to pursue common goals. Sometimes, however, gaps in communication and mutual understanding are mentioned, for example, when "some researchers have added in their project descriptions that materials will be handed to one of our archives, without letting us know about it [...]. This means some extra work for us" (Interview 2, ELM). To avoid potentially confusing or painful situations, public knowledge institutions have developed the position that even when they accept a visitor as stakeholder a limit is always imposed. As one interviewee mentions: "'suppliers' always need a filter—employees" (Interview 9, ELM). This implies that even when these stakeholders function within the close proximity of a public knowledge institution, their inclusion is never total.

The stakeholder interest in the public knowledge institution is strongly related to the third characteristic, where stakeholders have knowledge and expertise that is deemed to be lacking in public knowledge institutions. One of the resources mentioned is information, rendering the stakeholders information suppliers. The status of these suppliers varies based on their professional activity, ranging from voluntary correspondents to "professional researchers spending most of their working time in the knowledge institutions, working with materials these institutions can provide, and having contracts that oblige them to deposit their materials in public knowledge institutions" (Interview 2, ELM). Additionally, community representatives provide public knowledge institutions with information about "their" communities, in combination with expertise concerning ethical or ethnographic issues. "Expert customers" provide public knowledge institutions with valued knowledge about the fields they are experts in, helping to "develop the thesaurus" (Interview 15, UTL), or "selecting outdated books and having them removed from the collections" (Interview 10, UTL). Finally, in some cases, visitors-suppliers contribute more than information. This is mainly the case with donators, who supply the public knowledge institutions with material objects.

The stakeholders' position in the analyzed material is best described as partnership. This partnership is achieved by representation, interest (in the well-being and efficiency of the institution), and knowledge (that public knowledge institutions need). These are characteristics valued by the public knowledge institutions, the interest becomes shared, the bond with visitors represented by stakeholders stronger, and both the "quantity" and the "quality" of knowledge in public knowledge institutions are deemed to improve.

Logics of visitor governmentality

All three main visitor articulations are firmly embedded in the politics of governmentality as strategies (Dean 1999: 38) that exert power over visitors. From a Foucauldian perspective, this also implies that these governing strategies are both restrictive and generative, and entail forms of resistance. In Table 2, we can find a brief summary of how each visitor articulation is linked to a specific means of governance: disciplining, categorizing, excluding, and incorporating.

The first strategy, disciplining, has been previously analyzed in Bennett's (1995) and Black's (2005) works on museums and libraries, as both were opened to the public to improve "man's inner life" (Bennett 1995: 18), and "eradicate the social diseases" (Black 2005: 431). These tasks were undertaken for the sake of society, for all (by providing guidance on good behavior, the general nature of the progress of humanity, etc.). Although the "social diseases" logics have not entirely disappeared from society, the civilizing aspects of knowledge institutions are pushed to the background by educational aspects. The long-term success of the civilizing process also changes the inner dynamics of governmentality, as the conduct of visitors rarely poses a threat to the institution (by damaging the atmosphere, physical facilities, or collections). In these Estonian public knowledge institutions, we can see this disciplining educational logic at work when people are expected to ask and learn about the products and services the institutions provide; and to use these (by visiting exhibitions, participating in hands-on seminars, using databases, etc.) accordingly. Also, the power position of visitors-as-people is rather weak. Although their opinions and practices are sometimes researched, their impact on the institution is minimal, and they have no access to decision-making theaters. Third, disciplining still includes stimulating the proper behavior in and usage of public knowledge institutions, such as being quiet (UTL regulations) and sober (Regulations for using the ENM's collections), leaving personal belongings in the cloakroom (UTL regulations), not damaging collections (regulations for using ELM collections), etc. This form of discipline becomes more relevant if the numbers of visitors increase. Here, discipline not only aims to ensure the well-being of the institution, its objects, and its staff, but is also legitimized by generating "proper" conditions for other visitors. Simultaneously, we need to remember that the educational aspect of discipline has generative dimensions (present in management documents), for it is opening up new(er) ways in which visitors-as-people are articulated—such as the way in which the shift from "healing" to "educating" no longer articulates visitors as helpless "patients" but as active learners. Nevertheless, the level of agency remains limited, as we can also see when

Table 2: Visitor articulations, their characteristics, and means of governance.

Visitor articulation	People	Target groups	Stakeholders
The position among visitors	All	All as groups	Not all—represent and have legal power to represent
Degree of interest	Interested generally	Interested specifically	Interest in public knowledge institution
Relationship to knowledge	In need of guidance	In need of information/ knowledge	Not in need/have knowledge, resources
Relationship with the institution	Outsider	Outsider	Partner
Means of governance	Disciplining	Categorization (and disciplining)	Exclusion and incorporation (and disciplining)

looking at resistance. Visitors-as-people can (and sometimes do, as the interviewees explain) decide not to enter a public knowledge institution, show only limited interest having entered, or disrespect the rules. As the analysis indicates, visitors-as-people can also try to shift positions by becoming a target group member or stakeholder (by joining a group of tourists, or by becoming a correspondent or volunteer), but in general, their resistance is minimal.

This potential transformation (from people to target group) leads to the second governance strategy aimed at the visitor-as-target group: categorization. For this strategy, one of previously mentioned characteristics of the target group—being externally heterogeneous but internally homogeneous—is relevant. First, we should again emphasize that categorization has a generative component as it enables diversity among visitors: instead of treating visitors as people with general interests, the target group articulation allows consideration of various visitor characteristics. On the other hand, categorization also homogenizes the target group: one's members must act according to the requirements imposed by the target group definition. In this sense, target group members are treated similarly to the "people": their opinion is sought, and they are supposed to use the products and services of public knowledge institutions. As categorizing people into target groups is an entirely rationalized activity[9] (see Foucault 1983: 224), we can again find little resistance. One trace of that in the analyzed material is when students (one of the libraries' main target groups) refused to use the spatial environment intended to facilitate individual work (more specifically: booths), and started to "reorganize the furniture (sofas, chairs, even tables), and sat on the floor" (Interview 13, UTL) so that they could engage in group work. The library recognized their needs as a target group and responded by providing them with a new interior, including suitable furniture, which supported group work. Simultaneously, this still disciplined the students into the desired behavior.

The governing strategies relating to visitors-as-stakeholders involve both exclusion and incorporation. The strategy of exclusion is based on the distinction between stakeholders and non-stakeholders, as only a small number of visitors are labeled stakeholders based on the resources (knowledge, symbolic capital) they have, excluding other visitors from (the benefits of) this articulation. This logic of exclusion is also fed by the more general hesitance to allow for participation within the context of post-Soviet Estonia. There is a strong emphasis on the control exerted by members of staff, as it is them "who are appointed to decide" (Interview 1, ENM), which goes hand in hand with an identity of public knowledge institutions that is supporting the more traditional staff and visitors positions and which is only changing slowly; a change that will "probably take decades" (Interview 10, UTL). At the same time, this exclusion is also generative, as small groups of visitor-stakeholders, considered worthy partners, can become more closely involved within the institutions, which would not be possible if all visitors gained a similar discursive status. Still, the inclusion of stakeholders is only partial, as they are neither allowed, nor supposed, to participate in long-term decision-making or contributing to public knowledge institutions without specific knowledge of the relevance of the contribution. Second, through the strategy of incorporation, including "them into the dominant system and thus attempting to rob them of any oppositional meaning" (Fiske 1989: 18), stakeholders also become disciplined. For instance, their contributions are only accepted when deemed relevant (by/for the institution). These contributions are included in the collections on conditions defined by the public knowledge institution and its staff acting as a filter. This right to intervene is legitimized by the threat of chaos in the collections (and cultural heritage). These types of governance are difficult to resist. However, there are cases mentioned in the analyzed material (more specifically in the interviews) in which stakeholders contribute in the way they consider useful, or with the information they think is relevant. For example, the stakeholders may possess "materials they do not simply want to throw away, [...] they do not know exactly what to do with the materials, but they want the materials to be preserved" (Interview 2, ELM).

Conclusion

Three visitor articulations, people, target groups, and stakeholders, are seen to circulate within the Estonian public knowledge institutions, coexisting and overlapping. As public knowledge institutions do not exist in a social vacuum, this plurality of articulations reflects the developments both within museum and library culture and in Estonian society at large. This includes the development toward a more pluralist (institutional) culture and knowledge, with "multiple frames of reference, each with its own scheme of understanding and criteria of rationality" (Kliever 1982 cited in Bauman 1987: 128), and the need to consider complex processes that have impact on public knowledge institutions.

These articulations are not empty words in everyday rhetoric of the public knowledge institutions. They aim to provide meaning to the public knowledge institutions' complex relations with their outside worlds. Unavoidably, this also implies the regulation of the always slightly disruptive presence of these visitors entering the still sacred world of the public knowledge institution, and crossing the boundary between internal and external worlds. The visitor articulations play a key role in the facilitation of this generative process, allowing and structuring the entry of visitors into the public knowledge institution. These articulations also limit the agency of visitors, governing them by allowing and disallowing them to perform in particular ways. These restrictions, supported by visitor articulations, do not always function properly, as resistance remains possible—in Dean's words (1999: 37), we can find "the points at which regimes of government meet forms of resistance that reveal possibilities for doing things otherwise."

The three different visitor articulations also have different discursive affordances, and allow for different levels of visitor agencies. The notion of stakeholdership particularly brings in a more open and participatory model of the relations between the public knowledge institutions' interior and exterior worlds. Although here too we can see governance strategies at work, stakeholdership opens up the public knowledge institution for the knowledge and/or expertise of its outsiders, transgressing and disrupting the boundaries between the sacred inside and the profane outside. In doing so, stakeholders contribute to the democratization of the public knowledge institutions themselves, and also of society as a whole (Beck et al. 1994), strengthening the societal position of both parties. In the Estonian case, we can see that the Estonian National Museum especially had already gained some of its vitality by defining and involving stakeholders a 100 years ago, which facilitated and legitimized its significant role in the construction of the Estonian nation. Our research shows the slow continuation of, and even mild increase in, the presence (and practice) of the stakeholder concept in the selected public knowledge institutions, signifying the actual changes in museum and library culture.

However, the Estonian post-Soviet context also works against the stakeholder concept. In some situations (especially, when it concerns internal decision-making), it becomes evident that the cultural and political background of the three public knowledge institutions impacts on the role that the stakeholder concept was (and is) allowed to play. In the former Soviet republic of Estonia, the notion of the stakeholder is still very unknown and unused, in contrast with the cultural expert and national culture approaches (rendering, to use Marstine's (2005) words, public knowledge institutions into shrines) and marketing-driven approaches. The meaning of stakeholdership also was and still is blurred by the discursive alignment with the rhetoric of the former communist state. Concepts like democracy, participation, or communal activity, which also provide meaning to the notion of stakeholdership, gained negative meanings among the populations of the Soviet Union, and only after 20 years of independence did the attitudes of irony and suspicion begin to reveal signs of weakening, making space for the articulation and deployment of more democratic-participatory practices with in and by public knowledge institutions.

Acknowledgment

The authors are grateful for the support of the ETF research grant no. 8006.

References

Andriof, Jörg, Waddock, Sandra, Husted, Bryan, and Sutherland Rahman, Sandra (2002), "Introduction," in J. Andriof, S. Waddock, B. Husted, and S. Sutherland Rahman (eds), *Unfolding Stakeholder Thinking: Theory, Responsibility and Engagement*, Sheffield: Greenleaf, pp. 9–16.

Armstrong, Gary, Harker, Michael, Kotler, Philip, and Brennan, Ross (2009), *Marketing: An Introduction*, Harlow: Pearson Education.

Bauman, Zygmunt (1987), *Legislators and Interpreters*, Cambridge, MA: Polity Press.

Beck, Ulrich, Giddens, Anthony, and Lash, Scott (1994), *Reflexive Modernization: Politics, Tradition and Aesthetics in the Modern Social Order*, Cambridge, MA: Polity Press.

Bennett, Tony (1995), *The Birth of the Museum: History, Theory, Politics*, London: Routledge.

Black, Alistair (2005), "The library as clinic: A Foucauldian interpretation of British public library attitudes to social and physical disease, ca. 1850–1950," *Libraries & Culture*, 40, pp. 416–34.

Blaxter, Loraine, Hughes, Christina, and Tight, Malcolm (2010), *How to Research*, Buckingham: Open University Press.

Canovan, Margaret (2005), *The People*, Cambridge, MA: Polity.

Carpentier, Nico (2007), "Participation, access and interaction: Changing perspectives," in V. Nightingale and T. Dwyer (eds), *New Media Worlds*, Oxford: Oxford University Press, pp. 214–30.

—— (2010), "Deploying discourse theory: An introduction to discourse theory and discourse theoretical analysis," in N. Carpentier, I. Tomanić Trivundža, P. Pruulmann-Vengerfeldt, E. Sundin, T. Olsson, R. Kilborn, H. Nieminen, and B. Cammaerts (eds), *Media and Communication Studies Intersections and Interventions: The Intellectual Work of ECREA's 2010 European Media and Communication Doctoral Summer School*, Tartu: Tartu University Press, pp. 251–65.

Charmaz, Kathy (2006), *Constructing Grounded Theory: A Practical Guide through Qualitative Analysis*, London: Sage.

Commission of the European Communities (2005), *i2010: Digital Libraries*, http://eur-lex.europa.eu/LexUriServ/site/en/com/2005/com2005_0465en01.pdf. Accessed 12 June 2012.

Corrall, Sheila (2003), "Planning and policy-making," in M. Melling and J. Little (eds), *Building a Successful Customer-Service Culture: A Guide for Library and Information Managers*, London: Facet, pp. 27–52.

Couldry, Nick (2003), *Media Rituals: A Critical Approach*, London: Routledge.

Dalsgaard, Peter, Dindler, Christian, and Eriksson, Eva (2008), "Designing for participation in public knowledge institutions," *Proceedings of the 5th Nordic Conference on Human-Computer Interaction Building Bridges—NordiCHI '08*, New York: ACM Press, pp. 93–102.

Dean, Mitchell (1999), *Governmentality: Power and Rule in Modern Society*, London: Sage.

Falk, John (2009), *Identity and the Museum Visitor Experience*, Walnut Creek, CA: Left Coast Press.

Fiske, John (1989), *Understanding Popular Culture*, London: Routledge.

Foucault, Michel (1983), "Afterword: The subject and power," in H. L. Dreyfus and P. Rabinow (eds), *Michel Foucault: Beyond Structuralism and Hermeneutics*, Chicago: The University of Chicago Press, pp. 208–26.

—— (1991a), *Discipline and Punish: The Birth of the Prison*, London: Penguin Books.

—— (1991b), "Questions of method," in G. Burchell, C. Gordon, and P. Miller (eds), *The Foucault Effect: Studies in Governmentality*, London: Harvester Wheatsheaf, pp. 73–86.

—— (1991c), "Governmentality," in G. Burchell, C. Gordon, and P. Miller (eds), *The Foucault Effect: Studies in Governmentality*, London: Harvester Wheatsheaf, pp. 87–104.

Freeman, R. Edward (1984), *Strategic Management: A Stakeholder Approach*, Boston: Pitman.

Gordon, Colin (1991), "Governmental rationality: An introduction," in G. Burchell, C. Gordon, and P. Miller (eds), *The Foucault Effect: Studies in Governmentality*, London: Harvester Wheatsheaf, pp. 1–51.

Hjørland, Birger (2000), "Documents, memory institutions and information science," *Journal of Documentation*, 56:1, pp. 27–41.

Hooper-Greenhill, Eilean (1992), *Museums and the Shaping of Knowledge*, London: Routledge.

—— (1994), *Museums and Their Visitors*, London: Routledge.

—— (2000), *Museums and the Interpretation of Visual Culture*, London: Routledge.

—— (2007), *Museums and Education: Purpose, Pedagogy, Performance*, Abingdon: Routledge.

—— (2011), "Studying visitors," in S. Macdonald (ed.), *A Companion to Museum Studies*, Malden: Wiley-Blackwell, pp. 362–76.

ICOM (2006), *ICOM Code of Ethics for Museums*, Paris: International Council of Museums, http://icom.museum/fileadmin/user_upload/pdf/Codes/code2006_eng.pdf. Accessed 12 June 2012.

Kotler, Philip (1975), *Marketing for Nonprofit Organizations*, Englewood Cliffs: Prentice-Hall, Inc.

Kotler, Philip and Sidney, Levy J. (1969), "Broadening the concept of marketing," *Journal of Marketing*, 33:1, pp. 10–15.

Kuutma, Kristin (2011), "National museums in Estonia," in P. Aronsson and G. Elgenius (eds), *Building National Museums in Europe 1750-2010; Conference proceedings from EuNaMus, European National Museums: Identity Politics, the Uses of the Past and the European Citizen*, Bologna, 28–30 April, EuNaMus Report No. 1, Linköping: Linköping University Electronic Press, pp. 231–59.

Kuzio, Taras (2002), "History, memory and nation building in the post-Soviet colonial space," *Nationalities Papers: The Journal of Nationalism and Ethnicity*, 30, pp. 241–64.

Laclau, Ernesto (1988), "Metaphor and social antagonisms," in C. Nelson and L. Grossberg (eds), *Marxism and the Interpretation of Culture*, Urbana: University of Illinois Press, pp. 249–57.

Laclau, Ernesto and Mouffe, Chantal (1985), *Hegemony & Socialist Strategy: Towards a Radical Democratic Politics*, London: Verso.

Lampi, Elina and Orth, Matilda (2009), "Who visits the museums? A comparison between stated preferences and observed effects of entrance fees," *Kyklos*, 62:1, pp. 85–102.

Lauristin, Marju and Vihalemm, Peeter (2009), *Siirdeaeg: Sotsioloogiline Tagasivaade Eesti Arengutele 1988–2008*, unpublished manuscript.

Legget, Jane (2009), "Measuring what we treasure or treasuring what we measure? Investigating where community stakeholders locate the value in their museums," *Museum Management and Curatorship*, 24, pp. 213–32.

Lõhmus, Maarja, Lauristin, Marju, and Siirman, Eneli (2009), "The patterns of cultural attitudes and preferences in Estonia," *Journal of Baltic Studies*, 40, pp. 75–94.

Lupton, Mandy and Bruce, Christine (2010), "Windows on information literacy worlds: Generic, situated and transformative perspectives," in A. Lloyd and S. Talja (eds), *Practicing Information Literacy*, Wagga Wagga: Centre for Information Studies, pp. 3–27.

Marstine, Janet (ed.) (2005), *New Museum Theory and Practice: Introduction*, Malden: Blackwell.

Masso, Iivi A. (2001), "Eesti sotsiaalpoliitilisest arengust 1990-ndatel," *Vikerkaar*, 2–3, pp. 161–66, http://www.iivimasso.com/docs/eesti_sotsiaalpoliitilisest.html. Accessed 12 June 2012.

McLean, Fiona (2003), *Marketing the Museum*, London: Routledge.

McQuail, Denis (1994), *Mass Communication Theory: An Introduction*, 3rd ed, London: Sage.

Melucci, Alberto (1996), *Challenging Codes*, Cambridge: Cambridge University Press.

Miller, Peter and Rose, Nikolas (2008), *Governing the Present: Administering Economic, Social and Personal Life*, Cambridge, MA: Polity.

Morsing, Mette and Schultz, Majken (2006), "Corporate social responsibility communication: Stakeholder information, response and involvement strategies," *Business Ethics: A European Review*, 15, pp. 323–38.

Oldman, Christine (1977), "Marketing library and information services the strengths and weaknesses of a marketing approach," *European Journal of Marketing*, 11:6, pp. 460–74.

Õunapuu, Piret (2011), "Eesti Rahva Muuseumi loomine ja väljakujunemine" ("Foundation and evolution of the Estonian National Museum"), Ph.D. thesis, Tartu: Tartu Ülikooli Kirjastus.

Pateman, Carole (1970), *Participation and Democratic Theory*, Cambridge: Cambridge University Press.

Petersoo, Pille (2007), "Reconsidering otherness: Constructing Estonian identity," *Nations and Nationalism*, 13, pp. 117–33.

Pitman, Bonnie and Hirzy, Ellen (2010), *Ignite the Power of Art*, New Haven: Dallas Museum of Art & Yale University Press.

Pottage, Alain (1998), "Power as an art of contingency: Luhmann, Deleuze, Foucault," *Economy and Society*, 27, pp. 1–27.

Rentschler, Ruth and Hede, Anne-Marie (2007), "Introduction," in R. Rentschler and A.-M. Hede (eds), *Museum Marketing Competing in the Global Marketplace*, Oxford: Elsevier, pp. XIX–XII.

Ritzer, George (1992), *Sociological Theory*, New York: McGraw-Hill.

Runnel, Pille, Tatsi, Taavi, and Pruulmann-Vengerfeldt, Pille (2011), "Who authors the nation? The debate surrounding the building of the new Estonian National Museum," in S. J. Knell, P. Aronsson, A. B. Amundsen, A. J. Barnes, S. Burch, J. Carter, V. Gosselin, S. A. Hughes, and A. Kirwin (eds), *National Museums: New Studies from Around the World,* London and New York: Routledge, pp. 325–38.

Screven, Chandler G. (2004), "United States: A science in the making," in G. Anderson (ed.), *Reinventing the Museum: Historical and Contemporary Perspectives on the Paradigm Shift,* Walnut Creek, CA: Altamira Press, pp. 160–66.

Scupola, Ada and Nicolajsen, Hanne Westh (2010), "Service innovation in academic libraries: Is there a place for the customers?," *Library Management*, 31, pp. 304–18.

Sillaste, Juhan, Kirch, Aksel, and Kirch, Marika (1999), "People of foreign origin in Tallinn and Ida-Virumaa: Change in identity and prospects for development," *EBS Review*, 10, pp. 17–21.

Simon, Nina (2010), *The Participatory Museum*, Santa Cruz, CA: Museum 2.0, http://www.participatorymuseum.org/chapter1/. Accessed 12 June 2012.

Tankler, Hain (1997), "Erakogud Tartu Ülikooli Raamatukogu komplekteerimisallikana 19 Sajandil" ("Private collections as acquiring sources of the University of Tartu Library in the 19th century"), in R. Saukas (ed.), *Tartu Ülikooli Raamatukogu aastaraamat 1996 (The Yearbook of the University of Tartu Library)*, Tartu: Tartu Ülikool, pp. 115–32.

Toner, Lisa Jane (2008), "Non-use of library services by students in a UK academic library," *Evidence Based Library & Information Practice*, 3:2, pp. 18–29.

Tucker, Kenneth H. (1998), *Anthony Giddens and Modern Social Theory*, London: Sage.

UNESCO (1997), *Museums, Libraries and Cultural Heritage*, Hamburg: UNESCO Institute for Education, http://www.unesco.org/education/uie/confintea/pdf/7b.pdf. Accessed 12 June 2012.

Vihalemm, Peeter, Lauristin, Marju, and Tallo, Ivar (1997), "Development of political culture in Estonia," in M. Lauristin, P. Vihalemm, K. E. Rosengren, and L. Weibull (eds), *Return to the Western World: Cultural and Political Perspectives on the Estonian Post-Communist Transition*, Tartu: Tartu University Press, pp. 197–210.

Walker, Derek H. T., Bourne, Lynda M., and Shelley, Arthur (2008), "Influence, stakeholder mapping and visualization," *Construction Management and Economics*, 26, pp. 645–58.

Werther Jr., William B. and Chandler, David (2006), *Strategic Corporate Social Responsibility: Stakeholders in a Global Environment*, Thousand Oaks: Sage.

Williams, Raymond (1963), *Culture and Society 1780–1950*, Harmondsworth: Penguin Books.

Wilson, Alexander (1977), "Marketing of library services," *Canadian Library Journal*, 34, pp. 375–77.

Yorke, David A. and Jones, R. R. (1984), "Marketing and museums," *European Journal of Marketing*, 18, pp. 90–99.

Notes

1   In this analysis, the specific connotations of the signifier visitor (which are also manifold) are not problematized; the visitor is used here as a container concept, which is stabilized in order to allow for the analysis of the three articulations of the visitor, as people, target groups, and stakeholders.

2   Prior to this, in 1969, Kotler and Levy had migrated the concept to the world of non-business organizations.

3   These debates are usually supported by word *eestimaalane* (instead of *eestlane*, that is ethnic Estonian) referring to "the one living in Estonia" (Sillaste et al. 1999: 18) regardless of ethnicity. Compared to "Swedish, the Baltic Germans and the 'old' Russian minorities" (Petersoo 2007: 125) who were seen as "sufficiently similar to Estonians" (Petersoo 2007: 125), the perception of Russian minority in Estonia has needed more time for changing and improving (Petersoo 2007).

4   The Estonian National Museum, founded in 1909, then contained both oral and material heritage. It was divided in 1940 into the National Ethnography Museum and the National Literary Museum. The University of Tartu Library (as we know it now) was established in 1802 (Tankler 1997). All three institutions are open to the general public.

5   The following abbreviations are used: the Estonian National Museum (ENM), the Estonian Literary Museum (ELM), and the University of Tartu Library (UTL).

6   Charmaz (2006: 59–60) defines identifying moments as implicit notions that are at some point openly discussed.

7   All three institutions have, since their foundation, relied on their social networks and collaboration with their visitors to improve their collections either with the aid of correspondents or donors for whom helping is a manifestation of patriotism (Õunapuu 2011) or a matter of honour (Tankler 1997: 117). Yet the correspondents (and donors in the library context) are still regarded "rather as sources of information and authenticity for the museum" (Runnel et al. 2011: 333) than active interpreters of culture.

8   Exceptions mainly concern media professionals who use the collections of public knowledge institutions for research.

9   This concerns both "the effectiveness of the instruments and the certainty of the results" and its "proportion to the possible cost (be it the economic cost of the means brought into operation, or the cost in terms of reaction constituted by the resistance which is encountered)" (Foucault 1983: 224).

Chapter 10

To be a Common Hero: The Uneasy Balance between the Ordinary and Ordinariness in the Subject Position of Mediated Ordinary People in the Talk Show *Jan Publiek*

Nico Carpentier and Wim Hannot

To a common hero, an ubiquitous character, walking in countless thousands on the streets. In invoking here at the outset of my narratives the absent figure who provides both their beginning and their necessity, I inquire into the desire whose impossible object he represents.

(De Certeau 1984, in the preface to *The Practice of Everyday Life*)

Introduction

Because of the present-day tendency to focus on the participatory potential of new media (and especially on Web 2.0), we tend to forget that many different media technologies and genres allow ordinary people to participate in the generation of media content. Despite exceptions, like the attention paid to participation in the reality TV genre, the importance of "old" media remains structurally underestimated, and their cultural importance is ignored when it comes to mediated participatory processes. One of the main television genres that facilitates the participation of so-called ordinary people is audience discussion programs (ADPs). Being part of a broadcast tradition that has been celebrated for its emancipatory-democratic potential for quite some time now, ADPs are very much worth the same attention as the more fashionable Web 2.0-driven types of participation and the often more problematic types of participation in reality TV programming (Andrejevic 2004) or in quiz shows.

ADPs are culturally and politically relevant because they not only offer their audiences discourses on (mainstream media) participation, but also a series of subject positions by featuring a diversity of social categories engaged in public talk. A subject position is defined here—following Laclau and Mouffe (1985)—as the positioning of subjects within an overdetermined discursive structure that generates the conditions of possibility for this identity. Important for this analysis is that subject positions play key roles in discursive (political) struggles, leading to antagonistic subject positionings (for instance ordinary people versus the power-bloc) built on processes of othering. At the same time we should keep in mind that, for Laclau and Mouffe, antagonisms always have both negative and positive aspects, as antagonistic subject positions attempt to destabilize the "other" identity but desperately need that very "other" as a constitutive outside in order to stabilize their own identity.

Television is one of the many discursive machines that produce and reproduce a diversity of these subject positions, turning the on-screen and off-screen (inter)actions of media professionals, ordinary people, experts, and many other actors embedded in a wide range of social categories, into televised discourses that are in some cases highly fluid, multilayered, and sometimes contradictory, but in other cases more singular and rigid as they are embedded within specific hegemonies. These discourses not only relate to the topics being explicitly addressed; television talk shows for instance also (re)produce discourses on the articulation of participation, on the power relations that lie behind the participatory process, and on the conditions of possibility and limits of the participatory process, by representing the interactions between actors that, in turn, represent specific subject positions like the media professional, the ordinary person, the expert, and the celebrity (e.g., Bonner 2003, for a similar categorization).

As one of its main social categories, "ordinary people" is arguably the most important subject position supporting the emancipatory claims of the sub-genre of the ADP. In the academic literature on ADPs, two main approaches can be distinguished, the emancipation and the manipulation approach. The emancipation approach, which is often strongly influenced by community media theory, argues that the subject position of ordinary people gains a positive articulation through these ADPs by valuing ordinary people's common sense over expertise, by increasing the visibility of members of marginalized groups (Carpignano et al. 1990; Livingstone and Lunt 1996; Priest 1995) and by rendering political elites accountable to ordinary people, subjecting them to public scrutiny (McNair et al. 2003). These programs are seen to contribute to the democratization of the mass media (Hamo 2006: 428), give a voice to ordinary people, provide them with the symbolic resources to represent themselves and to resist existing power imbalances, and mobilize ordinary people to be(come) politically active (McNair et al. 2003). In contrast to this approach, a series of authors highlight the manipulative or pseudo-participatory nature of these programs, critiquing the emancipatory articulation of the ordinary people subject position (and ADP). The inability to criticize or undo the existing power imbalances in society (McLaughin 1993), and within the programs themselves (Carpentier 2001; Gruber 2004), the emphasis on the individual and the personal to the detriment of the structural and the social (Peck 1995), the instability of the debate and its many contradictions (Tomasulo 1984) are all considered problematic.

In both the emancipation and the manipulation approach toward ADPs, the majority of the analyses focus on the programs and their production processes. Despite their importance in evaluating the claims made by both approaches, reception analyses still remain rare, with some notable exceptions like Livingstone and Lunt's (1996) *Talk on Television*. This chapter explicitly aims to contribute to this discussion about the democratic potential of ADPs by looking at the reception of a north Belgian[1] talk show called *Jan Publiek*, and the way this talk show's audience interpret the televised subject position of ordinary people. This reception studies' approach (e.g., Staiger 2005) will allow us to further enrich the more textual readings of *Jan Publiek* (Carpentier 2001) by bringing in the voices of audience members.

As in participatory programming, the status of the audience is always profoundly complicated by the on-screen presence of representatives of the audience; this chapter combines a more traditional focus-group-based reception analysis with interviews with the "ordinary" participants in this talk show. Both sets of voices will be analyzed to see how the televised multilayered subject position of ordinary people is seen to support the more democratic-emancipatory discourse, and how this discourse is simultaneously infiltrated, weakened, and subverted by a reductionist articulation of the subject position of ordinary people in *Jan Publiek*, based on the discursive antagonism between ordinary people and an alliance of power-blocs (Hall 1981)—consisting of celebrities, experts, politicians, and media professionals—all represented in the talk show.

The everyday and the ordinary

Before addressing the mediated subject position of ordinary people, we need to look at the theoretical reflections on a related concept—everyday life. There are a number of reasons for this strategy: the everyday life concept has received much more theoretical attention than ordinary people, thus generating much richer theoretical frameworks. Following Gregg's and Sandywell's arguments, care should nevertheless be taken not to "erase" (Gregg 2007: 99) the ordinary through an unnecessary focus on the everyday, nor to "denigrate" the ordinary through "the very act of [it] being theorised as 'everyday life'" (Sandywell 2004: 174). Second, especially Lefebvre's work on the everyday in particular allows for an increase in the weight of the political in the ordinary. A third argument is that one of the main significations of the ordinary is grounded in the everyday, when the ordinary is defined through its articulation with everyday (authentic) experiences.

The everyday

When analyzing the everyday (and the ordinary) we can distinguish between more essentialist and relationist perspectives. The more essentialist approaches tend to see identities as stable, independent, and possessing a "true" essence. The more relationist approaches incorporate notions of fluidity and contingency, see identities as mutually dependent and ignore the existence of "true" essences. Despite the incorporation of these essentialist approaches in this chapter, identities are still—following Laclau and Mouffe (1985), as mentioned above—basically seen as relational, contingent, and the result of articulatory practices within a discursive framework.

The more essentialist frameworks that theorize the everyday stress the repetitive, the un-purposeful, the unnoticed, and the routine-based as the main characteristics of the everyday. One illustration is Felski's ([1999] 2000: 18) seminal definition of the everyday as:

grounded in three key facets: time, space and modality. The temporality of the everyday [...] is that of repetition, the spatial ordering of the everyday is anchored in a sense of home and the characteristic mode of experiencing the everyday is that of habit.

The difficulty of capturing the everyday has led many authors to define the everyday in a relationist way, or at least to generate some openings toward a relationist definition. In these relationist approaches, everyday life is seen as different from the exceptional, or the sublime and its enchantment. For instance De Certeau (1984: xx) refers to everyday "practices that produce without capitalizing," and Bennett and Watson (2002: x) mention that everyday life is depicted "as ordinary in the sense that it is not imbued with any special religious, ritual or magical significance." Even Lefebvre (1958: 97), who uses a more essentialist approach to the everyday, has proposed to define everyday life in relation to "exceptional" or "superior" activities like dreams, art, philosophy, politics, etc.

The advantage of these relationist approaches is that they allow an emphasis on the fluid construction of everyday life, and the impossibility of capturing this floating signifier (Laclau and Mouffe 1985: 112–13). On the downside, the risk of the relationist approaches is twofold. The old romantic dichotomy between the everyday "inauthentic" and the tragic "authentic," which for instance characterized the work of the early Lukács ([1911] 1974) is still threatening to contaminate any type of relationist approach toward the everyday. Second, hyper-relationist approaches bring with them the risks of cultural relativism, and the disarticulation of everyday life from its potentially empowering signification. For these reasons, it is crucial to keep the essentialist approaches linked to the study of the everyday, while simultaneously incorporating them in a more constructivist/relationist position that allows articulation of the fluid nature of everyday life.

The distinction that Lefebvre (1988) has made between the everyday (*le quotidien*) and everydayness (*la quotidiennité*) is especially worth salvaging, as this allows the incorporation of the tension between the emancipatory and manipulative approach discussed above. Lefebvre strongly emphasizes the critical, political, and emancipatory potential of the everyday as the site where social change resides. Roberts (2006: 13) summarizes Lefebvre's position as follows: "the everyday is that social or experimental space in which the relations between technology and cognition, art and labor are configured and brought to critical consciousness." It is not "simply the expression of dominant social relations, but the very place where critical thinking and action begins" (2006: 38). In order to theorize the difference between capital's administration of atomization and repetition, and the modality of social transformation and class resistance against this atomization and repetition, Lefebvre uses the distinction between the everyday and everydayness. This safeguards the critical-political potential of the everyday, which is seen as "lived experience (*le vécu*) elevated to the status of a concept and to language. And this is done not to *accept* it but, on the contrary, to *change* it" (Lefebvre 1988: 86, emphasis in original).

The ordinary

Similar to the above discussion on the everyday, the ordinary and, more specifically, ordinary people can also be approached from more essentialist perspectives. While the concept of ordinary people is sometimes seen as a synonym of the "people," in many other cases a class-based definition is used, where ordinary people are defined as "members of the working and middle classes" (Bennett and Watson 2002: x). Hartley (1994: 173) explicitly refers to the moments when the concept of ordinary people is used as "convenient 'erasures' or euphemisms for class."

But again the fluidity of the signifier ordinary people (and of class), and the difficulty of capturing the signifier (see Thumim 2006), need to be emphasized. De Certeau (1984: 2, emphasis in original) pointed out that ordinary people are "*Everyman*" and "*Nobody*," "*Chacun*" and "*Personne*," "*Jedermann*" and "*Niemand*." As was the case with everyday life, this fluidity has resulted in the development of a number of relationist approaches. In the case of ordinary people, the class-based background of the concept has not been erased, but was transformed into an elite versus the people relationship. For instance Hall (1981: 238) positions (ordinary) people versus this power-bloc, i.e., "the side with the cultural power to decide what belongs and what does not, an alliance of social forces which constitute what is not the people." Williams (1981: 226) refers to ordinary people as "a generalised body of Others ... from the point of view of a conscious governing or administrative minority." A number of authors writing from a media studies perspective have also used these relationist approaches. Syvertsen (2001: 319) defines ordinary people as people who are not media professionals, experts, celebrities, or newsworthy for any other reason. Ytreberg (2004: 679) describes ordinary people as non-professional and non-specialized performers.

Finally, Laclau (1977), who also uses this relational approach, emphasizes the conflictual and dominating nature of the relationship between ordinary people and the power bloc. He writes: "the 'people'/power bloc contradiction is an antagonism whose intelligibility depends not on the relations of production but the complex of political and ideological relations of domination constituting a determinate social formation" (1977: 166). The issue of domination unavoidably foregrounds the resistance debate. De Certeau especially has highlighted the tactical resistance of ordinary people, arguing that ordinary people find ways to beat the strong: "be that of powerful people, or the violence of things or of an imposed order" (1984: xix).

Another way to capture this resistance and to emphasize the political nature of the signifier ordinary people is by using Lefebvre's distinction between the everyday and everydayness. This distinction allows us to see the *ordinary* as a site of resistance against the workings of power elites, while *ordinariness* can then be used to refer to the administration, disciplining, and management of ordinary people by these power blocs. Through this distinction, the ordinary is invested with a clear emancipatory signification, which consists of resisting against the strategies of the societal elites and power blocs. Or, to put it in other words, this distinction allows emancipation to be seen as intrinsically linked to the ordinary, and not as something that is imposed by external actors or processes. As this semantic strategy again risks introducing a number of too essentialist positions, it remains a necessary condition to embed these concepts within a more constructivist/relationist model, where both the ordinary and ordinariness are seen as fluid and contingent (see also Sandywell 2004).

The ordinary and ordinariness in *Jan Publiek*

The above-discussed semantic-theoretical strategy allows the emancipation-manipulation debate to be enriched with regard to ADPs. On the one hand, the notion of the ordinary can be embedded within the emancipation discourse on ADPs, as the emancipatory articulation of the subject position of ordinary people. The notion of ordinariness is, on the other hand, linked to the manipulation discourse, as it articulates the subject position of ordinary people as disciplined and managed by a (number of) power bloc(s).

This strategy will structure our analysis of the articulations of the subject position of the ordinary people that featured in the ADP *Jan Publiek*, and the reception of their being ordinary and their ordinariness. As mentioned above, ADPs like *Jan Publiek* not only offer always-specific discourses on participation, but also a series of subject positions that—because of the specificity of the program format—are divided along the lines of ordinary people versus a fluid alliance of power blocs. Our analysis will not only focus on the ways that the focus group respondents and ordinary talk show participants accept (or reject) the being ordinary of the participants, but also on the ways that the antagonistic structure of the program affects the subject positions of all parties involved, including those of the ordinary participants.

The format of Jan Publiek

Jan Publiek[2] is a Dutch-language north Belgian ADP that was produced and broadcast by the public broadcaster VRT. Its first series had 21 broadcasts, which were aired live in the spring of 1997. Later, four more series, with each thirteen or sixteen broadcasts, were produced and broadcast in the fall of 1997 (second series), in 1998 (third and fourth series), and in the spring of 1999 (fifth series). In the 70-minute broadcasts of *Jan Publiek*, one specific topic was discussed on each occasion by the participants in the studio, with the host of the program, Jan Van Rompaey, standing at the front of an arena-shaped studio, while all participants were seated facing him. What makes *Jan Publiek* a slightly less traditional ADP was that in contrast to the first, the four other series used a panel of twenty ordinary people—ten women and ten men—who were invited to participate in an entire series of thirteen or sixteen broadcasts.

When it was broadcast for the first time, it was considered the flagship of north Belgian televised audience participation. Although previous human-interest programming—

mainly but not solely by the public broadcaster VRT (Dhoest and Van Den Bulck 2007)—had paid attention to offering ordinary people a voice, *Jan Publiek* was a turning point as it explicitly offered ordinary people the opportunity to debate social, political, and cultural issues. *Jan Publiek* triggered a number of other television programs (like *Eerlijk Gezegd* and *Advocaat van de Duivel*) in the five years after its final broadcast. After this period, the ADP format lost much of its attraction (with election programs as notable exceptions). Because of its prominent role, many of the specific choices made by the *Jan Publiek* editorial team (including the use and articulations of categories like ordinary people, celebrities, experts, and politicians) were copied by the programs that followed after *Jan Publiek*.

Through its format, *Jan Publiek* made use of, and articulated a series of specific subject positions. Apart from ordinary people, who were invited on the basis of their authentic experiences or who were part of the panel of ordinary people, the program included four more subject positions: the media professional (in this case, the host), the celebrity, the expert, and the politician. The production team of *Jan Publiek* carefully selected a number of individuals that fit these social categories, and built the entire program structure on the interventions these individuals were expected to make. During the actual broadcast, the moderator-host carefully selected the participants and combined traditional interview strategies with more open moderation strategies (which were all based on a pre-prepared script). The interaction of the individual participants (structured through their participant-categories and subject positions), the host (and his subject position[s] and scripts), the pre-prepared footage, the tele-voting interventions of the viewers at home, combined with the ideologies of participation and the ideologies of television production all contributed to the construction of a weekly broadcast media text.

Methodologies

The methodology of this chapter rests on two main approaches, which incorporate the two types of audiences ADPs have. First there is the regular or home audience, whose audience constructions are researched through a traditional reception analysis based on focus groups. Second, there is the studio audience, which participates in the actual debates. Here, the panel members, representing the audience in the actual ADP, were interviewed, both in 1999 and 2007.

For the reception analysis of the first series in 1999,[3] which intended to focus not only on participation but also on gender issues, four specific broadcasts from the first series of *Jan Publiek* were selected for eight focus group discussions in which 45 people participated. While the original reception analysis focused more on the participatory process and on gender issues, the material obtained was rich enough for a new analysis in relation to the topic that is discussed in this chapter.[4] These four programs discussed the topics shown in Table 1.

Table 1: The four *Jan Publiek* broadcasts (first series).

Date	Topic
13 Feb 97	A brief love affair should be acceptable
22 May 97	Porn should be banned
10 Apr 97	Women make better bosses
17 Apr 97	Children are always the victim of a divorce

The second methodological component is a series of interviews with the panel members of *Jan Publiek*'s second series. All 20 panel members who participated in *Jan Publiek* in 1997 were interviewed in 1999. In 2007, ten years after their participation in *Jan Publiek*, the panel members were traced and contacted again. Eventually thirteen of them were interviewed,[5] three other panel members had died, two were untraceable, and two refused to be interviewed. All thirteen former participants had very vivid and consistent memories of their participation, and had little trouble answering the questions, even if their participation in *Jan Publiek* took place ten years ago.

For the analysis of the reception focus groups and the interviews, a qualitative content analysis was used (Maso 1989; Wester 1995). We were careful not to fall into the trap of empiricist-universalist knowledge production. One of the main strategies for avoiding this trap was to use the notion of the subject position (and, more specifically, the interrelated, fluid, and sometimes antagonistic subject positions of the ordinary people, the celebrity, the expert, the politician, and the media professional) as sensitizing concepts (see Blumer 1969), guaranteeing an open perspective on the diversity of meanings and significations generated by the research subjects. Another potential problem was the time lag between the different research phases, but the outcomes of the reception focus groups and the interviews turned out to be very similar. For this reason they are also discussed together, and the focus groups and the interviews are distinguished only when there were structural differences between them.

Communication rights and pluralism

During the focus group discussions and the interviews, the ordinary and its presence in the television system in *Jan Publiek* are explicitly validated through two interrelated discourses. The first discourse is based on communication rights, and simply claims access for ordinary people to the television system as a basic (human) right. As this interview quote illustrates, the participants felt validated through this process of self-expression:

Just my opinion counts, and that's how it really was. Coming home and hearing reactions of people who had really watched and listened. People came up to me on the street with: sorry, I totally disagree with you, for this and that reason. Just talking. That moved me, it gave me some self-confidence, that's what I got out of it.

(Roeland, male, 21, interviewed in 1997)

The second (interrelated) discourse is based on pluralism. It is deemed important that the different views, as expressed by (among others) the ordinary participants, can gain publicness through *Jan Publiek*. However, these two discourses of communication rights and pluralism do not mean that the ordinary people's on-screen presence is unconditionally accepted. In order for their presence to be acceptable, the condition of relevance has to be met.

For the focus group participants, relevance is first of all generated by the representativeness of the ordinary participants in *Jan Publiek*. For that reason the ordinary participants need to be in group, so that they can speak on behalf of the population and generate the pluralism of ideas that is much valued. This articulation renders the ordinary people concept as always plural, articulating them as *the* public opinion.

But not surprisingly, the talk show participants take a different position here, as, inevitably, they emphasize their own individuality. As one of the participants puts it "Every person in him/herself was unique" (Betty, female, 58, interviewed in 2007). But even then they still stress the need for relevance, as one of the participants put it: "What's the use of having people talk about a topic with which they have nothing to do, and that want to give their opinion because they want to be on television?" (Fatiha, female, 34, interviewed in 2007). The tension between the participants' emphasis on individuality and the need for relevance is only resolved by reverting to another legitimizing concept: authenticity.

For both the focus group respondents and for the interviewees, authenticity is the main argument to support the relevance of the presence of ordinary people, as has been mentioned in other research as well (see Montgomery 2001; Scannell 2001; Thornborrow 2001). Montgomery (2001: 399) remarked that authenticity can be situated at the level of spontaneity, at the level of truthfulness of the lived experience, and at the level of the truthfulness of the performed self. In the *Jan Publiek* case, the importance of the authentic lived experience is especially emphasized. When this authentic experience is deemed absent, the legitimacy of the presence of ordinary people in *Jan Publiek* is questioned by their audiences. In a number of cases, both focus group participants and interviewees simply state how difficult it is to speak about issues participants have not experienced, but in other cases they revoke the access rights of ordinary talk show participants when there is no authentic experience to support their presence.

But when these authentic experiences become too intense, the same process of delegitimization also takes place. Ordinary people need to have authentic everyday life experiences, but when these experiences are considered (too) extraordinary, abundantly detailed, or even vulgar, their narrations also become disarticulated from the subject position of ordinary people and they are marginalized. Similarly, when ordinary people are seen to appear on screen only to become famous, they are again no longer considered authentic, and they become pseudo-celebrities.

The antagonistic position of ordinary people toward the other subject positions

The subject position of ordinary people is not only articulated through the simple presence of this social category in the studio, and the way the format defines them as being in possession of authentic experiences.[6] The subject position of ordinary people is also defined in an antagonistic relationship to a set of other subject positions, which also feature prominently in *Jan Publiek*: celebrities, experts, politicians, and media professionals. It is through the antagonistic relationship with these more elitist social categories that the subject position of ordinary people becomes intertwined with ordinariness.

Traditionally, antagonism is viewed as a collision of social agents that dispose of fully developed identities. Following Laclau and Mouffe (1985), antagonism is seen here as a struggle between different subject positions that can never be completely developed, because—to use Laclau and Mouffe's words (1985: 125)—"the presence of the Other prevents me from being totally myself." Applied to ADPs, a subject position in a talk show is constituted in relation to its counterparts, and the televised articulation of a subject position affects both itself and its counterparts.

But a too rigid interpretation of these subject positions should be avoided, as these antagonistic relationships can be fluid and mobile in some cases, for instance allowing people to shift from one position to another. Thornborrow (2001: 478) rightly observed that the dichotomy of broadly oppositional criteria "in practice often breaks down when the discursive roles and interactions of participants in these shows is examined more closely," which we can also observe in the case of *Jan Publiek*. But at the same time the rigid structure of *Jan Publiek*, with its media professionals protecting the pre-defined subject positions, and the sometimes equally rigid discursive frameworks used by the audiences, causes these subject positions to remain very present in articulating the identities of the Other and the self.

Celebrities

In constructing a three-level typology (famous, semi-famous, and anonymous), Hamo (2006: 430) points out that the level of renown is one of the main structuring elements of the subject position of the celebrity. This type of fame is (at least partially) generated through their frequent presence in popular public spaces, which has also allowed them to develop a wide range of communicative skills (Ytreberg 2004: 679).

Through the antagonistic relationship between the subject positions of celebrities and ordinary people, ordinary people are articulated as unknown (or anonymous), not having access to these popular public spaces and not being experienced or skilled. The element of authenticity, which characterizes ordinary people, also affects the identity of celebrities, as articulated in focus groups and interviews.

First, the lack of authentic experiences of the celebrities that participate in *Jan Publiek* is critiqued. Second, authenticity is seen as restricted by processes of commodification and image construction. Celebrities, in contrast to ordinary people, are part of a specific cultural-industrial system, which is seen to structurally limit their capacity to participate openly and to act spontaneously (and to be authentic). As one of the *Jan Publiek* participants remarks: "they wear masks" (Suzanne, female, 57, interviewed in 2007). These critiques first of all again strengthen the importance of authenticity, as the absence of authenticity also delegitimizes the participation of celebrities. They also position ordinary people as non-commodified, which can be added to their articulations as unknown and non-experienced.

There are nevertheless moments where these subject positions start to shift. First of all, celebrities are still allowed access to lived experience as well, rendering their identities semi-authentic, as the following citation illustrates: "I think that celebrities who talk about their divorce [...] that they come across much better" (Evelien, female, 23, FG [Focus Group] 4).

Second, ordinary people can gain access to celebrity status through their contributions in participatory programming. In the case of *Jan Publiek*, some focus group respondents know the other series fairly well. After the first series the format was changed and ordinary participants returned each series as members of a permanent panel. Although the focus groups discussed only the first series (which had no permanent panel), some viewers started comparing series (which also had been broadcast at the time the focus groups took place), claiming that the ordinary panel members became celebrities themselves.

In the interviews with these panel members, many anecdotes of them being recognized by people they don't know come up. For instance, Astrid (female, 27, interviewed in 2007) describes how she was recognized by the anesthetist who asked her (right before an appendix operation): "Hey, you're from *Jan Publiek*. How are you doing now?" Even ten years later, some people approach the participants, asking them how they know each other.

Experts

In the case of the expert subject position, legitimacy is provided by expertise (Van Leeuwen 2007: 94). Traditional genres like documentaries or current affairs programs valorize the expert for his or her objective, rational, and factual knowledge, but in ADPs this position is often inverted, as they are articulated as inauthentic, alienated, cold, and artificial (Livingstone and Lunt 1996: 101–02).

Despite the critical position of ADPs toward expert knowledge (which can also be found in their reception), the expert subject position is still very present in ADPs, and is again articulated in a specific fashion. Most importantly, experts are seen as knowledgeable (although this knowledgeability is sometimes valued negatively). This articulation again has its consequences for the identity of ordinary people, who are linked to authentic experiences, through the antagonistic relationship with the expert identity, as is illustrated in the citation below: "Yes, their experience is just their own experience and not the experience of other people. That's why they are not experts" (Jan B, male, 22, FG3).

Apart from being knowledgeable, experts are also individuated, embedded in professional systems, and considered to be experienced. The process of individuation is partially strengthened by the way experts are treated by media professionals who attribute names, rank, institutional affiliation, and status to them (Thornborrow 2001: 459). Through their affiliation, their institutional and organizational membership is also highlighted. In the reception focus groups, these people were indeed often referred to by their names or by their affiliations. Moreover, they are also considered to be more experienced (like the celebrities) in talking in public, again in contrast to the ordinary people.

As already indicated, the expert position (however present it is in the program) is not always valued positively. In some cases the respondents use a flexible definition of expert, attributing the label of expert to a science journalist (working for a magazine called *Knack*), or to a psychologist working for *Libelle*, a women's magazine. However, this attribution of the label is never wholehearted. In other cases, there is a perceived absence of "real" experts, which is fed by the need to ground knowledge in academia. But for yet another group, even the presence of these "real" experts—termed "superprofessors" by one participant (Jan B, male, 22, FG3)—is considered problematic. Again, these articulations of the expert identity have consequences for the subject position of ordinary people, which again articulates them with ordinariness. Through this antagonism, ordinary people are considered unknowledgeable but still authentic, unorganized but still part of a collective, and inexperienced. In contrast to the celebrities, there is little overlap between the subject positions of experts and ordinary people. They are still deemed very different categories, and the difference between knowledge and opinion remains very rigid. There is nevertheless one exception, and that is when ordinary panel members turn out to be experts. The most important case is the panel member Fatiha, who worked at the integration agency of the city of Leuven, and was initially approached by the editorial team of *Jan Publiek* to help locate potential panel members with a migrant background. Because of the lack of other candidates, she decided to participate as a panel member herself. Her professional expert background was hardly ever mentioned during the broadcasts, which renders her a hidden expert.

Politicians

The focus group discussions only rarely make reference to this third subject position, despite the fact that quite a number of politicians actually feature in the *Jan Publiek* broadcasts. The legitimacy of their presence is based on the notion of accountability toward the "people," through which politicians become articulated as representing the people in ADPs. Like experts, politicians do not escape from a number of negative and sometimes cynical connotations, articulating them as alienated and even corrupt.

The nature of the articulation of the identity of politicians is nevertheless different from the case of ordinary people: while politicians are known to us, ordinary participants represent the people anonymously, symbolically, and collectively. Traditional (political) representation becomes individuated and linked to power through the mechanism of delegation. Politicians are also defined as grounded in (political) organizations and as (political) experts, as they know how the political system works. This is again contrasted to ordinary people who—according to the focus group respondents—do not possess this kind of knowledge and expertise. Similar to the expert subject position, the antagonism between politicians and ordinary people articulates ordinary people as authentic, but at the same time unknowledgeable, un-organized, and inexperienced.

Again, the border between the subject position of the politician and the ordinary people turns out to be more fluid than expected. This is partially caused by the fact that one panel member was already a member of a city council before her participation in *Jan Publiek*. Also, the requests that panel members received from political parties after they had appeared in *Jan Publiek* generates fluidity. At least one panel member was a candidate at the local elections, one other panel member was also asked to stand (but refused), and a third panel member was nominated by the north Belgian liberal party VLD to represent them on the Management Board of the public broadcaster VRT, a position Rudi De Kerpel effectively held for five years.

Media professionals

The central role of the media professional in an ADP is based on the role of moderator, combined with an interviewing role (Carpentier 2001: 224). An important part of the critiques launched at ADPs is focused on the role of the host, as they are seen to play a key role in the management of the debate and of the participants (e.g., White 1992). This role articulates the host in *Jan Publiek* as professional, and as part of a professional media system. This focus can also be found in the focus group discussions, where both his identity and his actions are linked to professionalism.

Being professional also implies in some cases being embedded in the professional media system and culture. His on-screen presence first of all generates renown, which is not dissimilar to the fame of "other" celebrities. His on-screen moderating and interviewing role also articulates his subject position with power. The host (supported by the invisible production team) controls the setting and nature of the debate. In the antagonistic position of the media professional toward the ordinary people, ordinary people thus become positioned as unknown, powerless, unprofessional, and not part of a professional system or organization, again articulating them with ordinariness.

This again does not imply that the position of the media professional remains without critique. Especially the combination of professionalism and his being perceived as powerful generates strong critiques, which amount to the host (and his production team) not being professional enough, interrupting too much, keeping the debate superficial, not being neutral enough and even being manipulative. Most of the panel members (having experienced being professionally managed themselves) also indicate that they became more critical television viewers than before their participation. As Fatiha (female, 34, interviewed in 2007) puts it: "What I learned from it is that media cannot contain reality. It's always a representation, an image, and not reality."

Finally, the border between media professionals and ordinary people also becomes unstable, but this happens only after the broadcasts. A number of panel members used the fame generated by their appearance in *Jan Publiek* to become media professionals themselves. One of them presented a program about gardening on public radio, another did a show about dogs on Liberty TV for two years, and a third panel member started freelancing for a magazine (*Knack*).

Jan Publiek: The subject positions model

As a preliminary conclusion, the model shown in Figure 1 provides us with an overview of the antagonistic relations between ordinary people and the alliance of power blocs, at the discursive level of the different subject positions as they are articulated by the viewers in the reception analysis focus groups. Through these antagonisms, all subject positions become articulated with a wide range of elements that co-construct the identities of all individuals involved.

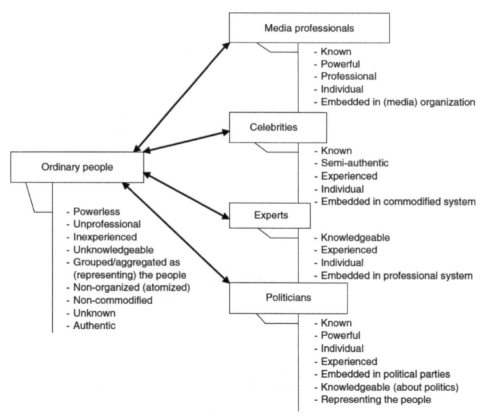

Figure 1: The articulations of the subject positions in *Jan Publiek*.

Conclusion

When talking about audience discussion programs, or about Web 2.0 participation, we should avoid taking an a-historical position. These analyses are part of a long history of debates on the democratic capacity of media technologies (see Figure 2). In the post–Second World War era, we can distinguish two major periods. In the 1970s, the UNESCO debates about the new world information and communication order (NWICO), and the community (and alternative) media movement, placed media participation on the agenda. After a period of relative silence, a second major upsurge of these participatory practices (and societal debates about them) was related to the internet and later Web 2.0, partially combined with the arrival of reality TV. But also outside these two major periods, we can find practices of, and debates about, mediated participation, like for instance mainstream television talk shows (including the audience discussion programs discussed in this chapter) that peaked in the 1980s and 1990s. Although their participatory intensity was relatively low, their emancipatory potential remained considerable. Moreover, none of these technologies (and the organizations in which they are embedded) has disappeared; all of them have managed to sustain themselves over time.

Each of the above-discussed examples of mediated participation has specific characteristics, (co-)determined by a matrix of technological, organizational, economic, social, and cultural features. Through this matrix, an always specific balance between emancipation and manipulation, between the ordinary and ordinariness is reached. So when looking at (the reception of) the emancipatory nature of *Jan Publiek*, or the perceived balance between the being ordinary and the ordinariness in these ADPs, the outcome is—not surprisingly—

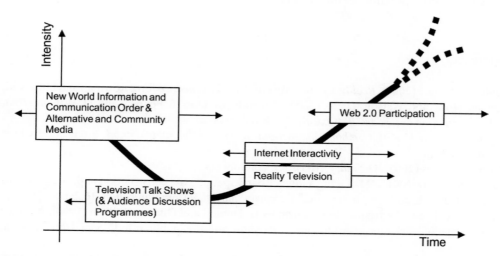

Figure 2: A selection of (debates on) participatory media technologies and their participatory intensity.

nuanced. Clearly, the focus group respondents and talk show participants emphasize the importance of public participation of ordinary people by invoking a communication rights discourse and a pluralism discourse. Their narrations of authentic experiences are highly valued and their interventions have positive connotations in a positive way, especially when compared with some of the other participant groups.

The relationist argument of the ordinary people versus the alliance of power blocs is not a mere theoretical construct, but is also (spontaneously) brought up in the focus groups and interviews. They articulate ordinary people in an antagonistic position toward the more elitist groups like celebrities, politicians, experts, and media professionals, and use that antagonism to expand their appreciation for the authenticity of ordinary people. In this sense, the ordinary—with its Lefebvrian emancipatory load—seems to be strongly present in *Jan Publiek*, and there seems to be little ordinariness (and the related administration, disciplining, and management of ordinary people).

But this antagonism also comes at a high price, as it traps the recipients and participants into linking other characteristics to both the ordinary people subject position and the other more elitist subject positions. The antagonism between media professionals and ordinary people, for instance, produces a powerful–powerless dimension. Moreover, the antagonism between experts and politicians on the one hand, and ordinary people on the other, supports the knowledgeable–unknowledgeable dimension. The antagonism between celebrities and ordinary people constructs the latter as unknown, while celebrities are constructed as famous and, thus, known. At a more generalized level, the antagonism between the power blocs and ordinary people constructs ordinary people as inexperienced, detached, and atomized, restricts them to the private, and traps them in their authenticity. Through this mechanism ordinary people are again reintroduced to their ordinariness, and cut off from the emancipatory potential of the ordinary.

References

Andrejevic, Marc (2004), *Reality TV: The Work of Being Watched*, Oxford: Rowman and Littlefield.

Bennett, Tony and Watson, Diane (2002), "Introduction," in T. Bennett and D. Watson (eds), *Understanding Everyday Life*, Oxford: Blackwell, pp. i–xxiv.

Blumer, Herbert (1969), *Symbolic Interactionism: Perspective and Method*, Englewood Cliffs: Prentice Hall.

Bonner, Frances (2003), *Ordinary Television*, London: Sage.

Carpentier, Nico (2001), "Managing audience participation: The construction of participation in an audience discussion programme," *European Journal of Communication*, 16:2, pp. 209–32.

Carpignano, Paolo, Anderson, Robin, Aronowitz, Stanley, and Difazio, William (1990), "Chatter in the age of electronic reproduction: Talk show and the 'public mind'," *Social Text*, 25&26, pp. 33–55.

de Certeau, Michel (1984), *The Practice of Everyday Life*, Berkeley: University of California Press.

Dhoest, Alexander and Van Den Bulck, Hilde (2007), *Publieke Televisie in Vlaanderen: Een Geschiedenis*, Ghent: Academia Press.

Felski, Rita ([1999] 2000), "The invention of everyday life," *New Formations*, 39, pp. 15–31.

Gregg, Melissa (2007), "The importance of being ordinary," *International Journal of Cultural Studies*, 10:1, pp. 95–104.

Gruber, Helmut (2004), "The 'conversation on Austria': A televised representation of Austria's internal condition after the national-conservative, 'Wende'," *Journal of Language and Politics*, 3:2, pp. 267–92.

Hall, Stuart (1981), "Notes on deconstructing the popular," in R. Samuel (ed.), *People's History and Socialist Theory*, London: Routledge and Kegan Paul, pp. 227–40.

Hamo, Michal (2006), "Caught between freedom and control: 'Ordinary' people's discursive positioning on an Israeli prime-time talk show," *Discourse & Society*, 17:4, pp. 427–45.

Hartley, John (1994), "Mass society/mass society theory," in T. O'Sullivan, J. Hartley, D. Saunders, M. Montgomery, and J. Fiske (eds), *Key Concepts in Communication and Cultural Studies*, London: Routledge, pp. 173–74.

Laclau, Ernesto (1977), *Politics and Ideology in Marxist Theory: Capitalism, Fascism, Populism*, London: New Left Books.

Laclau, Ernesto and Mouffe, Chantal (1985), *Hegemony and Socialist Strategy: Towards a Radical Democratic Politics*, London: Verso.

Lefebvre, Henri (1958), *Critique de la vie Quotidienne: Introduction*, Paris: L'Arche Éditeur.

—— (1988), "Towards a Leftist cultural politics: Remarks occasioned by the centenary of Marx's death" (trans. David Reifman), in C. Nelson and L. Grossberg (eds), *Marxism and the Interpretation of Culture*, Urbana: University of Illinois Press, pp. 75–88.

Livingstone, Sonia and Lunt, Peter (1996), *Talk on Television: Audience Participation and Public Debate*, London: Routledge.

Lukács, Georg ([1911] 1974), "The metaphysics of tragedy" (trans. Anna Bostock), *Soul and Form*, Cambridge, MA: MIT Press, pp. 152–74.

Maso, Ilja (1989), *Kwalitatief Onderzoek*, Amsterdam: Boom.

McLaughlin, Lisa (1993), "Chastity criminals in the age of electronic reproduction: Reviewing talk television and the public sphere," *Journal of Communication Inquiry*, 17:1, pp. 41–55.

McNair, Brian, Hibberd, Matthew, and Schlesinger, Philip (2003), *Mediated Access*, Luton: University of Luton Press.

Montgomery, Martin (2001), "Defining authentic talk," *Discourse Studies*, 3:4, pp. 397–405.

Peck, Janice (1995), "Talk shows as therapeutic discourse: The ideological labor of televised talking cure," *Communication Theory*, 5:1, pp. 58–81.

Priest, Patricia J. (1995), *Public Intimacies: Talk Show Participants and Tell-All TV*, Cresskill, NJ: Hampton Press.

Roberts, John (2006), *Philosophizing the Everyday: Revolutionary Praxis and the Fate of Cultural Theory*, London: Pluto Press.

Sandywell, Barry (2004), "The myth of everyday life: Toward a heterology of the ordinary," *Cultural Studies*, 18:2–3, pp. 160–80.

Scannell, Paddy (2001), "Authenticity and experience," *Discourse Studies*, 3:4, pp. 443–57.

Staiger, Janet (2005), *Media Reception Studies*, New York: New York University Press.

Syvertsen, Trine (2001), "Ordinary people in extraordinary circumstances: A study of participants in television dating games," *Media, Culture & Society,* 23:3, pp. 319–37.

Thornborrow, Joanna (2001), "Authenticating talk: Building public identities in audience participation broadcasting," *Discourse Studies,* 3:4, pp. 459–79.

Thumim, Nancy (2006), "Mediated self-representations: 'Ordinary people' in 'communities,'" *Critical Studies,* 28:1, pp. 255–74.

Tomasulo, Frank P. (1984), "The spectator-in-the-tube: The rhetoric of *Donahue,*" *Journal of Film and Video,* 36:2, pp. 5–12.

Van Leeuwen, Theo (2007), "Legitimation in discourse and communication," *Discourse & Communication,* 1, pp. 91–112.

Vandenberghe, Lies (2008), "Kan televisie werkelijk een mensenleven veranderen? Een bevraging van de participanten van het discussieprogramma *Jan Publiek,* 10 jaar na dato, over de impact van hun tv-programma," master's thesis, Brussels: Vrije Universiteit Brussel.

Wester, Fred (1995), "Inhoudsanalyse als kwalitatief-interpreterende werkwijze," in H. Hüttner, K. Renckstorf, and F. Wester (eds), *Onderzoekstypen in de Communicatiewetenschap,* Houten: Bohr Stafleur Van Loghum, pp. 624–49.

White, Mimi (1992), *Tele-Advertising: Therapeutic Discourse in American Television,* Chapel Hill: University of North Carolina Press.

Williams, Raymond (1981), *Keywords: A Vocabulary of Culture and Society,* London: Flamingo.

Ytreberg, Espen (2004), "Formatting participation within broadcast media production," *Media, Culture & Society,* 26:5, pp. 677–92.

Notes

1 In order not to resonate with the strong Flemish identity construction process, the use of the expression "north Belgium" is preferred, which actually approximates the transmission range of VRT quite well, as both the Flemish region and the Brussels capital region are covered by VRT.

2 The name of the program originates from a Dutch expression that can be translated as "Joe Public," which refers to the so-called "man in the street", aka "John Doe."

3 This analysis was organized in collaboration with Sonja Spee and Mieke De Clercq, and with the help of 24 Ghent University students. My warm thanks to all of them.

4 None of these reception analyses were ever published.

5 These thirteen panel members were traced and interviewed by Lies Vandenberghe. I wish to extend my gratitude to her for her appreciated help with the data gathering phase of this chapter. See also Vandenberghe (2008).

6 One could speculate about the reception of the authenticity of ordinary people if they were positioned differently (which partially happened in the other series of *Jan Publiek*), but in the case of the first series of *Jan Publiek*, both the format and the reception emphasize the articulation of authenticity with ordinary people.

Section 5

Activism and Resistance

Chapter 11

Online Barter and Counter-Hegemonic Resistance

Giulia Airaghi

Introduction

This chapter seeks to reveal the counter-hegemonic elements of barter as well as consider the ways in which it reproduces the hegemony of monetary exchange. The analysis will argue that barter conforms to the criteria de Certeau (1990) used to define a tactic, and that, as a tactic, it operates in a field where the rules have been decided by a dominant force, the force of the market. Barter is approached here from the perspective of discourse theory, which allows seeing the field of consumption as a political field. According to Mouffe (2005), the political, distinguished from the more narrow field of institutional politics, is a dimension of all spheres of human life. Across different spheres, she argues, different discourses, practices, or tactics struggle to gain the power to impose themselves on society. When a practice eventually manages to impose itself, it becomes hegemonic and its political nature becomes veiled. However, this hegemonic structure is ultimately contingent and can always be questioned by some counter-hegemonic practices (Mouffe 2005). Furthermore, Mouffe argues that the political confrontation between different alternatives is often related to collective identities. The latter can emerge from a "we/them" relationship that might turn out to be a friend/enemy relationship if the "other" is perceived as threatening the existence of the "we," triggering an antagonistic conflict between different identities.

As Beck (1992) emphasized with his description of "subpolitical" spheres, no matter how personal the choices and practices of a single consumer, she will always be mobilized inside the public sphere as part of a collective identity. From Simmel's (1996) description of the fashion mechanism to Bourdieu's (1980) studies on distinction and to cultural studies' analysis of subcultures (Hebdige 1979), we know consumption is a place where different identities emerge. In this sense, consumption is a political field where competing practices, performed and represented by collective identities, are engaged in a hegemonic struggle. In our societies, monetary exchange became the hegemonic practice of exchange. However, other forms of exchange did not simply die out, but became counter-hegemonic practices. As Mouffe (2005) suggested, when a hegemony is imposed, a choice is made between different alternatives, but these alternatives do not disappear.

Barter can be approached from this perspective. We know barter has been used throughout the entire history of humankind, long after money became the main accepted tool in goods exchanges. On the level of international trade, for example, barter has frequently been preferred to monetary exchange, both in commercial relations between the great colonial empires and their colonies, and later in the relationship between major economic powers, imposing itself as a "response to the growing number of barriers to international trade and finance" (Appadurai 1986: 10). Barter represents an alternative way not only to exchange goods, but also to give them value. It is for this reason that I will argue that barter, with its different and alternative practices, with its tactics that escape or even attempt to subvert the hegemonic system, and with its alternative associated discourses, is counter-hegemonic.

In the course of the chapter four dimensions of barter are explored, demonstrating how it is counter-hegemonic: its capacity to reject the use of money, to contrast the market, to support alternative consumption models, and to create alternative social relations.

The chapter is the result of a field research conducted with qualitative methods throughout six months. The researcher spent this time doing ethnographic observations in three barter websites[1] and conducting 22 in-depth interviews with barterers. As part of the ethnography, she created an account for each of the websites where she got involved in all the activities of the practices: from selecting objects to be exchanged, to negotiating with other people on the terms of exchange, to participation in discussion on public forum about the meaning of barter. Some of these exchanges resulted in face to face in-depth interviews about barter, which produced texts that were then analyzed through a discourse-theoretical approach (Carpentier and De Cleen 2007).

Barter rejects the idea of money

The history of money, its birth and diffusion, has been shown to be one of a political instrument employed by a political authority (whether the State or the king) to represent and exercise power (Bloch 1933; Bobbio 1985; Braudel 1981; Ingham 1996; Keynes 1971; Knapp 1924; Le Goff 1997, 2010; Smithin 1994; Turri 2009; Weber 1978). Far from being a mere unit of measure,[2] money is the representation of the economic value of an object exchanged in a market: it is the representation of a relation that involves all the commodities exchanged in the market. In this monetary system, the relation between the individuals that exchange commodities is not taken into consideration. For historical and political reasons, money developed to be the dominant system of exchange in contemporary societies. In this sense, the counter-hegemonic nature of barter is manifested by its enabling exchanges without the use of that instrument. Money represents the value of objects and is recognized as representing interchangeability with itself, meaning an instrument that is interchangeable with any other thing (Simmel 2011: 122). As a consequence, people place their trust in money (and in a third party, the State or the banking institution, which guarantees its value), instead of in the person they are exchanging with. Barter resists the hegemony of money by setting the value of the objects exchanged within the relation between people and by moving the location of trust to the subjects that exchange.

Rejection of money

It is by rejecting the use and the very idea of money that barter expresses its counter-hegemonic power: as barterers contend, the less the reference to money the better the barter mechanism works. There is an expression of resistance deriving from a consciousness of living in a world where the value of nearly everything is expressed in monetary terms. Even when this consciousness is less developed, many barterers described money as "dirty," "useless," "a-social."

However, the hegemonic power of money reveals itself in barter practices in different ways. The exchange of gold, for example, distorts the mechanism of negotiation because it exercises excessive power over other objects: as the value of gold immediately transforms into money, it is perceived as the "neutral object" (Simmel 1997a, 1997b) that can be exchanged with everything. There are barterers either offering gold to obtain as many objects as possible, or offering a high number of low-value objects against gold. Gold can then be exchanged for money in particular outlets.[3] In this manner, people who give away multiple objects in exchange only for gold can then turn it into money and make what interviewees described as "the deal." This attitude weakens the counter-hegemonic force of barter in contrasting money. Barter's resistance is therefore protected by those barterers who regard the practice of gold exchange as misbehavior.

"Making a deal" refers to a concept of accumulation (maximizing profit) typical of capitalist societies where the ultimate aim of economic action is to accumulate capital. In this sense, Simmel (1997b) argued that money became problematic in our societies, when it moved from being a mere means to an ultimate aim. Making a profit is perceived by some barterers as misbehavior and is considered one of the worst sin in barter philosophy. Profit-oriented actions are perceived as typical of a market system where the value of the individual is omitted and the aim is to acquire as much capital as possible, while in barter the action of a subject is driven by different aims (like satisfying the other's needs).

The second way that the hegemony of money enters barter is when objects are measured and/or described in monetary terms. Thus, the function of money is maintained unaltered: it establishes a value prior to the exchange relation. Barterers who declare the price of an object are seeking to signal a pre-determined value and to start the negotiation phase based on that value. Although the barter mechanism tries to resist money, the latter became so hegemonic that it is used also within barter exchange as a value reference. The term "hegemony" here refers to the capacity to conquer not only the practical dimension of everyday life but also its abstract, cultural dimension. The fact that people cannot judge the value of an object without referring to money means that money has achieved hegemonic power.

As for the use of gold, a protection mechanism is activated to preserve the counter-hegemonic dimension of barter. Describing objects in monetary terms is considered bad behavior among barterers. This can lead to exclusion as barterers showing this attitude are perceived as subjects who do not understand the "barter philosophy," and are unable to assimilate the implicit rules coordinating a barter community (cf. the "recipes" described by Schutz 1979).

Inside/outside value setting

According to Simmel (2011), value is generated within an exchange, but money establishes an aprioristic value that prevents individuals from engaging in an exchange relation to struggle over value. Therefore, the strong counter-hegemonic power of barter lies in its capacity to restore the power of the subject in an economic transaction, allowing her to determine the value of what is exchanged. The process leading to the establishment of values is the result of an agonistic struggle, where participants are not willing to eliminate the counter-part, as if they were enemies (Mouffe 2005), but their aim is to collaborate in order to balance the sacrifices they both have to make, to possess the object they want (Simmel 2011), as if they were adversaries.

Not all possessions are considered suitable for exchange. The reasons why an object may end up in the list of potential objects for exchange are various and these reasons are important keys to understand the entire process. Objects selected for exchange are not just objects individuals no longer use. Indeed, an essential characteristic of an exchangeable object must be that it can be useful to someone else.

Whenever a subject selects an object to exchange on a barter website from the many objects she owns, she establishes a relation with all the other members of the community who might potentially be interested in establishing an exchange relation with her. In a monetary exchange system, each object derives its value (price) from its relation with all other objects. This leaves the individual feeling out of place in a market economy and makes the market appear artificial and impersonal, since value is defined within a relation that the market objectifies and the subject–object relation is reduced to mere calculus of the work-hours necessary to acquire the object.

In a market exchange, value is already fixed and the subject can only decide whether the sacrifice is possible or not, she cannot decide the measure of the sacrifice—she cannot decide the price.

The second relational dimension is the one established between subject and object: deciding to give the object away (receiving something in exchange) already implies a form of sacrifice. Simmel (2011) describes the sacrifice involved in exchange as the sacrifice a subject must make to close the distance between the desired object and herself. It could be argued that, in barter, there is a previous step: the two subjects involved do not enter the relation from the same position. On the one side, there is a subject who does not desire an object, but who has the desire to separate from the object she owns. The subject will agree to separate from that object only if the object in return being offered is commensurate with this sacrifice, the latter object representing the other party's sacrifice, on the other side of the relation.

Barterers have space to decide together the measure of the sacrifice both are willing to make. This is what is meant by an exchange of sacrifices, and this is why barter exchange is described as an exchange of equal values. These equal values refer to the value of the sacrifice, not the value of the objects exchanged: the exchange can be concluded only if the sacrifices of both parties correspond. One of the clearest examples in this sense is an exchange described by this barterer:

> I found myself bartering a pressure cooker against two very old dvd's [sic]. I was giving the two old dvd's and I received the pressure cooker. This exchange was stuck in my mind since I felt uneasy in exchanging only two dvd's [sic] for a pressure cooker but I remember that the other person told me "look, I do not need that cooker in any case, I do not give it any value, or at least I do not give it the value I know it would have in the market place. But those two dvd's [sic] of yours, I was looking for them since a long time, hence they are far more valuable for me, compared to the cooker." Then, I understood she was looking for those objects with the same urgency [with which] I was looking for the cooker, that is what mattered, nothing else.

(Zr_29f)

Moving the location of trust

In the market economy people must trust money since market exchanges are not reciprocal, in the sense that they do not establish relations between parties. Theoretically, money eliminates the need for trust because it frees the individual from the reciprocity mechanism typical of gift (Anspach 2007): parties involved in a monetary exchange do not have to trust that the other will reciprocate. Nonetheless, this need is not removed from exchanges; it is just shifted to money (Anspach 2007: 58). Indeed, exchanges are performed only because each individual believes the money she is receiving from another individual will be accepted by a third party. Simultaneously, the third party will eventually accept money, because she thinks it will be accepted by another person, and so on, infinitely. In the end, the third party that guarantees the value of money, the instrument people use to exchange, is the State or the banking institute minting money. So, trust is located in that third party. The counter-hegemonic dimension of barter, in this case, refers to the fact that barterers are involved in reciprocal relations where no third party is involved: they must trust each other. Although this may imply a more complex and a less secure process, the fact of placing trust in another person and not another entity (State or bank) endows the exchange with a human side. Many barterers who have had negative experiences with exchange are still more satisfied with barter exchange compared to monetary exchanges since the "price" they face in barter (the risk of being cheated) is more affordable compared to the anonymity of the market (the price of feeling deprived of social relations).

Barter is not market

A market economy is an economy with a precise structure (the market), where the forces of aggregate demand meet the forces of aggregate supply in order to establish the price of commodities, dominating the process of resource allocation (Polanyi 2001). The hegemony of the market is exercised in two ways: it extends the idea of economic interest to any form of social production, and it imposes a certain way of circulating commodities. For its part, barter, to a certain extent, constitutes a way of resisting this hegemonic force. It does so, firstly, by using objects taken outside the circuit of commodities and objects that have never been commodified. Second, it works with what could be described as the "visible" hands of the barter exchange, that is, non-abstract subjects who establish the value of objects through their relations.

Ex-commodities

According to Kopytoff (1986) and Appadurai (1986), in a capitalist system the biography of an object is parallel with the process of commodification: it is produced to be sold at a certain price and it is related to all other objects by money. It can quit the commodities circuit, but can also get back in if bought again for a certain price (e.g., in the second-hand market). In its phase of non-commodity, it acquires a value not represented by monetary price.

Barter works mainly with ex-commodities, and during ethnographic observation, the author noticed that the ex-commodities category is a broad category that includes different sub-categories of objects:

a) "objects I do not use anymore," which can be books that have been already read or old versions of objects (usually technological goods). Objects such as clothes that no longer fit, baby clothes no longer appropriate, furniture from a previous house that does not fit the new one.
b) "objects I no longer want to own," usually things acquired as gifts,—presents from people with whom the subject no longer has (or does not want to have) a relation, or unwanted gifts.
c) "objects I want to share," usually books that the party very much enjoyed and hopes others might appreciate.

Although there are differences between these ex-commodities, they all have in common the characteristic that they are almost irreversible. That is, it is hard for them to return to the status of a commodity because there is no market that would award them monetary value. They have been through a process of singularization (Kopytoff 1986) that works at a personal level and gives to the object an individual value. Their specific status keeps them outside of the logic of commodification, and their role within the exchange relation refers to a completely different universe of meaning, far removed from that of the market exchange, in which their value is homogenized and reduced to a quantity of money. In the exchange relation, the status of ex-commodity assigns them a sort of uniqueness, which was hidden in the market. This gives subjects the opportunity to use them as instruments of power during the negotiation struggle that determines their situated value—the value determined by a condition of hic et nunc typical of non-commodified objects. These objects assume the role of the work of art described by Benjamin (1974) for the common consumers, who are sharing not only the object but also a piece of their identity. The unconscious personification of the object is the tactic (de Certeau 1990) adopted by consumers, in the struggle between singularization and commodification (Kopytoff 1986).

The counter-hegemonic power of barter, in any case, is limited by the fact that the objects circulating through this modality of exchange initially were commodities, and some resist the singularization process. In particular, there are some objects that clearly maintain their previous commodity status, which are defined as "brand-name" or "designer" objects. This is because the power of the brand, deriving from the market, is so strong it resists personification.

Although this hegemonic dimension comes into barter, it is limited by the fact that brand names are recognized as denoting valuable objects, but this value is considered negatively by some barterers. This counter-hegemonic side becomes evident if we consider both perspectives: on the one side, is the person exchanging the branded/designer object who is regarded as a particular type of person with whom others prefer not to exchange because of a supposed lack of shared values. On the other side, there is a widely diffused idea that exchanging branded objects is not in line with the philosophy of barter (testified by endless discussions on public forums).

Self-produced objects

Exchanged objects can also include self-produced objects. The counter-hegemonic nature of barter is fully exhibited by these products, since they have never been commodified. Their level of uniqueness is higher both because they are unique pieces and because they have never been compared or related to other commodities and their values have never been expressed through money. These objects not only embody a part of the person who possesses them, they hold a part of the person who created them, part of her creativity and knowledge. The value assigned to these objects is determined by a different mechanism: these objects are not valued by market means, but they acquire a value through the relation they establish with the subject, thus contrasting the alienation produced by the rupture of the subject/object relation (Marx and Engels 1988).

This counter-hegemonic dimension of barter is conditional to an extent. For example, the raw materials used to create self-produced objects were usually once commodities. But there are two considerations here: first, the ex-commodity material passes through a deep transformation when it is used to create something new. It could be said that it is completely removed from the process of commodification. Second, using this raw material represents another form of resistance against useless waste since it activates a process of recycling. Using commodities to produce non-commodities can be regarded as a tactic of craft consumers, who create and diffuse new cultural meaning thorough recycling (de Certeau 1990; Campbell 2005).

The visible hand of the barter exchange

Finally, the counter-hegemonic force of barter is exercised against Adam Smith's (1976) invisible hand of the market. Adam Smith's conception was that the aggregation of all demand and the aggregation of all supply interacted in the market to produce prices. This assumption suggests the idea of the market as an abstract place where, *theoretically*, all demand and supply meet: a place where the single individual has no possibility to determine the value of anything.

In contrast, a barter website is a place where it is not an abstract subject who decides about the value of an object, but two physical individuals related by their objects, the values of which are defined within the exchange relation between the individuals. It is the subject who decides whether to conduct a negotiation, whether to create a relational situation with the intention of struggling over the power of one's own objects. The result of each single exchange relation is unique, since objects are not exchanged against a common universal object, but are the result of an exchange of personal, individual sacrifices.

Barter supports alternative consumption models

The process of exchange represents an important phase in consumption practice, but it is only the beginning of what is meant by "consuming" the good. Anthropological and sociological theories seek to demonstrate the extent to which consumption is a cultural and political activity: it involves the creation and manipulation of shared values and meanings. Therefore, exchange through money and exchange through barter generate two different models of consumption. The model generated by market exchange is a consumption model that is seen by barterers to drive consumers to a constant state of purchase, stimulated by a process of desire activation. In this model, the focus is on acquiring things regardless of need and regardless of their underlying production process. The model generated by barter understands consumption differently, especially with regard to the concept of time. In barter, the moments of acquisition are less frequent, so the counter-hegemonic power of barter is exerted by shifting the attention from constant purchasing to careful perception about "real" needs. In addition, the act of bartering is perceived as an act that is lengthening the life of the objects being exchanged, by increasing the lapse of time between the moment of production and the moment of disposal. The counter-hegemonic force of barter is generated also by the fact that this consumption model forces the subject to ponder over the utility of an object, and drives the subject to reformulate the measure of value with which she constructs her evaluation. The ecological dimension of barter calls upon a sort of civil awareness related to the act of reducing waste production, which benefits present and future generations. Therefore, the model of consumption created through barter practice reflects the model of consumption described in the literature on critical or alternative consumption (Micheletti 2002; Di Nallo and Paltrinieri 2006; Leonini and Sassatelli 2008).

Lengthening the object's life-cycle

In the market economy commodities are meant to have short lives. The declared aim of barterers is to lengthen their lives. The short lives of commodities in a market economy are the consequence of two factors. First, they are less durable because they are constructed from inferior quality materials[4] (to lower the costs of production). Second, commodity lives are shortened by the market continuously producing new versions of the same item. This applies especially to technological objects such as phones, computers, and cars, but also appliances and textbooks, for example.

The objects bartered on websites usually are perfectly functioning objects; they are neither ruined nor worn out, which is fundamental for the object to be exchanged. Degree of usedness is evidently a relative concept that can cause misunderstandings between barterers. It is the reason for debates and confrontations, and social and political decisions about the biography of objects.

Redefinition of objects (biography)

In a market economy, the normal path of an object taken out of the circuit of commodities is used for a certain period (a period that is progressively becoming shorter, see above) and then disposal. Consequently, in the hegemonic model of consumption, the degree of usefulness represented by an object to the subject who owns it determines the life of the object. In the counter-hegemonic model generated by barter exchange, the degree of usefulness is judged not only by its owner, but also by the numerous other subjects who would find the object useful. The life of an object does not end when the subject who bought it stops using it; it can resume its life by entering a re-signification process activated by another subject/owner. From this perspective, barter represents a deviation from the normal path of commodities (Appadurai 1986). The majority of interviewed barterers and barterers discussing in public forums maintain that what they most appreciate in barter is the possibility of "giving back life to objects": in other words, the possibility of deciding about the life of objects. It is this political side of barter that drives people to persist with the practice, more than the economic saving that bartering brings with it. Barterers also indicate that such economic savings are often limited and sometimes absent.

Ecological dimension

One of the effects of over-production is more pollution because of waste produced during the production process and because the rapid substitution of objects forces subjects to dispose of perfectly functioning objects, which then must be destroyed at high environmental cost. Lengthening the life of objects is a counter-hegemonic practice because it ultimately results in reductions to the amount of disposal and the levels of pollution, because the number of objects that must be produced and destroyed decreases. Also, but less frequently, barter allows the circulation of self-produced objects, which often have been made using recycled materials.

As some barterers argued, this ecological dimension of barter is to an extent questioned by the number of postal and courier shipments entailed, which in turn entail use of polluting devices such as cars and trucks, to transport objects from one place to another.

However, all bartering websites are cognizant of this dimension and explicitly suggest that barterers should exchange with people geographically close to them so as not to involve shipment services. Several barterers said that they usually searched by geographical area rather than by product category when looking for something on a website. Some barterers even offer to provide a personal courier service: if they are travelling from one place to another, for personal or work reasons, they offer to collect objects from barterers in one area and deliver them to barterers in another.[5]

The role of consumption in everyday life

The counter-hegemonic dimension of barter is expressed by individuals participating in barter, who are redefining the role attributed to consumption in their lives. According to some barterers interviewed, there needs to be a redefinition of the role played by consumption in people's everyday lives. In their view, the society in which we live assigns an overly important role to consumption. They feel that people are being forced to consume and, although perfectly conscious that consumption is fundamental, they want to reduce its burden. They see consumption as a highly time-demanding activity and prefer to use their time for other forms of social activity.

Indeed, bartering gives them the feeling of reducing their consumption: although the time spent on a barter exchange is no less than time spent consuming, the means and meaning behind the practice changes. In particular, barterers complained about how the excessive number of objects they possess that leaves them feeling oppressed and trapped in a house full of useless stuff. They see barter as helping them to free themselves from this situation and to understand the "true" value of their objects. Furthermore, they enjoy the time spent bargaining with other people, since in those moments they are creating social relations. This confirms that consumption responds to subjects' social needs first and that their material needs are secondary. Indeed, critical consumers claim mainly that it is not consumption as a process (Leonini and Sassatelli 2008), but a certain model of consumption that they dislike. The negative aspect of consumerism is that it imposes such a rapid pace that it can cause consumers to lose the capacity to work with meaning and to passively accept the meaning assigned by the market. Indeed, consumption is not negative, as Douglas and Isherwood (1996) noted: it is essential to keep cultural meanings circulating and is also the first source of instruments to define a subject's identity. Although the political function of consumption is undeniable, in barter practice this political dimension reveals its democratic nature.

The democratic side of barter does not refer to the possibility for people to access goods without using money, but to the possibility for individuals to decide about the value of goods. What is intended here as democratic in nature pertains to the kind of political struggle (Mouffe 2005) that is fought over the definition of value and meaning: in a barter relation, the two parties engage in an agonistic not an antagonistic struggle to define the value of each other's objects.

It is important to note that the counter-hegemonic power of generating an alternative model of consumption is contrasted by moments of suspension. Barterers are aware that they cannot count on barter for every need. In these situations, barterers stop searching for goods on barter websites and come back to the market.

The moment and time of consumption

With regard to the role played by consumption in everyday life, the "time" and the "moment" of consumption are modified within the alternative model developed through barter. In classical consumerist culture, the act of consumption can be performed at any time, whereas in barter this is not the case.

The constant tension in purchasing typical of the market model is at the base of Bauman's (2000, 2007) critique of the "consumerist society." In this kind of society, the market tries to drive people to a constant state of consumption: 24-hour shops, 7-day opening are the result of this tendency—as is the phenomenon of e-commerce that is expanding consumption activity in both time and space. Bauman's (2002) critique of consumer society focuses on the fact that the market, especially through advertising, has distorted the ideas of "need" and "desire," transforming the latter into the former, to the point that consumers are desiring to desire. As a result, the idea of "urgency" has been drastically influenced by this change in perspective, and every need/desire is perceived as a matter of survival that must be satisfied as quickly as possible.

From this perspective, barter is counter-hegemonic in showing that, for certain kinds of goods, a waiting time before possessing them is acceptable. Nonetheless, because of this imposition of delay, barterers change their patterns of consumption and learn to plan certain purchases. This means that when they know they will need something in the future, they start searching on the barter website well in advance, and may activate their barter social network to find the particular good.

Furthermore, waiting to achieve the object of our desire is actually nothing than another form of distance created between subject and object. For this reason, the act of waiting is perceived even more as a real sacrifice. For those barterers who do not slow their consumption pace it is hard to accept this, and this usually results in debates and complaints about the time taken to exchange. Some barterers maintained that their idea of barter resembles a slow consumption model. This slow consumption model enacted by barter is a counter-hegemonic characteristic of barter practice, since it assigns a different value to time and, also, to the object.

This demonstrates how far the practice of barter contributes to creating a counter-hegemonic value for objects through a different temporality. Barterers have the possibility to establish value not only within the relation with another subject, but also by temporally separating from the objects of their desire.

Barter creates alternative social relations

The types of relations generated show another counter-hegemonic side to the practice. Relations in barter are constructed directly between the two parties involved in the exchange, without any third party intervening in the relation. This means that the two parties have the opportunity to construct social meaning together, by determining the value of objects exchanged, and by responding to shared social norms. Furthermore, barter exchanges require very well-balanced relations in order to be successfully concluded.

According to Simmel (2011), money does relate individuals with one another, since it allows a perfect division of labor, but these kinds of relations drive the subject to an extreme individuality generated by the anonymous nature of relations. If Durkheim (1947) underlines the anomie typical of complex societies characterized by the organic solidarity, Simmel goes further in describing the paradoxical nature of these societies. They form huge numbers of relations and networks of strongly related individuals that are dependent on each other in which the "other" is an abstract individual with whom the subject relates by means of money. Although highly interconnected, these modern individuals described by Simmel experience a mediated relation. Therefore, it would be a mistake to describe the market as an asocial and apolitical place: the market, similar to any other entity, is the result of a social construction of reality (Berger and Luckmann 1991), and therefore a political construction. The market is a social structure—and money is the representation of social relations—determined by political struggle. The functioning of this particular social structure is characterized by a high level of anonymity and anomie because those interdependent relations are between *abstract* subjects.

The fundamental difference, therefore, refers to the relational dimension of the two fields, revealing the strong barter capacity to give back to subjects the possibility to create personal, non-anonymous relations.

Balanced relations

In contrast to market exchanges, the aim of both parts in barter is to collaborate rather than compete. Barter works with reciprocity: barterers' relation is based only on confrontation to determine the values of their sacrifices, which eventually must be equal. Consequently, barter is about balancing sacrifice.

The agonistic struggle characterizing barter exchange is influenced in online barter by the level of trust each party places in the other. Within the online barter practice, trusting one another is a demanding part of the exchange; it can in fact be considered a proper sacrifice. Therefore, trustworthiness becomes a special form of capital and can be considered the symbolic capital that characterizes the field (Bourdieu and Wacquant 1992).

The peculiarity of the barter field is that it creates a space for potentially balanced relations. Since the struggle is fought between the objects while the subjects collaborate agonistically with each other, their capitals (economic, cultural, and social capital) do not matter for the exchange relation.

Nevertheless, in the online environment, the counter-hegemonic dimension of barter is distorted by the fact that a particular form of symbolic capital does influence the barterers' relations. Although social actors in this online field may not compete for economic or cultural capital, they must compete for social capital, which is at the base of trust capital. The competition so generated reintroduces a hegemonic element into a practice that otherwise is profoundly counter-hegemonic.

Inevitably, this produces an unbalanced relation, and the potential counter-hegemonic force of barter, which resists the typical liberal idea of diffused competition between social actors, is brought back in. Also, if placing trust in another barterer is considered a sacrifice, those with a lower level of trust capital will be making a smaller sacrifice.

In general, although barter creates space for potentially balanced relations, it should be remembered that there is always the possibility of free rider problems, that is, users can still engage in opportunistic behaviors. These kinds of behaviors are enabled by the presence of asymmetric information more characteristic of the online than the offline environment.

All interviewed barterers said they had negative experiences, ranging from a barterer who did not send the agreed object, to a barterer who sent a different object from the one agreed upon, to one who sent an extremely used object, to problems related to communication. This opportunistic attitude, typical of market economies, is opposed by a strong social sanctioning. The cost of engaging in opportunistic behavior equates to the cost of losing the capital specific to the field, trustworthiness.

Conclusion

This chapter showed that barter is political. Not only does it represent an activity that resists hegemonic models of consumption and exchange, it also constitutes a space for struggle between these hegemonic and counter-hegemonic models. Following de Certeau's (1990) definition, barter is a tactic. Barter represents a subtle resistance, exercised through an alternative use and an alternative process of objects' signification/evaluation. Furthermore, its political nature is revealed by the struggle generated within the practice itself.

As it was shown in the chapter, one of the counter-hegemonic dimensions of barter is its capacity of creating a space where individuals have the power, together with other individuals, to establish the value of the objects exchanged. In other words, they participate in a decision-making process that is agonistic in nature. Following Mouffe, "this means that, while in conflict, they see themselves as belonging to the same political association, as sharing a common symbolic space within which the conflict takes place" (2005: 20). The symbolic space they share is the counter-hegemonic space of resistance.

The political nature of barter testifies to the fact that struggle is an ontological dimension of reality (Mouffe 2005; Simmel 2009) and, above all, that each activity of resistance moves together with its hegemonic order, in the same space defined by the latter. According to de Certeau (1990) the subtle forces of resistance do not shout against a dominant order, but they silently insinuate in the meshes of the pre-constituted net, filling the spaces hegemonies left empty. Counter-hegemony represents a rupture in the symbolic space of hegemony, modifying meanings that apparently remain untouched but that depict different conceptual lines.

What is important to note is the fact that the resistance barter exercises does not generate from an outer symbolical space, but it is produced within the same field defined by the hegemony. Indeed, barter represents a good example of a "tactic," a moment that destabilizes the strategy of hegemonic powers. Barter represents the attempt of consumers to suspend a setting, a wide and organized space where they cannot create a new order but where they can confront with it and re-signify the order, so as to create a moment of rupture that emerges from a confrontation, leading to the participation in decision-making processes. The chapter thus confirms that resistance does not come from outside the field of hegemony. Instead, counter-hegemony develops and emerges within the same field and keeps on carrying with it hegemonic elements, exactly because it can express its force only by exploiting the same instrument adopted by the hegemony.

References

Anspach, Mark (2007), *A Buon Rendere: La Reciprocità nella Vendetta, nel Dono e nel Mercato*, Torino: Bollati Boringhieri.

Appadurai, Arjun (ed.) (1986), *The Social Life of Things: Commodities in Cultural Perspective*, Cambridge: Cambridge University Press.

Bauman, Zygmunt (2000), *Liquid Modernity*, Cambridge, MA: Polity Press.

—— (2007), *Homo Consumens: Lo Sciame Inquieto dei Consumatori e la Miseria Degli Esclusi*, Gardolo: Erikson.

Beck, Ulrich (1992), *Risk Society: Towards a New Modernity*, London: Sage.

Benjamin, Walter (1974), *L'Opera d'Arte nell'Epoca della sua Riproducibilità Tecnica*, Torino: Einaudi.

Berger, Peter and Luckmann, Thomas (1991), *The Social Construction of Reality*, London: Penguin Books.

Bloch, Marc (1933), "Le problème de l'or au Moyen Age," *Annales d'Histoire Économique et Sociale*, 5, pp. 1–34.

Bobbio, Norberto (1985), *Stato, Governo, Società: Per una Teoria Generale della Politica*, Torino: Giulio Einaudi Editore.

Bulow, Jeremy (1986), "An economic theory of planned obsolescence," *The Quarterly Journal of Economics*, 100:4, pp. 729–49.

Bourdieu, Pierre (1980), *La Distinction: Critique Sociale du Jugement*, Paris: Les Éditions de Minuit.

Bourdieu, Pierre and Wacquant, Loïc J. (1992), *Réponses: Pour une Anthropologie Réflexive*, Paris: Seuil.

Braudel, Fernand (1981), *Civilization and Capitalism 15th-18th Century: The Structures of Everyday Life, Vol. I*, London: William Collins Sons & Co.

Campbell, Colin (2005), "The craft consumer: Culture, craft and consumption in a postmodern society," *Journal of Consumer Culture*, 5:1, pp. 23–42.

Carpentier, Nico and De Cleen, Benjamin (2007), "Bringing discourse theory into media studies," *Journal of Language and Politics*, 6:2, pp. 265–93.

de Certeau, Michel (1990), *l'Invention du Quotidien*, Paris: Gallimard.

Di Nallo, Egeria and Paltrinieri, Roberta (eds) (2006), *Cum Sumo: Prospettive di Analisi del Consumo nella Società Globale*, Milan: Franco Angeli.

Douglas, Mary and Isherwood, Baron (1996), *The World of Goods: Towards an Anthropology of Consumption*, London: Routledge.

Durkheim, Emile (1947), *Les Règles de la Méthode Sociologique*, Paris: Presses Universitaires de France.

Ferrari, Andrea, Gualendri, Elisabetta, Landi, Andrea, and Vezzani, Paola (2012), *Il Sistema Finanziario: Funzioni, Mercati e Intermediari*, Torino: Giappicchelli.

Hebdige, Dick (1979), *Subculture: The Meaning of Style*, New York and London: Routledge.

Humphrey, Carline and Hugh-Jones, Stephen (eds) (1992), *Barter, Exchange, and Value: An Anthropological Approach*, Cambridge: Cambridge University Press.

Ingham, Geoffrey (1996), "Money is a social relation," *Review of Social Economy*, 54:4, pp. 507–29.

Keynes, John M. (1971), *A Treatise on Money*, London: Macmillan.

Knapp, Georg F. (1924), *The State Theory of Money*, London: MacMillan.

Kopytoff, Igor (1986), "The cultural biography of things: Commoditization as process," in A. Appadurai (ed.), *The Social Life of Things: Commodities in Cultural Perspective*, Cambridge: Cambridge University Press, pp. 64–94.

Le Goff, Jacques (1997), *La Bourse et la Vie: Économie et Religion au Moyen Age*, Paris: Hacette Littératures.

—— (2010), *Le Moyen Age et l'Argent: Essai d'Anthropologie Historiques*, Paris: Perrin.

Leonini, Luisa and Sassatelli, Roberta (eds) (2008), *Il consumo critico*, Bari: Editori Laterza.

Marx, Karl and Engels, Friedrich (1988), *The Economic and Philosophic Manuscripts of 1844 and the Communist Manifesto*, Amherst: Prometheus Books.

Micheletti, Michele (2002), "Consumer choice as political participation," *Statsvetenskaplig Tidskrift,* 105, pp. 218–34.

Mouffe, Chantal (2005), *On the Political*, New York: Routledge.

Polanyi, Karl (2001), *The Great Transformation*, Boston: The Beacon Press.

Schutz, Alfred (1979), *Saggi Sociologici*, Torino: UTET.

Simmel, Georg (1996), *La Moda,* Milan: SE.

—— (1997a), "Money in modern culture," in D. Frisby and M. Featherstone (eds), *Simmel on Culture*, London: Sage, pp. 243–54.

—— (1997b), "On the psychology of money," in D. Frisby and M. Featherstone (eds), *Simmel on Culture*, London: Sage, pp. 233–42.

—— (2011), *Philosophy of Money*, Kindle ed., London and New York: Routledge.

Smith, Adam (1976), *An Inquiry into the Nature and Causes of the Wealth of Nation*, Oxford: Clarendon Press.

Smithin, John (1994), *Controversies in Monetary Economics: Ideas, Issues and Policy*, Aldershot: Edward Elgar.

Turri, Maria G. (2009), *La Distinzione tra Denaro e Moneta*, Rome: Carocci.

Weber, Max (1978), *Economy and Society: An Outline of Interpretive Sociology,* Berkeley: University of California Press.

Notes

1 Italian websites: www.zerorelativo.it, www.e-barty.it, www.reoose.com. Accessed 28 December 2018.

2 Money has four functions: (a) it is a medium of exchange; (b) it is a measure of value or a unit of account (numeraire); (c) it is a store of value, which means it keeps its value over time; (d) it is a standard for deferred payment (an implicit function deriving from the other three) (Ferrari et al. 2012).

3 In Italy, "*compro oro*" shops.

4 There is a theory related to the planned obsolesce of commodities (Bulow 1986) that claims that commodities are intentionally produced with low quality so that they will break more frequently and consumers will be forced to replace them.

5 This is such common practice that one interviewee, living outside of Milan, asked the researcher at the end of the interview to take something back to Milan for another barterer who would meet up with her.

Chapter 12

Activist Fantasies on ICT-Related Social Change in Istanbul

Itır Akdoğan

Introduction

Some say society changed fundamentally as information and communication technologies (ICT) became ever more prominent. Others disagree. Whether society changes with ICTs or not is one discussion. How we make sense of that change is another. When change occurs in society, different groups and different discourses perceive and try to understand and conceptualize this change differently. For a better understanding of what using ICTs in various areas of the social means, we need a deeper analysis of the perceptions of the role that the Internet, mobile technology, and their diverse applications play in social change.

In this chapter, I adopt the conceptual framework of Lacanian fantasy in an analysis of how activists in Istanbul perceive the role ICTs has had in changing activism and of how they make sense of those purported changes. Istanbul, as the largest city of Turkey (larger than the capital Ankara), is the most prominent city in globalization projects of the Turkish central government, the city with the largest activist communities in Turkey, and the city with the best ICT-infrastructure. It is at the same time a city facing several challenges and limitations in its local political life.

The Lacanian notion of fantasy is adopted here as both a theoretical and analytical backbone, as it allows for fluidity in the various ways of observing and making sense of change. Lacan is the source of inspiration of critical theory and analysis, including discourse theory (Stavrakakis 2007), and as Glynos (2001) suggests, Lacanian concepts like *fantasy*, but also *lack, desire, Other,* and *enjoyment* provide useful tools for critical analysis—including the analysis of (the perception of) social change.

The chapter first introduces the notion of Lacanian fantasy. Second, the chapter uses this Lacanian framework to theorize the main three fantasies in the field of ICT-related social change that this research identified, namely the fantasies of harmony, technological power, and political power. Following a brief contextual background on Istanbul, the chapter then presents the analysis of how activists perceive and make sense of the role of ICTs in changing activism in Istanbul, with a focus on the three fantasies that underpin these views. The analysis is based on semi-structured in-depth interviews with 20 Istanbul activists, who were analyzed using the qualitative research procedures of grounded theory (Strauss and Corbin 1998).

The Lacanian concept of fantasy

A number of concepts are central to a Lacanian understanding of how fantasy works: split, lack, and enjoyment (*jouissance*). In Lacanian theory, the subject is split from the source of its enjoyment. The enjoyment is lost forever, causing a never-to-be-filled lack in the subject. The subject endlessly searches for the enjoyment but this turns out to be an impossible quest, even though this desire for the lack to be filled produces a key driving force for action. For the subject to be able to cope with this situation, they will imagine scenarios where they believe to have reached this enjoyment. This mechanism that helps coping with the lack is called fantasy. This implies that fantasy becomes a key driving force for social action, and thus a very positive force, but at the same time, the Real will intervene and frustrate the fantasies by demonstrating the impossibility of their full realization. This does not mean that fantasies will necessarily be destroyed by their frustrations; the dynamics between fantasies and frustrations will allow for their coexistence.

Fantasy is the promise of filling the lack and thus reaching enjoyment. Another key element of fantasy is the concept of desire. Desire too endlessly searches for and pushes the subject to enjoyment (fullness). If desire reaches full enjoyment, however, it loses its very existence. The paradox is that in order to keep this quest alive there is always a distance between the subject and enjoyment, the latter never being fully reachable (Stavrakakis 1999). Žižek (1989) illustrates this paradox, at the societal level, with anti-Semitism; the anti-Semite who hates the Jew and whose fantasy is a world without Jews paradoxically needs the Jew in order to continue to be an anti-Semite.

Lacan (1964) developed his psychoanalytical concept of fantasy referring to the subject. Yet the concept increasingly becomes a tool for critical scholars for explaining political hegemonies, thus shifting focus from the individual to the social and the political (Stavrakakis 2007). More specifically, the Lacanian concept of fantasy has been put to work in critical and poststructuralist political analysis. Stavrakakis (2007) names the group of critical scholars who use the concept of fantasy as *The Lacanian Left*. He categorizes in this group different theorists who refer to Lacan in different ways:

> At the epicentre of this emerging field one would locate the enthusiastic endorsement of Lacan by Žižek; next to him—at what some would call a healthy distance—the Lacan-inspired Laclau and Mouffe; at the periphery—negotiating a delicate balancing act between the outside and the inside of the field, often functioning as its intimate "others" or adversaries— we would have to locate the critical engagement of thinkers like Castoriadis and Butler.
>
> (Stavrakakis 2007: 3–4)

Žižek (1989), in bringing fantasy into the political sphere, points out how fantasy operates in ideology. He argues that fantasy helps the ideology to "take its own failure into account in advance" (Žižek 1989: 126), linking it to Laclau and Mouffe's (1985) theory of antagonism. In doing so, Žižek revises Marx's formula "they do not know it but they are doing it" (Marx quoted in Žižek 1989) by placing the illusion not on knowledge but on reality. The new formula for Žižek is: "they know very well how things really are, but still they are doing it as if they didn't know," and Žižek labels this unconscious overlooked illusion ideological fantasy (Žižek 1989: 32–33). He (Žižek 1999: 92–93) also explains that in fantasy there is always a multitude of "subject-positions." This implies that the subject flows among different identifications; they are not only/automatically identified with themself. Second, fantasy always involves an impossible gaze. Therefore, from the political point of view, he argues that it is important to know for which gaze the fantasy is created.

More recently, Stavrakakis (1999: 13, emphasis in original) has argued that the split subject as the "*locus* of an impossible identity" is the major contribution of Lacan to the analysis of political hegemonies and ideologies. Stavrakakis (1999), in his *Lacan and the Political*, explains how the various elements of fantasy relate to the political. He starts with the subordination in the being of the subject. He argues that from the very beginning there is an exercise of power in the being of the subject (Stavrakakis 1999: 20). The impossible-to-fill-in lack of the subject, according to Stavrakakis, indicates that the fullness of identity is impossible, but identification is not (Stavrakakis 1999: 29). Concerning the new forms of politics that take place outside of the traditional frames, "Politics is identical to political reality, and political reality, as all reality, first, is constituted at the symbolic level, and second, is supported by fantasy" (Stavrakakis 1999: 73).

Glynos and Stavrakakis (2008: 261–62) also illustrate how the concept of fantasy permits political analysis. They emphasize three components of fantasy to schematize the parallelism between the subject and the political: imaginary; enjoyment of the body; and the stolen enjoyment. The imaginary promise of reaching the lost enjoyment, according to them, is visible in the political discourse about a better future society without today's problems. This abstract fantasmatic promise, however, is not enough because the enjoyment of the body sustains the desire and motivation. That is why the subject/society also needs this enjoyment that is found, for instance, in the defeat of the national enemy or the victory of the national football team. This short-term enjoyment, however, is not enough to satisfy the desire and thus creates dissatisfaction. The enjoyment will never be reached because it is lost, stolen by the Other. Glynos and Stavrakakis use the stolen enjoyment and the Other to explain the Other in the nationalist narratives. One of their examples of this argument is the immigrant who comes and steals the jobs (which takes the enjoyment away). Glynos and Stavrakakis (2008: 262) underline the role fantasy plays in building national identity and desire:

It does this by structuring the social subject's partial enjoyment through a series of collective practices (celebrations, festivals, consumption rituals, etc.) and by reproducing itself at the level of representation in official and unofficial public discourse (as a beatific narrative and a traumatic scenario.

Glynos and Howarth (2008) have further brought Lacanian fantasy into the conceptual framework of the discourse theory of Laclau and Mouffe (1985). They argue that it is through fantasmatic logics that subjects relate to discourses. Fantasmatic logics, they argue, "furnish us with the means to explain the way subjects are gripped or held by a practice or regime of practices." Fantasy operates through identification. When individuals identify with a subject position provided to them by a discourse, they invest in the discourse and come to embody and enact it. But contingency lurks, as identifications are always incomplete and never fully coincide with the subject position (Glynos and Howarth 2008). Fantasy, then, functions in such a way that it is capable of "suturing the rift in the symbolic order" (Howarth and Stavrakakis 2000: 14).

Fantasies of ICT-related social change

A wide variety of fantasies can be distinguished, but in this chapter I want to focus on the field of social change and ICT, and how three intersecting fantasies operate within this field, namely, the fantasies of harmony, political power, and technological power. In the case study, which will be discussed below, each of the three fantasies operates in one particular subfield of the main field of ICT-related social change. As this case study analysis is grounded in a qualitative-iterative methodology, this part contains a theorization of these three fantasies—harmony, political, and technological power—in close relationship with their subfields: the relationship between the global and the local, the (de)centralization of political power, and (technological) determinism.

The fantasy of the harmony of the global and the local

Harmony is a key fantasy; Žižek (1999), for instance, argues that this fantasy produces a belief in solidarity and cooperation, in an otherwise inharmonious society. And Carpentier (2011: 119) writes that this fantasy beholds "the promise of the unachievable wholeness and the harmonious resolution of social antagonism." In the subfield of the relation between the global and local, this fantasy operates in particular ways, with globalization offering the possibility of a better, more harmonious world by enlarging it, and with localization aiming to maintain a harmonious world, by protecting the local community. The idea of the "global village" is one example built on the idea of one unified society where everybody is connected. The global city, the global public sphere, and the global citizen are all part of this globalization component of the fantasy of harmony. Localization, on the other hand, feeds into the fantasy of harmony through the romantic idea of rural peace. Tönnies (1955), for instance, constructs a harmonious "community" (Gemeinschaft) by juxtaposing it to the "society" (Gesellschaft), articulating community as characterized by close human ties and strong communitarian identities (Carpentier 2011). In this way of thinking, even if Tönnies (1955) acknowledges their coexistence in social practice, "society" becomes the Other of "community," a "mechanical aggregate and artefact" (Tönnies 1955: 38), of which one senses that "such mechanical aggregates can at most prove dysfunctional, and therefore produce devastating turmoil rather than conscious social change" (Ruggiero 2014: 9).

The global public sphere is another example of the dynamics of the globalization component of the harmony fantasy. The global public sphere is very much based on the idea of global harmony and global solidarity, where different voices, including those of activists and civil society, can be heard. Global communication and networking, enabled by ICTs, feed this fantasy, as these tools are seen to offer the resources for more democratic actors to support their struggle for global justice and democratic policy-making at the global level. This fantasy, however, is frustrated by the challenges of several digital divides, elitism among activists, the impossibility of a global democracy, the impossibility of global activist organizations, and the representational crisis of the global activist organizations in global processes. Translocal online network—linking different grass-roots or local activisms—is another example of attempts to create a more harmonious world. In this model, activists reach out, but remain simultaneously rooted in the local for their local cause/struggles, as the concept of rooted cosmopolitans (Tarrow 2005) illustrates.

The political fantasies of power

A second fantasy in the field of ICT-related social change deals with political power. Here we can find two opposing versions of the fantasy of political power. A first version is strongly related to the Nietzschean will to power, or "the extension of power," which is, for him, "the true, fundamental instinct of life" (Nietzsche 2012: 163). This version of the political power fantasy focuses on the concentration and centralization of power, which often results in the restriction of (the existence of legitimate) power relations to the political system (or, to use Mouffe's [2005] label: politics). As Stavrakakis (1999: 82) has argued, this fantasy also implies that the political is domesticated and brought into the political system:

> If, according to Laclau's Lacanian dictum, society does not exist (as a harmonious ensemble) this impossible existence is all the time constructed and reconstructed through the symbolic production of discourse and its fantasmatic investment, through the reduction of the political to politics.

Moreover, as Carpentier (2011) has suggested, this fantasy is also articulated with social makebility, or the idea that the exercise of power can trigger immediate and unmediated change.

The second version of the political power fantasy is, in a way, the inverse of the first (and its Other), with a strong focus on power-sharing and the decentralization of power, which is combined with the acknowledgment that power circulates throughout society, and cannot be restricted to the political system (Mouffe [2005] labels this the political). In order to describe this fantasy, we can also revert to Pateman's (1970: 71) notion of full participation, which she defines as "a process where each individual member of a decision-making body has equal power to determine the outcome of decisions." As Carpentier (2014: 1004) argues, "This end point [of full participation] is unreachable and utopian—phantasmagoric," "but it arguably also serves as a crucial driving force" for democratic renewal.

The technological fantasies of power

The third fantasy in the field of ICT-related social change explicitly features technology, which brings us into the discussions on determinism. And again, we can distinguish two variations of this fantasy. The first variation can be labeled technological determinism and is based on the idea that technology shapes society and social change. This version of the fantasy feeds the belief that technology is a value-free and politically neutral asset that causes social and political change, independently of any social and cultural dynamics (Servaes 2014). Indeed, the fantasy of technological determinism conveys "a vivid sense of the efficacy of technology as a driving force of history: a technological innovation suddenly appears and causes important things to happen" (Marx and Smith 1994: x). This version of the fantasy conceives of technology in virtually exclusively artifactual terms, where its very materiality reinforces "a tangible sense of its decisive role in history" (Marx and Smith 1994: xi).

The second variation of the fantasy of technological power is social determinism. This is the idea that society exercises full control over technology: "social, political, economic and cultural factors are the prime determinants of technological change" (Winston 1998: 341). Williams is one of the key critics of technological determinism, resisting the idea of a value-free and politically neutral conception of technology, but he also points to the existence of social determinism, which he refers to as "determined technologies" (1974: 7). In this latter model, technology is not determining, but is determined by a variety of social intentions at each stage of technology development. In this radical form, social determinism denies any role of technology in social change, and grants social institutions, and often social and political elites, absolute power over technology and thus power over society and social change.

Both deterministic fantasies become frustrated through the presence of the respective Other in the process of social, where technology has become a solid component of our social realities, while remaining firmly embedded in the social structures of these realities.

A case study of ICT-related activism for social change in Istanbul

Before analyzing how activists in Istanbul perceive the role of ICT in changing activism, the first section presents a contextual background of activism in Istanbul and its relation to the three areas of social change studied in this chapter.

Activism in Istanbul

Istanbul is situated in a country where activism, as well as media and ICTs, face several challenges and limitations at several levels. Turkey is a relatively new representative democracy. During the westernization reforms after the foundation of modern Turkey in 1923, people shifted from being subjects of the Ottoman Empire to citizens of the Republic of Turkey almost overnight. In the twentieth century, civil rights have been awarded to citizens, especially to women, without them having to fight extensively for those rights. Therefore, the concept of citizens-fighting-for-their-rights is absent while at the same time the tradition of over-respecting the head of state is still alive. Moreover, a tradition of centralized and strong governments prevents the development of a powerful civil society (Toksöz 2009). In addition to this government tradition, also the army's strong presence and interference in politics has muted civil society activity for a long time (Özbudun 2007). For instance, civil society organizations (associations, trade unions, and semi-public professional organizations) received severe limitations under the 1982's constitution, a product of the 1980 military coup. While in the West, with the new social movements, the space for the political (Mouffe 2005) enlarged, the boundaries between the public and the private became blurred, and there were more interactions between the political system and other political actors, in Turkey, politics was legally separated from (the rest of) the political. While the army started losing its political power, from 2002 onwards, civil society and activism continued to face challenges.

From the mid-1990s on, global events that took place especially in Istanbul, permitted Turkish civil society and activists to join global networks. This new era meant increased access to information and increased interaction between Turkish civil society organizations and their global counterparts. Turkish activists also learned and explored various participatory-democratic and other governance models. Even though civil society and activism in Turkey are still weak and their struggle against anti-democratic policies and practices continues, they are significantly transforming, in terms of engaging citizens in policy issues, creating new methods, and local–global interactions and partnerships (Civicus and Tüsev 2006). Globalization, however, does not always incite democratization. Anti-democratic social movements have also emerged, simultaneously using the space of civil society (Uğur and Akdoğan 2016).

Challenges in democracy and participation unavoidably also reflect on the Turkish media and ICT environment. The Turkish press (and in broader terms, the media) have never been totally free, as governments exercised different kinds of pressure to control the media landscape (Çatalbaş 2007). During the past decade, the Turkish media have been going through a very difficult period of pressure and censorship, including severe Internet censorship, which places Turkey on the *not free* list on international freedom indices (as, for instance, the Internet Freedom Index[1]). It is in this context that the activists were interviewed.

Activist fantasies in Istanbul

The interviewed activists resort to these fantasies of harmony, political power, and technological power in their narrations of ICT-related social change. The analysis presents how interviewees utilize these fantasies, but also how all fantasies are frustrated. For this chapter, I will use the interviews with 20 activists; these data were collected between 2008 and 2010. They were selected to maximize diversity in terms of demographic and socio-economic parameters, political views, ways of activism (from traditional to new forms), level of operation (local, global), and use of ICTs. I benefited from my various local networks in reaching some interviewees and I reached others randomly online and/or offline.

Using "fantasy" as the main sensitizing concept for the analysis, and deploying the qualitative research procedures of grounded theory (Strauss and Corbin 1998), I identified the activist's usage of these fantasies, activated in, and underpinning, their accounts. The three key fantasies (with their respective frustrations) were identified, and then the theoretical backbone was further strengthened, following an iterative procedure. Because of the linear narrative of an academic text, which always rests slightly uneasy with this iterative procedure, the theoretical discussion of the three fantasies precedes the analysis, even though they are produced simultaneously.

Fantasy 1: The technological power of ICTs
The fantasy of technological power becomes visible in discussions about how activism today has become easier and more effective through ICTs, compared to activism in the past. They display a strong belief in the capacity of ICTs to generate social change, at a number of levels.

First, political institutions, the activists point out, had a monopoly over information and did not share it with civil society. This phenomenon left activists without the information they needed in order to act. The centralized government culture, older activists argue, also had an impact on the traditional forms of activism such as the trade unions: "We couldn't go into details in our discussions or strategy planning because information was blocked. We didn't know everything" (Ceylan, 60, f). Today, ICTs are said to permit activists to access information online independently, without much restraints. This belief in unrestricted access is illustrated by anecdotes as the following: "Now on Facebook there are the videos that are broadcast nowhere else; videos of policemen killing a person. (Mainstream) media don't broadcast this, it is on Facebook" (Ali, 29, m).

A second element that feeds the fantasy of technological power is the increased interaction. ICTs are argued to increase interaction quantitatively, as well as in terms of who interacts with whom. Activists point to the interaction between activists and citizens, and among citizens, on social networking sites. In a political culture where citizens traditionally are reluctant to even say which party they vote for, the hope is raised that this public expression of political views not only implies increased interaction between the activists and citizens, but also the emergence of forms of online and public political deliberation. Moreover, activists argue that increased ICT-enabled interaction will consolidate partnerships among activists, thus leading to social change.

Higher efficiency is another element that supports the technological power fantasy of ICTs. This element includes both managerial and democratic components. Activists refer to efficiency in their office work, and in reaching and mobilizing more citizens, especially young people. In a city where the majority of the population is under 30 years old, this outreach is argued to imply cheaper and faster office-based communication. Online outreach is articulated with crowdfunding, and the potential of ICTs is again emphasized: "We fund-raised the 5 billion only from the supporters. That group (on Facebook) helped us with this" (Kaan, 30, m). Activists define ICTs as highly important, not only as practical facilitators, but also as tools for engagement in local political action.

The fantasy of technological power, to have ICTs solve the problems of activism, civil society, and more broadly of democracy, is, however, frustrated. Even if increased interaction is mentioned (see above), the interviewees continue to worry that "passive online activism" and the distance that the online creates, (will) harm(s) their work: "It (the Internet) is abstracting things. It already is a problem that people don't care, so making a fight virtual doesn't help activism. They (ICT) should complement not replace offline activism" (Esra, 27, f).

Also, activists seem to be well aware that they are not the only users of ICTs. They understand that their political adversaries may also benefit from the same technology to create counter-discourses. Moreover, even though activists use online tools and social media, they have to acknowledge that these tools are not always more efficient as their fantasies indicate, for instance, due to the required new skills and resources. Their hopes are countered by the difficulties they have in relying on online content and the online activities of their supporters, where the absence of trust limits the capacities of the online interaction.

Another element that frustrates the technological power fantasy (favoring activism) deals with the dominance of visual culture. Activists claim that the emphasis on the visual has eradicated the café tradition that used to permit activists to meet in person in order to share information. Once gathered, they discussed and planned strategies. Activists argue that online communication replaced this collectivity, and use it to explain why street demonstrations do not manage to mobilize as many people as they did in the past; they are concerned that the ICTs create passivity. In a city (or country) where the political agenda changes so very quickly and where the social memory is considered to be very weak, the lack of follow-up may frustrate the core objectives of activism. In particular here, but also in some of the previous elements, we can see how the fantasy of technological power is maintained, even though its power works against activism, and in favor of the powers that be.

The final element of frustration, the presence of (a) digital divide(s), is not present in interviews as a challenge for activists themselves, but for their societal target groups. That is why online activism is not always considered relevant or preferable by all activists, as one of them explains:

only one of them had access to the Internet. They normally are an undereducated, low income, and digitally divided population. That is why we had to go to the neighbourhood; we had to be physically there to fight against the municipality. This is how activism should be anyway.

(Ferda, female, 42)

ICTs seem to help activists in their work but ICTs may also harm it; that is why activists think that ICTs should be complementary when needed and that e-activism should not replace activism. This argument again links to the paradox that Lacanian theory identifies. While ICTs may be defined as tools that solve the problems and overcome the challenges and limitations of activism, once online, activism also becomes restricted and harmed— although in different ways—in its capacity to stimulate political activity, engagement, and democracy.

Fantasy 2: The fantasy of harmony, connecting the global with the local level

Online access to, and interaction with, global networks feeds into the idea for global solidarity and harmony, where local Istanbul activists can connect to a more global activist community, get support from them, and can, potentially, contribute to generating global social change. Different models for this linkage through ICTs are present in the interviews. It is activated when local actors need support from global partners, organizations, networks, as well as traditional actors such as the parliamentarians of other countries. This support may be related to specific information or advice that they need to solve a problem at the local level, as one of the activists illustrates: "I then right away contacted our sister organization in France and asked what we could do" (Esra, 27, f). Activists may also ask global organizations or individuals to support them and to help generate pressure, when dealing with problems at the local level.

Also, the global appreciation of local activism matters, for instance, through the inclusion of local activists in global success lists, as in the case of the 500 most influential Muslim or global projects like the Museum of Freedom of The Internet. During the interviews, activists state the names of several European or global traditional/mainstream media outlets that covered their campaigns and opinions. Moreover, global actors may link to locals when they need the support of the local activists in their project.

The third model of linking the two levels is by building bridges. This model is not only said to feed both sides with knowledge and experience, but it is also claimed that it empowers the activists who build this bridge:

the very first network I joined was a global network. It allowed me to link to the local, inform people in the local about what's happening at the global level, and link the local back to the global to inform about what's happening in the local. This experience allowed many opportunities for young people even from the least developed parts of Istanbul and Turkey. We also contribute to global decision-making and to global policies with our local experience.

(Selim, male, 52)

The interviews reveal yet another way of linking the local and the global, which can be called a step-by-step model. Local work becomes connected to related national networks, which in turn become linked in global processes. The links in this model, however, are rather scattered, spontaneous, irregular, and they are more based on the personal interests of the activists.

What these models share is that they all assume that this level of harmony and solidarity is possible, and actually occurs. Moreover, they also assume a genuine interest from the side of the Other, to collaborate or support, to exchange or share. But this fantasy of harmony is also frustrated, and these frustrations stem from challenges in the local Real. Activists still argue that linking the local and the global with ICTs has many advantages for them, but they have understood that more than ICTs are required to create and maintain these benefits.

One Istanbul activist refers to the lack of foreign language skills: "they write in their mother tongue. There is no need to spend extra time in forwarding a document that is already written in English. But I need to have time for translation (because I have limited skills)" (Güneş, 50, f). This problem repeatedly appears in the interviews, as a complaint, failure, or a situation to be improved. Without language skills, activists cannot access information or global networks online even though they have access to ICTs. Activists with limited language skills nevertheless know about global networks and some still join them, even if they can only be present and act as lurkers. Global networking is also claimed to require time. Activists say that they need to allocate time to follow different processes, and to interact within these networks in order to benefit. Small or informal groups, or individual activists, are said to be disadvantaged, in comparison to organizations that can practically (e.g., office space) or financially (e.g., salary) afford these investments. Finally, even though the local–global link is considered desirable, face-to-face (global) meetings are argued to be more important than online networking.

Fantasy 3: The political power fantasy

The third fantasy deals with political power, and, from the activists' perspective, with the decentralization of political systems and the sharing of power. Several reasons why activists feel more empowered and engaged in dealing with local politics provide the imaginary to mobilize this fantasy of political power. ICTs and ICT-enabled online global networks made activists learn about the relevance and importance of local politics and local political life, even if this process started much earlier:

> Turkey is a centralized country. Ankara solves all the problems. That's why before, activists used to talk only about national politics. As they entered global networks (especially during the Habitat II City Summit that took place in 1996 in Istanbul), they have seen that especially in the developed world, people think globally but act locally. They combine knowledge from their global networks and knowledge from their local work. This combination helps them to influence local policies and local authorities. This is how we discovered local politics.

> (Selim, male, 52)

These interactions are said to provide democratic learning experiences, and the activists argue that the more democratic structures of these processes at the global level, or the potential support they saw in their online interaction, encouraged them to fight in the local. The independent access to information, possible with ICTs, also makes activists discover the commitments of the Turkish government in global processes and agreements. This is how activists say that they can learn about their local rights and find the legal basis for their work. Activists also discover international organizations. The European Union, for instance, is an important regional organization for Turkey as a candidate country. Activists argue that access to alternative information and access to European networks permit them to learn about certain EU directives and regulations.

Moreover, they mention the opportunities to find allies and establish multi-stakeholder partnerships, also with the state, which have become more accessible through ICTs, but also more open and transparent in general (in the digital era). Activists claim that partnerships with political institutions at the local level, but also at the national level (with ministries or directorates), empower activists. The leading youth organization that works for local governance and youth capacity building is an example of this mechanism, as it became involved in the process of revising the law on local authorities, in order to make local politics more participatory. This change in the law on local authorities is not only important because it envisages a participatory structure in local politics but it also is claimed to be a participatory process in itself. Apart from this, activists also say that they feel more empowered when they see that they can use global actors to pressure the local authorities. They feel that ICTs have increased their self-confidence and the solidarity among activists in the local sphere.

This fantasy of (decentralized) political power, however, is confronted with its Other, and frustrated by the local political traditions. Even though ICTs are seen to help activists to improve their work, their interactions, and their relations, they still do not seem to be able to participate in decision-making processes in local politics in a meaningful way. The fantasy of participatory politics is frustrated by the contradictions between the written rules and laws, and the rather different applications of these rules and laws. As one of the activists mentions, these interactions do not always move beyond chatting: "We can say that those (online) networks are useful only if these people can influence local politics. Otherwise it doesn't go beyond chatting" (Ferda, 42, f). They point out that ICTs make it possible to pretend to allow for participation. Various online tools that activists may use look participatory at first sight, but activists desire for "meaningful participation" in local politics, which frequently becomes frustrated.

Conclusion

This chapter looked at the different fantasies that are mobilized in, and that underpin, activists' perceptions of ICT-related social change, through the conceptual framework of Lacanian fantasy. Slightly hidden in the voices of the interviewees, we could find three interconnected fantasies, namely those of harmony, political power, and technological power, but also many references to how these fantasies become endlessly frustrated.

It is important to stress that there is nothing wrong in creating and investing in fantasies. Fantasies are the driving forces that motivate different groups to take action for a better society and for a better world. The distance between the subject and the enjoyment, the unfulfilled desire, is what motivates different groups to keep on working for a better society. In practice, the fantasies of ICT-related social change provide imaginaries that are driving forces for the activists to work hard for a more democratic political life in Istanbul.

This also does not mean that the Istanbul activists are naïve and do not see the limits, or, the frustrations of the fantasy, but this does not annul the existence of these fantasies; it actually motivates the activists even more to counter the old limitations—that have been with them for a long time—and the new limitations—that have appeared on the horizon—in order to realize more of these fantasies, even if their full realization remains an impossibility.

It is in this acknowledgment of the driving force of fantasy, together with the perpetual dynamics of fantasy and its frustrations, that the theoretical and analytical strength of the fantasy concept can be found, adding to the repertoire of other (related) concepts, such as utopian discourse. Fantasy's capacity to produce deeply affective relationships with particular social horizons, and to have subjects cope with the endless disappointment of the unrealized fantasies, make it a valuable theoretical and analytical asset, and an important expansion for the discourse-theoretical repertoire.

References

Carpentier, Nico (2011), "Policy's hubris: Power, fantasy, and the limits of (global) media policy interventions," in R. Mansell and M. Raboy (eds), *The Handbook of Global Media and Communication Policy*, Malden: Wiley-Blackwell, pp. 113–28.

——— (2014), "'Fuck the clowns from *Grease*!!' Fantasies of participation and agency in the YouTube comments on a Cypriot Problem documentary," *Information, Communication & Society*, 17:8, pp. 1001–16.

Çatalbaş, Dilruba (2007), "Freedom of press and broadcasting," in Z. F. K. Arat (ed.), *Human Rights in Turkey*, Philadelphia: University of Pennsylvania Press, pp. 19–34.

Civicus and Tüsev (2006), *Civil Society in Turkey – An Era of Transition: Civicus Civil Society Index Report for Turkey*, Istanbul: TÜSEV.

Glynos, Jason (2001), "The grip of ideology: A Lacanian approach to the theory of ideology," *Journal of Political Ideologies*, 6:2, pp. 191–214.

Glynos, Jason and Howarth, David (2008), "Structure, agency and power in political analysis: Beyond contextualised self-interpretations," *Political Studies Review*, 6:2, pp. 155–69.

Glynos, Jason and Stavrakakis, Yannis (2008), "Lacan and political subjectivity: Fantasy and enjoyment in the psychoanalysis and political theory," *Subjectivity*, 24, pp. 256–74.

Lacan, Jacques (1964), *Four Fundamental Concepts of Psychoanalysis*, London: Penguin Books.

Laclau, Ernesto and Mouffe, Chantal (1985), *Hegemony and Socialist Strategy: Towards A Radical Democratic Politics*, London: Verso.

Marx, Merit Roe and Smith, Leo (1994), "Introduction," in M. R. Marx and L. Smith (eds), *Does Technology Drive History? The Dilemma of Technological Determinism*, Cambridge, MA: MIT Press, pp. ix–xvii.

Mouffe, Chantal (2005), *On the Political*, London: Verso.

Nietzsche, Friedrich (2012), *The Gay Science*, Mineola: Dover.

Özbudun, Ergun (2007), *Çağdaş Türk Politikasi, Demokratik Pekişmenin Önündeki Engeller* (*Contemporary Turkish Politics, Obstacles for Enforced Democracy*), Istanbul: Doğan Kitap.

Pateman, Carole (1970), *Participation and Democratic Theory*, Cambridge: Cambridge University Press.

Ruggiero, Vincenzo (2014), *Movements in the City: Conflict in the European Metropolis*, Milton Park: Routledge.

Servaes, Jan (ed.) (2014), *Technological Determinism and Social Change*, London: Lexington Books.

Stavrakakis, Yannis (1999), *Lacan & the Political*, London: Routledge.

—— (2007), *The Lacanian Left: Psychoanalysis, Theory, and Politics*, New York: University of New York Press.

Strauss, Anselm L. and Corbin, Juliette M. (1998), *Basics of Qualitative Research Techniques and Procedures for Developing Grounded Theory*, 2nd ed., London: Sage.

Tarrow, Sidney (2005), *The New Transnational Activism*, Cambridge: Cambridge University Press.

Toksöz, Fikret (2009), *Yerel Yönetim Sistemleri Türkiye Ve Fransa İspanya İtalya Polonya Çek Cumhuriyeti* (*Local Authorities Systems Turkey and France, Spain, Italy, Poland, Czech Republic*), Istanbul: TESEV.

Tönnies, Ferdinand (1955), *Community and Association*, London: Routledge and Kegan Paul.

Uğur, Aydın and Akdoğan, Itır (2016), "Türkiye'deki Sivil Toplumun Gelişimi: Bıçak Sırtında Bir Sergüzeşt" ("Development of civil society in Turkey: A delicate adventure"), in M. Kabasakal (ed.), *Türkiye'de Siyasi Yaşam Dün, Bugün, Yarın* (*Political Life in Turkey Yesterday, Today, Tomorrow*), Istanbul: Bilgi Üniversitesi Yayınları, pp: 253–73.

Williams, Raymond (1974), *Television: Technology and Cultural Form*, London: Routledge.

Winston, Brian (1998), *Media Technology and Society*, London: Routledge.

Žižek, Slavoj (1989), *The Sublime Object of Ideology*, London: Verso.

—— (1999), *The Ticklish Subject: The Absent Centre of Political Ontology*, London: Verso.

Note

1   See https://freedomhouse.org/report/freedom-net/freedom-net-2017. Accessed 28 December 2018.

Chapter 13

Contesting the Populist Claim on "The People" through Popular Culture: The 0110 Concerts versus the Vlaams Belang

Benjamin De Cleen and Nico Carpentier

Introduction

On 1 October 2006—one week before the Belgian local elections—a series of concerts "for tolerance, against racism, against extremism, and against gratuitous violence" (0110.be) were held in four Belgian cities: Antwerp, Brussels, Ghent, and Charleroi.[1] The initiative for the 0110 concerts was taken by Tom Barman—singer of Antwerp rock band dEUS—who wanted to organize a concert against the extreme-right party Vlaams Belang (VB) in Antwerp. Other artists joined in and organized similar events in other cities. 0110 evolved into a media event featuring a long list of Belgian artists (playing all kinds of musical genres, including the more popular ones). The estimates are that more than 100,000 people attended the 0110 concerts. The concerts received a huge amount of media attention, and sparked a fierce debate on the usefulness of artistic initiatives against the extreme right and on the relationship between culture and politics in general. The VB itself also reacted strongly against the concerts.

This chapter looks at the 0110 concerts to show that popular culture is not only a site in which a political-ideological struggle can be waged, but that popular culture can also function as a tool and strategy to fight an extreme-right political party. The starting point of our argument is based on the shared core structure of popular culture and populism, as we want to argue that both popular culture and populism build on the juxtaposition between people and elite. This does not imply that popular culture and populism can be equated, for populism is a concept that is (and needs to be) much more linked to the world of politics, political strategies, and political actors. But although they belong to different spheres, popular culture and populism arguably have a similar core structure, and can in some cases become intertwined and interlocked. This is especially the case because populist parties are often happy to make use of popular culture as this allows them to strengthen their bond with the (signifier) people. But as this link between the populist parties and the signifier people is not given and to be taken for granted, political opponents might attempt to disarticulate it.

This chapter looks at one of these attempts: it analyzes how the organization behind the 0110 concerts attempted to disarticulate the signifier "the people" from the populist extreme-right party VB by turning popular culture against them, and using the link between popular culture and the people to weaken this party's symbolic relationship with the signifier. Before discussing the discourse-theoretical analysis of the discursive struggle between 0110 and VB (inspired by Laclau and Mouffe's 1985 discourse theory [DT]), we will first discuss the conceptual links between people, popular culture, and populism. The chapter moves from the more traditional idea of popular culture as a site of struggle between people and elite (without disavowing it) to a discussion of how the link between popular culture and the people can make popular culture a weapon against a populist political party.

Popular culture and the people

In his seminal *Keywords*, Williams (1983: 237) identifies four meanings of the term popular in relation to culture, where the signifier people is (often) attributed a crucial role. These four meanings are: "well-liked by many people," "inferior kinds of work," "work deliberately setting out to win favor with the people," and "culture actually made by the people for themselves." These four definitions show that "the popular" is defined *vis-à-vis* the "non-popular." Even in its more neutral sense of "well liked" or "widely favored," there is the underlying opposition to that which is not liked by many. Therefore, Williams argues, "the popular" often has two negative connotations: inferiority (O'Sullivan et al. [1983: 174] refer to the connotations "gross, base, vile, riff-raff, common, low, vulgar, plebeian, cheap"), and "deliberately setting out to win favor" (Williams 1983: 237). Different from these meanings and more positive, according to Williams, is the meaning of popular culture as the culture made by the people for the people, which is related to Herder's ideas on the *Kultur des Volkes* (Herder [1784] 1966), a meaning that lives on in the concept of folk culture.

Popular culture has different meanings, but is always defined relationally, through its implicit or explicit antagonism to "other conceptual categories: folk culture, mass culture, dominant culture, working-class culture, etc." (Storey 2003: 1). The meaning of popular culture is not fixed but depends on its relation to the non-popular. As Hall argues:

> The structuring principle [of the relation between the popular and the non-popular] does not consist of the contents of each category—which I insist will alter from one period to another. Rather it consists of the forces and relations which sustain the distinction, the differences.
>
> (Hall 1981: 234)

Hall (1981) situates the political significance of popular culture exactly in this relation between the popular and the non-popular. The move to neo-Gramscian cultural studies, Oswell (2006: 85) writes, meant "popular culture was not to be measured through an anthropology of the people. Instead, popular culture was seen to provide the cultural and ideological space within which 'a people' could be politically constructed and mobilised." Or, as Storey (2003: 12) states, neo-Gramscian "theories of 'popular culture' [such as Hall's] are really theories about the construction of the people."

Zooming in on the people, we can make a number of similar arguments. First, "the people" is not a prefixed natural category, but a signifier that acquires meaning through a diversity of discourses. The idea that the signifier "people' is a discursive construct is illustrated by, for instance, theories on populism (see Canovan 2005; Laclau 2005a, 2005b) and nationalism (see Balibar 1991; Hobsbawm 1990), discourses in which "the people" has a pivotal role (rendering it a nodal point—see below). From this perspective, the essentializing and hegemonizing claims on "the people" can be seen as ways to generate coherent discursive structures that at the same time form strong interpellative forces to constitute political communities. Claims to speak for the people in an attempt to gain legitimacy and power are of course not limited to the field of politics, they are abound (and have been for centuries) within different societal fields—politics, religion, culture (see Bourdieu 1990). Second, like popular culture (following Storey's 2003 interpretation), the constructions of "the people" are often antagonistic; that is, based on the juxtaposition between the people and another identity (Bourdieu 1990; Laclau 2005a, 2005b; see below for the different antagonisms structuring nationalism and populism).

This chapter analyzes the struggle between competing claims on "the people" and popular culture, using Laclau and Mouffe's (1985) DT as a framework (see also Carpentier and De Cleen 2007; Carpentier and Spinoy 2008). The theoretical starting point of Laclau and Mouffe's DT is the proposition that all social phenomena and objects obtain their meaning(s) through discourse. Discourses and identities are not stable and fixed—unconnected elements can always be claimed, (re-)articulated by and integrated within that discursive structure, and this prevents the full saturation of meaning—but at the same time discourses have to be partially fixed, since the abundance of meaning would otherwise make any meaning impossible (Laclau and Mouffe 1985: 112). The points where the discourse is (partially) fixed, Laclau and Mouffe (1985: 112) call nodal points—privileged signifiers that fix the meaning of a chain of signifiers (or moments), and have a certain degree of rigidity.

In the case of popular culture, this nodal point is "the people," and as the discussion of popular culture above shows, it is the antagonism between "the people" and "the elite" that structures discourses about popular culture. We will argue below that the same goes for populist discourse. This shared nodal point and the shared mechanism of the construction of "the people"/the popular through a juxtaposition to "the elite" links populist discourses and discourses on popular culture.

From the struggle within popular culture to the struggle for the signifier people through popular culture

Much research that is situated within the neo-Gramscian tradition is concerned with the political struggle that takes place *within* popular culture.[2] Hall's ([1973] 1980) encoding/decoding model is exemplary of these concerns with how the meaning of popular culture depends on both the meanings that are inscribed at the moment of production and on the way these are read at the moment of consumption. Other authors focus almost exclusively on the moment of consumption. Fiske (1989: 15), for example, sees popular culture as that which the subordinate do with cultural commodities, which are resources out of which popular culture can be made. Or as Barker (2005: 69) formulates it: "Popular culture is constituted through the production of popular meaning located at the moment of consumption. Such meanings are the site of contestation over cultural and political values."

This chapter is not concerned with the political struggle within the arena of popular culture or with popular culture as a space for the construction of "the people," but with the discursive struggle *over* and *for* the signifier people through (political) claims on the field of popular culture. It is concerned with how political discourses—in their attempts to become hegemonic—attempt to associate themselves with popular culture, and how the "ownership" of popular culture (and its nodal point, "the people") becomes the object of a struggle. Although culture and institutionalized politics are relatively separate fields that function according to their own logics, institutionalized politics attempts to make use of popular culture in several ways (see Van Zoonen 2000, 2005). Cloonan and Street (1998: 36) argue that "politics feeds of popular culture, if only because of their common concern with notions of popularity and authenticity, and their shared desire for publicity." Political projects often try to speak to as many people as possible. In doing this, politicians and political parties sometimes associate themselves with artists (and other celebrities such as sports stars) that have a broad appeal in order to feed on their popularity. As Street (2000: 77) argues, being associated with artists is important as it says something about the politician (and about the kind of people they want to speak to and associate themselves with). From this perspective, the question of whether a political party associates itself with say a rock band or a *schlager* singer becomes politically relevant. But there is more: because of the centrality of the signifier "the people" for popular culture, associating with popular culture and popular artists can be a way for political projects, parties, or individual politicians to link themselves to the (ordinary) people. As will be argued below, establishing this link with the people is especially important to populist parties for the signifier "the people" is at the core of populist discourse.

A discourse-theoretical perspective on populism

Bourdieu (1990: 152) argues that "it is clearly in the political field that the use of 'the people' and the 'popular' is most directly profitable." Attempts to speak to, associate with, or represent the people can be found throughout the political spectrum, but are most systematic in and most crucial to populist parties. In order to discuss the relationship between populist politics and popular culture, we will first turn to Ernesto Laclau's work to define populism. We will use his work to develop a definition of populism that enables us to discuss the interrelations between popular culture and populist politics without treating all political uses of popular culture and all links between politics and popular culture as populist.

Laclau is obviously not the only contemporary author working on populism. On the contrary, the concept of populism is used in a wide range of contexts, and has been attributed a diversity of meanings. Populism is sometimes treated as a (thin) political ideology (for example, Mudde 2004) or a kind of political style (e.g., Jagers and Walgrave 2003), whereas in other cases it refers to positive evaluations of popular culture or is used as a label for any kind of culture aimed at a broad audience. Broadening the concept of populism to the sphere of media and culture has in some cases caused the term to become synonymous with popular or popularizing, which has negative consequences for the analytical value of populism as a concept (Carpentier 2007). In this chapter, populism is limited to the sphere of politics, but even in the literature that focuses on political populism there is no consensus about its meaning.

Much of the literature on (political) populism actually starts with the ambiguity of the concept's meaning. Taggart (2000: 1), for example, refers to "an essential impalpability, an awkward conceptual slipperiness." The lack of consensus on the meaning of populism can be explained by the different waves of populism and the differences between them (see Taguieff 1998), and by the use of the concept of populism on different levels of meaning (see Arditi 2007: 54–87; Jagers 2006: 19–76; Mudde 2004: 543; Taguieff 2002: 99–106). There is a certain degree of consensus on which movements or parties can be labeled populist, but not on what exactly makes a movement or party populist (Canovan 1999: 3). However, as the term "populism" already suggests, the concept of "the people" has a central position in many definitions. The difficulty lies in the fact that "the people" does not mean the same thing to all populist parties and that, as a consequence, the term "populism" does not suffice to characterize a political discourse. The use of terms such as "national populism" (Taguieff 1995) or "right-wing-populism" (Betz 2002) illustrates this.

In dealing with the conceptual diversity of populist discourses, we prefer to (at least partially) align ourselves with Laclau's (1977, 2005a, 2005b) work on populism. Laclau avoids the problems related to defining the contents of populist discourse by arguing that "the people" is an empty signifier and that populism as such is not an ideology. Laclau's perspective can be called "formalistic" (Stavrakakis 2004: 255–56): what counts is not the ideology behind the use of "the people," but the use of this signifier and the way it structures a discourse:

> A movement is not populist because in its ideology it presents actual contents identifiable as populist, but because it shows a particular logic of articulation of those contents—whatever those contents are.
>
> (Laclau 2005b: 33)

But the use of the signifier "the people" in itself does not suffice to speak of populism. In order to speak of a populist discourse, there has to be an antagonistic relation between the people and the elite (see also Canovan 2002; Mény and Surel 2000; Mudde 2004, 2007).

> The presence of popular elements in a discourse is not sufficient to transform it into a populist one. Populism starts at the point where popular-democratic elements are presented as an antagonistic option against the ideology of the dominant bloc.
>
> (Laclau 1977: 143)

Laclau's critique of essentialism leads him to the conclusion that "the people" is a relationist concept, which can only acquire meaning through antagonism. Different identities are grouped under the signifier "the people" by opposing them to a constitutive outside: the elite. What links "the people" is not something positive they have in common, but their opposition to the same outside. Put in discourse-theoretical terms: populism functions according to the logic of equivalence (Laclau 2005a, 2005b). Here Laclau reverts to a concept developed together with Chantal Mouffe in *Hegemony and Socialist Strategy* (Laclau and Mouffe 1985) to describe the logics that discourses use to establish their hegemony. In this logic, chains of equivalence are created, articulating a diversity of meanings, subject positions, and identities in the same discourse exactly by opposing them to another negative identity (or constitutive outside). The logic of equivalence thus brings together a number of identities in one discourse, without however totally eliminating their differences: chains of equivalence "can weaken, but they cannot domesticate differences" (Laclau 2005a: 79).

What complicates Laclau's work on populism is that his position on the nature of the populist logics of equivalence and the role of the signifier "the people" has changed over time (and is sometimes ambiguous). Whereas in his earlier work (Laclau 1977) on populism, Laclau stressed the centrality of the signifier "the people" for populism, in his more recent work (Laclau 2005a, 2005b) a discourse does not necessarily need to be centered around the signifier "the people" in order to qualify as populist. Stavrakakis says:

> Although the antagonistic dichotomisation of the social space remains central, the core reference to the signifier "the people" is replaced—more or less—by the production of empty signifiers in general. This is essential in moving from an ontic to an ontological conception of populism—Laclau's expressed aim. In other words, populism as a mode of discursive articulation is no longer associated with the location of the point de capiton "the people."
>
> (2004: 262)

We side with Stavrakakis' (2004: 263) critique that broadening the concept of populism to any kind of political discourse governed by the logic of equivalence (structured around any kind of empty signifier) threatens the analytical strength of the concept. For the sake of the concept's empirical usefulness, we think that the term populism is best reserved for those discourses centered around the antagonism between the people and the elite. However, we do accept that other signifiers can take a similar role, but only conditionally. It is not the signifier "the people" in itself that is crucial, but the up-down dimension (as Dyrberg 2003 calls the antagonism between the people and the "power-bloc" that defines it; Mény and Surel 2002 call it vertical). Whether it is structured around "the people" or around another signifier is not the point. We speak of populism when a discourse is governed by the logic of equivalence *and* pretends to speak for the underdog whose political identity is constructed by opposing it to an elite. In practice, most of these discourses will be centered around the signifier "the people," but this is not a necessary condition; it is the structural up-down dimension that defines a discourse as populist.

To summarize: this means that a discourse need not necessarily be built around the signifier "the people" to qualify as populist, and that not every discourse using the signifier "the people" qualifies as populist. This definition of populism allows us to make the distinction between nationalism and populism that is important to the analysis of extreme-right discourse. Nationalist discourses construct a nation/a people by creating an antagonism between that nation/people and other nations/peoples living within or outside the state. Nationalism's definition of the people/the nation is thus based on an in/out distinction, rather than an up/down distinction. Nationalism *can* be coupled with a populist logic—for example, in the case of separatist movements that juxtapose the nation against a centralist elite that does not represent the nation—but this is not necessarily the case.

Populism and the discursive struggle to align with popular culture

As mentioned before, associating with popular culture is a means for political parties in the battle for popularity (Cloonan and Street 1998; Van Zoonen 2000, 2005). This goes for any political party that aims to have a broad appeal. For populist politics, however, the importance of attaching itself to popular culture goes beyond the fact that popular culture is "well-liked by many people." Populist political parties present themselves as representatives of the people by creating an antagonism between the people and themselves, on the one hand, and the elite, on the other. It is in their strategic interest to build and protect a close symbolic relationship with the signifier "the people", in as many societal fields as possible. Aligning themselves with popular culture and its nodal point, the people, is one of the ways to achieve this connection. This does not imply that populist parties *necessarily* have links with popular culture or even attempt to establish such links, but it does imply that popular culture *can* become politically relevant to populist parties, and to their opponents.

Indeed, no single political discourse can exercise an exclusive and everlasting claim on popular culture (or on the people). After all, there is no pre-established connection between any kind of political discourse and popular culture (see Fiske 1989: 163). Because of its discursive connection with the people, the field of popular culture can become the object of struggle between competing political projects in their attempts to become hegemonic. In the case study presented below, we look at how the strong claim of an extreme-right populist political party on the signifier people is contested, and how—through their use of popular culture—the political opponents of that extreme-right populist political party (at least partially) manage to reclaim the signifier people from that party.[3]

The Vlaams Belang, the logic of populism, and popular culture

Despite the structural openness of the signifiers "the people" and "the elite," some European populist extreme-right political parties seem to have been rather successful at claiming "the people" and at defining the meaning of people and elite. The Flemish extreme-right party VB is one of the most successful European extreme-right parties, with impressive election results: in the 2004 Flemish elections the party won 24.15 percent of the votes, which resulted in 32 (out of the 124) seats in the Flemish Parliament.[4] In the 2007 national elections it obtained seventeen seats in the national chamber of representatives (out of a total of 150 seats),[5] but nevertheless suffered a loss of some 5 percent of the Flemish votes compared with the 2004 Flemish elections (Sinardet 2008: 1025).[6] On the level of the municipality, the party is especially strong in Antwerp, where it won no less than 33.51 percent in the 2006 municipal elections.[7]

Before turning to the analysis of 0110 as a discursive struggle between the VB and 0110, we first need to look at the VB's populist discourse and its ideas on (popular) culture. What do the signifiers "the people," "the elite," and "popular culture" mean in the VB's discourse?

The Vlaams Belang, "the people," and "the elite"

The relationship between the extreme right and populism is less straightforward than often assumed, and these two concepts cannot be equated. Populist discourses do not necessarily have an extreme-right character, and not every extreme-right discourse is populist, as for example the explicitly elitist French extreme right of the 1960s and 1970s shows (Mény and Surel 2000: 12). Nevertheless, populism is considered one of the main defining features of the contemporary extreme right, as the use of terms such as "populist radical right," "national populism," and "extreme-right populism" shows (e.g., Hainsworth 2000: 6; Mudde 2002: 13, 2007). This link between the extreme right and populism also applies to the VB. According to Mudde (2007: 43), "after its beginning as an old-style radical-right party, with some elitist elements, the VB developed into a well-organized populist radical-right party in the 1980s." Today, the signifiers "the people" and "the elite" are indeed central to the VB's discourse. This raises the question of how the people and the elite are articulated by the VB.

The VB is a Flemish-nationalist party. Its nationalist discourse is built around the demand for an independent Flemish state for the Flemish people/nation (Jagers 2006: 205–6). Like other extreme-right parties, the VB holds a specific view on who belongs to the nation and who does not. Mudde (2007: 22) calls this view nativist: a combination of nationalism and xenophobia. Both nationalism and xenophobia are ways of ingroup–outgroup differentiation that construct the (identity of) the people, where non-natives serve as constitutive outside(s) to the people. The VB considers internal differences subordinate to the unity of the people and simultaneously stresses the difference with other groups (Jacobs and Rummens 2003: 6). It constructs the Flemish people in opposition to a number of outgroups that do not share this people's "common history, language, culture, mores and values" (Jagers 2006: 205–07). One constitutive outside is the French-speaking population of Belgium, as the VB's main goal is the creation of an independent Flemish state for a ethnic-culturally defined Flemish people (see Jagers 2006: 214; Mudde 2007: 19; Swyngedouw and Ivaldi 2001: 4–5). To the VB, the people are an ethnic-cultural entity (Jagers 2006: 211; see Mény and Surel 2000: 177–222).

Because of this nationalist homogenizing strategy, the socio-economic differences within the Flemish people are not thematized by the VB.[8] Immigrants are a second constitutive outside: they are said to "destroy Flemish culture" (Swyngedouw 1998: 65–6). Swyngedouw and Ivaldi (2001: 4) argue that, because of taboos established in the aftermath of the Second World War and because of existing anti-racist laws, explicit biologically racist statements are not often to be found in the VB's formal discourse, but that "those arguments are plainly suggested" (see also Spruyt 1995: 105–47).

As we argued before, nationalism(/nativism) and populism share the notion of "the people," and construct "the people" differently, but can nevertheless be articulated. Indeed, in VB discourse these two ways of defining "the people" frequently overlap, Jagers (2006: 208–9) argues, for example, when the VB speaks of the French-speaking Belgian elite that dominated/dominates the Flemish people. The VB stresses the Flemish people's history of oppression and struggle for recognition and emancipation from the French-speaking Belgian elite. A similar articulation of nationalism and populism occurs when the government is criticized for taking care of immigrants while ignoring or even going against the needs of the autochthonous population. But the nativist and populist definition of "the people" need not necessarily overlap. The Flemish political parties/politicians that "collaborate" with the Belgian "regime" for example, are part of the elite in a populist discourse, but remain part of the people/the nation in a nativist sense—a tension that is resolved by articulating them as traitors of that nation (see Mudde 2007: 64–79).

For the VB, "the elite" consists first of all of its political opponents. The party presents itself as radically different from the "traditional" parties (Swyngedouw and Ivaldi 2001: 12–4). It is the sole defender of the interests of the Flemish people, the voice of the silent majority, a resistance movement (Jagers 2006: 219, 233, 251–2). But "the elite" also includes magistrates, media (almost all considered left-wing by the VB), academia (common sense is valued higher than intellectual knowledge), the monarchy (the symbol of Belgium), labor unions, and, sometimes, the church. All of these groups are lumped together in their opposition to the VB (Jagers 2006: 224–33). By contrasting itself with all of these elites, the VB presents itself as the party of the people.

The Vlaams Belang and popular culture

Now what do these definitions of the people and the elite imply for the VB's views on popular culture? As a party that bases its discourse on the notion of "the people," and distinguishes itself from political opponents through a populist discourse, the VB potentially has a political-strategic interest in aligning itself with popular culture—especially because the party departs from an (ethnic-)cultural definition of "the people."

Despite the possible importance of this connection, the VB's position on culture has rarely been analyzed in the academic literature. Most information on the VB's discourse on culture can be found in the more journalistic or semi-academic literature. These works (mainly Gijsels 1992: 123–36; Spruyt 2000: 119–22) argue that the VB's program hardly mentions culture and that the party does not produce texts that directly deal with culture. However, these authors list a series of controversies, incidents, and debates where the VB did voice its opinions about culture. These do give us an idea about the VB's views on culture as the VB's interventions about culture are characterized by a number of recurring (and interrelated) themes.

A first important theme is Flemish nationalism. For the VB, culture is first and foremost a means to stimulate Flemish nationalist consciousness, Spruyt (2000: 121) argues. Flemish-nationalist symbols—Flemish flags, singing the Flemish "national" anthem (the Flemish Lion) are prominently visible at meetings and manifestations (see also Gijsels 1992: 135). The VB also demands that cultural institutions focus their investments on Dutch-language, Flemish culture.

A second recurring theme is anti-multiculturalism. The support for Flemish culture goes hand in hand with critiques of "multicultural" cultural initiatives and of the subsidizing of such initiatives. The VB's ideas about an ethnic-culturally defined Flanders are clearly exemplified by violent VB protests against a number of performances at Flemish national holiday festivities: against the performance of Alida Neslo (who is of Suriname descent) in 1987 and against Willem Vermandere's performance of a song defending multicultural society in 1992. These incidents can be considered protests against the construction of Flanders as a multicultural region through (popular) culture.

A third recurring theme is conservatism. The VB criticizes what it considers progressive cultural decadence, and argues against the governments' financial support of such culture. Also, cultural events that explicitly show sexuality, homosexuality, abortion, and drug use have been the object of VB critique (Gijsels 1992: 123–36; Spruyt 2000: 121; see also Meuleman 2004).

The above-discussed existing reflections on the VB's views on culture are mainly based on the VB's critiques of specific forms of culture, but the VB also takes an explicitly positive stance toward other forms of culture, as the use of Flemish-nationalist symbols (e.g., the Flemish anthem and the Flemish flag) illustrates. The VB also expresses a positive appreciation for artists and books that played a role in the Flemish nationalist movement (who thus also become symbols of Flemish nationalism) or represent what the VB considers European culture. In 1991, for instance, then president and founder of the party, Karel Dillen, published a collection of European poems that, according to Gijsels (1992: 135), featured a list of "heimatpoets, militant collaborators, authors of caramel verses and of fascist prose." The VB's appreciation of these rather highbrow artists is thus based on these artists' political importance or political preferences. But popular culture also plays a role for the VB, as it attempts to associate itself with specific forms of popular culture by, for example, releasing a carnival song or by inviting popular artists—mainly *schlager* singers—to perform at party meetings. These performing artists predominantly have a degree of popular appeal. In these cases, not the explicit political opinions of the artists are important, but rather the fact that they appeal to and symbolically represent the ordinary people that the VB claims to represent. As Meuleman (2004) notes, not many artists like to be identified with the VB. Apart from a more general reluctance to engage in or be linked to party politics, and the fact that many popular artists do not support the VB, it can safely be assumed that the public disapproval for the VB also plays a role. A prominent case in this respect is that of the Strangers. On 24 November 1992, the band—which sings Antwerp dialect lyrics over well-known pop tunes—performed at a VB meeting. The band was heavily criticized for its performance and lost much of its support in the media. What is important for our argument is that the populist VB does attempt to associate itself with popular culture at some points. Our case study of 0110 asks the question what happens when popular artists perform *against* the VB.

A discourse-theoretical analysis of 0110

Method and research material

We have discussed the link between the people and popular culture, between populist political discourses and the people, and between populist political discourses and popular culture. This gives us the tools for an analysis of the discursive struggle between 0110 and the VB. Laclau and Mouffe's (1985) DT, and particularly Laclau's theory of populism, provides us with the concepts necessary to analyze 0110 as a discursive struggle for the people. However, DT offers no methodological guidelines. In this chapter, general DT concepts, and especially the DT concepts central to Laclau's theory of populism (empty signifier, antagonism, and chain of equivalence), are used as sensitizing concepts (Blumer 1969) in a discourse-theoretical analysis (see Carpentier and De Cleen 2007).

The discourse-theoretical analysis presented below is based on the external communication of the VB on 0110 and of the organization of 0110 that can be found on their websites[9] and on the coverage of the concerts in the Flemish press (see below). Several types of documents can be found on the VB website: there are the overviews of VB representatives' media appearances (called "In the media"), the press releases, the online journal *E-Magazine*, the weekly column of the (now ex-) party president (Frank Vanhecke) entitled "Common sense" ("Gezond Verstand"), and several comments per day on current events in politics and society in "Current events" ("Actualiteit"). All texts that refer to 0110 (directly or indirectly) were analyzed: two "In the media" texts, one "Press release" ("Persbericht"), five *E-Magazine* articles, two "Common sense" columns, and 23 "Current events" texts. This was supplemented by two external communication texts, whose publication were key interventions in the 0110 debate and that were (partly) published and discussed in the press: VB MP Filip Dewinter's open letter to the artists participating in 0110 and VB MP Francis Van den Eynde's open letter to Helmut Lotti, one of the artists participating in the concerts. Both texts could be found on the personal websites of the VB MP in question.

The 0110 website produced less material. Using the Internet Archive's Wayback Machine (www.archive.org), all of the different versions (updates) of the website were downloaded. The material to be found on the different versions of the 0110 website consisted of the general 0110 manifesto, the manifestos for each of the organizing cities, the 0110 line-up per city, news items from the 0110 organization on the new names that were added to the line-up, a list of sponsors, practical information on the 0110 concerts, and information on 0110-related events. In total, this generated 31 documents.

A second part of the corpus consists of the press coverage of 0110 between 6 April 2005—the day Tom Barman announced the concerts—and 31 December 2006, in the newspapers *Gazet Van Antwerpen* (78 articles), *Het Laatste Nieuws* (108 articles), *De Morgen* (199 articles), *Het Nieuwsblad* (171 articles), *De Standaard* (138 articles), *De Tijd* (20 articles), and the weeklies *Knack* (23 articles), *Focus Knack* (20 articles), and *Weekend Knack* (3 articles).

0110 and the symbolic reclaiming of "the people"

The 0110 concerts can be seen as part of a tradition of concerts with a political message such as Live Aid, Live8, and, thematically closer to 0110, Rock Against Racism (see Street 2003; Street et al. 2007). From the initial phase, the aim of the 0110 concerts (the name "0110" itself came only later) is to reach as many people as possible to give a strong "signal" against the extreme-right party VB. 0110 shares this motivation of showing the existence of a large counter-extreme-right force with a series of earlier anti-racist/anti-extreme-right initiatives in Belgium (see Detant 2005; Van Aelst 2000).

But 0110 also differs from these earlier anti-racist events, in that it keeps a clearer distance from institutionalized politics. First, the 0110 organization does not want to become involved in party-political debates. It presents 0110 as a cultural event with political relevance, but steers clear from the field of institutionalized politics. So 0110 formulates no precise political demands, is reluctant of political rhetoric, and does not side with any political party. The original 0110 manifesto written by Tom Barman—movie director, DJ, and the singer of one of Belgium's most successful and critically acclaimed rock bands, dEUS—says:

> There is no speeching, no patronizing, no condemnations, everyone is welcome. But the message is clear: Flanders deserves better than the extreme-right. In this way, we celebrate the complexity of life with a simple music party.
>
> (0110.be, 12 July 2006)

Second, 0110 avoids any kind of link with political parties or any other kind of politically affiliated organizations in terms of its practical organization. Belgian artists had spoken out against racism and the extreme right before the 0110 concerts, but 0110 differs from most of these earlier Belgian anti-racist/anti-extreme-right initiatives as concerns the relationship between artists and political actors. 0110 is organized by artists and their managers without the support of the actors that are usually involved in anti-racist events, such as labor unions, non-governmental organizations, and the peace movement. Also, political parties and affiliated organizations are not granted any visibility at the concerts. This distance from institutionalized politics makes it easier for 0110 to involve more artists and create a broad appeal. At the same time, this explicit distance from the political field (and the fact that most politicians respect this distance, sometimes because they are critical of 0110) makes it more difficult for the VB to disarm the initiative with the populist argument that 0110 is an attack on the VB organized by its political opponents, the political elite.

Whereas the distance to institutionalized politics is important to avoid a populist critique on the initiative, the main strength of 0110 as a contestation of the VB's claim on "the people" lies in the participation of a number of artists that are considered popular. From the outset, 0110 aimed to make a broadly supported statement, by including artists from different genres. In *Focus Knack* of 6 April 2005, Barman states:

> No, we want to provoke reactions, that's the whole point. It also has to be much more than a few rockers doing their left-wing thing, to put it a little disrespectfully. The goal is that we make it a big party. We want to show a different side of Antwerp: a tolerant Antwerp, that makes clear what it thinks about the Vlaams Belang.

A relation is presumed between musical preferences and political preference. Rock music and its fans are linked to left-wing politics and anti-racism; popular Flemish artists and their fans, by contrast, are not expected to be left-wing and anti-racist. So 0110 is presented not as a left-wing initiative against the extreme right, but as a message supported by a united group of people, spanning the political spectrum. Tom Barman makes the link between the participation of popular artists and the strength of the signal against the populist VB more explicit by stating that at 0110 "people's singers" (*volkszangers*) will perform against the "party of the people":

> In the last 15 years nothing happened before the elections, there was no positive signal from the world of artists and the Vlaams Belang just got bigger. Now we do something and yes, the party will probably grow even more. But the so-called "largest people's party" will know that it is not necessarily supported by some of the greatest "people's singers" in Flanders.

> (Barman 2006b)

At the level of artists' explicit stances against the VB, the picture is not clear-cut. The participation of more and more artists from different genres leads to a less explicit and more ambiguous message, at least for some of the participating artists. Tom Barman conceived 0110 as a concert against the VB, and intended that 0110 would be a clear political statement. The more artists join 0110, the more this explicit anti-VB stance moves to the background. Quite a number of artists are not willing to support an initiative that is explicitly directed against the VB (which does not mean they are not against the VB), while others keep silent or say very little about their participation in the concerts. Artists such as Tom Barman, however, do not want to give up the anti-extreme-right message. The solution is found in putting the signifier tolerance to the forefront. In the first interview on 0110 (*Focus Knack*, 5 April 2006), Tom Barman had already linked the idea of tolerance to the struggle against the VB when he said:

> We want to show a different face of Antwerp: a tolerant Antwerp that makes clear how it thinks about the Vlaams Belang.
>
> (Barman 2006a)

All artists unite under the banner of tolerance, a signifier that leaves enough space for individual artists to specify their personal motivation for participating in the concerts. The emptiness of the signifier tolerance makes it possible to link a number of different messages and concerns under one header. For some, performing for tolerance equals performing against the VB, while for others the extreme right is just one of the examples of intolerance to be found in contemporary society, besides for example road rage, and "gratuitous violence," a term coined by the media after a so-called surge of violent deaths.[10] The title of the concerts becomes "For tolerance," with "against racism, extremism, and gratuitous violence" as a sub-header.

The participation of so many artists from different genres leads to ambiguity regarding the explicit anti-VB stance of 0110. But 0110's timing (one week before the elections), the fact that 0110 was originally explicitly presented as a concert geared against the VB and that a stance against the VB was equated with a pro-tolerance message by, for example, Tom Barman, and the fact that even a broad message of tolerance is still utterly incompatible with the VB's ideology do imply that 0110 remains a more or less explicit form of resistance against the VB. This discursive framing unavoidably affects the artists' participation in the concerts, for they become aligned with both the pro-tolerance discourse and the resistance against the VB discourse. The 0110 line-up turns out to be an impressive list of Belgian artists including big rock names (on a Belgian scale, that is) such as dEUS, Hooverphonic, and Arno, and *schlager* and pop artists such as Laura Lynn, Helmut Lotti, Will Tura, and Clouseau. Most of the popular artists are careful to make (explicit) statements, but some popular artists do play songs that refer to the importance of tolerance, like Clouseau's "Het zit vanbinnen" ("It's on the inside"—which is about the insignificance of outer appearances) and Helmut Lotti's "Oaster iets scheelt" ("If something is wrong"—about the lack of tolerance in all of us).

0110 is threatening for the VB's populist logic because, especially through the popular artists' participation, the link between the VB and the ordinary Flemish people becomes disrupted. Even the mere presence of popular artists, the symbolic (cultural) representatives of the people, who take position against the (intolerance of the) party of the people, disrupts the naturalness of the VB's claim on the signifier people. Their presence also implies that 0110 cannot simply be dismissed as a performance of the politically correct leftist artistic elite performing against the party of the people.

The Vlaams Belang and 0110: Trying to protect a populist claim on "the people"

The VB reacts fiercely against the attempts to weaken its symbolic claim on the signifier people. When looking at the VB's external communication about 0110, it is clear that the party has problems with exactly those characteristics that give 0110 a broad appeal: the participation of popular artists, the ambiguous attitude toward explicitly speaking out against the VB, and the distance 0110 keeps from the field of institutionalized politics. The party deploys a number of strategies to criticize and to try to delegitimize 0110 and to (re-) establish the link between the VB and popular artists (and thus the people).

A first strategy is to present 0110 as a political propaganda tool used by the traditional political parties in their struggle against the VB. 0110 is presented as a way for the elite to criticize the party of the people. In the same movement, this critique against the VB is reduced to election propaganda.

> The 0110 festival is a covert political meeting where all kinds of artists, singers and rock bands are being recuperated by politically correct Flanders that wants to avoid a victory of the VB in the communal elections on 8 October 2006 at all costs.
>
> (Filip Dewinter, open letter, 4 July 2006)

As discussed above, 0110 was organized by artists, without the involvement of political actors of any kind. In its attempts to fit 0110 into its populist logic, the VB explicitly states that its political opponents are behind the concerts (although the other political parties are not involved in the organization of the concerts). Note the move from traditional parties to artists in the next extract.

> It is well known that really all means are suited to halt the rise of the Vlaams Belang. To that end the traditional parties are preparing all weapons to attack our party. On October 1st, one week before the local elections, a number of Flemish artists are organizing a real concert against the Vlaams Belang in Antwerp, Ghent and Brussels.
>
> (Vlaams Belang, Actualiteit, 4 July 2006)

In order to incorporate 0110 into a populist logic, the VB tries to reduce the ambiguity that characterizes 0110's message. The message of tolerance is contested and 0110 is presented as election propaganda.

> It should be clear by now that the entire plan has little or nothing to do with "tolerance" but everything with an operation orchestrated and paid for by the regime against a successful opposition party.
>
> (Vlaams Belang, Actualiteit, 14 July 2006)

To prove that 0110 is an anti-VB event, the VB constantly refers to, and often quotes, statements by artists involved in the organization of 0110 in which they speak out against the VB explicitly. The signifier tolerance itself is almost continuously questioned by putting it between brackets, adding "so-called" or referring to (in)tolerance. Another way to question the link between the VB and intolerance and to try to neutralize the 0110 discourse is to present the VB as the victim of intolerance. A *Current Events* text about the VB's 1 October election congress mentions Dewinter's speech:

> Dewinter referred to the "concerts for tolerance" that took place at the same time somewhere else in Antwerp, and said that the Vlaams Belang had been waiting for an invitation to 0110 for an entire week. "For one must admit that, as victims of intolerance we Vlaams Belangers are experts by experience."
>
> (Vlaams Belang, Actualiteit, 2 October 2006)

The VB even calls 0110 undemocratic and argues that artists' performances against the VB are a form of blackmail. But 0110 is not only "undemocratic," it is also useless, for "real democracy" (Vlaams Belang, Actualiteit, 2 October 2006) is not affected by concerts against the VB. The VB places 0110 in a tradition of leftist anti-VB campaigns and concludes that 0110 most probably will not affect the election results because voters do not follow voting advice.

> Ah well, it is probably not worth all the hassle. Let all those singers and little bands warble a politically correct little song. After all the anti-Vlaams Blok and anti-Vlaams Belang campaigns—including notorious Hitler posters—the organizers were faced with defeat. The chances that it will be different this time are extremely small. For the Antwerp and Flemish voters do not care for political patronizing. Let the left have its party on October 1st. We will throw one on October 8th!
>
> (Vlaams Belang, Actualiteit, 5 July 2006)

Whereas 0110 goes to great lengths to present 0110 as more than a left-wing event—through the participation of popular artists, the distance from political parties and the broader message of tolerance—the VB tries hard to reduce 0110 and its message of tolerance to ("useless") leftist election propaganda. However, the VB does not explicitly question the value of tolerance. Rather, it tries to break the connection between the message of tolerance and anti-racism, and the resistance against the VB.

> Of course it is a good thing that artists too commit and speak out against intolerance and racism. The perfidious attempt to link racism and intolerance to the Vlaams Belang and to dissuade the voter to vote Vlaams Belang by creating the impression that popular artists support this point of view however is unfair and unacceptable.
>
> (Filip Dewinter, open letter, 4 July 2006)

The VB is especially troubled by the "creation" of "the impression that popular artists support this point of view" through their performances at 0110. Indeed, the VB's reactions are the strongest when 0110 announces the participation of a number of popular artists in the concerts. Apparently, the disarticulation of popular artists from the VB and/or its ideology causes a serious strain on its populist discourse. Artists defined as politically correct or alternative do not cause any problems for its populist logic, for their statements against the VB can easily be dismissed as an attack by the (cultural) elite on the party of the people. However, the VB has trouble criticizing popular artists and defining them as part of "the elite." But their presence is still conceived as a problem. So how does the VB deal with their participation in the 0110 concerts?

The VB's basic strategy is to distinguish between the "small group of politically correct" organizers of 0110 and the popular artists performing at the concerts. The party attempts to disarticulate the popular artists from the message of 0110 by arguing that these artists are merely being used by the "extreme leftist" organizers of the concerts. In this fashion, the VB attempts to depoliticize the participation of popular artists at the concerts.

> Apart from alternative rock band also "traditional" artists such as Clouseau, Helmut Lotti, Will Tura, Johan Verminnen en Laura Lynn will perform. Quite a number of the artists participating are themselves from a Flemish-nationalist background, but apparently now they let themselves be used by the extreme left to battle against the biggest party of Flanders.
>
> (Vlaams Belang, Actualiteit, 4 July 2006)

In his open letter to the artists, Filip Dewinter—one of the VB's leaders and electoral strongholds—suggests that popular artists performing at 0110 do not know what they are performing for, as they have been misled. He warns them not to perform against the VB, and sends a message to their fans, claiming that this performance does not just imply an attack on the VB, but on its voters as well.

> May I point out that in the meantime the Vlaams Belang is the largest party of Flanders that represents almost one million Flemings. A lot of these Vlaams Belang voters are probably enthusiastic fans of yourself or of one of the other artists that are participating in these anti-Vlaams Belang concerts. Do you consider all of these Vlaams Belang voters intolerant racists? I am convinced that this is not the case. Even more, I have the impression that you hardly know what it is you are collaborating in on next October 1st. For that matter, I am convinced that as Flemish artist you want to keep a neutral party-political position. For that matter, I dare presume that as a Flemish artist you address all Flemings without distinction on the basis of political, religious or philosophical convictions. It is therefore very improbable that you would take the liberty to formulate a voting advise against a specific Flemish party, through which you go against an important part of the Flemish public opinion.
>
> (Filip Dewinter, open letter, 4 July 2006)

A second strategy is to claim that the artists yielded for the pressure of the media, a critique that chimes with the critique of mainstream media as part of "the elite" mentioned above. In much of its external communication, the VB criticizes the media's purported uncritical support of the 0110 concerts. It is this support that explains (for the VB) the success of 0110 both in terms of popular support (0110 is not "spontaneous popular anger"; Actualiteit, 2 October 2006) and in terms of the artists participating, not the fact that many people support 0110's message. The party suggests that at least some artists' performances can be explained by their fear of negative reactions from the "small leftist media world."

> And so we are not impressed. We only showed our displeasure about the fact that artists let themselves be dragged along in a dirty election campaign, secretly subsidised by the government and undoubtedly also under "soft compulsion" of the "us-knows-us" [ons-kent-ons] and "we-help-each other"-system of the small leftist media world.
>
> (Vlaams Belang, Gezond Verstand, 15 July 2006)

For the VB, it is this pressure that explains the impressive line-up of 0110. The VB refers to The Strangers case mentioned above as an example of how the media put pressure on artists that perform for the VB. In his open letter, Dewinter states:

> Evidently I realize very well that the *cordon sanitaire* does not count only for the Vlaams Belang. Singers, artists, writers, journalists and even sportsmen are the victim of it as well. May I give the example of the popular Antwerp band "The Strangers" who many years ago dared to perform at a Vlaams Belang manifestation. For years, they were boycotted by the public broadcaster, by all sorts of radio stations and by some concert organizers.
>
> (Filip Dewinter, open letter, 4 July 2006)

A third way the VB attempts to neutralize the critique against the party is by re-establishing the links between specific Flemish artists and the party of the people. For instance, VB MP Francis Van den Eynde writes an open letter to Helmut Lotti. In this letter Van den Eynde calls Lotti's father a "long-time propagandist" for the VB and refers to Lotti's alleged youth membership of the Vlaams Nationaal Jeugdverbond (the Flemish National Youth Alliance—an extreme-right-wing nationalist youth movement).

Van den Eynde's letter to Helmut Lotti and the above excerpt of Dewinter's open letter show how the VB puts pressure on the artists not to perform at the 0110 concerts by arguing that popular artists should not go against the largest party of Flanders and its voters, many of which are presumed to be fans of these artists. The assumption underpinning this argument is that popular artists simply cannot be against the VB, because that would mean that they would go against the people and as a consequence, would stop being popular.

> More and more, the political, cultural, and intellectual elite of our people locks itself inside a politically correct ivory tower. The distance between the man and woman in the street and the world of full and semi FF's [Famous Flemings] of all sorts is becoming bigger and bigger. I am convinced that you as a popular artist want to stand in between

and with the people instead of going against the people. I therefore do not doubt your honest and good intentions and am convinced that you will draw appropriate conclusions from my writings.

(Filip Dewinter, open letter, 4 July 2006)

This is the ultimate consequence of the VB's populist discourse: artists that go against the VB are not popular. However, throughout the corpus the VB shows a reluctance to call popular artists who perform at 0110 part of "the elite," which points to the strength of the discursive link between "the people" and popular culture.

Conclusion: 0110, popular culture, and the logics of populism

This chapter started from the argument that, because of their similar structure built around the nodal point, "the people," popular culture, and populist politics can become intertwined. The 0110 case study presented here showed how the struggle for the signifier people can be waged through a struggle over popular culture. Rather than a political project per se, 0110 is a cultural initiative with a political message. What 0110 does, first and foremost, is reclaim the signifier people from an extreme-right discourse by turning popular culture and its artists against the party, whilst remaining detached from institutionalized politics.

Feeling threatened, the VB deploys a number of strategies to re-establish the link between VB, popular culture, and its artists. One of the main strategies is to present 0110 as a tool used by competing parties against the VB. This counter-strategy turns out to be problematic as 0110 refuses to be claimed by any political party. This distance from institutionalized politics is important for the strength of 0110 as a political statement. If 0110 would have associated itself with other political parties, it would have made it easier for the VB to discredit 0110 as an attack by the political elite on the party of the people. In a sense, 0110 becomes a third space, being political and non-political at the same time. As we have seen, the VB still tries to do reduce 0110 to a party-political tool, but fails to make a convincing case.

More important than the argument that 0110 is part of an electoral campaign against the VB is the linking together of 0110 and the VB's political opponents as parts of the same politically correct elite that is far removed from the people. But this strategy also becomes problematic as the participation of popular artists in the 0110 concerts makes it difficult for the VB to discredit all participants as part of "the elite." Without explicitly claiming the signifier "the people," 0110 manages to destabilize the VB's populist discourse through the fact that popular artists perform at concerts that are still (sometimes implicitly, sometimes explicitly) seen as events geared against the VB. The party deploys a number of strategies to minimize the strain caused to its populist discourse by the participation of these popular artists in 0110. These counter-strategies consist of attempts to disarticulate the artists considered popular from the 0110 discourse and to rearticulate them into VB discourse. When the artists in question refuse this repositioning, the only remaining conclusion of the

VB's populist discourse is that these artists are not popular, which is difficult to maintain and communicate.

When we return to our definition of populism, we see that 0110 is dominated by the logic of equivalence with the VB functioning as a constitutive outside. 0110 cannot in itself be considered populist (according to the definition discussed above) because there is no up/down antagonism that structures its discourse. Rather, 0110 questions the up/down dimension crucial to the VB's populist discourse by breaking down the boundaries between alternative and popular music, as artists from all kinds of genres perform for tolerance. At the same time, 0110 of course only functions as an anti-extreme-right statement because all actors involved accept that there is a relation between cultural and political preferences and that there is an up/down dimension to this relation.

The discourse-theoretical analysis presented here cannot and does not aim to make claims about the electoral impact of 0110. It is quite simply impossible to measure 0110's direct electoral impact, not only for a discourse analysis. But 0110 did prove to be successful in questioning the naturalness of the VB's claim on the people by turning popular culture against the party. If we do look at the 8 October elections, one week after 0110, we see that the outcomes were not clear-cut. The VB lost or stagnated in a number of cities. In Antwerp, for example, the VB gained 0.5 percent but Filip Dewinter lost the popularity contest to social-democrat mayor Patrick Janssens; the VB lost in some of the districts that were its strongholds in Antwerp and, for the first time in many years, the VB was no longer the largest party in the city. In another large Flemish city, Ghent, the VB suffered a 1.5 percent loss and, like in Antwerp, the social-democrat party of the mayor won the elections. But the VB did make a leap forward in many smaller towns throughout Flanders, which shows that any linear connection between these elections and the 0110 concerts cannot be taken for granted. Still, the reclaiming of the signifier people through the 0110 can be considered an important moment in the political struggle against the extreme right in Belgium. What 0110 did undoubtedly show is that popular culture and the people are still very much linked, and that because of this link the field of popular culture can have a direct relevance to the world of politics and can become the object of political struggle.

References

Arditi, Benjamin (2007), *Politics on the Edges of Liberalism: Difference, Populism, Revolution, Agitation*, Edinburgh: Edinburgh University Press.

Balibar, Etienne (1991), "Preface," in E. Balibar and I. Wallerstein (eds), *Race, Nation, Class. Ambiguous Identities*, London: Verso, pp. 1–13.

Barker, Clive (2005), *Cultural Studies: Theory and Practice*, London: Sage.

Barman, Tom (2006a), interview, *Focus Knack*, 5 April.

—— (2006b), interview, Het Laatste Nieuws, 12 September.

Betz, Hanz-Georg (2002), "Conditions favoring the success and failure of radical right-wing populist parties in contemporary democracies," in Y. Mény and Y. Surel (eds), *Democracies and the Populist Challenge*, New York: Palgrave, pp. 197–213.

Blumer, Herbert (1969), *Symbolic Interactionism: Perspective and Method*, Englewood Cliffs, NJ: Prentice Hall.

Bourdieu, Pierre (1990), "The uses of the people," in *In other words. Essays Towards a Reflexive Sociology*, Stanford, CA: Stanford University Press, pp. 150–55.

Canovan, Margaret (1999), "Trust the people! Populism and the two faces of democracy," *Political Studies*, 47:1, pp. 2–16.

—— (2002), "Taking politics to the people: Populism as the ideology of democracy," in Y. Mény and Y. Surel (eds), *Democracies and the Populist Challenge,* Houndmills: Palgrave, pp. 25–44.

—— (2005), *The People*, Cambridge, MA: Polity Press.

Carpentier, Nico (2007), "Populaire toegang en toegankelijkheid in de massamedia: publiek debat of demagogisch populisme? Een (de)constructieve dialoog met 'Populisme'," *Advocare,* 15, pp. 47–74.

Carpentier, Nico and De Cleen, Benjamin (2007), "Bringing discourse theory into media studies," *Journal of Language and Politics*, 6:2, pp. 267–95.

Carpentier, Nico and Spinoy, Erik (2008), "Introduction: From the political to the cultural," in N. Carpentier and E. Spinoy (eds), *Discourse Theory and Cultural Analysis*, Creskill: Hampton Press, pp. 1–26.

Cloonan, Martin and Street, John (1998), "Rock the vote: Popular culture and politics," *Politics* 18:1, pp. 33–38.

Detant, Anja (2005), "The politics of anti-racism in Belgium: A qualitative analysis of the discourse of the anti-racist movement Hand in Hand in the 1990s," *Ethnicities*, 5:2, pp. 183–215.

Dyrberg, Torben Bech (2003), "Right/left in context of new political frontiers: What's radical politics today?," *Journal of Language and Politics*, 2:2, pp. 339–42.

Fiske, John (1989), *Reading the Popular,* London: Routledge.

Gijsels, Hugo (1992), *Het Vlaams Blok*, Leuven: Kritak.

Hainsworth, Paul (2000), "Introduction: The extreme right," in *The Politics of the Extreme Right. From the Margins to the Mainstream*, London: Pinter, pp. 1–17.

Hall, Stuart ([1973] 1980), "Encoding/decoding," *Culture, Media, Language: Working Papers in Cultural studies, 1972–79*, London: Hutchinson, pp. 128–38.

—— (1981) "Notes on deconstructing the popular," in R. Samuel (ed.), *People's History and Socialist Strategy*, London: Routledge and Kegan Paul, pp. 229–40.

Herder, Johan Gottfried ([1784] 1966), *Outlines of a Philosophy of the History of Man*, New York: Bergman.

Hobsbawm, Eric J. (1990), *Nations and Nationalism Since 1780: Programme, Myth, Reality*, Cambridge: Cambridge University Press.

Jacobs, Dirk and Rummens, Stefan (2003), "Wij zeggen wat ù denkt: Extreem-rechts in Vlaanderen en nieuw radicaal-rechts in Europa," *Krisis*, 4:2, pp. 41–59.

Jagers, Jan (2006), "De Stem van het Volk! Populisme als Concept Getest bij Vlaamse Politieke Partijen," Ph.D. thesis, Antwerp: Universiteit Antwerpen.

Jagers, Jan and Walgrave, Stefaan (2003), "Populism as political communication style: An empirical study of political parties' discourse in Belgium," *European Journal of Political Research*, 46, pp. 319–45.

Laclau, Ernesto (1977), *Politics and Ideology in Marxist Theory*, London: New Left Books.

—— (2005a), *On Populist Reason*, London: Verso.

—— (2005b), "Populism: What's in a name?," in F. Panizza (ed.), *Populism and the Mirror of Democracy*, London: Verso, pp. 32–49.

Laclau, Ernesto and Mouffe, Chantal (2001), *Hegemony and Socialist Strategy: Towards a Radical Democratic Politics*, 2nd ed, London: Verso.

Mény, Yves and Surel, Yves (2000), *Par le Peuple, Pour le Peuple: Le populisme et les Démocraties*, Paris: Fayard.

—— (2002), "The constitutive ambiguity of populism," in Y. Mény and Y. Surel (eds), *Democracies and the Populist Challenge*, Houndmills: Palgrave, pp. 1–21.

Meuleman, Bart (2004), "Het kunstbeleid van het Vlaams Blok," *De Witte Raaf,* 112, p. 28.

Mudde, Cas (2002), *The Ideology of the Extreme Right*, Manchester: Manchester University Press.

—— (2004), "The populist zeitgeist," *Government & Opposition*, 39:4, pp. 541–63.

—— (2007), *Populist Radical Right Parties in Europe*, Cambridge: Cambridge University Press.

Oswell, David (2006), *An Introduction to Cultural Studies*, Exeter: University of Exeter Press.

O'Sullivan, Tim, Hartley, John, Saunders, Danny, and Fiske, John (1983), *Key Concepts in Communication*, London: Methuen.

Sinardet, Dave (2008), "Belgian federalism put to the test: The 2007 Belgian federal elections and their aftermath," *West European Politics*, 31:5, pp. 1016–32.

Spruyt, Marc (1995), *Grove Borstels: Stel dat het Vlaams Blok Morgen Zijn Programma Realiseert, Hoe Zou Vlaanderen er Dan Uitzien?*, Leuven: Van Halewijck.

—— (2000), *Wat het Vlaams Blok Verzwijgt*, Leuven: Van Halewijck.

Stavrakakis, Yannis (2004), "Antinomies of formalism: Laclau's theory of populism and the lessons from religious populism in Greece," *Journal of Political Ideologies*, 9:3, pp. 253–67.

Storey, John (2003), *Cultural Theory and Popular Culture: An Introduction*, Harlow: Pearson Education.

Street, John (2000), "'Prime time politics': Popular culture and politicians in the UK," *Javnost—The Public*, 7:2, pp. 75–90.

—— (2003), "Fight the power: The politics of music and the music of politics," *Government & Opposition*, 38:1, pp. 113–30.

Street, John, Hague, Seth, and Savigny, Heather (2007), "Playing to the crowd: The role of music and musicians in political participation," *British Journal of Politics and International Relations*, 10:2, pp. 269–85.

Swyngedouw, Marc (1998), "The extreme-right in Belgium: Of a non-existent Front National and an omnipresent Vlaams Blok," in H.-G. Betz and S. Immerfall (eds), *The New Politics of the Right: Neo-Populist Parties and Movements in Established Democracies*, New York: St Martin's, pp. 59–75.

Swyngedouw, Marc and Ivaldi, Gilles (2001), "The extreme right utopia in Belgium and France: The ideology of the Flemish Vlaams Blok and the French Front National," *West European Politics*, 24:3, pp. 1–22.

Taggart, Paul (2000), *Populism*, Buckingham: Open University Press.

Taguieff, Pierre-André (1995), "Political science confronts populism," *Telos*, 103:1, pp. 9–43.

—— (1998), "Populismes et anti-populismes: Le choc des argumentations," *Mots: Les languages du Politique*, 55, pp. 5–26.

—— (2002), *L'illusion Populiste: De l'Archaique au Médiatique*, Paris: Berg International.

Van Aelst, Peter (2000), "De antiracistische protestgolf in België," in J.-W. Duyvendak, T. Sunier, S. Saharso, and F. Steijlen (eds), *Emancipatie en Subcultuur. Sociale Bewegingen in België en Nederland*, Amsterdam: Instituut voor Publiek en Politiek, pp. 98–119.

Van Zoonen, Liesbet (2000), "Popular culture as political communication: An introduction," *Javnost—The Public*, 7:2, pp. 5–18.

—— (2005), *Entertaining the Citizen: When Politics and Popular Culture Converge*, London: Rowman and Littlefield.

Williams, Raymond (1983), *Keywords: A Vocabulary of Culture and Society*, rev. ed, New York: Oxford University Press.

Notes

1 In the margins of the concerts, a number of other (much smaller) artistic initiatives were organized under the 0110 banner. Luc Tuymans organized an arts exposition entitled "Mute in Antwerp," at the location where, on 11 May 2006, Hans Van Themsche shot and killed a 2-year-old girl and her Malinese nanny, a murder that was considered to be inspired by racism. "Mute," the 0110 website states, means "'falling silent' or 'silencing something or someone.'" Also, a literary event called "0110 Literair" (0110 Literary) was held on 1 October. 95 authors wrote poetry to be published by the media under the header "Messages for the population."

2 This does not imply that they ignore the role of institutions in "disciplining and policing" the boundary between, for example, what is part of the great tradition and what is not (see Hall 1981: 236).

3 This chapter focuses on the struggle for the signifier "people" through the struggle over popular culture, but it should be clear that the signifiers "popular culture", "the people", and "power-bloc/elite" do not have a fixed meaning—politically or culturally—but are constructed in and through discourse. They are elements that can be articulated in different discourses, disarticulated from a certain discourse, and rearticulated in another discourse. The meaning of those signifiers depends on the discourse in which they are articulated. People, elite, and popular culture therefore have different meanings in different discourses. The struggle between competing discourses for popular culture (as a way of claiming the people) is, thus, simultaneously a struggle over the meaning of popular culture, people, and elite.

4 See http://verkiezingen2004.belgium.be/nl/vla/results/results_graph_etop.html. Accessed 28 December 2018.

5 See http://polling2007.belgium.be/nl/cha/seat/seat_etop.html. This implies a much higher percentage in Flanders as only the inhabitants of Flanders and Brussels can vote for the VB.

6   Also, compared with the 2003 national elections, the VB lost votes in some areas. In the Antwerp canton—traditionally the area where the VB is the strongest—the party won 28.43 percent compared with 30.46 percent in 2003.

7   See http://www.binnenland.vlaanderen.be/verkiezingen/verkiezingen2006/lijsten.html?type= GE&nis=11002#tabevent_tab_uitslagen_GE. Accessed 28 December 2018.

8   However, the socio-economic dimension does play a role in the VB's populist discourse as a way to oppose the Flemish people to the political establishment as well as to foreigners and Walloons. The political elite is criticized as being corrupt and in it for the money. The VB also systematically points to how the political establishment (also economically) favors foreigners and Walloons and disadvantages the Flemish (Jagers 2006: 211). At the same time, the VB sees Flanders' economic prosperity as the result of the Flemish' work ethos that is again juxtaposed to the Walloons' and foreigners' lack thereof (Jagers 2006: 217–18).

9   www.vlaamsbelang.be and www.0110.be, respectively. www.0110.be is actually the URL for a blog by a Belgian blogger who allowed the 0110 organization to temporarily use the URL. The 0110 website is no longer accessible.

10 This included the death of Joe Van Holsbeeck after being stabbed in an armed robbery of his MP3 player (12 April 2006), the murder of a 2-year-old and her Malinese nanny by Hans Van Themsche (9 May 2006), and the death of Guido De Moor after a violent incident with a number of youths of Moroccan descent on an Antwerp bus (24 June 2006).

Biographies

In order of appearance

Nico Carpentier is associate professor in media and communication studies at the Department of Media Studies of Charles University in Prague. In addition, he holds two part-time positions at the Communication Studies Department of the Vrije Universiteit Brussel (VUB-Free University of Brussels) and at the Department of Informatics and Media of Uppsala University. Moreover, he is a research fellow at the Cyprus University of Technology and Loughborough University. His latest monograph is *The Discursive-Material Knot: Cyprus in Conflict and Community Media Participation* (2017, Peter Lang).

Benjamin De Cleen is assistant professor at the Communication Studies Department of the Vrije Universiteit Brussel (VUB-Free University of Brussels) where he is the coordinator of the English-language master's on journalism and media in Europe. His research is situated within critical discourse studies, and has mainly been focused on radical-right rhetoric, and on the discourse-theoretical conceptualization of populism, nationalism, and conservatism.

Leen Van Brussel obtained her Ph.D. at the Vrije Universiteit Brussels (VUB–Free University of Brussels), where she adopted a discourse-theoretical framework to study death, illness, and health. She is currently a staff member of the Flemish Institute of Healthy Living (Vlaams Instituut Gezond Leven), where she works on health promotion ethics and health communication.

Yiannis Mylonas is assistant professor of media, sociology, and cultural studies at the School of Media, National Research University Higher School of Economics in Moscow. He has previously worked as a post-doctoral researcher at Lund University in Sweden, and as lecturer at Copenhagen University. His research interests depart from critical theory and post structuralism. He has published widely on politics, culture, and the media in various journals and edited volumes. His latest publications are included in the journals *Journal of Media and Cultural Studies*, *Race and Class*, and *Journal of Political Ideologies*. His coming monograph, *The "Greek Crisis" in Europe: Race, Class and Politics*, will be published in 2019 by Brill.

Kirill Filimonov is a Ph.D. candidate in media and communication studies at Uppsala University, Sweden. His research project explores participation in Russian alternative media communities from a post-structuralist and discourse-theoretical perspective. Previously, he has been involved in a study on the use of Instagram in Swedish electoral campaigning, published in *Social Media & Society*.

Jakob Svensson is holding a position of associate professor in media and communication studies at Malmö University, School of Arts & Communication. Dr Svensson directs the BA program, "media activism, strategy and entrepreneurship". His research focuses on the processes behind algorithms, political participation on digital media platforms, and mobile communication in developing regions.

Jo Bogaerts is a post-doctoral researcher at the Université libre de Bruxelles and a member of the university's Centre de Recherche en Philosophie. His main publications deal with the intersection of literature and philosophy, existentialism and Kafka. In the field of journalism studies, he focuses on journalistic values, discourse theory, and the performativity of journalistic identity. Currently, he is working on documenting the life and works of the French literary critic and psychoanalyst Marthe Robert.

Marit Trioen worked at the VUB-Free University of Brussels from 2008-2009, where she conducted research on journalistic identities. Currently, she is working at the Antwerp School of Education, where she teaches non-native students.

Guiquan Xu is associate professor at the School of Communication and Design of Sun Yat-sen University, Guangzhou, China. He obtained a joint Ph.D. at the Communication University of China and the Vrije Universiteit Brussel (VUB-Free University of Brussels) under the Erasmus Mundus framework. His research interests focus on the areas of discourse studies, audience research, and media sociology.

Krista Lepik is a lecturer in information sciences at the University of Tartu, Estonia. Since completing her Ph.D. dissertation on cultural participation and visitor governing in memory institutions in 2013, her research interests have involved museum and library communication and engagement. Besides academic activities, she has introduced the issues of participatory culture to Estonian librarians, and is a member of the community work-related sub-committee, awarding the Estonian Museum's annual award, "Museum Rat".

Wim Hannot studied audio-visual techniques at RITCS Brussels and communication sciences at the University of Antwerp. At the Free University of Brussels (VUB-Free University of Brussels), he researched the reception of audience participation programs. Currently, he teaches cultural and behavioral sciences.

Giulia Airaghi is an independent researcher. She received her co-joint Ph.D. in the sociology and methodology of social research from the Department of Sociology, Università Cattolica, Milan, and in media communication from the Faculty of Human Science, Vrije Universiteit, Brussels (VUB-Free University of Brussels). Her research has developed in the fields of sociology of conflict and economic sociology. She has taught the sociology of cultural processes and sociology of communication in different Italian universities.

Itır Akdoğan, after graduating from Notre Dame De Sion French lycée, completed her BA in communications at Galatasaray University, her MA in international politics at Université Libre de Bruxelles (ULB), and her Ph.D. in social sciences at Helsinki University. She has always enjoyed observing the interaction between new technologies and society. After her Ph.D., she worked as international e-democracy consultant with projects in northern Europe, with the Ministry of Justice, Finland, and in Africa, with the German Corporation for International Cooperation (GIZ). She worked in UNDP Turkey's program as an associate at the Habitat Center for Development and Governance from 2013-2015. She has also been the research director for the Turkish Economic and Social Studies Foundation since 2015. Her goal is to bridge academia and civil society.

Previous Publications

This volume gathers a selection of work by the members of the Brussels Discourse Theory Group. Therefore, the majority of texts included in the book have been published before. We thank the original publishers for granting us permission to re-use the texts.

Section 1: Political Ideologies
Yiannis Mylonas' contribution, "Crisis, Austerity, and Opposition in Mainstream Media Discourses in Greece", was first published as an article in *Critical Discourse Studies* (2014, 11:3, pp. 305–321). In 2016, *Nordicom Review* (37:2, pp. 51–66) published Kirill Filimonov and Jakob Svensson's article, "(Re)Articulating Feminism: A Discourse Analysis of Sweden's Feminist Initiative Election Campaign". Benjamin De Cleen's contribution, "The Stage as an Arena of Politics: The Struggle between the Vlaams Blok/Belang and the Flemish City Theatres", appeared first as a chapter in *Right-Wing Populism in Europe: Politics and Discourse*, edited by Ruth Wodak, Majid Khosravinik, and Brigitte Mral (2013, Bloomsbury Academic, pp. 209–222).

Section 2: The Politics of Everyday Life
Leen Van Brussel's contribution on the discourse-theoretical approach to death and dying was first published in 2014 in the edited volume, *The Social Construction of Death: Interdisciplinary Perspectives* (Palgrave, edited by Leen Van Brussel and Nico Carpentier, pp. 13–33). Nico Carpentier's contribution, "Putting Your Relationship to the Test: Constructions of Fidelity, Seduction, and Participation in *Temptation Island*", appeared in *Social Journalism Review* (2009, 2, pp. 321–345).

Section 3: Production
"The Postmodern Challenge to Journalism: Strategies for Constructing a Trustworthy Identity", by Jo Bogaerts and Nico Carpentier, was originally published as a chapter in the edited volume *Rethinking Journalism: Trust and Participation in a Transformed News Landscape*, authored by C. Peters and M. J. Broersma (2012, Routledge, pp. 60–72). Two years earlier, "The Particularity of Objectivity: A Poststructuralist and Psychoanalytical Reading of the Gap Between Objectivity-as-Value and Objectivity-as-Practice in the 2003 Iraqi War Coverage" (Nico Carpentier and Marit Trioen) appeared as an article in *Journalism* (2010, 11:3, pp. 311–328).

Section 4: Audiences and Participation

In 2014, Richard Butsch and Sonia Livingstone included Guiquan Xu's "The Articulation of 'Audience' in Chinese Communication Research" in their edited volume, entitled *Meanings of Audiences: Comparative Discourses* (Routledge, pp. 151–169). Krista Lepik and Nico Carpentier's "Articulating the Visitor in Public Knowledge Institutions" was published originally as an article in *Critical Discourse Studies* (2012, 10:2, pp. 136–153). In 2009, the *International Journal of Cultural Studies* (12:6, pp. 597–616) published "To be a Common Hero: The Uneasy Balance between the Ordinary and Ordinariness in the Subject Position of Mediated Ordinary People in the Talk Show *Jan Publiek*" (Nico Carpentier and Wim Hannot).

Section 5: Activism and Resistance

Benjamin De Cleen and Nico Carpentier's contribution, entitled "Contesting the Populist Claim on 'The People' through Popular Culture: The 0110 Concerts versus the Vlaams Belang", was first published as an article in *Social Semiotics* (2010, 20:2, pp. 175–196).

The book also includes a number of new texts. In section five, "Online Barter and Counter-Hegemonic Resistance" (by Giulia Airaghi) and "Activist Fantasies on ICT-Related Social Change in Istanbul" (by Itır Akdoğan) are new texts. Furthermore, the introduction, "Discourse Theory, Media and Communication, and the work of the Brussels Discourse Theory Group" is a new text, even if some of its parts have been published before. The introduction was written with the aim of reflecting on the interaction between discourse theory and the study of media and communication, and the group's present and future contribution to it.